Worker Trait Group Guide

Appalachia Educational Laboratory, Inc.
Charleston, West Virginia
David W. Winefordner, Director
Division of Career Guidance

MERIDIAN EDUCATION CORPORATION
BLOOMINGTON, ILLINOIS

Foreword

This *Worker Trait Group Guide* is part of the new *Career Exploration and Planning Program* (CEPP) developed by the Appalachia Educational Laboratory, Inc. (AEL). The CEPP is a revised and updated version of AEL's original Career Decision-Making (CDM) program. AEL's Board of Directors authorized investment of corporate funds for development of CEPP as a part of the Lab's continuing commitment to the improvement of education through research and development in the field of career education.

The staff of AEL's Career Guidance Division has a long record of outstanding performance in the development and dissemination of quality products. More than 100 products have been used successfully by literally millions of students and adults in career exploration and educational planning. As a valid extension of these earlier successes, the *Career Exploration and Planning Program* is a major revision of CDM that incorporates significant new content and updated instructional technology.

We are indeed fortunate to have the Meridian Education Corporation join with AEL in the publication and dissemination of CEPP. This merger of the Lab's R & D capacity with Meridian's publishing and marketing expertise provides a major new resource for schools. CEPP will have an immediate impact on students' educational planning and an ongoing impact on their career planning and decisions.

Terry L. Eidell, D.Ed.
Executive Director
Appalachia Educational Laboratory, Inc.
Charleston, West Virginia

Contents

Preface

The *Worker Trait Group Guide,* Revised Edition, is a basic career information reference. It is an educational version of the *Guide for Occupational Exploration* (GOE) produced by the Department of Labor (DOL). The *Worker Trait Group Guide* describes the 12 Career Areas and 66 Worker Trait Groups (WTG), an occupational classification system used by the DOL.

As part of the research and development work on the Career Decision-Making (CDM) Program, the Appalachia Educational Laboratory (AEL) rewrote the GOE to a reading level and format appropriate for use by students and others in a variety of settings. The WTG Guide includes basic information about the work factors and worker characteristics not given in the GOE. Another major difference between the WTG Guide and the GOE is the listing of occupations associated with each Group. The GOE lists over 12,000 occupational titles. The Guide lists only "core" occupations, those providing the major employment opportunities nationally. This provides a more useful list for career exploration.

This Revised Edition of the *WTG Guide,* part of the new AEL *Career Exploration and Planning Program* (CEPP), has several improvements and changes. The major ones are:

1. The Career Area and Worker Trait Group descriptions have been expanded to include more detailed information important for career orientation and exploration.

2. Each of the 12 Career Areas is divided into smaller "clusters" of Worker Trait Groups. Descriptions of these clusters are included to provide for a broader Career Area description.

3. The "core" list of occupations includes those in state career information delivery systems and commonly used career guidance computer systems.

4. Occupations with military counterparts are identified. An appendix lists these occupations by WTG· and identifies the branches of service where training or experience is available.

5. The Profile Section, including the work factors and worker characteristics associated with each WTG description, has been refined to reflect only information about the core and not the thousands of other miscellaneous or obscure occupations.

6. Information about education and training has been expanded.

The expanded and improved Worker Trait Group Guide, Revised Edition, is a valuable information resource to assist youth and adults in the critical process of career exploration and planning.

David W. Winefordner, Director
Division of Career Guidance
Appalachia Educational Laboratory

Introduction to the User

The *Worker Trait Group Guide* is a basic career information reference. You can use it in your career exploration and educational planning. It has information about groups of occupations that provide many kinds of career opportunities.

There are over twenty thousand different occupations. These thousands of occupations are arranged into groups of similar occupations. Information about the occupations in each group has been summarized into general descriptions. Thus, in a short period of time, it is possible to get an overview of the entire world of work.

Before using the Worker Trait Group Guide you should read and become familiar with the following information. It describes how the Guide is organized and provides an overview of the information it contains.

Organization

The *Worker Trait Group Guide* has two major sections: (1) descriptions of the 12 Career Areas and the 66 Worker Trait Groups and (2) a series of nine appendices. The Career Area and Worker Trait Group descriptions provide the basic information you need for career exploration. The appendices provide detailed definitions of the work factors and worker characteristics used as part of the Career Area and Worker Trait Group descriptions.

The twelve Career Areas are related to the basic types of interests people have. In the Guide these areas are numbered from 01 through 12. A zero is used as a first digit on numbers less than ten. This makes all Career Area numbers two digits for computer use. The twelve Career Areas are listed below.

01 Artistic
02 Scientific
03 Nature
04 Authority
05 Mechanical
06 Industrial
07 Business Detail
08 Persuasive
09 Accommodating
10 Humanitarian
11 Social/Business
12 Physical Performing

A second kind of occupational grouping structure used in the Guide is called the Worker Trait Group Arrangement. This structure organizes occupations into groups that have common work factors and worker traits. This is why they are called Worker Trait Groups.

The work factors and worker traits are related to job success and worker satisfaction. Job success depends upon the abilities and skills of workers. Worker satisfaction is related to the interests and other characteristics of workers. You can use this information to help you identify those groups related to your interests and abilities.

In the Guide, the descriptions of the Worker Trait Groups are organized by the Career Area to which each belongs. For example, the following is a list of the Worker Trait Groups belonging to Area 01.

CAREER AREA 01: ARTISTIC

01.01 Literary Arts
01.02 Visual Arts
01.03 Performing Arts: Drama
01.04 Performing Arts: Music
01.05 Performing Arts: Dance
01.06 Technical Arts
01.07 Amusement
01.08 Modeling

Note that each Worker Trait Group (WTG) has a four-digit number. The first two digits represent the area to which the Worker Trait Group belongs. The second two digits represent the group within the area.

The Worker Trait Groups are numbered from 01.01 (Literary Arts) through 12.02 (Physical Feats). The WTG descriptions are in the sequence of these numbers. You can use the WTG numbers to locate specific Worker Trait Groups in the Guide. The WTG number and title are located at the top of each page of the description.

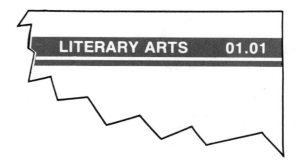

The pages containing the Career Area descriptions also have the area number located at the top for easy reference.

The second major section of the Guide, the Appendices, is located in the back of the book. The Appendices are labeled A through I. They also are referenced with letters of the Appendices at the top of the pages. You may use these Appendices for more details about information presented in the area and WTG descriptions.

Content

The major content of the Guide is the Career Area and Worker Trait Group descriptions. These descriptions provide the kind of information you need for career exploration and educational planning. Each Career Area and Worker Trait Group is described in the same format to make it easier for you to compare them.

The Career Area descriptions provide an overview of the Worker Trait Groups belonging to them. Each Career Area description contains:
1. A statement that identifies the basic type of interest related to the area.
2. An overview of the kind of work the area represents.
3. Cluster descriptions (the clusters are smaller groups of Worker Trait Groups belonging to the Career Area. For example, Area 01, ARTISTIC, is divided into two clusters — the "Creative Arts" and the "Performing Arts").

The Worker Trait Group descriptions provide more specific information about the world of work. Each Worker Trait Group has three parts:
1. A description of the group.
2. A qualifications profile.
3. A list of common occupations in the group.

The first part, the WTG description, provides a brief overview of the type of work related to the group. Then, subgroups of occupations belonging to the Worker Trait Group are given and described. These subgroups represent different kinds of work within a WTG. For example, WTG 01.01, LITERARY ARTS, includes the subgroups of Editing, Creative Writing, and Critiquing.

The group description also provides information to help you answer the following questions:
1. What skills and abilities would help you succeed in this kind of work?
2. Do you have or can you develop an interest in this kind of work?
3. What else should you know about this group of occupations?
4. How can you prepare for this kind of work?

The information presented and your response to these questions will help you identify related experiences and provide clues as to your interest in the type of work represented by the Worker Trait Group.

The second part, Qualifications Profile, provides a summary of the worker traits and work factors important to occupations in each WTG. The qualifications shown are those needed for *average successful job performance.* This means that some workers in occupations within a group may have higher qualifications. It also means that other workers with lower qualifications may be successful workers.

Keep in mind that a Worker Trait Group describes a group of related occupations, never a single occupation. Not all of the qualifications shown for a group will apply to every occupation in the group. An asterisk (*) marks those traits and factors related to more than 60% of the occupations listed. The other traits and factors are important, but relate to fewer occupations. The asterisk does not mean the trait is more important but that it is related to more occupations. Remember that Appendices B - G provide definitions and descriptions of all the traits and factors used.

The last part of each WTG description identifies common occupations belonging to the group. Most occupations listed represent major employment opportunities. Some are included because they are listed in commonly used sources of occupational information, state career information systems, or computerized guidance systems.

The occupations are listed with the subgroup to which each belongs. The following illustration shows the occupations belonging to the Editing subgroup of WTG 01.01 Literary Arts.

Editing

131.087-014	Reader
132.037-022	Editor, Publications (M)
132.037-026	Story Editor
132.067-014	Editor, Book
132.067-022	Editor, Greeting Card
187.167-174	Producer (M)
962.264-010	Editor, Film (M)

In the first column under the subgroup title "Editing" is the nine-digit code for the occupational title that follows. This code is used to locate specific information about the occupation in some sources such as the Dictionary of Occupational Titles (DOT). The DOT is a source you may wish to use frequently. Information about how to use the DOT is found in Appendix I, "Use of the WTG Guide With Other Career Exploration Resources".

Look again at the list of occupations in the illustration above. Three of the occupational titles have an (M) following the title. This means one or more branches of the military services offer training and experience in a military job that is directly related to the civilian occupation. More information about military training and experience opportunities may be found in Appendix A, "Occupations With Military Counterparts."

Use the Worker Trait Group Guide as a basic career information resource. As you use it you will become more familiar with the vocabulary of the world of work and gain understanding about groups of occupations related to your own interests and abilities. The time and effort you use now in career exploration and planning will help you make more meaningful career decisions later. Your future job success and satisfaction is dependent upon the decisions you make.

ARTISTIC

People with artistic interest enjoy work where they can apply their creative talents. They like to interpret and express ideas and feelings to others. Their work may interpret social and cultural values or be an expression of their own ideas. They gain personal satisfaction from the forms of art they create. Their work provides others with visual and listening enjoyment.

It takes a lot of time, study, and education to develop the skills needed for some jobs. But, there are opportunities for some workers who develop their natural talents through experience.

Work in the Artistic area is divided into two clusters: Creative Arts and Performing Arts.

Creative Arts

The Creative Arts cluster includes the literary, visual, and craft arts. Workers gather and organize information. They are involved with processes and methods, or they work on and produce a form of art. Workers need to be able to form a mental image of what their final product will look like. They often use their personal judgment to make decisions.

The Literary Arts express ideas and feelings through words to be read or performed. This work requires a good vocabulary and the ability to use words in creative ways. Ideas and feelings are expressed in the Visual and Craft Arts through paintings, sculptures, and products with artistic designs. These workers are skillful with their hands and fingers as they use the tools of their trade. They also have an eye for beauty.

Performing Arts

The Performing Arts cluster includes drama, music, and dance. Modeling and amusement jobs also are included. This type of work involves performing to entertain or amuse an audience. This may be in the form of serious drama where actors play their roles with feeling. Or, it may be as light and colorful as circus clowns amusing children.

A good voice and verbal skills are needed by Actors, Singers, and Announcers. Even Barkers are skilled in the use of words as they lure people into a side show. Some workers such as Instrumental Musicians and Dancers do not need these verbal skills. Models also have a silent role when posing for an artist or photographer. Workers in the Performing Arts have one thing in common. They feel at ease with their audiences and enjoy the recognition and appreciation they receive from their work.

The following Worker Trait Groups and Subgroups are related to the Creative Arts and Performing Arts clusters.

2

01

Artistic: an interest in creative expression of feelings and ideas.

Creative Arts

01.01 Literary Arts
Editing
Creative Writing
Critiquing

01.02 Visual Arts
Instructing and Appraising
Studio Art
Commercial Art

01.06 Technical Arts (Craft Arts)
Graphic Arts and Related Crafts
Arts and Crafts
Hand Lettering, Painting, and
  Decorating.

Performing Arts

01.03 Performing Arts: Drama
Instructing and Directing
Performing
Narrating and Announcing

01.04 Performing Arts: Music
Instructing and Directing
Composing and Arranging
Vocal Performing
Instrumental Performing

01.05 Performing Arts: Dance
Instructing and Choreography
Performing

**01.07 Amusement
    (Elemental Arts)**
Psychic Science
Announcing
Entertaining

01.08 Modeling
Personal Appearance

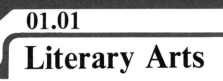

01.01
Literary Arts

Literary Arts is the creative expression of ideas and feelings in written form. This includes novels, short stories, plays, poems, and nonfiction. It also includes scripts for radio, TV, or motion pictures. This group includes the subgroups of:

Editing
Creative Writing
Critiquing

Editing is to correct or revise the writing of others. Editors may plan and direct the development of books, magazines, or scripts. They review materials from writers and select those of value. They edit for content and how the ideas are put together. They may rewrite the copy or tell the writers what changes to make.

Creative Writing expresses original ideas. A writer may select a topic of interest or be given an assignment. A writer usually must research a topic. In addition, some writers prepare ads, humorous materials, or song lyrics (words).

Critiquing is to examine and make judgments. Critics attend art exhibits, plays, read books, or view motion pictures or TV programs. They write reviews and base their opinions on knowledge, judgment, and experience.

Jobs may be found with companies which publish books, magazines, greeting cards, or newspapers. They also may be found with ad agencies, and radio, TV, and movie studios. Many writers are self-employed and sell their works to publishers.

Film editing requires special abilities and the use of technical equipment as in this videotape studio.

What Skills and Abilities Would Help You Succeed in This Kind of Work?

The most important skills are listed below. All of those listed do not apply to each occupation. As you explore occupations you should identify the specific ones needed.

Reading Comprehension – to understand what you read.

Leadership (in Editing) – to plan and direct the work of others.

Critical Thinking – to form opinions and make decisions based upon knowledge, judgment, and experience.

Esthetic Perception – to know quality or beauty in art and literature.

Creative Thinking – to develop original ideas.

Interpretation – to explain ideas, information, and feelings.

Proper Form – to use the rules of grammar when writing.

Vocabulary – to use many different words to write clearly and in an interesting way.

Organization – to arrange ideas, thoughts, and information in a way that can be understood.

Do You Have or Can You Develop an Interest in This Kind of Work?

Review the following questions. Your answers can give you clues as to your interest in the Literary Arts field.

Have you written an original story? Can you create characters and situations that interest and entertain others? Do you enjoy making up jokes or funny stories?

Do you enjoy word games? Do you like to solve crossword puzzles? Do you have a large vocabulary?

Have you used the library to look up information for a project? Do you enjoy writing? Do you have a pen pal or keep a diary?

Do you try to analyze the movies or TV programs you watch? Do you like to discuss them with your friends?

Do you like to read novels, short stories, or poems? Do you belong to a book club?

Do you like English courses? How are your grades?

Have you edited or written articles for a school paper? Have you written verses for a greeting card?

Have you written words for a song? Have you made up ideas for posters?

A conference helps copy writer and layout artist meet the requirements of the production manager.

What Else Should You Know About This Group of Occupations?

Literary Arts is not the only Worker Trait Group that involves writing. Group 11.08 (Communications) includes workers who deal with factual information. This differs from the creative expression of ideas related to the Literary Arts field.

Sometimes, a worker must start with an entry level job that requires few skills. This helps one to gain experience and to become known by the employer. Examples of published materials or writing samples may be required for some jobs. Some workers in the Literary Arts field may use their experience as a background for teaching.

The military services offer training and experience related to some occupations in this group. These occupations are included in the list at the end of this group description. They are identified by an (M) following the occupational title. More information about the military training and experience opportunities may be found in Appendix A.

How Can You Prepare for This Kind of Work?

Most occupations in Literary Arts require two to four years of training and experience. Others may require up to ten years. Two to four years of college is the most common way to prepare for this field. You may need several years of experience to advance to some jobs. For example, many skills of an editor are developed through experience as a writer.

As you plan your high school program, you should include courses related to Literary Arts. Next, you should include courses needed to enter college. The following list of courses and skills can help you plan your education.

Language Skills – grammar, spelling, punctuation; and communication skills such as speaking, listening, reading, and writing.

Composition – expressing information in writing; organizing, clarifying, and expressing ideas and feelings; writing styles such as creative, narrative, and persuasive.

Literature – study of different types of writing during periods of history.

Communications/Journalism – methods of gathering, processing, evaluating, and writing facts about current events and other topics for publication, radio, or TV.

Creative Writing – methods of writing short stories, poems, and drama.

Speech – speaking skills including debate, persuasion, discussion, criticism, and interpretation.

Editors and creative people frequently utilize word processing.

Some writers, editors, or critics may require a special background. For example, art, music, or drama may be involved in their work. Another example is *Copywriters*, who prepare advertising for goods and services. They may need a background in advertising/marketing. Social Science courses such as history, geography, and government also may be useful as background information for writing. You may identify other related programs as you explore specific occupations.

Qualifications Profile

This section is a summary of the worker traits and work factors related to successful job performance and worker satisfaction. Try to relate your interests, abilities, aptitudes, and preferences to these traits and factors. An asterisk (*) marks those traits and factors that are related to more than 60% of the occupations listed at the end of this group. The other traits and factors listed are as important, but relate to fewer occupations. See Appendices B-G for information about all of the worker traits and work factors.

Work Situations

Workers must be willing to:

3. Plan and direct an entire activity.
4. Deal with people.
5. Influence people's opinions, attitudes, and judgments.
* 7. Make decisions using personal judgment.
* 9. Interpret and express feelings, ideas, or facts.

Work Activities

The most important activities related to this group involve:

2. Business contact.

5. Recognition or appreciation from others.
* 6. Communication of ideas and information.
* 8. Creative thinking.
10. Working on or producing things.

Data-People-Things

This chart shows the levels for these three basic elements of work as related to this group. Level means the degree of difficulty of job tasks rather than the amount of time involved. The terms low, average, and high indicate the highest level at which occupations are involved. Compare your interests and abilities with the levels checked.

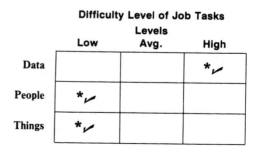

	Difficulty Level of Job Tasks		
	Low	**Avg.**	**High**
Data			*✓
People	*✓		
Things	*✓		

Drama critics attend performances and use their judgment in preparing reviews.

Physical Demands

Workers in this group of occupations must be able to do:

*S – Sedentary work

Working Conditions

These are the physical surroundings in which work is done. In occupations belonging to this group, work is performed:

*I – Inside — workers spend most of their time inside protected from weather conditions but not always from temperature changes.

Educational Skills

This chart shows the levels of reasoning, math, and language skills related to this group. These skills are usually developed in an educational setting. There are six levels ranging from the simple (1) to the most complex (6).

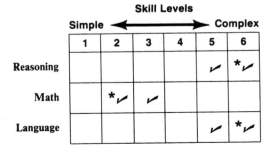

	Skill Levels					
	Simple ⟵ ⟶ Complex					
	1	2	3	4	5	6
Reasoning					✓	*✓
Math		*✓	✓			
Language					✓	*✓

8

Aptitudes

This chart presents the most important aptitudes related to this group. The levels checked compare aptitudes needed for success in this group to aptitudes of the general working population in all occupations. For example, level 5 is low and represents the bottom 10% of the working population. Level 1 is high and represents the top 10%.

APTITUDE LEVELS COMPARED TO ALL WORKERS						
Related Aptitudes (Ability to Learn)		Lower 1/3		Middle 1/3	Upper 1/3	
		Level 5	Level 4	Level 3	Level 2	Level 1
Code	Title	10%	23%	34%	23%	10%
G	General Learning Ability				✔	*✔
V	Verbal				✔	*✔

Common Occupations

A full listing of all occupations belonging to this group may be found in the Guide for Occupational Exploration.

The following occupations have been selected to represent this group. They provide the major employment opportunities. However, specific job opportunities will vary according to locations of industry, geographical region, and other factors.

Information may be found in common sources of occupational information, state career information systems, and computerized guidance systems.

An (M) follows the occupational title where the military services offer training and experience.

Editing

131.087-014	Reader
132.037-022	Editor, Publications (M)
132.037-026	Story Editor
132.067-014	Editor, Book
132.067-022	Editor, Greeting Card
187.167-174	Producer (M)
962.264-010	Editor, Film (M)

Creative Writing

131.067-014	Copy Writer
131.067-022	Editorial Writer (M)
131.067-026	Humorist
131.067-034	Lyricist
131.067-038	Playwright
131.067-042	Poet
131.067-046	Writer, Prose, Fiction and Nonfiction
131.087-010	Continuity Writer
131.087-018	Screen Writer (M)

Critiquing

131.067-018	Critic

Visual Arts

Visual Arts communicate ideas and feelings with original works of art. This includes paintings, designs, photographs, and sculptures. Workers in this group are very skillful in using the tools of their trade. Artists often refine their skills by working with others more experienced. This group includes the subgroups of:

Instructing and Appraising
Studio Art
Commercial Art

Instructing and Appraising require in-depth knowledge of the field of art. Art teachers instruct in the correct ways to paint, sketch, design, and sculpt. They observe their students at work to make comments and corrections. They may help their students become known by arranging art contests and exhibits. Art appraisers examine pieces of art to determine if they are original and to place a value on them. This process requires a knowledge of art history. Works of art are examined for such things as color value and style of brushstroke. This helps to establish the art period or to identify the artist.

Studio Art includes workers who paint or sculpt (carve) objects to be viewed for their esthetic (beauty) value. Some artists may specialize in a form of art such as stained glass. Painters use watercolors, oils, acrylics, and charcoal. They paint landscapes, portraits, still lifes, and abstracts. Sculptors carve objects from stone, concrete, plaster, or wood. They also form objects out of clay or wax. These objects are then cast in bronze or concrete, or fired in a kiln (oven) to harden.

A greeting card company cartoonist adds final touches to a drawing. All of his tools are close at hand.

Commercial Art is to design, layout, and illustrate materials, products, or services. Designers use their creative ideas to draw or sketch plans for products. These include such things as furniture, furs, clothes, and product packages. Cartoonists draw pictures for use in animated motion pictures or TV. They also draw cartoons to be used in books or magazines. They use their ideas or interpret written materials to amuse the public. Illustrators draw or paint pictures for books, magazines, or films. They may specialize and illustrate medical or other technical publications. Photographers take pictures of people, places, and events. They may specialize in still photography or motion picture camera work. Commercial Art also includes the display of products in windows, showcases, or on the floor of a retail store. Displays are used to attract the attention of customers.

Employment may be found with advertising agencies, printing and publishing firms, industrial firms, art schools, and retail stores. Some workers are self-employed and work in their homes or studios.

What Skills and Abilities Would Help You Succeed in This Kind of Work?

The most important skills are listed below. All of those listed do not apply to each occupation. As you explore occupations you should identify the specific ones needed.

Imagination – to form mental images (pictures) of things not present or not experienced before.

Spatial Perception – to form a mental image of how shapes and forms can be combined in three dimensions - height, width, and depth.

Color Discrimination – to recognize different shades and tones of color.

Dexterity – to move the fingers and hands quickly and correctly to use brushes, pens, pencils, chisels, or cameras.

Esthetic Perception – to know quality or beauty in art.

Visualization – to form a mental image of what the final work of art will look like.

Form Perception – to see details in objects or drawings and notice differences in shapes or shadings.

This merchandise displayer must make fresh produce attractive to the consumer.

A graphic designer working on a rough layout.

Do You Have or Can You Develop an Interest in This Kind of Work?

Review the following questions. Your answers can give you clues as to your interest in the Visual Arts field.

Have you taken art courses or private lessons? Have you entered art shows? Did any of your work sell or win awards?

Have you carved objects out of wood, stone, clay, or other material? Do you enjoy creating designs and figures? Do others admire your work?

Do you like to make sketches or drawings? Can you draw objects so others can tell what they are? Have you drawn posters?

Have you helped design or paint scenery for plays? Did the scenery achieve the desired effect?

Do you take photographs of family, friends, or other activities? Are they of good quality and pleasing to the eye? Have you started a scrapbook for the photos you have taken?

Have you visited art shows and galleries? Do you try to judge the quality of the exhibits or the works of art? Do you regularly read articles or magazines about art?

Have you made a floral arrangement using live or artificial flowers? Do you enjoy creating original designs with flowers?

Do you create cartoons for the school paper or as a hobby? Are you able to convey a message through your characters? Does your work amuse others?

Do you enjoy looking at window displays? Have you ever built a display to attract people's attention? Have you helped to arrange items for display at a garage sale?

What Else Should You Know About This Group of Occupations?

Although talent is the major skill needed, technical skills are becoming more important. For example, industrial designers often use computer aided design (CAD). This new technology (method) helps them design new products or to improve existing ones. Also, computers are used by illustrators to generate images for TV.

Some well-known artists sell enough work to support themselves. However, most add to their incomes with earnings from another job. Some artists display their work in community settings to make people aware of their talents. Artists who have a variety of skills may find jobs more easily than those who specialize.

Artists usually develop a file of the best examples of their work. This file is called a portfolio. Artists usually show their portfolios when applying for jobs.

The military services offer training and experience related to some occupations in this group. These are included in the list at the end of this group description. They are identified by an (M) following the occupational title. More information about the military training and experience opportunities may be found in Appendix A.

How Can You Prepare for This Kind of Work?

Most occupations in Visual Arts require four to ten years of training and experience. However, in the subgroup of Commercial Art only two to four years are needed for most jobs.

Some high school courses can help you decide if you have interest in and talent for the Visual Arts field. Vocational or technical programs can help you get started in some jobs. Colleges and art schools provide more advanced programs.

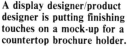

A display designer/product designer is putting finishing touches on a mock-up for a countertop brochure holder.

As you plan your high school program you should include courses related to Visual Arts. Next, you should include courses needed to enter college or the art program or school you select. There is a difference in the knowledge and skills needed between commercial art and fine art (Studio Art and Instructing and Appraising). Because of this difference you may need to determine which one you prefer before you select courses. Listed below are courses and skills related to commercial and fine art.

Commercial Art – courses related to product and package design; visual advertisements and displays; communications technology; and graphic illustrations and pictures used in printed materials. The knowledge and skills related to illustration and design are very important. Drawing, sketching, drafting, or the use of computer software packages may be needed. In addition, you may need to know about the products or information to be presented. For example, a medical illustrator needs to know anatomy and other background information.

Fine Art – Important courses are art history, appreciation, and conservation. These provide the basic background needed by artists, painters, sculptors, appraisers, restorers, and teachers. They also must know about the materials and techniques used to prepare a work of art. Intermedia (the use of a variety of materials) might be part of the preparation. Kinetics (using materials in motion, including light) is another form of fine art.

In addition to programs and courses related to commercial or fine art, you may wish to consider: Home Economics (clothing, textiles, home furnishings, and floral design); Industrial Arts (wood and metal working, textiles/leather, upholstering, ceramics, and photography); and Vocational Programs such as Distributive Education (merchandising and marketing).

Qualifications Profile

This section is a summary of the worker traits and work factors related to successful job performance and worker satisfaction. Try to relate your interests, abilities, aptitudes, and preferences to these traits and factors. An asterisk (*) marks those traits and factors that are related to more than 60% of the occupations listed at the end of this group. The other traits and factors listed are as important, but relate to fewer occupations. See Appendices B-G for information about all of the worker traits and work factors.

Work Situations

Workers must be willing to:

3. Plan and direct an entire activity.

4. Deal with people.

* 7. Make decisions using personal judgment.

* 9. Interpret and express feelings, ideas, or facts.

10. Work within precise limits or standards of accuracy.

Work Activities

The most important activities related to this group involve:

* 6. Communication of ideas and information.
* 8. Creative thinking.
*10. Working on or producing things.

Data-People-Things

This chart shows the levels for these three basic elements of work as related to this group. Level means the degree of difficulty of job tasks rather than the amount of time involved. The terms low, average, and high indicate the highest level at which occupations are involved. Compare your interests and abilities with the levels checked.

This designer of patterns for china is painting a master from which production patterns will be made.

Difficulty Level of Job Tasks

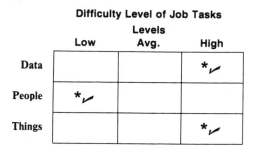

	Low	Avg.	High
Data			*✔
People	*✔		
Things			*✔

Educational Skills

This chart shows the levels of reasoning, math, and language skills related to this group. These skills are usually developed in an educational setting. There are six levels ranging from the simple (1) to the most complex (6).

Working Conditions

These are the physical surroundings in which work is done. In occupations belonging to this group, work is performed:

* I – Inside — workers spend most of their time inside protected from weather conditions but not always from temperature changes.

  B – Both inside and outside — workers spend about equal time in each setting.

Skill Levels

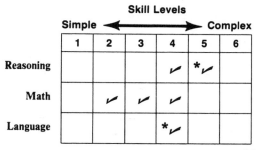

	Simple → Complex					
	1	2	3	4	5	6
Reasoning				✔	*✔	
Math		✔	✔	✔		
Language				*✔		

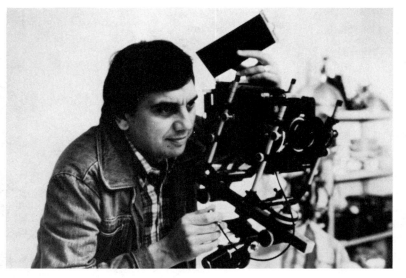

In his studio, this photographer has complete control over the lighting needed to make a successful photo.

Physical Demands

Workers in this group of occupations must be able to do:

S – Sedentary work
L – Light work

Aptitudes

This chart presents the most important aptitudes related to this group. The levels checked compare aptitudes needed for success in this group to aptitudes of the general working population in all occupations. For example, level 5 is low and represents the bottom 10% of the working population. Level 1 is high and represents the top 10%.

APTITUDE LEVELS COMPARED TO ALL WORKERS						
Related Aptitudes (Ability to Learn)		**Lower 1/3**		**Middle 1/3**	**Upper 1/3**	
		Level **5**	Level **4**	Level **3**	Level **2**	Level **1**
Code	Title	10%	23%	34%	23%	10%
G	General Learning Ability				*✔	
S	Spatial				*✔	✔
P	Form Perception				*✔	✔
K	Motor Coordination			✔	✔	
F	Finger Dexterity			✔	✔	✔
M	Manual Dexterity			✔	✔	

Common Occupations

A full listing of all occupations belonging to this group may be found in the Guide for Occupational Exploration.

The following occupations have been selected to represent this group. They provide the major employment opportunities. However, specific job opportunities will vary according to locations of industry, geographical region, and other factors.

Information may be found in common sources of occupational information, state career information systems, and computerized guidance systems.

An (M) follows the occupational title where the military services offer training and experience.

Instructing and Appraising
149.021-010	Teacher, Art
191.287-014	Appraiser, Art

Studio Art
142.061-034	Ornamental-Metalwork Designer
142.061-054	Stained Glass Artist
144.061-010	Painter
144.061-018	Sculptor
149.041-010	Quick Sketch Artist

Commercial Art
141.031-010	Art Director
141.061-010	Cartoonist
141.061-014	Fashion Artist
141.061-018	Graphic Designer (M)
141.061-022	Illustrator (M)
141.061-026	Illustrator, Medical and Scientific (M)
141.067-010	Creative Director
141.081-010	Cartoonist, Motion Pictures
141.081-014	Commercial Designer
142.031-010	Art Director
142.031-014	Manager, Display
142.051-010	Display Designer
142.051-014	Interior Designer
142.061-014	Cloth Designer
142.061-018	Clothes Designer
142.061-022	Furniture Designer
142.061-026	Industrial Designer
142.061-042	Set Decorator
142.061-050	Set Designer
142.081-010	Floral Designer
142.081-014	Fur Designer
142.081-018	Package Designer
143.062-010	Director of Photography (M)
143.062-022	Photographer, Motion Picture (M)
143.062-030	Photographer, Still (M)
143.062-034	Photojournalist (M)
149.061-010	Audiovisual Production Specialist (M)
298.081-010	Displayer, Merchandise
976.667-010	Photographer Helper

01.03
Performing Arts: Drama

Drama is the creative use of words or actions to entertain an audience. Body movements, facial expressions, and tones of voice are used. Some workers may perform on stage as actors. Others may not face an audience, but perform for TV, movie, or radio. Drama involves more than acting. It also includes the creative use of words to describe events in an entertaining way. This group includes the subgroups of:

Instructing and Directing
Performing
Narrating and Announcing

Instructing and Directing is working with actors to teach and direct them in the methods of acting. This helps them to put feelings into

the roles they play. Teachers and Directors read and interpret scripts to be performed. They help actors to understand the ideas and emotions to be expressed. A Producer selects a play and determines the budget needed to produce it. The Producer also must obtain the finances needed.

Performing is to act in serious or comic roles. Actors rehearse for many hours to learn their lines and cues. Clowns and comedians may dress in costumes and makeup to do funny routines. Magicians perform acts to mystify audiences. They use props such as cards, rabbits, and jewelry.

Narrating and Announcing involves talking to an audience. This may be during a radio

A popular children's television show features clowns.

or TV broadcast, or as part of a motion picture. Narrators describe or explain the action taking place. They also may write their scripts. Announcers give station breaks, commercials, or public service information. They may talk with guests or describe public events such as parades.

The major sources for jobs include radio and TV stations, motion picture studios, nightclubs, and theaters. Schools and colleges also employ teachers and directors.

What Skills and Abilities Would Help You Succeed in This Kind of Work?

The most important skills are listed below. All of those listed do not apply to each occupation. As you explore occupations, you should identify the specific ones needed.

Interpretation – to explain ideas, information, and feelings.

Verbalization – to put thoughts and actions into words.

Memorization – to learn scripts or other written materials by heart.

Performance – to express ideas and emotions through facial expressions, body motions, and voice.

Elocution – to deliver words effectively, showing emotion and expression.

Proper Form – to use the rules of grammar when speaking.

Vocabulary – to use a variety of words to speak clearly and in an interesting way.

Poise – to be calm and self-confident in front of an audience.

Leadership (in Instructing and Directing) – to plan and direct the work of others.

Do You Have or Can You Develop an Interest in This Kind of Work?

Review the following questions. Your answers can give you clues as to your interest in the Drama field.

Have you attended plays or movies? Do you enjoy them? Can you judge the quality of acting?

Have you acted in or directed a school play or skit? Do you like to perform before an audience? Do you like to instruct others?

Have you done impersonations for friends or family members? Can they guess who or what you are impersonating? Do you enjoy entertaining at parties or other events?

Have you been on a debate team? Are you able to control your voice and speak loudly and clearly?

Have you been a master of ceremonies or spoken before a group? Were you at ease before the audience?

Are you able to memorize easily? Can you remember lines and cues when you act in a play?

Have you had courses in speech? Did you enjoy them?

What Else Should You Know About This Group of Occupations?

Acting requires a special talent as well as practice and hard work. Only a few actors become famous. To become known in the field may require starting out by taking minor

University productions can be valuable preparation for actors and producers.

roles. Beginners may need to work as stagehands in small theaters. Several auditions may be required to get a job.

Jobs in the dramatic arts field often have demanding work schedules. Rehearsals and performances may start early or run late every day. Frequent travel may be necessary.

Radio and TV station managers, college teachers, and theatrical agents often know about job openings. Many are willing to help people who have an interest in this field.

The military services offer training and experience related to some occupations in this group. These occupations are included in the list at the end of this group description. They are identified by an (M) following the occupational title. More information about the military training and experience opportunities may be found in Appendix A.

20

How Can You Prepare for This Kind of Work?

Most occupations in Drama require six months up to ten years of training and experience. The occupations related to directing and instructing need the most time. Those related to narrating and announcing, and some performing jobs, require the least time.

For some jobs training can be obtained in special schools of the performing and dramatic arts. These are usually located in or near large cities. Community and two-year colleges also offer related courses. Many of these courses are accepted for credit at universities.

To advance in this field usually requires formal training, hard work, and a lot of experience. Sometimes, getting an important role may be based upon the people you know, a personal trait, or a special ability.

As you plan your high school program you should include the courses related to Drama. Next, you should include courses needed to enter college or schools of the performing and dramatic arts. The following list of courses and skills can help you plan your education.

Language – grammar and other basic composition skills.

Speech – speaking skills including debate, persuasion, discussion, criticism, and interpretation.

Drama – acting, directing, play production, dramatic literature, history of the theater, scenic and stage design, and costuming.

Communications – design and production of programs for radio, TV, or motion pictures.

Broadcasting and Motion Picture Technology – equipment, processes, and production procedures.

Instruction – methods of teaching and demonstrating.

Although indirectly related, music may be helpful for occupations such as a Director, Producer, and Disk Jockey.

Qualifications Profile

This section is a summary of the worker traits and work factors related to successful job performance and worker satisfaction. Try to relate your interests, abilities, aptitudes, and preferences to these traits and factors. An asterisk (*) marks those traits and factors that are related to more than 60% of the occupations listed at the end of this group. The other traits and factors listed are as important, but relate to fewer occupations. See Appendices B-G for information about all of the worker traits and work factors.

Work Activities

The most important activities related to this group involve:

   2. Business contact.
 * 5. Recognition or appreciation from others.
 * 6. Communication of ideas and information.
   8. Creative thinking.

Physical Demands

Workers in this group of occupations must be able to do:

*L – Light work

Watching a bank of television monitors, TV producers must make quick decisions about which picture will be shown.

Data-People-Things

This chart shows the levels for these three basic elements of work as related to this group. Level means the degree of difficulty of job tasks rather than the amount of time involved. The terms low, average, and high indicate the highest level at which occupations are involved. Compare your interests and abilities with the levels checked.

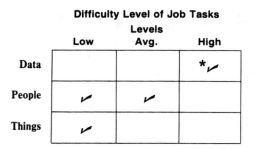

Difficulty Level of Job Tasks

	Low	Avg.	High
Data			*✓
People	✓	✓	
Things	✓		

Working Conditions

These are the physical surroundings in which work is done. In occupations belonging to this group, work is performed:

*I – Inside — workers spend most of their time inside protected from weather conditions but not always from temperature changes.

Educational Skills

This chart shows the levels of reasoning, math, and language skills related to this group. These skills are usually developed in an educational setting. There are six levels ranging from the simple (1) to the most complex (6).

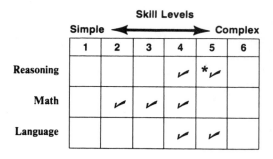

Skill Levels

Simple ◄———► Complex

	1	2	3	4	5	6
Reasoning				✓	*✓	
Math		✓	✓	✓		
Language				✓	✓	

Work Situations

Workers must be willing to:

* 1. Perform duties which change frequently.
* 3. Plan and direct an entire activity.
* 4. Deal with people.
* 7. Make decisions using personal judgment.
  9. Interpret and express feelings, ideas, or facts.
 10. Work within precise limits or standards of accuracy.

Aptitudes

This chart presents the most important aptitudes related to this group. The levels checked compare aptitudes needed for success in this group to aptitudes of the general working population in all occupations. For example, level 5 is low and represents the bottom 10% of the working population. Level 1 is high and represents the top 10%.

		APTITUDE LEVELS COMPARED TO ALL WORKERS				
Related Aptitudes (Ability to Learn)		**Lower 1/3**		**Middle 1/3**	**Upper 1/3**	
		Level 5	Level 4	Level 3	Level 2	Level 1
Code	**Title**	10%	23%	34%	23%	10%
G	General Learning Ability			✔	*✔	✔
V	Verbal				*✔	

Common Occupations

A full listing of all occupations belonging to this group may be found in the Guide for Occupational Exploration.

The following occupations have been selected to represent this group. They provide the major employment opportunities. However, specific job opportunities will vary according to locations of industry, geographical region, and other factors.

Information may be found in common sources of occupational information, state career information systems, and computerized guidance systems.

An (M) follows the occupational title where the military services offer training and experience.

Instructing and Directing

150.027-010   Dramatic Coach
150.027-014   Teacher, Drama
150.067-010   Director, Stage
159.067-010   Director, Motion Picture (M)
159.067-014   Director, Television (M)
159.117-010   Producer (M)
159.167-014   Director, Radio (M)
159.167-018   Manager, Stage
159.267-010   Director, Casting
187.167-178   Producer

Performing

150.047-010   Actor
159.041-010   Magician
159.047-010   Clown
159.047-014   Comedian

Narrating and Announcing

150.147-010   Narrator
159.147-010   Announcer (M)
159.147-014   Disk Jockey (M)

01.04
Performing Arts: Music

Music is sounds that have rhythm, harmony, and melody. It is a form of art. Music is a creative way to express feelings and emotions through singing or playing a musical instrument. This group includes the subgroups of:

Instructing and Directing
Composing and Arranging
Vocal Performing
Instrumental Performing

Instructing and Directing involves helping others to learn musical skills. This includes score and sight reading, harmony, and music theory. It also involves leading vocal or instrumental music groups. Conductors and Directors select music, hold auditions, and lead groups at rehearsals and performances. They also may schedule tours and other activities.

Composing and Arranging includes writing original music such as popular songs, operas, or symphonies. It also includes arranging music so it can be played or sung in different ways. Composers use symbols and words as the language of music to express feelings and ideas. Arrangers adapt music for a style of voice, or to achieve the desired sound effects from instruments.

Vocal Performing is singing. Singers interpret music using their knowledge of melody, harmony, and rhythm. As a member of a vocal group they may need to conform to a set style. As a soloist they may use their own style to perform. Singers are usually known by their voice range such as tenor, soprano, or bass. They may be known for one type of music. This may be opera, rock, folk, or country and western.

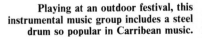
Playing at an outdoor festival, this instrumental music group includes a steel drum so popular in Carribean music.

Instrumental Performing involves playing a musical instrument. This may be solo, or with an orchestra, band, rock group, or jazz combo. Musicians play from memory or follow notes printed on sheet music. They study and rehearse to learn and interpret scores. Classical music is usually played on string, brass, woodwind, or percussion instruments. The trumpet, trombone, drums, flute, guitar, and piano are examples of instruments also used for popular music.

Music is performed in a variety of settings. Jobs may be found with theaters, concert halls, nightclubs, and restaurants. Schools and colleges, recording studios, and music publishing companies also employ musicians.

Do You Have or Can You Develop an Interest in This Kind of Work?

Review the following questions. Your answers can give you clues as to your interests in the field of Music.

Have you had lessons in singing or in playing an instrument? Did you practice regularly? Did you take part in recitals?

Have you sung in a school glee club or church choir? Were you chosen for a solo?

Have you sung or played with a rock or country group? Have you performed in an amateur musical play or a variety show? Do you enjoy performing before an audience?

What Skills and Abilities Would Help You Succeed in This Kind of Work?

The most important skills are listed below. All of those listed do not apply to each occupation. As you explore occupations you should identify the specific ones needed.

Dexterity – to move the hands and fingers skillfully to play a musical instrument.

Performance – to express ideas and feelings by singing, or by playing a musical instrument.

Form Perception – to recognize musical notes and symbols.

Poise – to be calm and self-confident in front of an audience.

Persistence – to practice and rehearse music for long periods of time.

Memorization – to learn words or music symbols by heart.

Interpretation – to express creative thoughts and feelings through music.

After many years of training and practice, this young woman is auditioning for a part in a musical.

Have you played in a school band or orchestra? Can you read music? Can you memorize music notes easily?

Have you directed a musical group? Do you have an ear for music? Can you tell when a singer or player is off-key?

Have you composed or arranged vocal or instrumental music? Did others enjoy it?

What Else Should You Know About This Group of Occupations?

Musicians often spend many years in training. They need talent and must be willing to practice. To get a job, many musicians must audition to demonstrate their skills. Also, many jobs require frequent travel. Because of the competition, many musicians are not able to find enough work to be employed full time. Many add to their incomes by teaching music, or by working in other jobs.

The quality of a singer's voice may change with age. As a result, a singing career may not last long. Sometimes personal singing styles become outdated or unpopular. This also may lead to a short career. Singers who can dance or act are preferred for some jobs.

Most conductors and directors have prior experience as performers. Their work is usually on a more permanent basis. Composers are usually self-employed. They may write music to be published, or performed and recorded. They may also write music for TV commercials, or other special purposes.

The military services offer training and experience related to some occupations in this group. These occupations are included in the list at the end of this group description. They are identified by an (M) following the occupational title. More information about the military training and experience opportunities may be found in Appendix A.

How Can You Prepare for This Kind of Work?

Most occupations in Music require from four years up to ten years or more of training and experience. Instrumental musicians usually start to develop their talent at an early age. They begin by taking lessons in elementary or junior high school. Many students also take private lessons. They develop their skills through many hours of practice. This practice must continue to maintain and improve their skills.

Singers usually start their training after their voices mature. They also must continue to practice as long as they perform. School music classes or vocal groups may provide initial training. Some students may take private lessons.

Formal programs may be taken in a college or music conservatory. These programs provide a background in music theory and composition needed for some jobs in this field. Composers, conductors, and arrangers need this background as well as more advanced training.

Experience is important for many jobs in this field. Most teachers and directors have prior experience as singers or instrumental musicians. Also, most composers, conductors, and arrangers have had other music experience.

As you plan your high school program, you should include courses related to music. Next, you should include courses needed to enter college or a school of music. The following list of courses and skills can help you plan your education.

Music – General background courses related to enjoying, performing, and creating music; activities such as choir, chorus, band, and orchestra.

Music Performance – courses to develop skills to play a musical instrument or to develop one's voice.

Music History and Appreciation – courses to study music and its relationship to history and current events, the lives of musicians, and the development of musical styles.

Music Theory and Composition – courses to study the basic elements and forms of music, and the techniques of creating and arranging music.

Courses such as speech and drama may be helpful. They can help build poise and self-confidence important for performing before an audience. Courses such as dancing can provide a related skill. Also, for some singers, a foreign language may be helpful.

Qualifications Profile

This section is a summary of the worker traits and work factors related to successful job performance and worker satisfaction. Try to relate your interests, abilities, aptitudes, and preferences to these traits and factors. An asterisk (*) marks those traits and factors that are related to more than 60% of the occupations listed at the end of this group. The other traits and factors listed are as important, but relate to fewer occupations. See Appendices B-G for information about all of the worker traits and work factors.

Physical Demands

Workers in this group of occupations must be able to do:

S – Sedentary work
*L – Light work

Work Activities

The most important activities related to this group involve:

  2. Business contact.
* 5. Recognition or appreciation from others.
* 6. Communication of ideas and information.
* 8. Creative thinking.

Work Situations

Workers must be willing to:

  3. Plan and direct an entire activity.
* 4. Deal with people.
* 7. Make decisions using personal judgment.
* 9. Interpret and express feelings, ideas, or facts.

Data-People-Things

This chart shows the levels for these three basic elements of work as related to this group. Level means the degree of difficulty of job tasks rather than the amount of time involved. The terms low, average, and high indicate the highest level at which occupations are involved. Compare your interests and abilities with the levels checked.

Difficulty Level of Job Tasks

	Low	Avg.	High
Data			✔
People	✔	✔	
Things	✔		

Working Conditions

These are the physical surroundings in which work is done. In occupations belonging to this group, work is performed:

*I – Inside — workers spend most of their time inside protected from weather conditions but not always from temperature changes.

Educational Skills

This chart shows the levels of reasoning, math, and language skills related to this group. These skills are usually developed in an educational setting. There are six levels ranging from the simple (1) to the most complex (6).

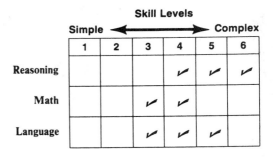

Skill Levels

Simple ← → Complex

	1	2	3	4	5	6
Reasoning				✔	✔	✔
Math			✔	✔		
Language			✔	✔	✔	

After completing a musical score at his desk, this composer checks his arrangement at the piano. Like many composers, he does not compose while seated at a piano.

Aptitudes

This chart presents the most important aptitudes related to this group. The levels checked compare aptitudes needed for success in this group to aptitudes of the general working population in all occupations. For example, level 5 is low and represents the bottom 10% of the working population. Level 1 is high and represents the top 10%.

APTITUDE LEVELS COMPARED TO ALL WORKERS						
Related Aptitudes (Ability to Learn)		Lower 1/3		Middle 1/3	Upper 1/3	
		Level **5**	Level **4**	Level **3**	Level **2**	Level **1**
Code	Title	10%	23%	34%	23%	10%
G	General Learning Ability				✔	* ✔
V	Verbal				* ✔	✔
Q	Clerical Perception			✔	* ✔	
K	Motor Coordination		✔	✔	✔	
F	Finger Dexterity		✔	✔	✔	

Common Occupations

A full listing of all occupations belonging to this group may be found in the Guide for Occupational Exploration.

The following occupations have been selected to represent this group. They provide the major employment opportunities. However, specific job opportunities will vary according to locations of industry, geographical region, and other factors.

Information may be found in common sources of occupational information, state career information systems, and computerized guidance systems.

An (M) follows the occupational title where the military services offer training and experience.

Instructing and Directing

152.021-010   Teacher, Music
152.047-010   Choral Director (M)
152.047-014   Conductor, Orchestra (M)
152.047-018   Director, Music
159.167-010   Artist and Repertoire

Composing and Arranging

152.067-010   Arranger (M)
152.067-014   Composer (M)
152.067-022   Orchestrator

Vocal Performing

152.047-022   Singer (M)

Instrumental Performing

152.041-010   Musician, Instrumental (M)

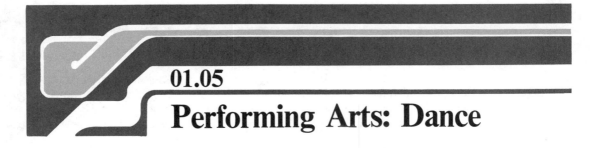

01.05
Performing Arts: Dance

Dance is the movement of the body to rhythm and sound. It involves creating, performing, or teaching dance routines and techniques. Dance is often used in drama and musical productions to enhance the performance. It adds to the creative expression of feelings and emotions. This group includes the subgroups of:

Instructing and Choreography
Performing

Instructing and Choreography is to teach or create dances such as ballet, ballroom, tap, or jazz. Teachers and choreographers explain and demonstrate techniques and methods used to dance correctly. Choreographers create dances to be performed on stage or screen. They may hold auditions to select dancers. Managers of dance studios also are included in this subgroup.

Performing includes dancers. They use music and graceful body movements to interpret a story, or to express ideas, feelings or emotions. They perform classical, modern, or acrobatic dances to entertain an audience. Dancers practice long hours in order to perfect a routine. In addition to dancing some may sing or act.

Jobs may be found with TV and movie studios, theaters, and nightclubs. Schools and colleges may also employ these workers.

Dance studio managers and teachers must be skilled in many forms of dance and aerobics to lead a class confidently.

Concentration is required to execute the precise movements of an interpretive dance.

What Skills and Abilities Would Help You Succeed in This Kind of Work?

The most important skills are listed below. All of those listed do not apply to each occupation. As you explore occupations you should identify the specific ones needed.

Memorization – to learn instructions and dance routines by heart.

Physical Stamina – to have the strength to endure long hours of practice and rehearsals.

Performance – to express ideas and emotions through body movements.

Poise – to be calm and self-confident in front of an audience.

Accuracy – to make precise body movements in rhythm with music and in timing with other dancers.

Dexterity – to move the hands and feet together in response to music or visual instructions.

Visualization – to form a mental image (picture) of body movements for a dance routine.

Interpretation – to express creative thoughts and ideas through dance.

Creative Thinking – to make up new dance routines.

Do You Have or Can You Develop an Interest in This Kind of Work?

Review the following questions. Your answers can give you clues as to your interest in the Dance field.

Have you taken dance lessons? Do you learn dance steps quickly? Do you like to learn new dances?

Have you performed in a school or amateur musical? Can you move your body gracefully? Do you enjoy performing before an audience?

Have you attended dances? Can you lead or follow dance steps easily? Do you have a sense of rhythm?

Have you created dance routines for an amateur musical? Can you teach dance steps to others?

Have you marched in a school band? Have you been a cheerleader or on a drill team? Do you enjoy this type of activity?

Have you done freestyle or interpretive dancing? Do you like this kind of expression?

What Else Should You Know About This Group of Occupations?

Dancing is strenuous (hard) and requires a lot of energy. Dancers must have strong feet, ankles, and legs. Daily practice is a must to develop and maintain the physical condition needed. Most shows take place in the evening and on weekends. Dancers must work late hours and may be required to travel.

Many dancers cannot make dancing a lifetime job because of the physical demands. By their thirties, they may change jobs and become choreographers or dance teachers, or find other work.

Dancers most often work with a partner or as part of a group. Only the best dance solo. Dancers usually audition for jobs and there is a lot of competition. Some dancers combine stage work with teaching. Many are self-employed and give private lessons.

Dancing in unison requires all members of the troupe to memorize the entire routine.

How Can You Prepare for This Kind of Work?

Jobs in this field require two to ten years of training and experience. Training as a dancer usually starts at an early age and continues throughout one's career. Dance instructors and choreographers require the most training and have experience as performers. A college degree is usually needed for teaching in a university. Although helpful, a degree is not necessary for work in private studios.

Initial training in dance is usually received in private studios. Taking part in dance recitals, or church, school, and other dance programs provides early experience. Advanced training and experience can be obtained in dance academies, colleges, and theater art schools. Programs in these schools provide a background in the theory, history, and techniques of dance.

As you plan your high school program you should include courses related to this field. Next you should include courses needed, if you plan to enter college or a dance academy. The following list of courses and skills can help you plan your education.

Physical Education – courses to develop muscle strength and coordination; gymnastics, aerobics, and different types of dance.

Liberal Arts – courses such as music, drama, theater, art, literature, history, and philosophy (helpful in the interpretation of stories, ideas, feelings, and emotions).

Dance – introductory courses; specific types of dance such as ballet, folk, tap, jazz, modern, and acrobatic; dance techniques, choreography, and stagecraft.

Instruction – courses in methods of teaching and demonstrating.

Business – courses related to the operation of a dance studio.

Qualifications Profile

This section is a summary of the worker traits and work factors related to successful job performance and worker satisfaction. Try to relate your interests, abilities, aptitudes, and preferences to these traits and factors. An asterisk (*) marks those traits and factors that are related to more than 60% of the occupations listed at the end of this group. The other traits and factors listed are as important, but relate to fewer occupations. See Appendices B-G for information about all of the worker traits and work factors.

Work Activities

The most important activities related to this group involve:

   2. Business contact.

* 5. Recognition or appreciation from others.

* 6. Communication of ideas and information.

* 8. Creative thinking.

A choreographer "composes" a dance routine, teaches it to the dancers, then continues to work with them to be sure the performance is effective.

Physical Demands

Workers in this group of occupations must be able to do:

L – Light work

H – Heavy work

Data-People-Things

This chart shows the levels for these three basic elements of work as related to this group. Level means the degree of difficulty of job tasks rather than the amount of time involved. The terms low, average, and high indicate the highest level at which occupations are involved. Compare your interests and abilities with the levels checked.

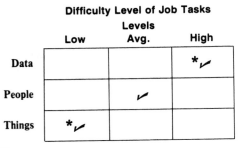

Difficulty Level of Job Tasks

	Low	Avg.	High
Data			*✔
People		✔	
Things	*✔		

Educational Skills

This chart shows the levels of reasoning, math, and language skills related to this group. These skills are usually developed in an educational setting. There are six levels ranging from the simple (1) to the most complex (6).

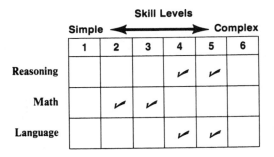

Skill Levels

Simple ⟵⟶ Complex

	1	2	3	4	5	6
Reasoning				✔	✔	
Math		✔	✔			
Language				✔	✔	

Work Situations

Workers must be willing to:

* 3. Plan and direct an entire activity.
  4. Deal with people.
* 7. Make decisions using personal judgment.
* 9. Interpret and express feelings, ideas, or facts.
*10. Work within precise limits or standards of accuracy.

Working Conditions

These are the physical surroundings in which work is done. In occupations belonging to this group, work is performed:

*I – Inside — workers spend most of their time inside protected from weather conditions but not always from temperature changes.

Aptitudes

This chart presents the most important aptitudes related to this group. The levels checked compare aptitudes needed for success in this group to aptitudes of the general working population in all occupations. For example, level 5 is low and represents the bottom 10% of the working population. Level 1 is high and represents the top 10%.

APTITUDE LEVELS COMPARED TO ALL WORKERS						
Related Aptitudes **(Ability to Learn)**		Lower 1/3		Middle 1/3	Upper 1/3	
		Level **5** 10%	Level **4** 23%	Level **3** 34%	Level **2** 23%	Level **1** 10%
Code	Title					
G	General Learning Ability			✔	*✔	
S	Spatial			✔	✔	
K	Motor Coordination		✔	✔	✔	

Common Occupations

A full listing of all occupations belonging to this group may be found in the Guide for Occupational Exploration.

The following occupations have been selected to represent this group. They provide the major employment opportunities. However, specific job opportunities will vary according to locations of industry, geographical region, and other factors.

Information may be found in common sources of occupational information, state career information systems, and computerized guidance systems.

Instructing and Choreography
151.027-010   Choreographer
151.027-014   Instructor, Dancing
187.167-086   Manager, Dance Studio

Performing
151.047-010   Dancer

Technical Arts (Craft Arts)

Technical Arts is to make, design, repair, or process art products. Workers use special skills to do fine handwork. They work with materials such as wood, clay, stone, metal, or gemstones. Some workers do hand lettering, etching, engraving, or painting. They use engraving and etching equipment, knives, chisels, paint brushes, and power tools. This group includes the subgroups of:

Graphic Arts and Related Crafts
Arts and Crafts
Hand Lettering, Painting, and Decorating

Graphic Arts and Related Crafts include a broad range of jobs. Most of the work is not usually thought of as art. However, there is an element of art in the product, its design, or the manufacturing process. Some workers engrave designs or lettering into the surface of flat or curved metal objects. Other workers make plates for printing presses. These plates are made by chemical and manual etching or by a photographic process. Some workers follow sketches or blueprints to develop plate designs. Others photograph drawings to make negatives for transfer to the printing plates.

Arts and Crafts include workers who design, produce, or repair handmade products. They use special hand tools and power tools in their work. They use their artistic ability as they carve designs, make models, and to make or repair art objects and jewelry. They work with a variety of materials such as stone, wood, glass, precious metals, and leather. The products range from novelty items to expensive jewelry. They may make stained glass windows or mosaic patterns in tile and other materials.

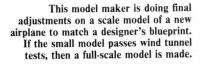

This model maker is doing final adjustments on a scale model of a new airplane to match a designer's blueprint. If the small model passes wind tunnel tests, then a full-scale model is made.

Hand Lettering, Painting, and Decorating includes workers who do freehand artistic work. They may paint or letter signs. Some workers retouch photographs or negatives, or add oil colors to portraits. Others may sketch and paint designs on products such as pottery and glassware.

Jobs may be found with industries such as printing and publishing, engraving, signs, jewelry, and photofinishing. Jobs also are found with companies making furniture, glass, pottery, or ceramic tile products. Some workers are self-employed and sell their own products.

What Skills and Abilities Would Help You Succeed in This Kind of Work?

The most important skills are listed below. All of those listed do not apply to each occupation. As you explore occupations you should identify the specific ones needed.

Esthetic Perception – to know quality or beauty in art.

Spatial Perception – to form a mental image (pictures) of how shapes and forms can be combined in three dimensions - height, width, and depth.

Visualization – to form a mental image of what the final work of art will look like.

Color Discrimination – to recognize different shades and tones of color.

Dexterity – to coordinate the movement of the hands and fingers skillfully.

Critical Thinking – to use personal judgment to make decisions.

Accuracy – to work within precise limits using standards that can be measured or checked.

Do You Have or Can You Develop an Interest in This Kind of Work?

Review the following questions. Your answers can give you clues as to your interest in the Technical Arts field.

Have you decorated a cake for a birthday or other event? Did you create your own designs?

Have you used a wood-burning tool to etch a preprinted design? Have you completed a paint-by-number picture? Do you have a steady hand for this kind of activity?

Have you applied makeup for a school or amateur play? Did it produce the desired change in the performer's appearance?

Do you have a craft hobby such as jewelry making, wood carving, or leather tooling? Have you entered your work in an arts and crafts show? Did any of your work sell?

Have you taken industrial arts or other courses which give training in the use of hand tools? Can you skillfully use screwdrivers, pliers, chisels, and files?

Have you had a mechanical drawing course? Can you draw things to scale? Do you like to do lettering?

Have you assembled plastic models, made pottery, or pieced a quilt? Do you enjoy working with your hands and making things?

What Else Should You Know About This Group of Occupations?

Some artistic talent is needed for most jobs in this group. However, the chance to use creative expression varies from job to job. Skills and abilities are developed through related entry level jobs, apprenticeships, or on-the-job training. Less time and money is required for training to enter the Technical Arts field. Some workers with experience open their own businesses and sell the products they make. They also may contract to do work for others.

The military services offer training and experience related to some occupations in this group. These occupations are included in the list at the end of this group description. They are identified by an (M) following the occupational title. More information about the military training and experience opportunities may be found in Appendix A.

**How Can You Prepare
for This Kind of Work?**

Years of on-the-job training and experience are required to become a skilled worker for many jobs in this group. However, some jobs require as little as six months. But,

most jobs require over two years and up to ten years of training and experience.

The following list of courses and skills can help you plan your education.

Graphics and Printing – courses in photography, lithographic plate making, silk screening, drafting, letterpress, and offset printing.

Precision Metalworking – courses in pattern-making, metal fabrication, welding, brazing, and soldering.

Craft Arts – courses such as model making, leather work, sewing, sculpting, and lapidary (cutting and polishing gem stones).

Art – courses in sketching, painting, lettering, etching, and freehand drawing.

Woodworking – courses in wood shop, cabinetmaking, and carving.

Other helpful courses include General Math, Applied Math, General Science, and Industrial Arts.

Qualifications Profile

This section is a summary of the worker traits and work factors related to successful job performance and worker satisfaction. Try to relate your interests, abilities, aptitudes, and preferences to these traits and factors. An asterisk (*) marks those traits and factors that

are related to more than 60% of the occupations listed at the end of this group. The other traits and factors listed are as important, but relate to fewer occupations. See Appendices B-G for information about all of the worker traits and work factors.

Work Activities

The most important activities related to this group involve:

* 1. Things and objects.
  8. Creative thinking.
* 9. Processes, methods, or machines.
*10. Working on or producing things.

Work Situations

Workers must be willing to:

1. Perform duties which change frequently.
7. Make decisions using personal judgment.
* 8. Make decisions using standards that can be measured or checked.
*10. Work within precise limits or standards of accuracy.

Data-People-Things

This chart shows the levels for these three basic elements of work as related to this group. Level means the degree of difficulty of job tasks rather than the amount of time involved. The terms low, average, and high indicate the highest level at which occupations are involved. Compare your interests and abilities with the levels checked.

Physical Demands

Workers in this group of occupations must be able to do:

  S – Sedentary work
*L – Light work

Working Conditions

These are the physical surroundings in which work is done. In occupations belonging to this group, work is performed:

*I – Inside — workers spend most of their time inside protected from weather conditions but not always from temperature changes.

This computer console is the control center of a laser scanner which makes color separations at a newspaper.

Difficulty Level of Job Tasks

	Low	Avg.	High
Data		*✓	
People	*✓		
Things			*✓

Educational Skills

This chart shows the levels of reasoning, math, and language skills related to this group. These skills are usually developed in an educational setting. There are six levels ranging from the simple (1) to the most complex (6).

Skill Levels

Simple ←——————→ Complex

	1	2	3	4	5	6
Reasoning			✓	*✓		
Math		✓	✓			
Language		✓	✓			

Aptitudes

This chart presents the most important aptitudes related to this group. The levels checked compare aptitudes needed for success in this group to aptitudes of the general working population in all occupations. For example, level 5 is low and represents the bottom 10% of the working population. Level 1 is high and represents the top 10%.

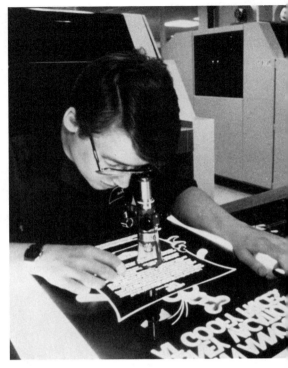

Making the final quality control check on an advertising layout before printing, this photolithographic stripper is using a special magnifying tool to see even the smallest imperfections.

APTITUDE LEVELS COMPARED TO ALL WORKERS						
Related Aptitudes (Ability to Learn)		Lower 1/3		Middle 1/3	Upper 1/3	
		Level **5**	Level **4**	Level **3**	Level **2**	Level **1**
Code	Title	10%	23%	34%	23%	10%
G	General Learning Ability			*✓	✓	
S	Spatial			✓	✓	
P	Form Perception			✓	*✓	
K	Motor Coordination			*✓	✓	
F	Finger Dexterity			✓	✓	
M	Manual Dexterity			*✓	✓	

Common Occupations

A full listing of all occupations belonging to this group may be found in the Guide for Occupational Exploration.

The following occupations have been selected to represent this group. They provide the major employment opportunities. However, specific job opportunities will vary according to locations of industry, geographical region, and other factors.

Information may be found in common sources of occupational information, state career information systems, and computerized guidance systems.

An (M) follows the occupational title where the military services offer training and experience.

Graphic Arts and Related Crafts

142.061-010	Bank-Note Designer
143.062-014	Photographer, Aerial (M)
704.381-026	Engraver, Hand, Hard Metals
704.381-030	Engraver, Hand, Soft Metals
970.361-010	Form Designer
970.381-030	Retoucher, Photoengraving
971.381-014	Etcher, Photoengraving
971.381-018	Offset-Plate Maker
971.381-022	Photoengraver
971.381-030	Photoengraving Finisher
971.382-014	Photographer, Photoengraving
972.281-010	Process Artist
972.281-014	Process Stripper
972.381-010	Lithographic Plate Maker (M)
972.381-018	Sketch Maker 2
972.382-014	Photographer, Lithographic (M)
979.381-018	Paste-Up Copy-Camera Operator
979.382-018	Graphic Arts Technician (M)
979.581-010	Engraver, Rubber

Arts and Crafts

102.167-010	Art Conservator
102.381-010	Museum Technician
199.261-010	Taxidermist
333.071-010	Make-Up Artist
700.281-010	Jeweler
700.281-022	Silversmith
700.381-034	Mold Maker 1
700.381-046	Sample Maker 1
704.381-010	Chaser
709.381-018	Model Maker
739.381-050	Souvenir and Novelty Maker
761.281-010	Carver, Hand
770.381-010	Bead Maker
771.281-014	Stone Carver
772.381-010	Glass Bender
777.261-010	Model Maker 1
777.281-014	Model Maker
779.381-010	Glazier, Stained Glass
779.381-014	Mosaic Worker
779.381-018	Repairer, Art Objects
781.381-018	Leather Stamper
962.382-014	Sound Cutter (M)

Hand Lettering, Painting, and Decorating

652.130-010	Supervisor, Decorating
740.381-010	Decorator
772.381-014	Patternmaker
773.381-010	Tile Decorator
970.281-010	Airbrush Artist
970.281-018	Photograph Retoucher
970.281-022	Sign Writer, Hand
970.381-010	Colorist, Photography
970.381-022	Painter, Hand
970.381-026	Painter, Sign
970.381-034	Spotter, Photographic
970.661-014	Letterer
972.381-022	Stripper, Photolithographic (M)

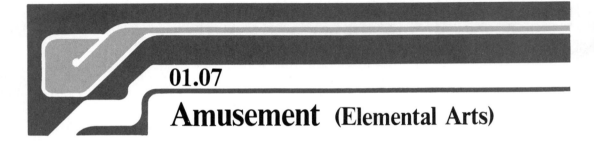

01.07

Amusement (Elemental Arts)

Amusement is to entertain people. Workers perform an act for a group of people in a setting such as a circus. Others shout, gesture (use body movement), or wear a costume to get attention. Some workers forecast the future or inform people about their traits. This group includes the subgroups of:

Psychic Science
Announcing
Entertaining

Psychic Science is the use of mystic powers. Psychic Readers tell about past, present, or future events. People in these jobs claim to have visions, intuition, or ESP (ex-trasensory perception). Graphologists study handwriting to describe the traits of a person. Astrologers prepare horoscopes to advise people of future trends and events. They suggest what course of action to follow and the chances of success or failure.

Announcing is to get attention and to inform. Announcers use a public address system to describe an entertainment event as it takes place. Barkers call out to get people to attend an event. Some workers dress in costumes and pretend to be storybook characters to promote an event, or to amuse a group. And, during a circus there is always a Ring Conductor to announce each act.

People who wish to find out about their future sometimes consult with a psychic reader who may use a "crystal ball."

A ring conductor directs the audience's attention to each new act during a circus performance.

Entertaining is a form of amusement. Workers may eat fire, swallow a sword, or charm a snake as a special act. Other workers operate games of chance, or guess weights or ages. They attract a crowd by talking loudly about their skills or by calling attention to a winner.

Jobs may be found with street fairs, amusement parks, or sporting events.

What Skills and Abilities Would Help You Succeed in This Kind of Work?

The most important skills are listed below. All of those listed do not apply to each occupation. As you explore occupations you should identify the specific ones needed.

Verbalization – to put thoughts and actions into words.

Poise – to be calm and self-confident in front of an audience.

Communication – to give or exchange information.

Persuasiveness – to use words to influence the thinking and actions of others.

Imagination (in Psychic Science) – to use information about clients to form a mental image of future events to amuse or advise them.

Do You Have or Can You Develop an Interest in This Kind of Work?

Review the following questions. Your answers can give you clues as to your interest in the Amusement field.

Have you been a cheerleader or a school mascot? Do you like to wear costumes in front of strangers?

Have you performed magic or card tricks at parties or other events? Do you like to amuse others?

43

Have you worked at a school fair or carnival? Were you able to get people to play the games or watch the shows?

Have you entertained others by trying to read their minds? Do you feel you have ESP (extrasensory perception)?

Have you read or prepared horoscopes for your friends or at a party? Do you like this type of activity?

Have you been an emcee or announced a program? Do you like to perform in front of an audience?

What Else Should You Know About This Group of Occupations?

Many jobs in this field are part-time. Also, many of the jobs are short-term, such as summer or Christmas. Work with a circus, or other kinds of shows, requires frequent travel. It also requires late night and weekend work.

Newcomers may have a hard time starting out in this field. A hobby such as fortune telling can help develop a talent. Some workers in the Psychic Sciences have their own places of business. Many use their homes.

How Can You Prepare for This Kind of Work?

Most jobs in this group can be entered through on-the-job training. This training may range from a short demonstration up to six months. Becoming an Announcer or Ring Conductor can require from one to two years of related experience. Also jobs in Psychic Science require special instruction, practice, and experience.

Courses that may be helpful are: General English, Speech, Psychology, Drama, Sports and Physical Education.

School activities and hobbies that develop self-confidence in performing or talking with people also can be helpful.

Qualifications Profile

This section is a summary of the worker traits and work factors related to successful job performance and worker satisfaction. Try to relate your interests, abilities, aptitudes, and preferences to these traits and factors. An asterisk (*) marks those traits and factors that

are related to more than 60% of the occupations listed at the end of this group. The other traits and factors listed are as important, but relate to fewer occupations. See Appendices B-G for information about all of the worker traits and work factors.

In a colorful costume and makeup, this clown is a roving entertainer in a theme park.

Work Activities

The most important activities related to this group involve:

2. Business contact.
5. Recognition or appreciation from others.
* 6. Communication of ideas and information.

Work Situations

Workers must be willing to:

* 4. Deal with people.
5. Influence people's opinions, attitudes, and judgments.
* 7. Make decisions using personal judgment.
9. Interpret and express feelings, ideas, or facts.

Data-People-Things

This chart shows the levels for these three basic elements of work as related to this group. Level means the degree of difficulty of job tasks rather than the amount of time involved. The terms low, average, and high indicate the highest level at which occupations are involved. Compare your interests and abilities with the levels checked.

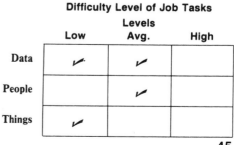

Difficulty Level of Job Tasks

	Low	Avg.	High
Data	✔	✔	
People		✔	
Things	✔		

45

Physical Demands

Workers in this group of occupations must be able to do:

S – Sedentary work
*L – Light work

Educational Skills

This chart shows the levels of reasoning, math, and language skills related to this group. These skills are usually developed in an educational setting. There are six levels ranging from the simple (1) to the most complex (6).

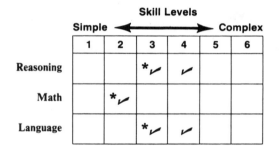

Skill Levels

Simple ◄────────► Complex

	1	2	3	4	5	6
Reasoning			*✓	✓		
Math		*✓				
Language			*✓	✓		

Working Conditions

These are the physical surroundings in which work is done. In occupations belonging to this group, work is performed:

I – Inside — workers spend most of their time inside protected from weather conditions but not always from temperature changes.
O – Outside — workers spend most of their time outside with little protection from weather conditions.
B – Both inside and outside — workers spend about equal time in each setting.

Aptitudes

This chart presents the most important aptitudes related to this group. The levels checked compare aptitudes needed for success in this group to aptitudes of the general working population in all occupations. For example, level 5 is low and represents the bottom 10% of the working population. Level 1 is high and represents the top 10%.

APTITUDE LEVELS COMPARED TO ALL WORKERS						
Related Aptitudes (Ability to Learn)		Lower 1/3		Middle 1/3	Upper 1/3	
		Level **5**	Level **4**	Level **3**	Level **2**	Level **1**
Code	Title	10%	23%	34%	23%	10%
G	General Learning Ability		✓	*✓	✓	
V	Verbal			*✓	✓	

Common Occupations

A full listing of all occupations belonging to this group may be found in the Guide for Occupational Exploration.

The following occupations have been selected to represent this group. They provide the major employment opportunities. However, specific job opportunities will vary according to locations of industry, geographical region, and other factors.

Information may be found in common sources of occupational information, state career information systems, and computerized guidance systems.

Psychic Science

159.207-010   Astrologer
159.247-018   Graphologist
159.647-018   Psychic Reader

Announcing

159.347-010   Announcer
159.367-010   Ring Conductor
299.647-010   Impersonator, Character
342.657-010   Barker

Entertaining

159.647-010   Amusement Park Entertainer
342.357-010   Weight Guesser

01.08

Modeling

Modeling is to appear before an audience in a silent role, or to pose for an artist or photographer. This group includes the subgroup of:

Personal Appearance

Personal Appearance is to model hair styles, clothes, and other products. Models appear at fashion shows for news media, buyers from retail stores, sales people, and customers. Models often pose for paintings, sculptures, or other types of art. They also pose for pictures used in advertising. They may stand-in for movie stars as cameras and lights are adjusted. Some models may work as extras and appear in crowd scenes on TV or in movies. Some workers instruct others in techniques and methods of self-improvement. This includes poise, wardrobe coordination, and cosmetic application.

Jobs may be found with stores, motion picture studios, and artists' and photographers' studios.

Modeling instructor helps student with make-up techniques.

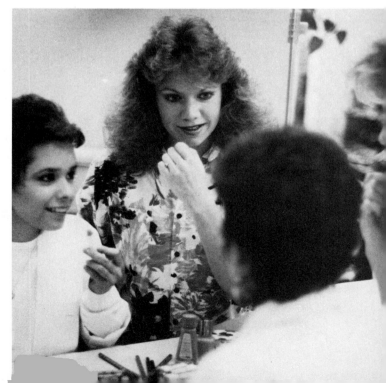

Modeling for an optometrist's ad, the angle must be just right, as well as the expression.

What Skills and Abilities Would Help You Succeed in This Kind of Work?

The most important skills are listed below. All of those listed do not apply to each occupation. As you explore occupations you should identify the specific ones needed.

Poise – to be calm and self-confident in front of an audience.

Performance – to pose or use body movements to express ideas and emotions or promote products and services.

Dexterity – to make graceful body movements; to use fingers and hands skillfully to apply makeup and style hair.

Physical Stamina – to stand, sit, walk, or pose for long periods of time.

Esthetic Perception – to know quality or beauty in personal appearance.

Do You Have or Can You Develop an Interest in This Kind of Work?

Review the following questions. Your answers can give you clues as to your interest in the Modeling field.

Have you appeared in a school or community style show? Do you enjoy appearing before groups?

Have you modeled for an artist or photographer? Can you hold a pose for a half-hour or longer?

Have you taken part in athletic events? Did you enjoy training for these events?

Have you been in a beauty or photographic contest? Did you win or receive honorable mention?

49

What Else Should You Know About This Group of Occupations?

The key to success in this field is an attractive physical appearance. Many jobs are short-term or seasonal. There is little chance for advancement.

It is difficult to get started in this field for there is a lot of competition. People who hire models usually do so through agencies. Models may hold other jobs and work on a part-time basis. Models are sometimes hired because of their unique looks or size. A few may be in constant demand and earn large fees.

How Can You Prepare for This Kind of Work?

Preparation for some jobs in modeling may consist of demonstrations or on-the-job training. Positions such as Photographer's Model and Modeling Instructor require more training and experience. Specialty modeling schools, usually found in larger cities, can provide training and help in getting started in this field. Initial experience can be gained by working at local clothing or department stores.

Helpful courses include:

Physical Education – courses to develop muscle strength, coordination, and graceful body movements.

Dance, Dramatics, and Speech – courses to develop poise and graceful body movements.

Home Economics – courses in clothing and textiles.

Distributive Education – courses in sales and general merchandising, for sometimes models also work in sales.

Qualifications Profile

This section is a summary of the worker traits and work factors related to successful job performance and worker satisfaction. Try to relate your interests, abilities, aptitudes, and preferences to these traits and factors. An asterisk (*) marks those traits and factors that are related to more than 60% of the occupations listed at the end of this group. The other traits and factors listed are as important, but relate to fewer occupations. See Appendices B-G for information about all of the worker traits and work factors.

Working Conditions

These are the physical surroundings in which work is done. In occupations belonging to this group, work is performed:

I – Inside — workers spend most of their time inside protected from weather conditions but not always from temperature changes.

*B – Both inside and outside — workers spend about equal time in each setting.

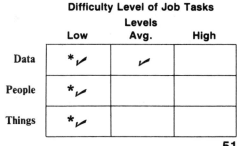

With casual attire — a casual stride is appropriate during a fashion show. Compare the street attire at right.

Work Activities

The most important activities related to this group involve:

2. Business contact.
3. Tasks of a routine, definite nature.
* 6. Communication of ideas and information.
9. Processes, methods, or machines.

Work Situations

Workers must be willing to:

2. Perform routine tasks.
* 4. Deal with people.
* 9. Interpret and express feelings, ideas, or facts.

Physical Demands

Workers in this group of occupations must be able to do:

*L – Light work

Data-People-Things

This chart shows the levels for these three basic elements of work as related to this group. Level means the degree of difficulty of job tasks rather than the amount of time involved. The terms low, average, and high indicate the highest level at which occupations are involved. Compare your interests and abilities with the levels checked.

Difficulty Level of Job Tasks

	Levels		
	Low	Avg.	High
Data	*✔	✔	
People	*✔		
Things	*✔		

Educational Skills

This chart shows the levels of reasoning, math, and language skills related to this group. These skills are usually developed in an educational setting. There are six levels ranging from the simple (1) to the most complex (6).

Skill Levels

Simple ←——————→ Complex

	1	2	3	4	5	6
Reasoning		✔	*✔			
Math	*✔	✔				
Language	✔	✔				

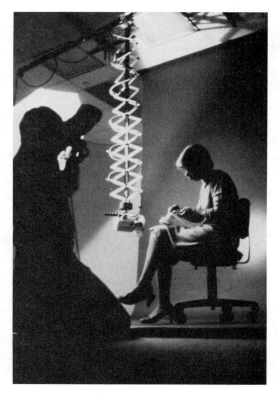

This model must be able to follow directions well so this commercial photographer can take good pictures to show the use of a new product.

Aptitudes

This chart presents the most important aptitudes related to this group. The levels checked compare aptitudes needed for success in this group to aptitudes of the general working population in all occupations. For example, level 5 is low and represents the bottom 10% of the working population. Level 1 is high and represents the top 10%.

APTITUDE LEVELS COMPARED TO ALL WORKERS						
Related Aptitudes (Ability to Learn)		Lower 1/3		Middle 1/3	Upper 1/3	
		Level **5** 10%	Level **4** 23%	Level **3** 34%	Level **2** 23%	Level **1** 10%
Code	**Title**					
G	General Learning Ability			* ✓		
K	Motor Coordination		* ✓	✓		
M	Manual Dexterity		* ✓	✓		

Common Occupations

A full listing of all occupations belonging to this group may be found in the Guide for Occupational Exploration.

The following occupations have been selected to represent this group. They provide the major employment opportunities. However, specific job opportunities will vary according to locations of industry, geographical region, and other factors.

Information may be found in common sources of occupational information, state career information systems, and computerized guidance systems.

Personal Appearance

099.227-026	Instructor, Modeling
159.647-014	Extra
297.667-014	Model
961.364-010	Double
961.367-010	Model, Photographers'
961.667-010	Model, Artists'
961.667-014	Stand-In

SCIENTIFIC

People with a scientific interest enjoy doing research on living and nonliving things. Through research, scientists seek to discover, expand, and apply knowledge. They use creative thinking to develop new theories, products, and processes. They do tests under controlled conditions. They may test theories that already exist.

The work of scientists is very demanding. It requires a high level of numerical and verbal skills. These skills are important to both scientists and to the lab workers who help them. They use these skills as they conduct tests, study the results, and report the findings.

The world of discovery is the world of science. The Physical, Life, and Medical Sciences provide the settings for work in this Area. Laboratory Technology is important in all three of these scientific fields.

Physical Science

The Physical Sciences involve nonliving things such as rocks, metals, and chemicals. Some workers examine the physical makeup of the earth. Others may conduct research to solve the mysteries of space and the universe. Workers in fields such as geology, astronomy, and oceanography may create new knowledge. Other workers apply this knowledge as they develop new or improved processes and materials for use in construction or to produce products.

Life Sciences

The Life Sciences are concerned with living things. This includes both plants and animals. Some workers conduct research to expand the knowledge about life. They may develop methods of disease control or work to improve plants and animals. For example, they might develop new cross-breeding and pollinating methods.

Medical Sciences

The Medical Sciences involve providing health care for people and animals. This work includes prevention, diagnosis, and treatment of diseases, disorders, and injuries. Workers usually specialize in one area of medicine, such as dentistry. Some specialize in veterinary medicine and are involved with animals only. Others may specialize in a specific part of the body (heart) or body function (speech). The Medical Sciences can combine an interest in science with a desire to help people.

The following Worker Trait Groups and Subgroups are related to the Physical Sciences, Life Sciences, and Medical Sciences clusters.

Scientific: an interest in conducting research or applying research findings.

Physical Sciences

02.01 Physical Sciences
Theoretical Research
Technology

02.04 Laboratory Technology
Physical Sciences
Life Sciences

Life Sciences

02.02 Life Sciences
Animal Specialization
Plant Specialization
Plant and Animal Specialization
Food Research

02.04 Laboratory Technology
Physical Sciences
Life Sciences

Medical Sciences

02.03 Medical Sciences
Medicine and Surgery
Dentistry
Veterinary Medicine
Health Specialties

02.04 Laboratory Technology
Physical Sciences
Life Sciences

02.01
Physical Sciences

Physical Science is the study of nonliving matter. This includes materials such as rocks and metals. Workers study the physical and chemical make up of matter and how it interacts with energy. This has led to the discovery of what are known as the laws of nature. A knowledge of math, physics, and chemistry is used to perform this type of research. The results are used to conduct more research and to develop new products. The results of this research also are used in everyday life. For example, information about wind, temperature, and humidity is used to predict the weather. This group includes the subgroups of:

Theoretical Research
Technology

Theoretical Research involves the development of new knowledge. Workers con-duct experiments to test theories or procedures. Their findings help solve specific problems or add new knowledge to the field of science. Some occupations in mathematics, astronomy, chemistry, physics, geology, and meteorology are involved in Theoretical Research.

Technology is the use of scientific methods to develop new or improved materials or processes. Some workers study the earth's crust to locate natural resources. Others study the structure and make up of such things as metals, alloys, and ceramics. This provides research data to improve or to develop products. Workers also conduct research on pollution to develop ways to control it.

Jobs may be found in research facilities with private industries, government agencies, or large universities.

Seismologists may have difficult working conditions, as this crew which is measuring a fault for movement of the earth.

What Skills and Abilities Would Help You Succeed in This Kind of Work?

The most important skills are listed below. All of those listed do not apply to each occupation. As you explore occupations you should identify the specific ones needed.

Comprehension – to read and understand formulas, tables, charts, and graphs dealing with chemistry and math.

Accuracy – to follow rules and work without error.

Critical Thinking – to form opinions and make decisions based upon knowledge, judgment, and experience.

Organization – to present information clearly and in sequence.

Interpretation – to understand and express complex, technical, and scientific information.

Spatial Perception – to form a mental image (picture) of how shapes and forms can be combined in three dimensions - height, width, and depth.

Numerical – to use concepts in advanced mathematics and statistics.

Creative Thinking – to develop original ideas.

Communication – to give and exchange information to teach or demonstrate scientific findings.

Do You Have or Can You Develop an Interest in This Kind of Work?

Review the following questions. Your answers can give you clues as to your interest in the Scientific field.

Do you read scientific books or magazines? Do you understand the terms and symbols used?

Do you own a chemistry set or microscope? Do you like to do experiments?

Have you collected rocks or minerals as a hobby? Can you tell the differences in ores and minerals?

Have you belonged to a science club? Have you taken part in a research project that involved math? Have you taken a geology field trip?

Have you taken part in a science fair? Did you enjoy designing and making your project?

Do the weather reports on TV interest you? Do you understand the terms used?

Do you like science or math courses? Do you make good grades?

Are you interested in such problems as air and water pollution? Would you like to help solve these problems?

Using a "sniffer" to check core samples of rock for petroleum deposits, this geologist's test results will help her company decide where to drill for oil.

This geologist catalogs mineral samples from around the world for future reference and study.

What Else Should You Know About This Group of Occupations?

Some workers in this group may work irregular hours. They have to meet research deadlines or observe events in nature when they occur. Sometimes this requires field work. They may travel to remote areas such as excavation sites or near volcano craters. Workers may be outside for long periods of time and may have to 'rough it.' Workers must keep up-to-date with research in their field. They often attend seminars and read professional journals.

The military services offer training and experience related to some occupations in this group. These occupations are included in the list at the end of this group description. They are identified by an (M) following the occupational title. More information about the military training and experience opportunities may be found in Appendix A.

How Can You Prepare for This Kind of Work?

Most occupations in Physical Sciences require four to ten years of training and experience. Others may require over ten years. Four years of college is the most common way to prepare for this field. To advance usually requires more formal training and extensive experience. A graduate degree is needed for most research work or to teach. Advanced study or a doctorate is usually required for work in basic research.

As you plan your high school program, you should include courses related to Physical Sciences. Next, you should include courses needed to enter college. The following list of courses and skills can help you plan your education.

Physical Science – courses in areas such as physics, astronomy, geological science, oceanography, and earth science. These courses are examples of special areas related to specific occupations. This group contains occupations that may require different physical science backgrounds.

Mathemathics – courses in algebra, geometry, and trigonometry provide a background for the more advanced mathematics courses such as calculus, analytic geometry, differential equations, and statistics. Occupations in the Theoretical Research subgroup require more advanced courses. Specific occupations such as Mathematician, Physicist, and Computer Application Engineer need an extra program of math courses.

Chemistry – courses in general chemistry provide a background for the more advanced courses such as analytical, inorganic, organic, and physical chemistry that relate to some occupations. The Chemist and Perfumer need an extensive background.

Courses in history and geography can be important for occupations such as Geophysicist and Geodesist. Helpful courses include technical and business writing and computer science.

Qualifications Profile

This section is a summary of the worker traits and work factors related to successful job performance and worker satisfaction. Try to relate your interests, abilities, aptitudes, and preferences to these traits and factors. An asterisk (*) marks those traits and factors that are related to more than 60% of the occupations listed at the end of this group. The other traits and factors listed are as important, but relate to fewer occupations. See Appendices B-G for information about all of the worker traits and work factors.

Work Situations

Workers must be willing to:

 1. Perform duties which change frequently.
* 3. Plan and direct an entire activity.
* 7. Make decisions using personal judgment.
* 8. Make decisions using standards that can be measured or checked.
*10. Work within precise limits or standards of accuracy.

Work Activities

The most important activities related to this group involve:

 1. Things and objects.
 6. Communication of ideas and information.
* 7. Tasks of a scientific and technical nature.
 8. Creative thinking.
 9. Processes, methods, or machines.

Working Conditions

These are the physical surroundings in which work is done. In occupations belonging to this group, work is performed:

I – Inside — workers spend most of their time inside protected from weather conditions but not always from temperature changes.

B – Both inside and outside — workers spend about equal time in each setting.

Data-People-Things

This chart shows the levels for these three basic elements of work as related to this group. Level means the degree of difficulty of job tasks rather than the amount of time involved. The terms low, average, and high indicate the highest level at which occupations are involved. Compare your interests and abilities with the levels checked.

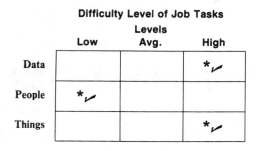

Difficulty Level of Job Tasks

	Levels		
	Low	**Avg.**	**High**
Data			*✓
People	*✓		
Things			*✓

Physical Demands

Workers in this group of occupations must be able to do:

*L – Light work

Educational Skills

This chart shows the levels of reasoning, math, and language skills related to this group. These skills are usually developed in an educational setting. There are six levels ranging from the simple (1) to the most complex (6).

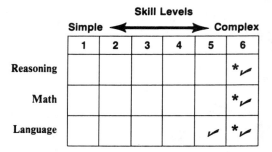

Skill Levels

Simple ⟵⟶ Complex

	1	2	3	4	5	6
Reasoning						*✓
Math						*✓
Language					✓	*✓

Aptitudes

This chart presents the most important aptitudes related to this group. The levels checked compare aptitudes needed for success in this group to aptitudes of the general working population in all occupations. For example, level 5 is low and represents the bottom 10% of the working population. Level 1 is high and represents the top 10%.

APTITUDE LEVELS COMPARED TO ALL WORKERS						
Related Aptitudes (Ability to Learn)		Lower 1/3		Middle 1/3	Upper 1/3	
		Level 5	**Level 4**	**Level 3**	**Level 2**	**Level 1**
Code	**Title**	10%	23%	34%	23%	10%
G	General Learning Ability					*✓
V	Verbal					*✓
N	Numerical				✓	*✓
S	Spatial				*✓	✓
P	Form Perception			✓	✓	✓

Working with massive telescopes and other very technical equipment, the findings of astronomers are useful to other scientists, as in predicting changes in the weather due to solar flares.

Common Occupations

A full listing of all occupations belonging to this group may be found in the Guide for Occupational Exploration.

The following occupations have been selected to represent this group. They provide the major employment opportunities. However, specific job opportunities will vary according to locations of industry, geographical region, and other factors.

Information may be found in common sources of occupational information, state career information systems, and computerized guidance systems.

An (M) follows the occupational title where the military services offer training and experience.

Theoretical Research

020.062-010   Computer-Applications Engineer
020.067-014   Mathematician (M)

021.067-010   Astronomer
022.061-010   Chemist (M)
023.061-014   Physicist (M)
023.067-010   Physicist, Theoretical
024.061-014   Geodesist
024.061-018   Geologist (M)
024.061-030   Geophysicist (M)
024.061-034   Hydrologist (M)
024.061-038   Mineralogist
024.061-046   Petrologist
024.061-050   Seismologist
024.061-054   Stratigrapher
025.062-010   Meteorologist (M)
029.067-010   Geographer
029.067-014   Geographer, Physical

Technology

011.061-022   Metallurgist, Physical
024.061-022   Geologist, Petroleum
024.061-026   Geophysical Prospector
029.081-010   Environmental Analyst (M)
029.081-014   Materials Scientist
029.167-010   Aerial-Photograph Interpreter (M)
029.167-014   Project Manager, Environmental Research

02.02
Life Sciences

Life Sciences involve the study of plants, animals, and humans. Scientists in this group are concerned with how living things function. They conduct tests on living matter to study its origin, growth, reproduction, and behavior. Some may study diseases and develop ways to control them. Other workers study how the environment affects living things. Life Scientists use their research results to develop such things as drugs, special types of plants, and ways to make and keep the environment clean. This group includes the subgroups of:

Animal Specialization
Plant Specialization
Plant and Animal Specialization
Food Research

Animal Specialization includes research on animals and humans. Workers may study live animals in controlled (laboratory) or natural settings. Some may conduct research on the selection, breeding, and feeding of domestic animals. Other workers may dissect dead animals to study their cells and cell structure. The results are used to help in the diagnosis, prevention, and treatment of animal disorders. Human remains also are studied to help in the diagnosis and treatment of human diseases. Workers conduct research to determine the origin and development of the human race. They compare the physical features of fossilized (rigid or fixed) human remains with those of existing racial groups.

This botanist is pollinating a tomato blossom, searching for new varieties of tomatoes.

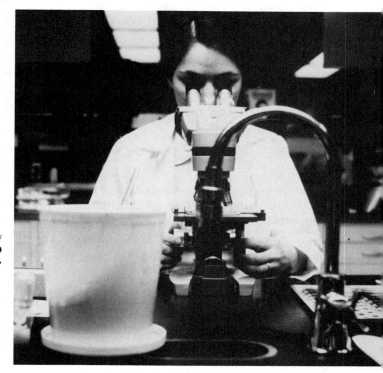

This microbiologist works in a laboratory setting, examining tissue samples to help a doctor make a diagnosis.

Plant Specialization involves research on plant growth and diseases. Also included are soil and water conservation. Some workers may conduct tests to find new ways to increase crop yields or use less labor. They also seek ways to control pests and weeds more effectively. Other workers conduct studies to find the best soil types for different plants. Still others may study soil erosion control.

Plant and Animal Specialization includes research on plants and animals. The job titles generally include "Bio" such as the title Biologist. This means the study of the two forms of life - plants and animals. Workers in this subgroup perform the same type of functions as those in Animal Specialization and Plant Specialization.

Food Research is concerned with the way food is processed and its nutrition value. Some workers study ways to improve the quality of food. This includes its color, texture, or flavor. Other workers conduct research to improve quality control, packaging, and distribution of food products. This subgroup also includes Research Dietitians. They study ways to improve the nutrition of people. They interpret their research for the public through reports and publications.

Jobs may be found in research facilities with hospitals, government agencies, private industries, or universities.

63

What Skills and Abilities Would Help You Succeed in This Kind of Work?

The most important skills are listed below. All of those listed do not apply to each occupation. As you explore occupations you should identify the specific ones needed.

Comprehension – to understand reports of technical and scientific data.

Leadership – to plan and direct the work of others.

Dexterity – to move eyes, hands, and fingers together to handle sensitive or delicate instruments.

Form Perception – to observe details and identify differences in shapes and structures.

Accuracy – to follow rules and work without error.

Critical Thinking – to form opinions and make decisions based upon knowledge, judgment, and experience.

Numerical – to use concepts (ideas) in advanced mathematics and statistics.

Do You Have or Can You Develop an Interest in This Kind of Work?

Review the following questions. Your answers can give you clues as to your interest in the Life Sciences field.

Have you belonged to a 4-H or nature club? Did you have a project to raise or study plants or animals.

Have you walked along a nature trail to observe plants and wildlife? Did you recognize and identify different plants and animals?

Have you had courses in biology, botany, or zoology? Did you like performing experiments to learn more about plants and animals?

Have you worked in a plant nursery or in an animal clinic? Do you enjoy this type of activity?

Have you belonged to a scout troop? Did you take part in efforts to clean up or preserve forests, parks, or campgrounds?

Have you owned a pet? Do you enjoy raising animals? Can you tell when an animal is ill?

This zoologist is observing turtles to make sure that the zoo setting is similar to their natural habitat.

These food technologists are checking the quality of cooked catfish that was raised in a controlled environment at a fish farm.

What Else Should You Know About This Group of Occupations?

Most Life Scientists work regular hours in a lab or office. However, some are required to live or work in remote areas. Some jobs require workers to dissect animals to study tissues or organs. Others may conduct biopsies on living tissues or autopsies to determine the cause of death. It is important that workers keep informed of developments in their field. They often attend seminars and read professional journals.

The technical background required for occupations in this group could lead to employment in related sales positions. Employers sometimes hire people with technical knowledge and train them in Business and Marketing.

The military services offer training and experience related to some occupations in this group. These occupations are included in the list at the end of this group description. They are identified by an (M) following the occupational title. More information about the military training and experience opportunities may be found in Appendix A.

This pathologist, dissecting fish to determine what caused their death, must make a quick response to disease to keep it from spreading throughout an entire fish hatchery.

How Can You Prepare for This Kind of Work?

Most occupations in Life Sciences require four to ten years of training and experience. Others may require over ten years. Four years of college with a major in biology or another life science is needed to enter this field. A graduate degree is needed for most research work. Advanced studies or a doctorate is usually required for work in basic research.

As you plan your high school program you should consider courses related to Biological or Agricultural Sciences. Biological Sciences provide a background for occupations related to research and laboratory work. Courses in Agriculture such as soil, plant, and animal sciences provide a background for conservation and other agriculture related occupations. The combination of Biological and Agricultural (animal) courses may be considered for occupations related to the veterinary research field. Next, you should include courses needed to enter college. The following list of courses and skills can help you plan your education.

Life Sciences – courses in areas such as biology, zoology, biochemistry, biophysics, botany, and microbiology.

Health Sciences – courses in Public Health Laboratory Sciences, such as principles and practices of public health and laboratory procedures; Veterinary Medicine courses, such as nutrition and parasitic diseases of domestic animals.

Agricultural Sciences – courses related to animal, food, plant, and soil sciences; horticulture, forestry, and related natural resources.

Mathematics – courses in algebra provide a background for the more advanced mathematics courses such as differential equations and statistics used in research.

Chemistry – courses in general chemistry provide a background for the more advanced courses such as physiological and soil chemistry.

Technical writing may be helpful for some occupations in this group. Food science and human nutrition are important areas for Research Dietitians.

Qualifications Profile

This section is a summary of the worker traits and work factors related to successful job performance and worker satisfaction. Try to relate your interests, abilities, aptitudes, and preferences to these traits and factors. An asterisk (*) marks those traits and factors that are related to more than 60% of the occupations listed at the end of this group. The other traits and factors listed are as important, but relate to fewer occupations. See Appendices B-G for information about all of the worker traits and work factors.

Work Situations

Workers must be willing to:

1. Perform duties which change frequently.
* 3. Plan and direct an entire activity.
7. Make decisions using personal judgment.
* 8. Make decisions using standards that can be measured or checked.
*10. Work within precise limits or standards of accuracy.

Work Activities

The most important activities related to this group involve:

1. Things and objects.
* 7. Tasks of a scientific and technical nature.
8. Creative thinking.

Data-People-Things

This chart shows the levels for these three basic elements of work as related to this group. Level means the degree of difficulty of job tasks rather than the amount of time involved. The terms low, average, and high indicate the highest level at which occupations are involved. Compare your interests and abilities with the levels checked.

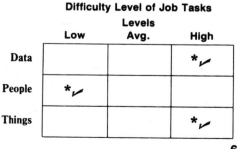

	Difficulty Level of Job Tasks		
	Levels		
	Low	Avg.	High
Data			*✓
People	*✓		
Things			*✓

Physical Demands

Workers in this group of occupations must be able to do:

*L – Light work

Educational Skills

This chart shows the levels of reasoning, math, and language skills related to this group. These skills are usually developed in an educational setting. There are six levels ranging from the simple (1) to the most complex (6).

Skill Levels

Simple ←————→ Complex

	1	2	3	4	5	6
Reasoning					✔	*✔
Math				✔	✔	*✔
Language					✔	*✔

Working Conditions

These are the physical surroundings in which work is done. In occupations belonging to this group, work is performed:

*I – Inside — workers spend most of their time inside protected from weather conditions but not always from temperature changes.

B – Both inside and outside — workers spend about equal time in each setting.

Aptitudes

This chart presents the most important aptitudes related to this group. The levels checked compare aptitudes needed for success in this group to aptitudes of the general working population in all occupations. For example, level 5 is low and represents the bottom 10% of the working population. Level 1 is high and represents the top 10%.

APTITUDE LEVELS COMPARED TO ALL WORKERS						
Related Aptitudes (Ability to Learn)		Lower 1/3		Middle 1/3	Upper 1/3	
		Level 5	Level 4	Level 3	Level 2	Level 1
Code	Title	10%	23%	34%	23%	10%
G	General Learning Ability					*✔
V	Verbal				✔	*✔
N	Numerical				✔	✔
S	Spatial			✔	✔	✔
P	Form Perception			✔	✔	✔
F	Finger Dexterity			✔	✔	✔
M	Manual Dexterity			✔	✔	✔

Common Occupations

A full listing of all occupations belonging to this group may be found in the Guide for Occupational Exploration.

The following occupations have been selected to represent this group. They provide the major employment opportunities. However, specific job opportunities will vary according to locations of industry, geographical region, and other factors.

Information may be found in common sources of occupational information, state career information systems, and computerized guidance systems.

An (M) follows the occupational title where the military services offer training and experience.

Animal Specialization

019.061-010	Biomedical Engineer (M)
040.061-014	Animal Scientist
041.061-010	Anatomist
041.061-046	Entomologist (M)
041.061-050	Geneticist
041.061-054	Histopathologist
041.061-070	Parasitologist (M)
041.061-074	Pharmacologist (M)
041.061-090	Zoologist
041.061-094	Staff Toxicologist (M)
041.167-010	Environmental Epidemiologist (M)
055.067-014	Anthropologist, Physical

070.061-010	Pathologist (M)
073.061-010	Veterinarian, Laboratory Animal Care (M)
073.061-014	Veterinary Anatomist (M)
073.061-018	Veterinary Bacteriologist (M)
073.061-022	Veterinary Epidemiologist (M)
073.061-026	Veterinary Parasitologist (M)
073.061-030	Veterinary Pathologist (M)
073.061-034	Veterinary Pharmacologist (M)
073.061-038	Veterinary Physiologist (M)
073.061-042	Veterinary Virologist (M)
079.021-014	Medical Physicist (M)
168.161-010	Coroner

Plant Specialization

040.061-010	Agronomist (M)
040.061-038	Horticulturist
040.061-046	Range Manager
040.061-054	Soil Conservationist
040.061-058	Soil Scientist
040.061-062	Wood Technologist
041.061-038	Botanist
041.061-086	Plant Pathologist

Plant and Animal Specialization

041.061-022	Aquatic Biologist
041.061-026	Biochemist (M)
041.061-030	Biologist
041.061-034	Biophysicist
041.061-058	Microbiologist (M)
041.061-078	Physiologist (M)

Food Research

040.061-022	Dairy Technologist
041.081-010	Food Technologist
077.061-010	Dietitian, Research

02.03
Medical Sciences

Medical Sciences involve the diagnosis and treatment of human and animal diseases, disorders, or injuries. Medical workers may specialize in one area of the body or specific kinds of illnesses. Some are involved in research to find cures for illnesses and diseases or to develop ways to prevent them. This group includes the subgroups of:

Medicine and Surgery
Dentistry
Veterinary Medicine
Health Specialists

Medicine and Surgery is the health care of humans. Doctors examine patients to diagnose their illnesses. They may request various tests or x-rays to help make a diagnosis. They may give or prescribe medicine as part of their treatment. They also advise their patients on how to stay healthy through proper diet, exercise, and hygiene. Some doctors are general practitioners, but most are specialists. The general practitioner is involved in a variety of medical cases. There are many types of medical specialties, an example is surgery. Surgeons correct defor-

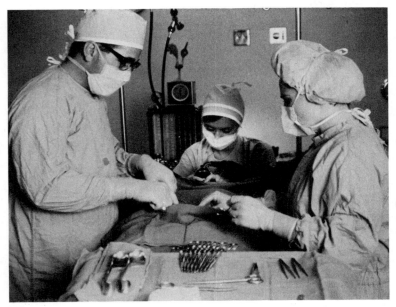

Surgeons work carefully and quickly to repair damage from injuries.

Many city veterinarians specialize in small-animal care, but in more agricultural areas, veterinarians care for farm animals.

mities, repair injuries, or remove diseased organs.

Dentistry is the care, treatment, and repair of gums and teeth. Dentists order or take x-rays, fill cavities, straighten teeth, repair fractured teeth, and treat gum disease. When necessary, dentists pull teeth and fit their patients with dentures. Dentists also clean teeth and provide other preventive care. Some dentists may specialize in surgery or in straightening teeth. Another example of a specialty is dentistry for children.

Veterinary Medicine is to diagnose, treat, and prevent animal disorders. Veterinarians examine and prescribe or administer medicine or perform surgery. Most vets are involved in private practice and some limit this practice to the care of pets. Some vets work for government agencies. They inspect animals for the presence of disease. They may set up and enforce laws for the import, export, and movement of livestock between states.

Health Specialties involve the treatment and rehabilitation of persons with physical disorders. Some workers may treat people who have trouble talking. This may be caused from total or partial hearing loss, brain injury, or vocal cords that do not function properly. Another specialty involves hearing. These workers conduct hearing tests and treat problems. They may fit and dispense hearing aids. Other specialists examine eyes and prescribe glasses or contact lenses to improve vision. Another type of specialty involves radiation. These workers operate equipment used in the therapy (treatment) of patients. And some specialists adjust parts of the body, mostly the spine, to correct problems with the nervous system.

Jobs are found in a variety of settings. Many workers in this field are self-employed and treat patients in private offices. They may also see patients in a clinic or hospital setting. Some may be employed by medical schools or in research facilities. Public health clinics, schools, prisons, and business firms also are employment settings. Many jobs are found with public health service agencies.

What Skills and Abilities Would Help You Succeed in This Kind of Work?

The most important skills are listed below. All of those listed do not apply to each occupation. As you explore occupations you should identify the specific ones needed.

Critical Thinking – to form opinions and make decisions based upon knowledge, judgment, and experience.

Dexterity – to move the hands and fingers skillfully to use surgical instruments.

Comprehension – to understand complex, technical, and scientific information.

Form Perception – to observe detail in objects or drawings and notice differences in shapes or shadings.

Verbalization – to put thoughts and actions into words.

Leadership – to plan and direct the work of others.

Accuracy – to work within precise limits using standards that can be measured or checked.

Spatial Perception – to form a mental image (picture) of how shapes and forms can be combined in three dimensions - height, width, and depth.

Composure – to be calm and self-confident in emergency situations.

Concentration – to focus attention on detailed tasks and remain alert for long periods of time.

This family practice physician uses a stethoscope to examine a patient.

Do You Have or Can You Develop an Interest in This Kind of Work.

Review the following questions. Your answers can give you clues as to your interest in the Medical Sciences field.

Have you taken courses in biology, anatomy, or zoology? Have you dissected an animal? Can you handle small instruments skillfully?

Have you been trained in first aid? Have you treated an accident victim? Are you calm during emergencies?

Have you done volunteer work in a hospital? Did you enjoy the work?

Do you watch medical shows on TV? Do you understand the medical terms used? Do you enjoy such programs?

Have you assembled a plastic model of a human or animal? Do you have an interest in how internal body structures or systems work?

Do you own a pet? Can you tell when an animal is sick? Have you cared for a sick or injured animal?

Have you taken care of a sick relative or friend? Were you able to stay alert and be patient for long periods of time?

What Else Should You Know About This Group of Occupations?

Most workers in this group earn high incomes. However, the training needed to enter this type of work is costly in time and money. These workers must be sincere and gain the confidence of others. They gain satisfaction from their work knowing that it contributes to the well-being of others. They usually are respected and have prestige (status) in their communities.

Workers must adjust to irregular hours and weekend and holiday work. Some are required to be on call any time of the day or night.

Workers must keep their knowledge and skills up-to-date. They do this by reading journals, attending seminars, and taking advanced courses.

The military services offer training and experience related to some occupations in this group. These occupations are included in the list at the end of this group description. They are identified by an (M) following the occupational title. More information about the military training and experience opportunities may be found in Appendix A.

How Can You Prepare for This Kind of Work?

Most occupations in Medical Sciences require four to ten years of training and experience. Some may require over ten years. Doctors of medicine, veterinary medicine, and dentistry must have four years of advanced study. They also serve one to two years as interns in approved hospitals. To specialize in a specific field, physicians spend several more years in study and training as residents or interns. Some dentists may specialize, teach, or perform research in specific fields. To do so, they take postgraduate courses or serve as

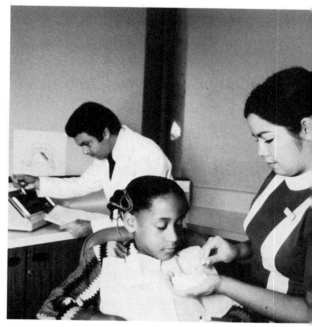

Dentists work with patients to prevent problems with their teeth.

residents in hospitals. All states require medical doctors, dentists, and veterinarians to have licenses to practice. Occupations such as Radiation-Therapy Technologist and Animal Health Technician require up to two years of training.

As you plan your high school program, you should include courses related to Medical Sciences. Next, you should include courses needed to enter college. The following list of courses and skills can help you plan your education.

Health Sciences – courses that teach how to restore or preserve health through the use of medicine, surgery, or other related methods. Specific courses should be taken related to the field of specialization desired.

Life Sciences – courses in areas such as biology, zoology, anatomy, embryology, histology, toxicology, pathology, physiology, and nutritional sciences.

Chemistry – courses in general chemistry provide background for the more advanced courses such as organic, biochemistry, and physiological chemistry.

Mathematics – courses in algebra and geometry provide a background for the more advanced mathematics courses such as calculus and statistics.

A course in Latin is important to the medical profession. Also, courses in technical writing are helpful for some occupations in this group.

Qualifications Profile

This section is a summary of the worker traits and work factors related to successful job performance and worker satisfaction. Try to relate your interests, abilities, aptitudes, and preferences to these traits and factors. An asterisk (*) marks those traits and factors that

are related to more than 60% of the occupations listed at the end of this group. The other traits and factors listed are as important, but relate to fewer occupations. See Appendices B-G for information about all of the worker traits and work factors.

Work Activities

The most important activities related to this group involve:

* * 4. Direct personal contact to help or instruct others.
* * 5. Recognition or appreciation from others.
* * 7. Tasks of a scientific and technical nature.

Physical Demands

Workers in this group of occupations must be able to do:

*L – Light work

Work Situations

Workers must be willing to:

3. Plan and direct an entire activity.
* * 4. Deal with people.
* * 7. Make decisions using personal judgment.
* * 8. Make decisions using standards that can be measured or checked.

Working Conditions

These are the physical surroundings in which work is done. In occupations belonging to this group, work is performed:

*I – Inside — workers spend most of their time inside protected from weather conditions but not always from temperature changes.

Data-People-Things

This chart shows the levels for these three basic elements of work as related to this group. Level means the degree of difficulty of job tasks rather than the amount of time involved. The terms low, average, and high indicate the highest level at which occupations are involved. Compare your interests and abilities with the levels checked.

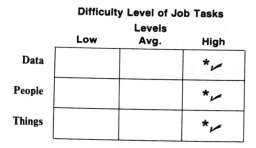

	Difficulty Level of Job Tasks		
	Low	Avg.	High
Data			*✓
People			*✓
Things			*✓

Educational Skills

This chart shows the levels of reasoning, math, and language skills related to this group. These skills are usually developed in an educational setting. There are six levels ranging from the simple (1) to the most complex (6).

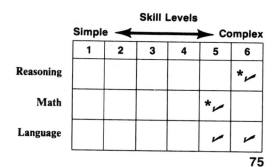

	Skill Levels					
	Simple ← → Complex					
	1	2	3	4	5	6
Reasoning						*✓
Math					*✓	
Language					✓	✓

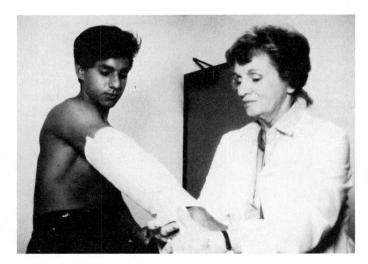

Orthopedic specialists treat patients with injured or diseased bones.

Aptitudes

This chart presents the most important aptitudes related to this group. The levels checked compare aptitudes needed for success in this group to aptitudes of the general working population in all occupations. For example, level 5 is low and represents the bottom 10% of the working population. Level 1 is high and represents the top 10%.

APTITUDE LEVELS COMPARED TO ALL WORKERS						
Related Aptitudes (Ability to Learn)		Lower 1/3		Middle 1/3	Upper 1/3	
		Level 5	Level 4	Level 3	Level 2	Level 1
Code	Title	10%	23%	34%	23%	10%
G	General Learning Ability					*✔
V	Verbal				✔	*✔
N	Numerical				✔	✔
S	Spatial				✔	*✔
P	Form Perception				✔	✔
K	Motor Coordination			✔	✔	
F	Finger Dexterity				✔	✔
M	Manual Dexterity				✔	✔

Common Occupations

A full listing of all occupations belonging to this group may be found in the Guide for Occupational Exploration.

The following occupations have been selected to represent this group. They provide the major employment opportunities. However, specific job opportunities will vary according to locations of industry, geographical region, and other factors.

Information may be found in common sources of occupational information, state career information systems, and computerized guidance systems.

An (M) follows the occupational title where the military services offer training and experience.

Medicine and Surgery

070.101-010	Anesthesiologist (M)
070.101-014	Cardiologist (M)
070.101-018	Dermatologist (M)
070.101-022	General Practitioner (M)
070.101-026	Family Practitioner (M)
070.101-030	Flight Surgeon (M)
070.101-034	Gynecologist (M)
070.101-038	Intern (M)
070.101-042	Internist (M)
070.101-046	Medical Officer (M)
070.101-050	Neurologist (M)
070.101-054	Obstetrician (M)
070.101-058	Ophthalmologist (M)
070.101-062	Otolaryngologist (M)

070.101-066	Pediatrician (M)
070.101-070	Physiatrist (M)
070.101-074	Physician, Head (M)
070.101-078	Physician, Occupational (M)
070.101-086	Proctologist
070.101-090	Radiologist (M)
070.101-094	Surgeon 1 (M)
070.101-098	Urologist (M)
070.107-010	Allergist-Immunologist (M)
070.107-014	Psychiatrist (M)
071.101-010	Osteopathic Physician
079.101-022	Podiatrist (M)

Dentistry

072.061-010	Oral Pathologist (M)
072.101-010	Dentist
072.101-014	Endodontist
072.101-018	Oral Surgeon
072.101-022	Orthodontist (M)
072.101-026	Pedodontist (M)
072.101-030	Periodontist (M)
072.101-034	Prosthodontist (M)
072.101-038	Public-Health Dentist (M)
072.117-010	Director, Dental Services (M)

Veterinary Medicine

073.101-010	Veterinarian (M)
073.101-018	Zoo Veterinarian (M)
073.161-010	Veterinary Livestock Inspector
073.264-010	Veterinary Meat-Inspector

Health Specialties

076.101-010	Audiologist (M)
076.107-010	Speech Pathologist (M)
078.361-034	Radiation-Therapy Technologist (M)
079.101-010	Chiropractor
079.101-018	Optometrist (M)

02.04
Laboratory Technology

Laboratory Technology is the use of special equipment and methods to perform tests in fields such as chemistry, biology, or physics. Results from these tests are recorded and used by doctors, scientists, researchers, and engineers. This type of work usually takes place in a laboratory. This group includes the subgroups of:

Physical Sciences
Life Sciences

Physical Sciences (Laboratory Technology) involve the study of nonliving things. Workers may arrange and run equip-ment to conduct chemical and physical tests on metal ores. Other workers may study mud to determine the presence of oil or gas. Some may test petroleum (oil) products or man-made fibers to find out if they meet quality standards. And, some workers set up equip-ment to test fire a gun. This helps them to gather evidence for a criminal investigation. However, not all workers conduct tests. Some prepare and dispense prescription drugs. Others measure the rainfall and river flow at metering stations. Still others set up equip-ment and photograph material to illustrate or record scientific data.

This pharmacist works in a grocery store drug department.

Life Sciences (Laboratory Technology) involve the study of living things. Some workers test blood, tissue, or other samples to help in the diagnosis and treatment of diseases. This may be through the use of chemical tests or slides viewed through microscopes. Not all jobs in this subgroup are related to health care. Some workers may use special equipment to record people's answers to a series of questions. Their answers help to determine if they are telling the truth. Some workers may prepare bodies for burial in accordance with the law.

Jobs in this group are primarily laboratory type jobs. In the Physical Sciences, those laboratories are found in a variety of settings. These range from research facilities where new materials and products are being tested to water treatment and power generating stations. Also, many jobs are found in government agencies. In the Life Sciences, hospitals and other medical facilities provide most of the jobs. However, the food and animal food industries also provide many jobs.

This weather testing equipment will be carried into the upper atmosphere to track wind and pressure conditions.

Organization – to arrange information in a way that can be understood.

Comprehension – to understand scientific and technical language and symbols.

What Skills and Abilities Would Help You Succeed in This Kind of Work?

The most important skills are listed below. All of those listed do not apply to each occupation. As you explore occupations you should identify the specific ones needed.

Accuracy – to work within precise limits using standards that can be measured or checked.

Dexterity – to move the hands and fingers skillfully to operate testing equipment and use delicate instruments.

Form Perception – to see slight differences in form or texture of substances being tested.

Do You Have or Can You Develop an Interest in This Kind of Work?

Review the following questions. Your answers can give you clues as to your interest in the Laboratory Technology field.

Have you experimented with a chemistry set? Did you enjoy that type of activity?

Have you taken courses in algebra or other advanced math? How were your grades? Can you read and understand charts and graphs?

Have you collected rocks? Could you recognize the different minerals present in the rocks?

Do you like to read scientific or technical magazines or books? Can you understand the language and symbols used?

Have you performed experiments during a science fair? Did you win an award?

Have you taken physics or earth or space science courses? Did you enjoy doing experiments?

What Else Should You Know About This Group of Occupations?

Many medical and technical labs operate 24 hours every day. Workers' hours may vary from week to week, or they may work at night. They may spend a great deal of time on their feet. Although labs, as a rule, are well lighted and clean, some jobs can be stressful. In some cases, a patient's life or the type of treatment may depend on quick and accurate analysis of tests.

The military services offer training and experience related to some occupations in this group. These occupations are included in the list at the end of this group description. They are identified by an (M) following the occupational title. More information about the military training and experience opportunities may be found in Appendix A.

How Can You Prepare For This Kind of Work?

Occupations in Laboratory Technology require one to four years of training and experience. Most of these jobs require workers to have a two- or four-year degree from a technical school or a university. In industry, some workers may move into laboratory or testing work from production areas. They make this move with on-the-job training.

As you plan your high school program, you should include courses related to Laboratory Technology. Next you should include courses needed to enter technical school or college. The following list of courses and skills can help you plan your education.

Science Technology – laboratory courses in the Physical and Life Sciences that develop skills needed to support and assist scientists and engineers.

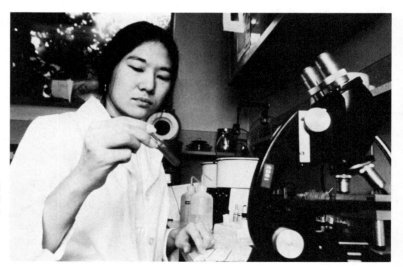

A laboratory technologist works in a laboratory with test tubes and microscopes.

Medical Technology – technical courses related to the diagnosis, treatment, and control of diseases. Also includes instruction in the use of technical equipment.

Life Sciences – courses in biology, zoology, anatomy, microbiology, cell biology, and pharmacology.

Physical Sciences – courses in areas such as physics, oceanography, metallurgy, atmospheric sciences, and meteorology.

Mathematics – courses in algebra, geometry, and trigonometry provide a background for the more advanced mathematics courses such as calculus and statistical methods.

Chemistry – courses in general chemistry provide background for the more advanced courses such as organic, organic synthesis, quantitative and qualitative, and physical chemistry.

Photographic Technology – basic and advanced courses in photography, including film development and related laboratory work, are needed for the occupations of Film Laboratory Technician, Scientific Photographer, and Biological Photographer.

Courses in Technical Writing can be helpful for some occupations in this group.

Qualifications Profile

This section is a summary of the worker traits and work factors related to successful job performance and worker satisfaction. Try to relate your interests, abilities, aptitudes, and preferences to these traits and factors. An asterisk (*) marks those traits and factors that are related to more than 60% of the occupations listed at the end of this group. The other traits and factors listed are as important, but relate to fewer occupations. See Appendices B-G for information about all of the worker traits and work factors.

Physical Demands

Workers in this group of occupations must be able to do:

*L – Light work

Work Activities

The most important activities related to this group involve:

1. Things and objects.
* 7. Tasks of a scientific and technical nature.
* 9. Processes, methods, or machines.

Work Situations

Workers must be willing to:

1. Perform duties which change frequently.
7. Make decisions using personal judgment.
* 8. Make decisions using standards that can be measured or checked.
*10. Work within precise limits or standards of accuracy.

Working Conditions

These are the physical surroundings in which work is done. In occupations belonging to this group, work is performed:

*I – Inside — workers spend most of their time inside protected from weather conditions but not always from temperature changes.

Data-People-Things

This chart shows the levels for these three basic elements of work as related to this group. Level means the degree of difficulty of job tasks rather than the amount of time involved. The terms low, average, and high indicate the highest level at which occupations are involved. Compare your interests and abilities with the levels checked.

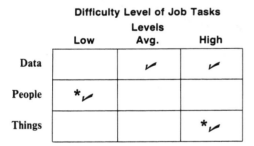

Difficulty Level of Job Tasks

	Low	Avg.	High
Data		✔	✔
People	*✔		
Things			*✔

Educational Skills

This chart shows the levels of reasoning, math, and language skills related to this group. These skills are usually developed in an educational setting. There are six levels ranging from the simple (1) to the most complex (6).

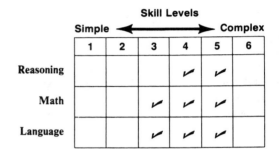

Skill Levels

Simple ⟷ Complex

	1	2	3	4	5	6
Reasoning				✔	✔	
Math			✔	✔	✔	
Language			✔	✔	✔	

Aptitudes

This chart presents the most important aptitudes related to this group. The levels checked compare aptitudes needed for success in this group to aptitudes of the general working population in all occupations. For example, level 5 is low and represents the bottom 10% of the working population. Level 1 is high and represents the top 10%.

APTITUDE LEVELS COMPARED TO ALL WORKERS						
Related Aptitudes (Ability to Learn)		Lower 1/3		Middle 1/3	Upper 1/3	
		Level 5	Level 4	Level 3	Level 2	Level 1
Code	Title	10%	23%	34%	23%	10%
G	General Learning Ability			✔	✔	
N	Numerical			✔	✔	
P	Form Perception			✔	✔	
F	Finger Dexterity			*✔	✔	

Common Occupations

A full listing of all occupations belonging to this group may be found in the Guide for Occupational Exploration.

The following occupations have been selected to represent this group. They provide the major employment opportunities. However, specific job opportunities will vary according to locations of industry, geographical region, and other factors.

Information may be found in common sources of occupational information, state career information systems, and computerized guidance systems.

An (M) follows the occupational title where the military services offer training and experience.

Physical Sciences

011.261-010	Metallurgical Technician
011.281-010	Laboratory Assistant, Metallurgical
011.281-014	Spectroscopist (M)
012.261-014	Quality-Control Technician
019.281-010	Calibration Laboratory Technician
022.261-010	Chemical-Laboratory Technician (M)
022.281-010	Assayer
022.281-018	Laboratory Tester
025.264-010	Hydrographer
025.267-010	Oceanographer, Assistant (M)
025.267-014	Weather Observer (M)
029.261-010	Laboratory Tester (M)

029.261-022	Tester
029.280-010	Photo-Optics Technician
029.281-010	Criminalist
074.131-010	Director, Pharmacy Services (M)
074.161-010	Pharmacist (M)
074.161-014	Radiopharmacist
074.381-010	Pharmacist Assistant (M)
078.364-010	Ultrasound Technologist
143.062-026	Photographer, Scientific
199.267-010	Ballistics Expert, Forensic (M)
199.384-010	Decontaminator (M)
375.387-010	Fingerprint Classifier (M)
579.484-010	Sampler
976.381-010	Film Laboratory Technician 1

Life Sciences

019.261-010	Biomedical Equipment Technician (M)
029.361-014	Food Tester
040.361-010	Laboratory Technician, Artifical Breeding
049.384-010	Biological Aide
073.361-010	Laboratory Technician, Veterinary
078.161-010	Medical Technologist, Chief
078.221-010	Immunohematologist (M)
078.261-010	Chemistry Technologist
078.281-010	Cytotechnologist (M)
078.361-014	Medical Technologist (M)
078.361-030	Tissue Technologist (M)
078.381-010	Medical-Laboratory Assistant (M)
078.381-014	Medical-Laboratory Technician (M)
078.687-010	Laboratory Assistant, Blood and Plasma
079.364-022	Phlebotomist
143.362-010	Biological Photographer (M)
199.267-026	Polygraph Examiner (M)
338.371-014	Embalmer
355.667-010	Morgue Attendant

03 NATURE
(Plants and Animals)

People with an interest in Nature can satisfy their interest by working in settings where plants and animals are raised or cared for. Most work in this area is outdoors. This provides workers contact with the natural beauty and peace of nature. But, it also can expose them to heat, cold, rain, and snow. Although most work is in rural settings, there are some jobs in urban areas. And some work is inside. Most jobs are found in farming, fishing, and forestry. Some jobs are related to animal training and service.

Farm workers raise and harvest crops. They raise livestock and poultry. Some farming takes place on ranches where horses, beef cattle, and sheep are raised.

Fishing involves more than catching fish to sell as food. Some workers raise fish in hatcheries.

Forestry work involves raising trees for lumber or paper products. Some jobs are with large logging firms. Care of forests in state and national parks is also included in the area. Some jobs are found with landscape nurseries where shrubs and houseplants are raised as well as trees.

Animal training and service workers feed and groom animals. Others may train them for helping people or for entertainment.

Work in the Nature area is divided into two clusters: Management and Manual Work.

Management

The Management cluster involves workers who manage programs and supervise workers. They must be able to plan and direct projects. For example, some study market trends to plan the type and amount of crops to plant. They arrange for the purchase of supplies needed. And, they also may be involved in keeping financial and production records. They must be able to solve problems and make decisions. This type of work also includes supervising other workers. It may require them to train workers.

Manual Work

The Manual Work cluster includes jobs that require workers to perform active physical tasks. They must work with their hands, use tools, and operate equipment. While modern technology and scientific methods reduce the amount of heavy work, physical fitness is still important. Many of the jobs require long hours of hard work at certain times of the year. Most work is routine and organized. Training is not required to enter most jobs. Training is provided when workers are hired or their duties change. With experience workers are given more complex tasks. Some advance to supervise other workers.

The following Worker Trait Groups and Subgroups are related to the Management and Manual Work clusters.

Nature: an interest in the care of plants and animals, usually in an outdoor setting.

Management

03.01 Managerial Work: Nature (Managerial Work: Plants and Animals)
Farming
Specialty Breeding
Specialty Cropping
Forestry and Logging

03.02 General Supervision: Nature (General Supervision: Plants and Animals)
Farming
Forestry and Logging
Nursery and Groundskeeping
Services

Manual Work

03.03 Animal Training and Care (Animal Training and Service)
Animal Training
Animal Service

03.04 Elemental Work: Nature (Elemental Work: Plants and Animals)
Farming
Forestry and Logging
Hunting and Fishing
Nursery and Groundskeeping
Services

Managerial Work: Nature
(Plants and Animals)

Managerial Work: Nature involves the operation and management of plant and animal businesses. This includes farming, ranching, fishing, plant nurseries, and forestry. Managers have a great deal of responsibility. Their duties are varied and range from analyzing market conditions to obtaining buyers for their products. They may hire workers and be responsible for training and supervising them. They often do physical work with the people they direct. In addition, managers may need to keep records and prepare written reports. This group includes the subgroups of:

Farming
Specialty Breeding
Specialty Cropping
Forestry and Logging

Farming is to raise and sell crops, livestock, and poultry. Farm operators may own or rent their farms. Their duties vary and depend upon what they are raising. A farmer who raises crops may plan and direct the purchase of supplies such as seed and fertilizer. On small farms, they may plant, cultivate, and harvest the crops. They also may be responsible for selling these products. Some farmers raise poultry for meat and eggs. They must feed the poultry and keep the coops clean and repaired. Dairy Farmers and Livestock Ranchers raise cattle and other livestock for milk, meat, and other animal products.

Specialty Breeding is to breed, raise, and protect animals other than livestock. It also includes fish and shellfish. Most animals are

Fish farmers must make careful checks of water quality in the ponds where fish are raised.

This grower is showing customers poinsettias in his greenhouse.

raised to sell or for their products such as fur pelts or honey. Workers must feed and water animals. They also keep pens, cages, hatchery trays, or hutches clean. Some may examine animals to see if they are ill or have been injured. If so, they may treat them. Some workers raise and sell fish or cultivate shellfish such as clams or oysters. Other workers may manage public or private fish hatcheries. They oversee trapping and spawning of fish and their movement to lakes, ponds, and streams. Some workers control animal populations and investigate crop and property damage done by wildlife. They recommend changes in hunting seasons and relocate animals to help control over populated areas. During hunting season they keep track of the number of animals killed. This helps determine if their methods of

animal control are working. They also may advise property owners how to prevent animal damage to their crops.

Specialty Cropping is to grow and sell horticultural products. These products include trees, shrubs, flowers, vegetables, and ornamental plants. Managers may determine the types and quantities of plants to grow. They may select and purchase the seeds and help with the planting. They supervise workers and keep personnel and production records. Some workers landscape the grounds of houses, industrial sites, and areas around highways. They determine where and what to plant and what it will cost. They provide the seeds, shrubs, flowers, or trees and do the planting. They also may maintain them.

Farmers who are owner-operators utilize expensive equipment, such as this combine, as well as plan and finance their operation.

Forestry and Logging is to manage and develop forest lands and their resources. This is done to provide recreation areas, habitats for wildlife, and to supply lumber. Foresters map forest areas and estimate the standing timber and its future growth. They research ways to cut and remove timber with little damage or waste. They plan campsites and direct workers as they build and maintain cabins, fences, telephone lines, and roads. They also help to plan and carry out projects to control floods, soil erosion, tree diseases, and insects. Foresters also direct fire fighting efforts and conduct fire prevention programs.

Jobs in this group may be found on farms and ranches. They also may be found with landscape nurseries, fish hatcheries, and state or federal forestry services. Many workers are self-employed. Co-op farm businesses, big companies, mortgage holders, banks, and large farm owners hire workers with management training and farm experience. Some of these workers form contracting companies which provide farm services or products.

What Skills and Abilities Would Help You Succeed in This Kind of Work?

The most important skills are listed below. All of those listed do not apply to each occupation. As you explore occupations you should identify the specific ones needed.

Leadership – to plan and direct the operation of a business in a way that obtains the cooperation and support of workers.

Organization – to organize the major elements involved in operating a business.

Communication – to give or exchange information in records and writen reports to supervisors or workers.

Numerical – to compute and keep business records.

Persuasiveness – to use words to influence the thinking and actions of others.

Rapport – to deal with people in an effective way and maintain harmony among workers.

Critical Thinking – to use personal judgment and information to make business decisions and solve problems.

Do You Have or Can You Develop an Interest in This Kind of Work?

Review the following questions. Your answers can give you clues as to your interest in this field.

Have you been a member of a 4-H Club or Future Farmers of America? Have you planned and directed a project? Did you like that type of responsibility?

Have you grown a flower or vegetable garden? Did you enjoy caring for the plants? Do you enjoy working outside?

Have you mowed grass for others or worked on a farm? Could you do or supervise this type of work everyday?

Have you taken science classes? Did you enjoy studying about plants and animals?

Have you held an office in a club? Were you required to keep records? Do you enjoy record keeping?

Have you visited a fish hatchery? Were you interested in how fish spawn and are raised?

This game farm manager will raise these pheasant hatchlings, which will be released in game preserves.

A landscaper gives finishing touches to a new planting of trees.

What Else Should You Know About This Group of Occupations?

As the world population increases so will the demand for food, fiber, and wood. Although the forestry, agricultural, and fishing industries can meet this demand, jobs will be limited. This is due to increased foreign competition. Also, technology and equipment is reducing the need for farm labor. However, managers will be in demand as farming becomes more complex. Jobs in farm management are found in all parts of the country. The climate and the land determine the location of jobs related to special crops, such as citrus fruits or cotton. The timber producing areas of the Pacific Northwest and the South provide most of the forestry and lumbering jobs. States which stock lakes and streams for fishing provide a few jobs in fish hatchery management. Jobs with plant nurseries, land-

scaping companies, and tree service firms are usually found in city and suburban areas. Many workers in this group are in business for themselves. Federal loans are sometimes offered to qualified people who wish to start a farm or horticultural service business. Workers can start this type of business at home. A few firms hire people in animal breeding, beekeeping, or fish farming.

How Can I Prepare for This Kind of Work?

Most occupations in Managerial Work: Nature require two to four years of training and experience. Some require up to ten years. Related work experience is also required for most of the jobs in this group. Growing up on a farm provides this experience for many workers. High schools often offer courses in vocational agriculture. Many colleges and

90

technical schools offer such programs as agribusiness, animal husbandry, and forest management. They also provide courses in small business management. Each state has at least one college which offers four and five-year programs in agriculture and related fields.

As you plan your high school program, you should include courses related to Managerial Work: Nature. Next, you should include courses needed to enter college, technical school, or other special program you are considering. The following list of courses and skills can help you plan your education.

Agricultural Production – courses in areas such as animal production, aquaculture, crop production, and game farm management.

Agricultural Business and Management – a course in general agricultural business and management provides background for the more advanced courses such as agricultural business, agricultural economics, farm and ranch management, and other related areas.

Agricultural Sciences – courses in general animal sciences, animal breeding and genetics, animal nutrition, livestock, poultry, general plant sciences, agronomy, and soil sciences.

Agricultural Products and Processing – courses in general agricultural products and processing, food products, and nonfood products.

Horticulture – courses related to producing, processing, and marketing plants, shrubs, and trees used for commercial purposes. Also includes instructions on how to establish, maintain, and manage a horticultural business.

Mathematics – courses in general and business mathematics.

Courses in agriculture, general science, life sciences, and economics can be helpful for occupations in this group.

Qualifications Profile

This section is a summary of the worker traits and work factors related to successful job performance and worker satisfaction. Try to relate your interests, abilities, aptitudes, and preferences to these traits and factors. An asterisk (*) marks those traits and factors that are related to more than 60% of the occupations listed at the end of this group. The other traits and factors listed are as important, but relate to fewer occupations. See Appendices B-G for information about all of the worker traits and work factors.

Work Activities

The most important activities related to this group involve:

1. Things and objects.
2. Business contact.
5. Recognition or appreciation from others.
7. Tasks of a scientific and technical nature.
* 9. Processes, methods, or machines.
*10. Working on or producing things.

Educational Skills

This chart shows the levels of reasoning, math, and language skills related to this group. These skills are usually developed in an educational setting. There are six levels ranging from the simple (1) to the most complex (6).

Skill Levels

Simple ⬅➡ Complex

	1	2	3	4	5	6
Reasoning				*✔		
Math			✔	✔		
Language			✔	✔		

Working Conditions

These are the physical surroundings in which work is done. In occupations belonging to this group, work is performed:

O – Outside — workers spend most of their time outside with little protection from weather conditions.

B – Both inside and outside — workers spend about equal time in each setting.

Work Situations

Workers must be willing to:

* 1. Perform duties which change frequently.
* 3. Plan and direct an entire activity.
  4. Deal with people.
* 7. Make decisions using personal judgment.
  8. Make decisions using standards that can be measured or checked.

Physical Demands

Workers in this group of occupations must be able to do:

L – Light work
M – Medium work
H – Heavy work

Aptitudes

This chart presents the most important aptitudes related to this group. The levels checked compare aptitudes needed for success in this group to aptitudes of the general working population in all occupations. For example, level 5 is low and represents the bottom 10% of the working population. Level 1 is high and represents the top 10%.

APTITUDE LEVELS COMPARED TO ALL WORKERS							
Related Aptitudes (Ability to Learn)		Lower 1/3		Middle 1/3	Upper 1/3		
		Level 5	Level 4	Level 3	Level 2	Level 1	
Code	**Title**	10%	23%	34%	23%	10%	
G	General Learning Ability			✔	✔		
V	Verbal			*✔	✔		
N	Numerical		✔	*✔			

Data-People-Things

This chart shows the levels for these three basic elements of work as related to this group. Level means the degree of difficulty of job tasks rather than the amount of time involved. The terms low, average, and high indicate the highest level at which occupations are involved. Compare your interests and abilities with the levels checked.

Difficulty Level of Job Tasks

	Levels		
	Low	Avg.	High
Data			*✓
People	*✓		
Things			*✓

Common Occupations

A full listing of all occupations belonging to this group may be found in the Guide for Occupational Exploration.

The following occupations have been selected to represent this group. They provide the major employment opportunities. However, specific job opportunities will vary according to locations of industry, geographical region, and other factors.

Information may be found in common sources of occupational information, state career information systems, and computerized guidance systems.

An (M) follows the occupational title where the military services offer training and experience.

Farming

180.167-018	General Manager, Farm
180.167-026	Manager, Dairy Farm
180.167-050	Migrant Leader
401.161-010	Farmer, Cash Grain
402.161-010	Farmer, Vegetable
403.161-010	Farmer, Tree-Fruit-And-Nut Crops
403.161-014	Farmer, Vine-Fruit Crops
404.161-010	Farmer, Field Crop
407.161-010	Farmer, Diversified Crops
410.161-018	Livestock Rancher
411.161-018	Poultry Farmer
421.161-010	Farmer, General

Specialty Breeding

169.171-010	Gamekeeper
180.167-030	Manager, Fish Hatchery
379.267-010	Wildlife Control Agent
410.161-010	Animal Breeder
410.161-014	Fur Farmer
413.161-010	Beekeeper
446.161-010	Fish Farmer
446.161-014	Shellfish Grower

Specialty Cropping

180.167-042	Manager, Nursery
182.167-014	Landscape Contractor
405.161-014	Horticultural-Specialty Grower, Field
405.161-018	Horticultural-Specialty Grower, Inside
408.161-010	Landscape Gardener
408.181-010	Tree Surgeon

Forestry and Logging

040.061-034	Forester

General Supervision: Nature
(Plants and Animals)

General Supervision: Nature is to oversee and direct the activities of workers engaged in farming, fishing, and forestry. Supervisors determine what needs to be done and discuss it with management. They may hire workers and train them. They plan work schedules, assign duties, and observe the work to make sure it is done right. Although their main responsibility is to supervise others, they may, at times, work along with them. Depending on the size of the business, they may purchase and issue supplies, keep records, and prepare reports. This group includes the subgroups of:

Farming
Forestry and Logging
Nursery and Groundskeeping
Services

Workers in the four subgroups of *General Supervision: Nature* perform duties that are very much alike. They differ in the knowledge and skills needed for the type of work they supervise.

Farming is concerned with vegetables, fruits, nuts, animals, poultry, and fish. *Forestry and Logging* involve planting trees (forest propagation), fighting fires, and preventing fires. It also involves felling (cutting down) and bucking (moving and loading) trees for lumber. *Nursery and Groundskeeping* includes lawn and tree services, parks and playgrounds, nurseries, greenhouses, and specialty farming. *Services* work includes the care of stables and horses and the care and movement of livestock in stockyards.

A supervisor records data while fish hatchery workers transfer fingerlings.

A working supervisor and helper use a leaf vacuum to gather leaves.

Jobs may be found with farms, ranches, landscape nurseries, fish hatcheries, shellfish farms, and federal and state forestry services.

What Skills and Abilities Would Help You Succeed in This Kind of Work?

Verbalization – to give clear directions and teach workers job skills.

Organization – to arrange work tasks and schedules.

Numerical – to do math quickly and correctly in keeping time and production records.

Rapport – to deal with people in an effective way and maintain harmony among workers.

Critical Thinking – to use personal judgment and information to make decisions and solve problems.

Leadership – to use authority in a way that develops group unity and effective work.

Do You Have or Can You Develop an Interest in This Kind of Work?

Review the following questions. Your answers can give you clues as to your interest in the field of Supervision.

Have you belonged to a 4-H Club or Future Farmers of America? Did you have a project involving plants or animals?

Have you raised or cared for animals? Have you nursed a sick pet back to health? Did you like this type of activity?

Do you like to camp, fish, or hunt? Do you like to be outdoors?

Have you planted trees or bushes? Have you designed and planted a flower garden? Have you raised vegetables in a home garden?

Have you worked all day mowing lawns, cutting weeds, or picking fruit? Would you like this type of work every day? Could you supervise others?

Have you been in charge of a group for a clean-up day? Did they follow your directions?

Have you used rakes, shovels, saws, or other tools? Do you like to work with your hands?

What Else Should You Know About This Group of Occupations?

Some work is seasonal or there are peak periods requiring overtime work. Working hours may vary. And, in some cases, a job or task must be completed before stopping for the day.

There is a lot of physical activity involved. Supervisors help do many of the tasks they supervise. They may be exposed to all types of weather and to natural hazards. In some jobs this could include storms, fires, or extreme temperatures.

How Can You Prepare for This Kind of Work?

Most occupations in General Supervision: Nature require one to four years of training and experience. Most workers are required to have experience in doing the work they supervise. They must know about tools and methods used in the work. Many workers in this group start out in routine jobs. They may advance after showing they have job knowledge and skills and leadership ability. Vocational and technical courses in agriculture, forestry, or related fields also can help experienced workers move into these jobs.

Gathering tree seedlings for shipment from tree farm.

As you plan your high school program, you should include courses related to General Supervision: Nature. Next, you should include courses needed to enter a related vocational or technical program after high school. The following list of courses and skills can help you plan your education.

General Agriculture – courses in agriculture including animal, food, plant, and soil sciences.

Agricultural Production – courses in agricultural production, animal production, aquaculture, crop production, and game farm management.

Courses in horticulture, agricultural mechanics, and agricultural services can be helpful for some occupations in this group. Basic math courses also can be helpful. In addition, general and life science courses can provide an introduction to plant and animal life. These courses might help you decide if you have an interest in this field.

Qualifications Profile

This section is a summary of the worker traits and work factors related to successful job performance and worker satisfaction. Try to relate your interests, abilities, aptitudes, and preferences to these traits and factors. An asterisk (*) marks those traits and factors that are related to more than 60% of the occupations listed at the end of this group. The other traits and factors listed are as important, but relate to fewer occupations. See Appendices B-G for information about all of the worker traits and work factors.

Work Activities

The most important activities related to this group involve:

* 2. Business contact.
* 5. Recognition or appreciation from others.
* 9. Processes, methods, or machines.

Data-People-Things

This chart shows the levels for these three basic elements of work as related to this group. Level means the degree of difficulty of job tasks rather than the amount of time involved. The terms low, average, and high indicate the highest level at which occupations are involved. Compare your interests and abilities with the levels checked.

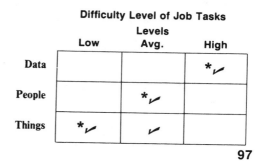

Difficulty Level of Job Tasks		
Levels		
Low	Avg.	High
Data			*✓
People		*✓	
Things	*✓	✓	

This crew chief explains log markings to a new worker.

Work Situations

Workers must be willing to:

* * 1. Perform duties which change frequently.
* * 3. Plan and direct an entire activity.
* * 4. Deal with people.
*   7. Make decisions using personal judgment.
* * 8. Make decisions using standards that can be measured or checked.

Working Conditions

These are the physical surroundings in which work is done. In occupations belonging to this group, work is performed:

* I – Inside — workers spend most of their time inside protected from weather conditions but not always from temperature changes.
* *O – Outside — workers spend most of their time outside with little protection from weather conditions.
* B – Both inside and outside — workers spend about equal time in each setting.

Physical Demands

Workers in this group of occupations must be able to do:

L – Light work
*M – Medium work

Educational Skills

This chart shows the levels of reasoning, math, and language skills related to this group. These skills are usually developed in an educational setting. There are six levels ranging from the simple (1) to the most complex (6).

Skill Levels

Simple ⟵⟶ Complex

	1	2	3	4	5	6
Reasoning				*✔		
Math		✔	*✔			
Language			*✔	✔		

Aptitudes

This chart presents the most important aptitudes related to this group. The levels checked compare aptitudes needed for success in this group to aptitudes of the general working population in all occupations. For example, level 5 is low and represents the bottom 10% of the working population. Level 1 is high and represents the top 10%.

APTITUDE LEVELS COMPARED TO ALL WORKERS						
Related Aptitudes (Ability to Learn)		**Lower 1/3**		**Middle 1/3**	**Upper 1/3**	
		Level 5	Level 4	Level 3	Level 2	Level 1
Code	**Title**	10%	23%	34%	23%	10%
G	General Learning Ability			*✔		
K	Motor Coordination		✔	*✔		
M	Manual Dexterity			*✔		

Common Occupations

A full listing of all occupations belonging to this group may be found in the Guide for Occupational Exploration.

The following occupations have been selected to represent this group. They provide the major employment opportunities. However, specific job opportunities will vary according to locations of industry, geographical region, and other factors.

Information may be found in common sources of occupational information, state career information systems, and computerized guidance systems.

Farming

402.131-010   Supervisor, Vegetable Farming
403.131-010   Supervisor, Tree-Fruit-And-Nut Farming
403.131-014   Supervisor, Vine-Fruit Farming
407.131-010   Supervisor, Diversified Crops
410.131-022   Supervisor, Stock Ranch
411.131-010   Supervisor, Poultry Farm
411.137-010   Supervisor, Poultry Hatchery
446.133-010   Supervisor, Shellfish Farming
446.134-010   Supervisor, Fish Hatchery

Forestry and Logging

452.364-010   Forester Aide
459.133-010   Supervisor, Logging

Nursery and Groundskeeping

405.131-010   Supervisor, Horticultural-Specialty Farming
406.134-014   Supervisor, Park Workers
408.131-010   Supervisor, Spray, Lawn And Tree Service

Services

410.131-010   Barn Boss
410.134-010   Supervisor, Livestock-Yard

Animal Care and Training
(Animal Training and Service)

Training and Animal Care is to train animals and to give them general care. They may be trained to protect people and property, to serve the handicapped, or to entertain. A wide variety of animals are raised and sold as pets or for medical research. This group includes the subgroups of:

Animal Training
Animal Service

Animal Training is to train animals for a variety of purposes. Trainers condition and prepare horses for racing. They also instruct and supervise others in the exercising, feeding, and grooming of the horses. Some workers train other animals to follow commands, compete in shows, or perform tricks. This includes training guard dogs and guide dogs. They also train animals to perform acts for motion pictures, TV, and the circus. Other workers may train animals for people to ride. They may manage a stable of animals and train them to walk, trot, or gallop. They also supervise workers who provide care for the animals, sell tickets, and help people to ride the animals.

Animal trainers work with porpoises to prepare shows in this aquatic amusement park.

Animal groomers must be familiar with many breeds of dogs and styles of clips — some groomers prepare dogs for competition in dog shows.

Animal Service is to take care of the basic needs of animals on a daily schedule. Workers feed and water animals. They keep cages and pens clean and make repairs when needed. They observe animals for signs of illnesses and may help to care for them when they are sick. Some workers bathe and groom dogs. They comb, clip, trim, and shape their coats of hair. Some workers fit, shape, and nail shoes (plates) to horse's hooves. Other workers assist people to mount and ride animals. They also may collect payment for rides and lead the animals.

Jobs may be found in a variety of settings. These include pet shops, pet grooming parlors, animal shelters, testing laboratories, and veterinarians' offices. Animal training and obedience schools, kennels, stables, and riding academies also offer employment. Other examples are: zoos, race tracks, aquariums, and the circus. Places that exhibit animals or use them to entertain an audience are still other work settings.

What Skills and Abilities Would Help You Succeed in This Kind of Work?

The most important skills are listed below. All of those listed do not apply to each occupation. As you explore occupations you should identify the specific ones needed.

Judgment – to understand the feeling, condition, or health of an animal by the way it looks or acts.

Coordination – to move the body, hands, and fingers easily in handling or grooming animals.

Persistence – to repeat signals and actions many times while training animals.

Physical Stamina – to do physical work to keep animal quarters clean or in leading or controlling animals.

Composure – to be calm and self-confident around animals.

101

Do You Have or Can You Develop an Interest in This Kind of Work?

Review the following questions. Your answers can give you clues as to your interest in the Training and Animal Care field.

Have you trained a pet to do tricks? Did you have patience when you had to repeat commands? Did the animal learn what you were trying to teach?

Have you belonged to a 4-H club? Did you have a project to raise and care for an animal? Did you always remember to feed, water, and groom it?

Have you worked on a farm? Did you clean barns, stables, or pens? Could you do this type of work every day?

Have you taken care of a sick or injured animal? Can you tell if an animal is getting sick or better by the way it looks or acts?

Have you had a hobby raising fish? Did you use eyedroppers, strainers, or other tools to feed, treat, or care for them?

What Else Should You Know About This Group of Occupations?

Workers in this group should like animals. Taking care of them involves more than feeding, watering, and grooming. Sometimes workers must remove waste from cages, stables, animal shelters, or from the animals themselves. Treating sick or injured animals may expose workers to bites, scratches, or kicks.

An increase in the number of household pets will create jobs for animal groomers and other pet-care workers. In addition, the number of people needed to care for laboratory animals will increase. This will be due to the expansion in the testing of foods and drugs by government agencies.

Little or no experience may be needed for some animal care jobs. However, farm experience or caring for animals at home may help in getting a job. Also courses in agriculture that involve animals can be very helpful. Part-time or temporary jobs are sometimes available. Carnivals and the circus

Grooming is an important activity at riding stables and horse boarding businesses.

hire temporary help where they perform. Full time jobs with carnivals require travel and may be seasonal.

How Can You Prepare for This Kind of Work?

Most occupations in Training and Animal Care require thirty days to two years of training and experience. Most beginning workers are given simple duties. As they gain experience, other duties are added. Special skills are required for some jobs in this group. For example, workers may need to know how to swim to work for aquariums. And, workers who train horses must know how to ride. Workers experienced in the care of certain animals may obtain jobs in training them as performers, guide dogs, or saddle horses.

As you plan your high school program, you should include courses related to Training and Animal Care. The following list of courses and skills can help you plan your education.

Agricultural Services – courses in pet services, animal hospital services, animal training, pet grooming, horse handling and care, animal breeding, and horseshoeing.

General Agriculture – courses in agriculture including animal, food, plant, and soil sciences.

Agricultural Production – courses in agricultural production, animal production, crop production, game farm management, and aquaculture.

Courses in biology, zoology, anatomy, and agricultural production (animals) can be helpful for occupations in this group.

Qualifications Profile

This section is a summary of the worker traits and work factors related to successful job performance and worker satisfaction. Try to relate your interests, abilities, aptitudes, and preferences to these traits and factors. An asterisk (*) marks those traits and factors that are related to more than 60% of the occupations listed at the end of this group. The other traits and factors listed are as important, but relate to fewer occupations. See Appendices B-G for information about all of the worker traits and work factors.

Work Situations

Workers must be willing to:

1. Perform duties which change frequently.
* 4. Deal with people.
7. Make decisions using personal judgment.
8. Make decisions using standards that can be measured or checked.
10. Work within precise limits or standards of accuracy.

Educational Skills

This chart shows the levels of reasoning, math, and language skills related to this group. These skills are usually developed in an educational setting. There are six levels ranging from the simple (1) to the most complex (6).

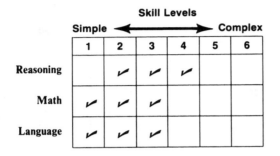

Data-People-Things

This chart shows the levels for these three basic elements of work as related to this group. Level means the degree of difficulty of job tasks rather than the amount of time involved. The terms low, average, and high indicate the highest level at which occupations are involved. Compare your interests and abilities with the levels checked.

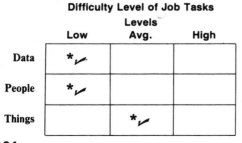

Work Activities

The most important activities related to this group involve:

3. Tasks of a routine, definite nature.
5. Recognition or appreciation from others.
6. Communication of ideas and information.
9. Processes, methods, or machines.

Physical Demands

Workers in this group of occupations must be able to do:

L – Light work
M – Medium work
H – Heavy work

Working Conditions

These are the physical surroundings in which work is done. In occupations belonging to this group, work is performed:

I – Inside — workers spend most of their time inside protected from weather conditions but not always from temperature changes.
O – Outside — workers spend most of their time outside with little protection from weather conditions.
B – Both inside and outside — workers spend about equal time in each setting.

Aptitudes

This chart presents the most important aptitudes related to this group. The levels checked compare aptitudes needed for success in this group to aptitudes of the general working population in all occupations. For example, level 5 is low and represents the bottom 10% of the working population. Level 1 is high and represents the top 10%.

APTITUDE LEVELS COMPARED TO ALL WORKERS							
Related Aptitudes (Ability to Learn)		**Lower 1/3**		**Middle 1/3**	**Upper 1/3**		
		Level **5**	Level **4**	Level **3**	Level **2**	Level **1**	
Code	**Title**	10%	23%	34%	23%	10%	
G	General Learning Ability			* ✔			
K	Motor Coordination		✔	* ✔			
M	Manual Dexterity			* ✔			

Common Occupations

A full listing of all occupations belonging to this group may be found in the Guide for Occupational Exploration.

The following occupations have been selected to represent this group. They provide the major employment opportunities. However, specific job opportunities will vary according to locations of industry, geographical region, and other factors.

Information may be found in common sources of occupational information, state career information systems, and computerized guidance systems.

Animal Training

153.224-014	Racehorse Trainer
159.224-010	Animal Trainer
349.224-010	Animal-Ride Manager

Animal Service

349.674-010	Animal-Ride Attendant
410.674-010	Animal Caretaker
410.674-022	Stable Attendant
412.674-010	Animal Keeper
418.381-010	Horseshoer
418.674-010	Dog Groomer
418.677-010	Dog Bather

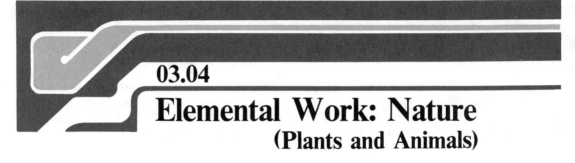

03.04

Elemental Work: Nature
(Plants and Animals)

Elemental Work: Nature is to use physical strength to do basic duties related to plants and animals. Most workers assist others who have more training. Active and sometimes heavy work is involved. Workers use hand tools such as shovels or axes. They also may operate equipment and machinery. They usually work outside. This group includes the subgroups of:

> Farming
> Forestry and Logging
> Hunting and Fishing
> Nursery and Groundskeeping
> Services

Farming is to raise crops, livestock, and poultry. Workers have a variety of duties. They may drive and operate farm machinery to plant, cultivate, and harvest crops. Some workers may need to repair farm equipment, buildings, and fences. Others take care of livestock. They mix food and feed and water them. They also may examine animals to detect diseases or injuries and help vaccinate them. They may milk cows by hand or use machines. Some workers may brand (mark) livestock to show ownership. These workers also clean pens and equipment. Other workers pick, sort, and pack fruit or produce. The job duties of workers depend on the type of farm.

Workers in cattle feedlots and stockyards move animals from pens to loading ramps or other pens.

Forestry and Logging involves developing and protecting forest lands and cutting trees for lumber or pulpwood. Forestry workers plant seedling trees. They also spray trees to protect them from diseases. They cut out diseased, weak, or undesirable trees. They also cut and clear brush and put up signs and fences. They may clean kitchens, restrooms, and campsites. Some workers put out forest fires by cutting down trees and digging trenches. They also patrol burned areas after a fire. Logging workers fell (cut down) timber trees. They cut these trees into log lengths. They fasten cables to the logs to skid them to roads for loading and transportation. They may brand (mark) logs to show ownership. Other workers operate logging tractors or drive trucks to haul logs to the mill. Some sort and inspect logs.

Hunting and Fishing is to trap animals, catch fish, or harvest shellfish. Hunters and trappers catch animals for pelts (skins), to sell them alive, or to relocate them. Workers in fishing jobs catch fish to sell or raise them to release as game fish. Some fishers catch fish by using a net or a line. Some work on a fishing boat and do a variety of duties. This may include standing lookout, steering, or engine-room watch. They may remove fish from nets and hooks to clean and sort them. Workers in fish hatcheries also perform a variety of duties. They trap spawning fish and incubate their eggs. They feed the fingerlings (young fish), monitor their growth, and release them in streams and lakes. They may clean ponds and troughs and make minor repairs to hatchery equipment. Some fishery workers cultivate and harvest shellfish such as clams and oysters.

Nursery and Groundskeeping include the raising of flowers, bulbs, shrubs, and turf grass. Most workers have outside jobs. They care for areas such as gardens, grounds, parks, and cemeteries. Many workers mow grass, trim and edge around walks, flower beds, and walls. They prune shrubs and trees, rake and burn leaves, and clean up litter. Some workers have inside jobs in greenhouses. They plant,

Stacking logs at a saw mill may be one of many tasks of this heavy equipment operator.

Harvesting a crop at a catfish farm.

General farming jobs are found in most sections of the country. Forestry and lumbering work is found mostly in the timber producing areas of the Pacific Northwest and the South. Most fishing jobs are located along the coasts and in the Great Lakes region. Jobs with nurseries, landscape companies, and lawn and tree service firms are usually found in city and suburban areas. Jobs may be found with golf clubs and private households. Jobs also may be found caring for the grounds of industrial, commercial, or public property.

What Skills and Abilities Would Help You Succeed in This Kind of Work?

The most important skills are listed below. All of those listed do not apply to each occupation. As you explore occupations you should identify the specific ones needed.

Coordination – to move the body, hands, and fingers in using tools or operating equipment.

Physical Stamina – to do active physical work each day.

Comprehension – to understand oral or written instructions.

cultivate, and harvest special flowers and shrubs. They also fertilize, water, weed, and transplant, or thin plants in growing areas. Some workers have additional kinds of duties. They may paint, repair, or clean the facilities where they work.

Services are support jobs concerned with plants and animals. For example, some workers capture and impound stray, unlicensed, or sick animals. Some workers drive draft animals (mules, horses) to pull materials such as logs or wagons. They also may need to feed and water the animals and clean their stables. Some workers provide other kinds of services. They trim or prune trees to clear a path for power and telephone lines. Some may cut away dead and excess branches from trees around homes or in an orchard.

Do You Have or Can You Develop an Interest in This Kind of Work?

Review the following questions. Your answers can give you clues as to your interest in Elemental Work: Nature.

Have you picked fruit or vegetables, cut grass, or pulled weeds? Did you like this type of physical work? Could you do it every day?

Have you raised an animal? Did you remember to feed and water it each day? Did you enjoy taking care of it?

Do you like to camp, fish, or hunt? Do you like to be outdoors?

Have you delivered newspapers or shoveled snow? Did you mind working outside in all kinds of weather?

Have you raised fish as a hobby? Did you keep the fish bowl clean?

Have you used rakes, shovels, saws, or other tools? Do you like to work with your hands?

Have you lived on a farm? Did you have daily chores? Did you mind doing them?

What Else Should You Know About This Group of Occupations?

Jobs in this group may have duties that are routine. The amount of heavy work may be reduced with the use of tools, machines, or equipment. Workers may put in long hours during certain times of the year. This could be at planting or harvesting time. Workers are faced with such hazards as storms, severe winter weather, or forest fires. Many jobs are seasonal and do not provide full time employment. This often requires workers to find other jobs during the off-season.

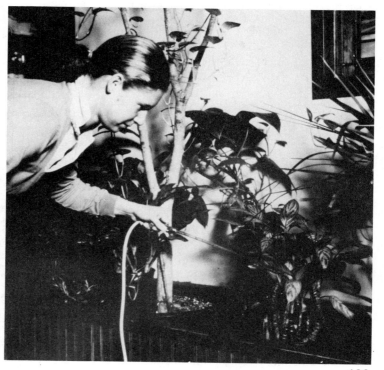

Using a knowledge of many plants and their environmental conditions, this plant care worker is employed by a business that provides plants and keeps them in good condition.

The military services offer training and experience related to one occupation in this group – Logger, All-Round. More information about the military training and experience opportunities may be found in Appendix A.

How Can You Prepare for This Kind of Work?

Most occupations in Elemental Work: Nature require only a short period of training and experience. This may be as little as one to six months. Employers may train workers when they are hired or when their duties change. Some jobs in local, state, or national parks are Civil Service. Farm experience is helpful in getting a full-time farm job. Experience in fishing, hunting, or camping also can be helpful. Many schools and training programs offer courses such as animal science, dairy science, forest management, and wildlife and fisheries management.

As you plan your high school program, you should include courses related to Elemental Work: Nature. The following list of courses and skills can help you plan your education.

General Agriculture – courses in agriculture including animal, food, plant, and soil sciences.

Agricultural Production – courses in agricultural production, animal production, crop production, game farm management, and aquaculture.

Natural Resources – courses in the conservation and/or improvement of natural resources such as air, soil, water, land, fish, and wildlife.

A course in general science can be helpful for occupations in this group.

Qualifications Profile

This section is a summary of the worker traits and work factors related to successful job performance and worker satisfaction. Try to relate your interests, abilities, aptitudes, and preferences to these traits and factors. An asterisk (*) marks those traits and factors that are related to more than 60% of the occupations listed at the end of this group. The other traits and factors listed are as important, but relate to fewer occupations. See Appendices B-G for information about all of the worker traits and work factors.

Work Activities

The most important activities related to this group involve:

* * 1. Things and objects.
* * 3. Tasks of a routine, definite nature.
  9. Processes, methods, or machines.

Work Situations

Workers must be willing to:

1. Perform duties which change frequently.
2. Perform routine tasks.
10. Work within precise limits or standards of accuracy.

Working Conditions

These are the physical surroundings in which work is done. In occupations belonging to this group, work is performed:

*O – Outside — workers spend most of their time outside with little protection from weather conditions.

B – Both inside and outside — workers spend about equal time in each setting.

Physical Demands

Workers in this group of occupations must be able to do:

M – Medium work
H – Heavy work

Data-People-Things

This chart shows the levels for these three basic elements of work as related to this group. Level means the degree of difficulty of job tasks rather than the amount of time involved. The terms low, average, and high indicate the highest level at which occupations are involved. Compare your interests and abilities with the levels checked.

Difficulty Level of Job Tasks

	Low	Avg.	High
Data	*✓		
People	*✓		
Things	✓	*✓	

A logging worker cuts branches from a felled tree.

Educational Skills

This chart shows the levels of reasoning, math, and language skills related to this group. These skills are usually developed in an educational setting. There are six levels ranging from the simple (1) to the most complex (6).

Skill Levels

	Simple ⟵			⟶ Complex		
	1	2	3	4	5	6
Reasoning		✔	✔			
Math	*✔	✔				
Language	✔	✔	✔			

In a free-flight pen at a game farm, this worker tags ring-necked pheasants.

Aptitudes

This chart presents the most important aptitudes related to this group. The levels checked compare aptitudes needed for success in this group to aptitudes of the general working population in all occupations. For example, level 5 is low and represents the bottom 10% of the working population. Level 1 is high and represents the top 10%.

APTITUDE LEVELS COMPARED TO ALL WORKERS							
Related Aptitudes **(Ability to Learn)**		Lower 1/3		Middle 1/3	Upper 1/3		
		Level **5**	Level **4**	Level **3**	Level **2**	Level **1**	
Code	**Title**	10%	23%	34%	23%	10%	
G	General Learning Ability		✔	✔			
K	Motor Coordination		✔	*✔			
M	Manual Dexterity			*✔			

Common Occupations

A full listing of all occupations belonging to this group may be found in the Guide for Occupational Exploration.

The following occupations have been selected to represent this group. They provide the major employment opportunities. However, specific job opportunities will vary according to locations of industry, geographical region, and other factors.

Information may be found in common sources of occupational information, state career information systems, and computerized guidance systems.

An (M) follows the occupational title where the military services offer training and experience.

Farming

401.683-010	Farmworker, Grain 1
401.683-014	Farmworker, Rice
402.663-010	Farmworker, Vegetable 1
403.683-010	Farmworker, Fruit 1
407.663-010	Farmworker, Diversified Crops 1
409.683-010	Farm-Machine Operator
410.664-010	Farmworker, Livestock
410.674-014	Cowpuncher
410.674-018	Livestock-Yard Attendant
410.684-010	Farmworker, Dairy
410.685-010	Milker, Machine
411.584-010	Farmworker, Poultry
421.683-010	Farmworker, General 1
529.687-186	Sorter, Agricultural Produce
920.687-010	Apple-Packing Header
920.687-134	Packer, Agricultural Produce

Forestry and Logging

452.687-010	Forest Worker
452.687-014	Forest-Fire Fighter
452.687-018	Tree Planter
454.384-010	Faller 1
454.684-010	Bucker
454.684-018	Logger, All-Round (M)
454.684-026	Tree Cutter
455.684-010	Log Sorter
455.687-010	Log Marker
459.687-010	Laborer, Brush Clearing
667.687-014	Log Inspector
669.687-026	Tie Inspector
929.683-010	Logging-Tractor Operator

Hunting and Fishing

441.684-010	Fisher, Net
442.684-010	Fisher, Line
446.684-010	Fish Hatchery Worker
446.684-014	Shellfish-Bed Worker
446.687-010	Clam Sorter
449.667-010	Deckhand, Fishing Vessel
461.684-014	Trapper, Animal

Nursery and Groundskeeping

301.687-018	Yard Worker
405.684-014	Horticultural Worker 1
406.137-010	Greenskeeper 1
406.684-010	Cemetery Worker
406.684-014	Groundskeeper, Industrial-Commercial
406.684-018	Garden Worker
406.687-010	Groundskeeper, Parks and Grounds
406.687-014	Laborer, Landscape

Services

379.673-010	Dog Catcher
408.664-010	Tree Trimmer
408.684-018	Tree Pruner
409.687-014	Irrigator, Gravity Flow
418.384-010	Artificial Inseminator
919.664-010	Teamster

04 AUTHORITY
(Protective)

Workers with an interest in protecting people and property enjoy work in the Authority area. Some jobs involve action, thrills, and adventure. This might be fighting a fire, making an arrest, or solving a crime. These jobs require an ability to work under pressure or in the face of danger. Workers must be able to talk and deal with all kinds of people. They must be able to think clearly and react quickly during a crisis.

Workers are usually required to wear uniforms. Their work hours may be irregular and they may need to work nights or weekends. Some jobs require skill in the use of guns, safety devices, or other equipment.

Authority work includes two clusters: Safety and Law Enforcement and Security Services.

Safety and Law Enforcement

The Safety and Law Enforcement cluster involves enforcing laws and regulations. Workers may investigate crimes, issue tickets, and make arrests. This cluster includes workers who manage or suervise, such as Fire Captain and Police Sergeant. Work is found mostly with local, state, and federal governments and most jobs are with police and fire departments.

Security Services

The Security Services cluster also involves the enforcement of laws and regulations. In addition, workers prevent crime and maintain order. They guard, patrol, and monitor property and people. Business and industry provide a variety of jobs. Jobs also are found with local, state, and federal agencies. Bodyguards and private detectives are included in this cluster.

The following Worker Trait Groups and Subgroups are related to the Safety and Law Enforcement and Security Services clusters.

04

Authority: an interest in providing protective services for people and property.

Law Enforcement

04.01 Safety and Law Enforcement
Managing
Investigating

Security Services

04.02 Security Services
Detention
Property and People
Law and Order
Emergency Responding

Safety and Law Enforcement

Safety and Law Enforcement is to protect the public against crimes, fires, and accidents. Workers have the authority to enforce rules that promote public welfare and safety. They prevent crimes and arrest law breakers. And they protect people and property from the hazards of fire. This group includes the subgroups of:

Managing

Investigating

Managing is to coordinate the services of a department and to direct the tasks of workers.

Titles such as chief and captain are given to these management positions. Their duties may involve training new recruits. They prepare reports and keep records. They help decide what supplies and equipment to purchase. They control business details and submit budgets. And they review and resolve complaints about the services of their department and of their workers. As part of their public relations work, they may give lectures or prepare newspaper releases.

Conservation law-enforcement officers have police authority and receive regular training on new laws and regulations.

Investigating is to look for, gather, and evaluate facts to be used as evidence. This may be to determine causes of a fire or traffic accident. It may be to detect or prevent smuggling or game law violations. It may be to prevent crime or solve criminal cases. Workers may patrol areas by foot or in a car, boat, or aircraft. They use search warrants and question suspects. They arrest people and testify in a court of law. They also keep records and prepare reports.

Most jobs in this group are found with federal, state, or local government agencies. Police and fire departments are major employers. Businesses offer a few job openings.

What Skills and Abilities Would Help You Succeed in This Kind of Work?

The most important skills are listed below. All of those listed do not apply to each occupation. As you explore occupations you should identify the specific ones needed.

Leadership – to plan and direct the work of others.

Communication – to direct workers, write reports, and question suspects.

Critical Thinking – to use personal judgment to make decisions.

Reasoning – to observe details, examine evidence, and draw conclusions.

Comprehension – to understand laws and safety rules.

Organization – to arrange ideas, thoughts, and information in a way that can be understood.

Physical Stamina – to use strength during emergency situations.

This leader prepares his oil refinery team during a practice drill.

Rapport – to relate with people in an understanding way and maintain harmony among workers.

Composure – to be calm and self-confident in emergency situations and to work under pressure.

Do You Have or Can You Develop an Interest in This Kind of Work?

Review the following questions. Your answers can give you clues as to your interest in the Safety and Law Enforcement field.

Have you been a member of the school safety patrol? Have you been a hall monitor? Did you like protecting people and enforcing rules?

Have you watched mystery shows on TV? Do you read detective stories? Do you try to solve the mysteries?

Have you used a gun for hunting or target practice? Are you a good shot?

Have you made speeches in public? Would you like work that requires some public speaking?

Have you had lessons in wrestling, karate, or judo? Would you like to use these physical skills in your work?

Have you had courses in government, civics, or in the study of crime? Did you find these subjects interesting? How were your grades?

Have you seen an accident? Did it bother you? Do you think you could give first-aid to a person that was hurt?

Have you helped to direct traffic at a community event? Did you remain calm when it became busy?

What Else Should You Know About This Group of Occupations?

People seeking jobs in this group should desire to serve the community. They must be U.S. citizens and may be required to be within certain height and weight ranges. Written, oral, or physical tests may be required of applicants. They may be tested for physical strength and the ability to move quickly and easily. All applicants are investigated to make sure they do not have criminal records.

Many jobs in this group require night and weekend work. They also require overtime work during emergencies. Although most of these jobs are routine, workers may be exposed to injury or death. Many of these workers have a great deal of responsibility and work with little supervision.

The military services offer training and experience related to some occupations in this group. These occupations are included in the list at the end of this group description. They are identified by an (M) following the occupational title. More information about the military training and experience opportunities may be found in Appendix A.

Game wardens check licenses of hunters and fishers, as part of enforcing fish and game regulations.

How Can You Prepare for This Kind of Work?

Most occupations in this group require more than one year of training and experience. Some require as much as ten years. Jobs with federal law enforcement agencies usually require a college degree. For example, FBI agents need a degree in law or accounting. Those with accounting degrees must have at least one year of related work experience. Most of the management jobs are filled through promotions. Civil service laws usually require written exams and job performance ratings.

Most police departments prefer to hire people with at least a high school education or its equal. Related experiences such as military service may help in getting a job. Police work is entered as a cadet or trainee.

As you plan your high school program, you should include any courses related to Safety and Law Enforcement. Next, you should include courses needed to enter college or a technical program. The following list of courses and skills can help you plan your education.

Protective Services – courses in criminal justice, law enforcement, law enforcement administration, security services, fire protection, safety technology, and firefighting.

Public Affairs – courses in community services, public administration, public policy studies, and social work.

Law/Accounting – courses in pre-law, law, legal assisting, and accounting. (FBI)

Courses in general English, speech, technical/business writing, math, government and civics, physical education, and criminology can be helpful for occupations in this group. Courses in general science and social studies can help you determine your interest in this field.

Qualifications Profile

This section is a summary of the worker traits and work factors related to successful job performance and worker satisfaction. Try to relate your interests, abilities, aptitudes, and preferences to these traits and factors. An asterisk (*) marks those traits and factors that are related to more than 60% of the occupations listed at the end of this group. The other traits and factors listed are as important, but relate to fewer occupations. See Appendices B-G for information about all of the worker traits and work factors.

Work Situations

Workers must be willing to:

* 1. Perform duties which change frequently.
  3. Plan and direct an entire activity.
* 4. Deal with people.
* 7. Make decisions using personal judgment.
  8. Make decisions using standards that can be measured or checked.

Work Activities

The most important activities related to this group involve:

* * 2. Business contact.
* * 5. Recognition or appreciation from others.
* * 6. Communication of ideas and information.

Working Conditions

These are the physical surroundings in which work is done. In occupations belonging to this group, work is performed:

I – Inside — workers spend most of their time inside protected from weather conditions but not always from temperature changes.

B – Both inside and outside — workers spend about equal time in each setting.

Physical Demands

Workers in this group of occupations must be able to do:

S – Sedentary work
L – Light work
M – Medium work

Educational Skills

This chart shows the levels of reasoning, math, and language skills related to this group. These skills are usually developed in an educational setting. There are six levels ranging from the simple (1) to the most complex (6).

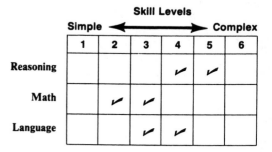

Aptitudes

This chart presents the most important aptitudes related to this group. The levels checked compare aptitudes needed for success in this group to aptitudes of the general working population in all occupations. For example, level 5 is low and represents the bottom 10% of the working population. Level 1 is high and represents the top 10%.

APTITUDE LEVELS COMPARED TO ALL WORKERS							
Related Aptitudes (Ability to Learn)		Lower 1/3		Middle 1/3	Upper 1/3		
		Level **5**	Level **4**	Level **3**	Level **2**	Level **1**	
Code	Title	10%	23%	34%	23%	10%	
G	General Learning Ability			✔	* ✔		
V	Verbal			✔	* ✔		
Q	Clerical Perception		✔	* ✔			

Data-People-Things

This chart shows the levels for these three basic elements of work as related to this group. Level means the degree of difficulty of job tasks rather than the amount of time involved. The terms low, average, and high indicate the highest level at which occupations are involved. Compare your interests and abilities with the levels checked.

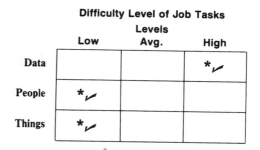

Difficulty Level of Job Tasks

	Low	Avg.	High
Data			*
People	*		
Things	*		

Common Occupations

A full listing of all occupations belonging to this group may be found in the Guide for Occupational Exploration.

The following occupations have been selected to represent this group. They provide the major employment opportunities. However, specific job opportunities will vary according to locations of industry, geographical region, and other factors.

Information may be found in common sources of occupational information, state career information systems, and computerized guidance systems.

An (M) follows the occupational title where the military services offer training and experience.

Managing

169.167-022	Fire Assistant
188.117-118	Police Commissioner 1
188.167-062	Park Superintendent
372.167-014	Guard, Chief
373.117-010	Fire Chief
373.134-010	Fire Captain
373.167-018	Fire Marshal
375.117-010	Police Chief (M)
375.133-010	Police Sergeant, Precinct 1
375.167-022	Detective Chief
375.167-026	Harbor Master (M)
375.167-034	Police Captain, Precinct (M)
376.137-010	Manager, Internal Security
376.167-010	Special Agent-In-Charge
377.117-010	Sheriff, Deputy, Chief (M)
377.137-014	Deputy Sheriff, Commander, Criminal and Patrol Division (M)
377.167-010	Deputy Sheriff, Chief (M)

Investigating

059.267-014	Intelligence Specialist (M)
168.167-010	Customs Patrol Officer (M)
373.267-014	Fire Marshal
375.167-042	Special Agent (M)
375.263-014	Police Officer 1 (M)
375.263-018	State-Highway Police Officer (M)
375.267-010	Detective (M)
375.267-014	Detective, Narcotics and Vice
376.267-018	Investigator, Private (M)
377.263-010	Sheriff, Deputy (M)
377.267-010	Deputy United States Marshall
378.267-010	Counterintelligence Agent (M)
379.167-010	Fish and Game Warden
379.263-014	Public-Safety Officer
452.167-010	Fire Warden

04.02
Security Services

Security Services protect people and property from fires, accidents, and crimes. Workers enforce the law. They prevent acts that are against the law and maintain order and safety. This group includes the subgroups of:

Detention
Property and People
Law and Order
Emergency Responding

Detention is to guard people in such places as jails and prisons. Workers' duties may vary due to the type of prisoner or the security needed. The most security (maximum) is used for prisoners guilty of serious crimes. Prison guards must check locks, bars, and doors for tampering. They search inmates and their cells. They watch inmates while they work and during meals. They patrol entrances and screen visitors. Other workers are involved in less secure settings such as courtrooms and detention homes. Some are involved in detaining people until they have a hearing. They may question prisoners. They may gather evidence and write arrest reports. Some work with females or juveniles only. They may provide care for runaway or lost children until their parents are found.

Property and People include protecting people, homes, and business places. Some workers guard government property. Their work may require travel. Some workers drive armored cars. They deliver and pick-up money and other things of value from

122

business places. They write receipts, keep records, and deposit money. Other workers escort people to protect them from harm or invasion of privacy. Still others may guard entrance gates to industrial plants or warehouses. They check credentials (IDs) of people coming in. They direct people to where they need to go. They also check permits for tools or other things going out.

Some security workers guard against fire, theft, and illegal entry. They patrol the area to check doors, windows, and gates to make sure they are secure. Some workers inspect

Rescue personnel and police officers coordinate efforts to get injured individuals safely to emergency care facilities.

premises to detect and get rid of fire hazards. These workers also may instruct employees in fire safety practices. Other workers check airline passengers. They inspect carry-on luggage for weapons or explosives. Some workers plan security systems. They oversee the installation of security devices. Other workers inspect these devices as well as fire alarms. They make sure they are set to operate. This subgroup also includes workers who protect retail stores from illegal acts. They may apprehend and question suspects. They file complaints. They write reports and alert other businesses of suspects. They also may be called to testify in court.

Law and Order is to protect people and property in a variety of settings. Some workers patrol the U.S. border or seacoast. They may do this to stop illegal entry into the country. Some patrol hotel or business premises to keep order. These workers may detain and question suspects or warn troublemakers. Others patrol public beaches, pools, or ski trails to provide help or prevent accidents. Some workers monitor (watch) people's activities to maintain discipline and safety. This may be on school buses. Or, they patrol state and national parks. Some monitor public bus, train, and airport terminals. Other workers maintain order in courtrooms during trials. They also guard the jury from outside contact.

Emergency Responding is to act quickly in response to alarms that signal distress. Workers may control and put out fires. They give first aid if needed. These workers may also drive and operate firefighting vehicles and equipment. Some workers may respond to air crash emergencies. They prevent or put out fires and rescue plane crews and passengers. They may also render first aid. Some homes and businesses have special

All law enforcement is not "out on the streets" — a lot of paperwork is needed to document events.

alarms installed. When this system goes off, workers respond to investigate. They work closely with the police and fire departments. They may also adjust and repair these systems.

What Skills and Abilities Would Help You Succeed in This Kind of Work?

The most important skills are listed below. All of those listed do not apply to each occupation. As you explore occupations you should identify the specific ones needed.

Composure – to be calm and self-confident in emergency situations and work under pressure.

Critical Thinking – to use personal judgment to make decisions and solve problems.

Dexterity – to move the eyes and hands or fingers together to perform a task rapidly and quickly.

Physical Stamina – to have physical strength in emergency situations.

Rapport – to relate with people in an understanding way and maintain harmony among workers.

Do You Have or Can You Develop an Interest in This Kind of Work?

Review the following questions. Your answers can give you clues as to your interest in the Security Services field.

Have you directed people at school or community events? Did you stay calm when it became crowded?

Have you been a member of a school safety patrol? Did you instruct others in observing traffic regulations? Can you follow rules yourself?

Have you taken care of brothers, sisters, or other children? Did they behave?

Have you taken a first aid course? Can you treat injuries quickly and skillfully?

A four-wheel drive vehicle can speed a beach lifeguard to the rescue of swimmers.

Have you worked as a camp counselor or other group leader? Did you like enforcing safety rules?

Have you used a gun for hunting or target practice? Are you a good shot?

Have you been a member of a volunteer fire or rescue squad? Did you like helping people? Did you stay calm during emergencies?

What Else Should You Know About This Group of Occupations?

Most jobs in this group have routine duties. However, there is an element of danger involved. Workers run the risk of injury by lawbreakers and suspects. This risk is higher when the worker is arresting or guarding such persons. Security Agents may work alone with no help nearby in case of accident or injury.

Some jobs involve night work. On other jobs, workers take turns working nights, days, weekends, and holidays. Workers also must be on call for emergencies.

For some jobs, applicants must provide character references and have no police record. A few jobs may require skill in using firearms. Some workers need to be bonded. This means they need special insurance to assure employers or customers of their honesty. They also may be fingerprinted.

The military services offer training and experience related to some occupations in this group. These occupations are included in the list at the end of this group description. They are identified by an (M) following the occupational title. More information about the military training and experience opportunities may be found in Appendix A.

How Can You Prepare for This Kind of Work?

Most occupations in this group require from thirty days to two years of training and experience. Many of these jobs are open to those who have little work experience. Some employers prefer people who have worked for military, local, or state police. People applying for government jobs may need to take written and physical tests.

As you plan your high school program, you should include courses related to Security Services. The following list of courses and skills can help you plan your education.

Protective Services – courses in criminal justice, law enforcement, fire protection, fire control, safety technology, and firefighting.

Health – courses in first aid and safety practices.

Physical Education – courses to build stamina and body coordination. Some jobs require specific physical skills. For example: lifeguards and ski patrols.

Courses in government, civics, and report writing can be helpful for some occupations in this group.

Jobs in this group may be found with Federal, State, or local governments. Jobs also may be found with hotels, stores, resorts, and industries. Some of these workers are self-employed and may be bodyguards or private detectives.

Qualifications Profile

This section is a summary of the worker traits and work factors related to successful job performance and worker satisfaction. Try to relate your interests, abilities, aptitudes, and preferences to these traits and factors. An asterisk (*) marks those traits and factors that are related to more than 60% of the occupations listed at the end of this group. The other traits and factors listed are as important, but relate to fewer occupations. See Appendices B-G for information about all of the worker traits and work factors.

Work Activities

The most important activities related to this group involve:

1. Things and objects.
* 2. Business contact.
3. Tasks of a routine, definite nature.
6. Communication of ideas and information.

Work Situations

Workers must be willing to:

1. Perform duties which change frequently.
* 4. Deal with people.
* 6. Work under pressure.
7. Make decisions using personal judgment.

Physical Demands

Workers in this group of occupations must be able to do:

*L – Light work
M – Medium work

Working Conditions

These are the physical surroundings in which work is done. In occupations belonging to this group, work is performed:

I – Inside — workers spend most of their time inside protected from weather conditions but not always from temperature changes.

O – Outside — workers spend most of their time outside with little protection from weather conditions.

B – Both inside and outside — workers spend about equal time in each setting.

Educational Skills

This chart shows the levels of reasoning, math, and language skills related to this group. These skills are usually developed in an educational setting. There are six levels ranging from the simple (1) to the most complex (6).

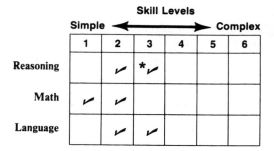

Aptitudes

This chart presents the most important aptitudes related to this group. The levels checked compare aptitudes needed for success in this group to aptitudes of the general working population in all occupations. For example, level 5 is low and represents the bottom 10% of the working population. Level 1 is high and represents the top 10%.

APTITUDE LEVELS COMPARED TO ALL WORKERS						
Related Aptitudes (Ability to Learn)		Lower 1/3		Middle 1/3	Upper 1/3	
		Level **5**	Level **4**	Level **3**	Level **2**	Level **1**
Code	Title	10%	23%	34%	23%	10%
G	General Learning Ability			* ✓		
V	Verbal		✓	* ✓		
K	Motor Coordination		✓	✓		

Data-People-Things

This chart shows the levels for these three basic elements of work as related to this group. Level means the degree of difficulty of job tasks rather than the amount of time involved. The terms low, average, and high indicate the highest level at which occupations are involved. Compare your interests and abilities with the levels checked.

Difficulty Level of Job Tasks

	Low	Avg.	High
Data	✔	✔	
People	*✔		
Things	*✔	✔	

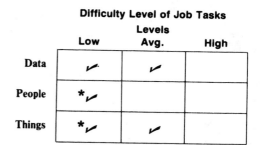

Common Occupations

A full listing of all occupations belonging to this group may be found in the Guide for Occupational Exploration.

The following occupations have been selected to represent this group. They provide the major employment opportunities. However, specific job opportunities will vary according to locations of industry, geographical region, and other factors.

Information may be found in common sources of occupational information, state career information systems, and computerized guidance systems.

An (M) follows the occupational title where the military services offer training and experience.

Detention
372.367-014   Jailer
372.667-018   Correction Officer (M)
375.367-010   Police Officer 2

Property and People
189.167-054   Security Consultant
372.363-010   Protective Officer

372.563-010   Armored-Car Guard and Driver
372.567-010   Armored-Car Guard
372.667-010   Airline Security Representative
372.667-014   Bodyguard
372.667-030   Gate Tender
372.667-034   Guard, Security (M)
372.667-038   Merchant Patroller (M)
373.367-010   Fire Inspector (M)
375.587-010   Parking Enforcement Officer
376.367-014   Detective 1
452.367-014   Fire Ranger

Law and Order
169.167-042   Park Ranger
372.667-042   School Bus Monitor
375.363-010   Border Guard
376.367-018   House Officer
376.667-014   Detective 2
377.667-010   Bailiff
379.364-014   Beach Lifeguard
379.367-010   Surveillance-System Monitor
379.664-010   Ski Patroller
379.667-014   Lifeguard

Emergency Responding
373.364-010   Fire Fighter (M)
373.663-010   Fire Fighter, Crash, Fire, and Rescue (M)
376.367-010   Alarm Investigator

MECHANICAL

People with mechanical interest enjoy working with machines and tools. Some workers design and develop new machines, tools, and processes. They apply basic physics principles such as wheels, gears, and levers to build complex machines and to improve tools. Other workers are involved in the skilled use of these machines and tools to help them in their work.

The Mechanical area includes over twenty percent of the occupations in the world of work. Jobs are found in a variety of nonfactory settings. These range from quiet offices in modern buildings to dirty and noisy places found on construction jobs and in mines. Factory jobs using machines and tools are included in Area 06 – Industrial.

The Mechanical area is divided into four clusters: Engineering and Management; Vehicle and Equipment Operation/Control; Quality/Materials Control; and Crafts.

Engineering and Management

These workers use math, science, and communication skills. Some analyze, design, construct, and evaluate as part of the work tasks they perform. Others plan, direct, and manage. Engineers solve problems in construction, manufacturing, and other industries. They design ways to convert energy into a mechanical force to do work. They usually specialize in one field, such as electrical, civil, or mechanical. Technicians support engineers in their work, performing tasks such as drafting and surveying. Management work uses engineering knowledge to direct the operations of systems and plants.

Vehicle and Equipment Operation/Control

This work involves the operation of heavy equipment, and the control of mechanical systems. This includes the operation or control of land, air, and water vehicles. Some workers operate heavy equipment to drill, hoist, mine, or dredge. Some control such equipment as pumps and boilers. Some operate boats or planes to move cargo or people. Others operate land vehicles such as trucks, vans, and railroad engines.

Quality/Materials Control

This work involves the flow of materials and products being shipped, received, or stored. Some workers inspect and check equipment to see if repairs are needed. Some inspect and test products or materials to be sure they meet standards. Some workers inventory (count) products and keep records. Some control the flow of materials to where they are needed.

Crafts

This includes highly skilled custom hand and machine work. Special training and experience is needed to develop craft skills. A variety of work is included in this cluster. Work might range from making a repair on a car engine to preparing food in a large hotel. Workers use their hands and hand tools skillfully as they process, install, and repair parts or products. Unskilled work related to crafts is also included in this cluster.

The following Worker Trait Groups and Subgroups are related to the Engineering and Management, Vehicle and Equipment Operation/Control, Quality/Materials Control, and Crafts clusters.

05

Engineering and Management

05.01 Engineering
  Research and Design
  Sales
  Installation and Operation

05.02 Managerial Work: Mechanical
  Systems
  Maintenance and Construction
  Processing and Manufacturing
  Communications
  Mining, Logging, and Petroleum
      Production
  Services
  Materials Handling

05.03 Engineering Technology
  Surveying
  Drafting
  Expediting and Coordinating
  Petroleum
  Electrical - Electronic
  Industrial and Safety
  Mechanical
  Environmental Control

Vehicle and Equipment Operation/Control

05.04 Air and Water Transportation
  Air
  Water

05.06 Systems Operation
  Electricity Generation and
      Transmission
  Stationary Engineering
  Oil, Gas, and Water Distribution
  Processing

**05.08 Land and Water Vehicle
  Operation**
  Truck/Services Delivery
  Rail Vehicle Operation
  Boat Operation

05.11 Equipment Operation
  Construction
  Mining and Quarrying
  Drilling and Oil Exploration
  Materials Handling

Quality/Materials Control

05.07 Quality Control
  Structural
  Mechanical
  Electrical
  Petroleum
  Logging and Lumber

05.09 Material Control
  Shipping, Receiving, and Stock
      Checking
  Estimating, Scheduling, and Record
      Keeping
  Verifying, Recording, and Marking

Mechanical: an interest in applying mechanical principles to practical situations.

Crafts

05.05 Craft Technology
  Construction and Maintenance
  Electrical/Electronic
  Fine Fabrication and Repair
  Food Preparation
  Metal Fabrication and Machine Work
  Mechanical
  Woodworking
  Printing

**05.10 Skilled Hand and Machine
  Work**
  Structural-Mechanical-Electrical-
      Electronic
  Reproduction
  Blasting
  Painting, Dyeing, and Coating
  Food Preparation
  Environmental

05.12 Elemental Work: Mechanical
  Services
  Materials Movement
  Fabrication and Structural Work

05.01
Engineering

Engineering is the use of science and math to solve problems in construction, manufacturing, and other industries. Some workers conduct research, but most are involved with producing goods and services. Workers usually specialize in one or more fields of engineering. Technicians are also included in this group. They provide support services for engineers. This group includes the subgroups of:

Research and Design
Sales
Installation and Operation

Research and Design involves the design of structures, products, equipment, and processes. Some workers design and direct the building of bridges, dams, and roads. Some conduct research to develop or improve products or the materials from which they are made. They develop new processes and systems as they conduct tests to solve problems. Some workers design new equipment and tools. Others work in the design and testing of aircraft and space vehicles. Engineers are involved in the manufacture of chemicals and related products, electronics, and mining.

Sales involve engineers who use their background in engineering to sell equipment, supplies, or service. They need to know what is cost effective for their customers. They review plans and blueprints to judge costs or increase production. Some draw up sales or service contracts. They also may train others in the use of their products or equipment.

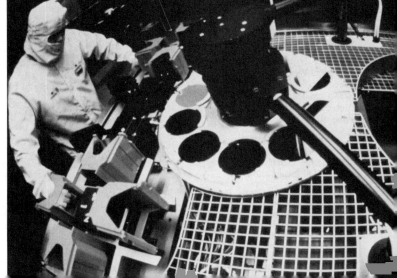

This aeronautical design engineer is at work on a satellite.

A chemical engineer controls a complex process from two control stations with screen readouts.

Installation and Operation involves facilities, equipment, materials, products, operating systems, and health and safety standards. Some workers design and install equipment and systems. Others are involved in operations and maintenance work. They plan production schedules and develop operating standards and procedures. Some workers monitor health and safety conditions to ensure that state and federal laws are being met. Others test products to ensure safety and quality control. Some may write training manuals or conduct safety programs.

Jobs may be found in manufacturing, construction, mining, communications, energy and power production, and in research labs. Some workers have their own engineering firms and accept work from individuals or companies. Federal, state, and local governments also offer employment.

What Skills and Abilities Would Help You Succeed in This Kind of Work?

The most important skills are listed below. All of those listed do not apply to each occupation. As you explore occupations you should identify the specific ones needed.

Comprehension – to know and use the basic principles of science and engineering.

Critical Thinking – to form opinions and make decisions based upon knowledge, judgment, and experience.

Spatial Perception – to form a mental image (picture) of objects or structures by looking at drawings.

Interpretation – to understand and explain technical ideas to others.

131

Leadership – to plan and direct the work of others.

Numerical – to use math to solve engineering problems.

Persuasiveness – to persuade, advise, and assist customers in purchasing engineering products or services.

Form Perception – the ability to make drawings to illustrate machine designs, factory layouts, or highway plans.

Rapport – to relate with people in an understanding way and maintain harmony among workers.

Do You Have or Can You Develop an Interest in This Kind of Work?

Review the following questions. Your answers can give you clues as to your interest in Engineering.

Have you done experiments with a chemistry set? Did you enjoy this type of activity?

Have you taken courses in advanced math or science? Did you like these subjects? How were your grades?

Have you built a model airplane or car? Can you look at drawings or read directions and picture the final structure?

Have you read mechanical or automotive design magazines? Did you understand the technical terms used? Did you enjoy reading them?

Have you taken physics courses? Did you like to study energy and matter?

Have you built a radio, TV, or amplifier using a commercial kit? Did you understand the terms and drawings used in the directions? Do you enjoy working with electrical or electronic products?

A team of design engineers studies the systems diagram of a submarine.

What Else Should You Know About This Group of Occupations?

Engineering is considered to be the second largest profession. Most jobs are located in modern offices and labs. However, some jobs require workers to visit construction sites, plants, mines, and other work areas. This may require a lot of time away from home. Engineers in sales are required to travel frequently.

The military services offer training and experience related to some occupations in this group. These occupations are included in the list at the end of this group description. They are identified by an (M) following the occupational title. More information about the military training and experience opportunities may be found in Appendix A.

College graduates trained in science or math may qualify for some beginning jobs. Experienced technicians with courses in engineering are sometimes advanced to engineering jobs.

All states require engineers whose work affects the life, health, or property of others to be licensed. An engineering degree and four years of experience are usually required for a license. License applicants may also need to pass a state exam.

As you plan your high school program you should include courses related to Engineering. Also, you should include courses needed to enter college. The following list of courses and skills can help you plan your education.

How Can You Prepare for This Kind of Work?

Most occupations in this group require four to ten years of education and training. A few require over ten years. Technician level jobs require two to four years. Workers usually need a bachelor's degree in engineering to enter this type of work. A background in math, physics, and chemistry is needed to enter most engineering schools. Some engineering schools have agreements with liberal arts colleges. Students spend three years in the college and two years in the engineering school. A degree is granted by each school. Some engineering schools offer work-study programs. Students earn a part of their tuition and get experience as they learn. These programs take five or six years to complete.

This electronics test engineer is using an oscilloscope.

Tracing a problem in a central office equipment room is the task of these engineers.

Engineering – programs and courses in the field of an engineering specialty such as chemical, civil, electronics, mining, mechanical, and safety.

Mathematics – courses in algebra, geometry, trigonometry, calculus, statistics, and other engineering/research mathematics.

Science – courses in physics, chemistry, and other science areas related to the field of specialization.

Drafting and Design – courses in mechanical drawing, basic drafting, design graphics, computer assisted design (CAD), surveying and mapping, and architectural design.

Communications – courses in composition, technical writing, speech, and debate can be useful for report writing, sales, and conducting training programs.

Industrial Arts – basic courses involving power systems, electrical circuits, electronics, metals, and manufacturing.

Sales and Business – accounting, salesmanship, distribution, marketing, cost analysis and budgeting, and computer programming.

Health and Safety – courses in life sciences, industrial hygiene, environmental control, radiation safety, fire protection, air pollution, sanitation, and occupational safety.

Qualifications Profile

This section is a summary of the worker traits and work factors related to successful job performance and worker satisfaction. Try to relate your interests, abilities, aptitudes, and preferences to these traits and factors. An asterisk (*) marks those traits and factors that are related to more than 60% of the occupations listed at the end of this group. The other traits and factors listed are as important, but relate to fewer occupations. See Appendices B-G for information about all of the worker traits and work factors.

Work Activities

The most important activities related to this group involve:

1. Things and objects.
6. Communication of ideas and information.
* 7. Tasks of a scientific and technical nature.
8. Creative thinking.
9. Processes, methods, or machines.

Work Situations

Workers must be willing to:

* 1. Perform duties which change frequently.
* 3. Plan and direct an entire activity.
   4. Deal with people.
   7. Make decisions using personal judgment.
* 8. Make decisions using standards that can be measured or checked.
*10. Work within precise limits or standards of accuracy.

Data-People-Things

This chart shows the levels for these three basic elements of work as related to this group. Level means the degree of difficulty of job tasks rather than the amount of time involved. The terms low, average, and high indicate the highest level at which occupations are involved. Compare your interests and abilities with the levels checked.

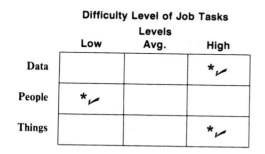

Difficulty Level of Job Tasks

	Low	Avg.	High
Data			*✔
People	*✔		
Things			*✔

Physical Demands

Workers in this group of occupations must be able to do:

  S – Sedentary work
*L – Light work

Working Conditions

These are the physical surroundings in which work is done. In occupations belonging to this group, work is performed:

*I – Inside — workers spend most of their time inside protected from weather conditions but not always from temperature changes.
B – Both inside and outside — workers spend about equal time in each setting.

Educational Skills

This chart shows the levels of reasoning, math, and language skills related to this group. These skills are usually developed in an educational setting. There are six levels ranging from the simple (1) to the most complex (6).

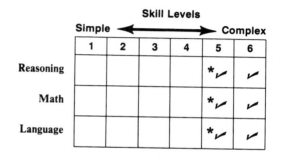

Skill Levels

Simple ⟵⟶ Complex

	1	2	3	4	5	6
Reasoning					*✔	✔
Math					*✔	✔
Language					*✔	✔

Aptitudes

This chart presents the most important aptitudes related to this group. The levels checked compare aptitudes needed for success in this group to aptitudes of the general working population in all occupations. For example, level 5 is low and represents the bottom 10% of the working population. Level 1 is high and represents the top 10%.

APTITUDE LEVELS COMPARED TO ALL WORKERS						
Related Aptitudes (Ability to Learn)		Lower 1/3		Middle 1/3	Upper 1/3	
		Level 5	Level 4	Level 3	Level 2	Level 1
Code	Title	10%	23%	34%	23%	10%
G	General Learning Ability				*✓	✓
V	Verbal				*✓	✓
N	Numerical				*✓	✓
S	Spatial				*✓	✓
P	Form Perception			✓	*✓	

Common Occupations

A full listing of all occupations belonging to this group may be found in the Guide for Occupational Exploration.

The following occupations have been selected to represent this group. They provide the major employment opportunities. However, specific job opportunities will vary according to locations of industry, geographical region, and other factors.

Information may be found in common sources of occupational information, state career information systems, and computerized guidance systems.

An (M) follows the occupational title where the military services offer training and experience.

Research and Design

001.061-010 Architect (M)
001.061-014 Architect, Marine (M)
001.061-018 Landscape Architect
001.167-010 School-Plant Consultant
002.061-010 Aerodynamist (M)
002.061-014 Aeronautical Engineer (M)
002.061-022 Aeronautical-Design Engineer (M)
002.061-026 Aeronautical-Research Engineer (M)
002.167-018 Aeronautical Project Engineer (M)
003.061-010 Electrical Engineer (M)
003.061-026 Electrical-Research Engineer
003.061-030 Electronics Engineer (M)
003.061-034 Electronics-Design Engineer (M)
003.161-010 Electrical Technician
003.161-014 Electronics Technician
003.161-018 Semiconductor-Development Technician
003.167-070 Engineering Manager, Electronics
003.261-010 Instrumentation Technician

005.061-014	Civil Engineer (M)
005.061-026	Railroad Engineer
005.061-034	Structural Engineer
005.061-038	Transportation Engineer
006.061-014	Ceramic Engineer
007.061-010	Automotive Engineer
007.061-014	Mechanical Engineer
007.061-022	Mechanical-Design Engineer, Products
007.061-026	Tool Designer
007.061-038	Applications Engineer, Manufacturing
007.161-026	Mechanical-Engineering Technician
007.161-030	Optomechanical Technician
007.167-014	Plant Engineer
008.061-018	Chemical Engineer
008.261-010	Chemical-Engineering Technician
010.061-018	Petroleum Engineer
011.061-026	Welding Engineer
011.261-014	Welding Technician
013.061-010	Agricultural Engineer
014.061-010	Design Engineer, Marine Equipment (M)
014.061-018	Research Engineer, Marine Equipment (M)
015.061-018	Research Engineer, Nuclear Equipment (M)
024.161-010	Engineer, Soils
142.061-038	Safety-Clothing-And-Equipment Developer

Sales

002.151-010	Sales Engineer, Aeronautical Products
003.151-010	Electrical Products
003.151-014	Electronics Products and Systems
006.151-010	Ceramic Products
007.151-010	Mechanical Equipment
010.151-010	Mining-And-Oil-Well Equipment And Services
013.151-010	Agricultural Equipment
014.151-010	Marine Equipment

Installation and Operation

002.061-018	Aeronautical Test Engineer (M)
002.061-030	Stress Analyst (M)
003.061-014	Electrical Test Engineer
003.061-042	Electronics-Test Engineer (M)
003.061-046	Illuminating Engineer
003.061-050	Planning Engineer, Central Office Facilities
003.167-018	Electrical Engineer, Power System
003.167-030	Engineer-In-Charge, Studio Operations

003.167-034	Engineer-In-Charge, Transmitter
003.167-062	Systems Engineer, Electronic Data Processing (M)
003.187-010	Central-Office Equipment Engineer
005.061-030	Sanitary Engineer (M)
005.061-042	Waste-Management Engineer, Radioactive Materials
005.167-018	Forest Engineer
007.061-042	Stress Analyst
007.161-034	Test Engineer, Mechanical Equipment
007.167-018	Tool Programer, Numerical Control
010.061-014	Mining Engineer
010.061-026	Safety Engineer, Mines
011.061-018	Metallurgist, Extractive
012.061-010	Product-Safety Engineer
012.061-014	Safety Engineer (M)
012.067-010	Metrologist (M)
012.167-010	Configuration Management Analyst
012.167-018	Factory Lay-Out Engineer
012.167-026	Fire-Protection Engineer (M)
012.167-030	Industrial Engineer (M)
012.167-034	Industrial-Health Engineer (M)
012.167-042	Manufacturing Engineer (M)
012.167-046	Production Engineer (M)
012.167-050	Production Planner (M)
012.167-054	Quality-Control Engineer (M)
012.167-058	Safety Manager (M)
012.167-070	Time-Study Engineer
012.167-074	Tool Planner
012.167-078	Documentation Engineer
014.061-014	Marine Engineer (M)
014.061-022	Test Engineer, Marine Equipment (M)
014.167-014	Port Engineer (M)
015.061-014	Nuclear Engineer (M)
015.061-030	Nuclear-Fuels Research Engineer
015.067-010	Nuclear-Criticality Safety Engineer
015.137-010	Radiation-Protection Engineer
018.167-018	Land Surveyor (M)
019.061-014	Materials Engineer
019.061-022	Ordnance Engineer (M)
019.061-026	Reliability Engineer
019.081-018	Pollution-Control Engineer
019.161-014	Test Technician
019.167-010	Logistics Engineer (M)
019.261-018	Facilities Planner
079.021-010	Health Physicist (M)
161.167-010	Management Analyst (M)
161.267-010	Clerical-Methods Analyst

05.02
Managerial Work: Mechanical

Managerial Work: Mechanical is to plan, organize, and direct technical functions and systems. This work may be in an industry, utility, or government agency. Workers use an in-depth knowledge of equipment, methods, and systems for the work they direct. These workers are concerned with solving production problems and keeping the flow of work efficient.

They manage or directly supervise workers. They interview, hire, and often train workers. They take disciplinary (corrective) action when needed. They may negotiate grievances (complaints) with a union, prepare budgets, and oversee the spending of monies. They order equipment, tools, and supplies needed on the job. They also write progress reports. This group includes the subgroups of:

Systems
Maintenance and Construction
Processing and Manufacturing
Communications
Mining, Logging, and Petroleum
　　Production
Services
Materials Handling

Workers in the seven subgroups of Managerial Work: Mechanical perform basic duties that are very much alike. They differ in the knowledge and skills needed for the type of work they direct.

Systems involve the flow of oil, gas, electric, water, and sewage through pipelines. It also includes telephone and telegraph systems.

Maintenance and Construction involves directing workers who construct such things as dams, roads, and pipelines. It also involves maintenance and repair work. This includes aircraft and other transportation equipment, as well as facilities and equipment in lodging or office buildings.

Processing and Manufacturing involves production and quality control. This includes control of production from start to finish and follow-up of customer complaints and claims.

Communications involve workers in services such as radio, TV, telephone, telegraph, and airline flight control.

Mining, Logging, and Petroleum Production includes underground mines, pits, quarries, and surface operations.

Services involve land surveying projects. Work includes writing survey reports and legal descriptions of land. It also involves coordinating survey work with engineering, architectural, and other project staff involved.

Materials Handling involves managing plants, terminals, and other facilities where ammunition or petroleum products are stored and distributed. The handling of these products requires special safety and security procedures and systems.

Jobs may be found in mining, construction, communications, manufacturing, transportation, and fuel production.

This superintendent of drilling and production is on his way to inspect an off-shore site.

Organization – to arrange ideas, thoughts, and information in a way that can be understood.

Judgment – to make decisions that involve a great deal of money or the safety of workers and to react quickly in emergency situations.

Visual Perception – to use charts, maps, and blueprints.

Physical Stamina – to stand or walk for long periods of time to observe work progress or problems.

Rapport – to relate with people in an understanding way and maintain harmony among workers.

Composure – to work under pressure or stress in critical, unusual, or dangerous situations.

Versatile – to perform a variety of duties which often change.

What Skills and Abilities Would Help You Succeed in This Kind of Work?

The most important skills are listed below. All of those listed do not apply to each occupation. As you explore occupations you should identify the specific ones needed.

Comprehension – to know and understand the technical details of a field such as construction or mining.

Communication – to speak and write clearly in giving oral directions and writing technical or progress reports.

Numerical – to use math to plan budgets or solve production problems.

Critical Thinking – to make judgments based on data that can be measured.

Leadership – to plan the work of others and encourage them to work in an efficient manner.

Do You Have or Can You Develop an Interest in This Kind of Work?

Review the following questions. Your answers can give you clues as to your interest in Managerial Work.

Have you read mechanical or automotive design magazines? Did you understand the terms and drawings used?

Have you owned a chemistry set? Did you conduct experiments? Did you enjoy testing new ideas?

Have you had courses in chemistry, physics, and advanced math? Did you enjoy these courses? How were your grades?

Have you collected rocks or minerals? Can you identify them?

Have you planned and supervised a project or a group activity? Did it go well? Did you enjoy directing the activities of others?

Can you solve puzzles or problems easily? Do you use logical thinking in solving them?

Do you like activities involving people? Do you communicate easily with them?

Have you built high fidelity equipment? Do you like technical activities?

Have you taken courses in industrial arts? Can you deal with mechanical and technical problems?

What Else Should You Know About This Group of Occupations?

Workers in this group have a great deal of responsibility. They must make many decisions and their jobs can be stressful. They may stand on their feet for long periods of time. They usually tour work sites and are subject to hazards. These include falling objects, cave-ins, poor ventilation, noise, and the grime of machinery. These workers may have to work overtime without additional pay. However, they may receive bonuses, stock options, and profit sharing plans.

Workers usually specialize in one technical field. If they change companies, it is usually to other firms in the same field. Some industries, such as construction and petroleum, require workers to travel. Some have to move their homes to other cities or foreign countries.

The military services offer training and experience related to some occupations in this group. These occupations are included in the list at the end of this group description. They are identified by an (M) following the occupational title. More information about the military training and experience opportunities may be found in Appendix A.

How Can You Prepare For This Kind of Work?

Most jobs in this group require four to ten years of education and training. College courses in the specific technical field and in management are usually needed. Training often includes instruction in computer science, and in data storage and retrieval systems.

Most workers promoted to jobs in this group are skilled engineers or technicians with five to ten years of experience in the technical field. They usually have supervisory experience and training in management. Some employers provide management training for workers they plan to promote to these jobs. Clerical workers who plan production and work schedules may be promoted to some jobs if they have the technical training.

As you plan your high school education you should include courses related to Managerial Work: Mechanical. Next, you should include courses needed to enter college. The following list of courses and skills will help you plan your education.

A construction superintendent discusses a production method with a job foreman.

140

Engineering – courses in the engineering specialty (mining, petroleum, civil, etc.) that provide technical background for the area of management.

Business and Management – courses in business administration, contract management, procurement/purchasing, product management, labor/industrial relations, management information systems, marketing management, organizational behavior, personnel management, industrial management.

Mathematics – courses in algebra, trigonometry, and advanced math (engineering related).

Communications – courses in composition, technical and business writing, and speech.

Science – courses in physics, chemistry, or other science areas related to the field of specialization.

Industrial Arts – basic courses involving machines, equipment, and power systems.

Engineering Technology –courses in quality control, safety and health, industrial production, environmental control, and other technologies directly related to the field of specialization.

Qualifications Profile

This section is a summary of the worker traits and work factors related to successful job performance and worker satisfaction. Try to relate your interests, abilities, aptitudes, and preferences to these traits and factors. An asterisk (*) marks those traits and factors that are related to more than 60% of the occupations listed at the end of this group. The other traits and factors listed are as important, but relate to fewer occupations. See Appendices B-G for information about all of the worker traits and work factors.

Work Activities

The most important activities related to this group involve:

* 2. Business contact.
* 5. Recognition or appreciation from others.

6. Communication of ideas and information.

9. Processes, methods, or machines.

Work Situations

Workers must be willing to:

1. Perform duties which change frequently.

* 3. Plan and direct an entire activity.

* 4. Deal with people.

7. Make decisions using personal judgment.

8. Make decisions using standards that can be measured or checked.

10. Work within precise limits or standards of accuracy.

Educational Skills

This chart shows the levels of reasoning, math, and language skills related to this group. These skills are usually developed in an educational setting. There are six levels ranging from the simple (1) to the most complex (6).

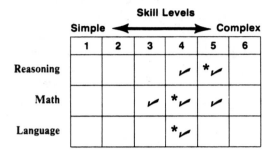

Skill Levels

	Simple ←				→ Complex	
	1	2	3	4	5	6
Reasoning				✔	*✔	
Math			✔	*✔	✔	
Language				*✔		

Physical Demands

Workers in this group of occupations must be able to do:

S – Sedentary work
L – Light work

Working Conditions

These are the physical surroundings in which work is done. In occupations belonging to this group, work is performed:

*I – Inside — workers spend most of their time inside protected from weather conditions but not always from temperature changes.

B – Both inside and outside — workers spend about equal time in each setting.

Aptitudes

This chart presents the most important aptitudes related to this group. The levels checked compare aptitudes needed for success in this group to aptitudes of the general working population in all occupations. For example, level 5 is low and represents the bottom 10% of the working population. Level 1 is high and represents the top 10%.

APTITUDE LEVELS COMPARED TO ALL WORKERS						
Related Aptitudes (Ability to Learn)		Lower 1/3		Middle 1/3	Upper 1/3	
		Level 5	Level 4	Level 3	Level 2	Level 1
Code	Title	10%	23%	34%	23%	10%
G	General Learning Ability				*✔	✔
V	Verbal				*✔	
N	Numerical			✔	*✔	
S	Spatial		✔	✔	✔	
P	Form Perception		✔	*✔	✔	
Q	Clerical Perception		✔	*✔		

Data-People-Things

This chart shows the levels for these three basic elements of work as related to this group. Level means the degree of difficulty of job tasks rather than the amount of time involved. The terms low, average, and high indicate the highest level at which occupations are involved. Compare your interests and abilities with the levels checked.

Difficulty Level of Job Tasks

	Levels		
	Low	Avg.	High
Data			*✓
People	*✓		
Things	*✓		

Common Occupations

A full listing of all occupations belonging to this group may be found in the Guide for Occupational Exploration.

The following occupations have been selected to represent this group. They provide the major employment opportunities. However, specific job opportunities will vary according to locations of industry, geographical region, and other factors.

Information may be found in common sources of occupational information, state career information systems, and computerized guidance systems.

An (M) follows the occupational title where the military services offer training and experience.

Systems

010.167-018 Superintendent, Oil-Well Services
181.167-014 Superintendent, Drilling And Production
184.117-082 Superintendent, Communications (M)
184.161-014 Superintendent, Water-And-Sewer Systems
184.167-038 Dispatcher, Chief 1
184.167-162 Superintendent, Electric Power
914.167-014 Dispatcher, Oil (M)

Maintenance and Construction

182.167-026 Superintendent, Construction
184.167-174 Superintendent, Maintenance (M)

184.167-266 Transportation-Maintenance Supervisor (M)
187.167-190 Superintendent, Building
189.167-046 Superintendent, Maintenance
891.137-010 Maintenance Supervisor

Processing and Manufacturing

012.167-014 Director, Quality Control
169.167-054 Tooling Coordinator, Production Engineering
182.167-022 Superintendent, Concrete-Mixing Plant
183.117-014 Production Superintendent
183.167-022 General Supervisor
183.167-026 Manager, Food Processing Plant
189.117-018 Manager, Customer Technical Services

Communications

184.167-062 Manager, Communications Station (M)
184.167-066 Manager, Flight Control (M)
184.167-230 Supervisor of Communications (M)
193.167-018 Superintendent, Radio Communications (M)
962.162-010 Director, Technical

Mining, Logging, and Petroleum Production

181.117-014 Mine Superintendent
181.167-018 Supervisor, Mine

Services

018.167-022 Manager, Land Surveying (M)

Materials Handling

181.117-010 Manager, Bulk Plant (M)
184.167-186 Superintendent, Marine Oil Terminal (M)
189.167-038 Superintendent, Ammunition Storage (M)

143

05.03
Engineering Technology

Engineering Technology involves the detail work required to apply engineering principles to practical situations. Workers provide technical support services for engineers and managers. Their work includes surveying, drafting, and engineering technology. Also included is communications control and materials scheduling. This group includes the subgroups of:

Surveying
Drafting
Expediting and Coordinating
Petroleum (Prospecting)
Electrical/Electronic
Industrial and Safety
Mechanical
Environmental Control

Surveying is to measure and record the outline, size, elevation, and location of land or water. This confirms the official boundaries. Surveys are conducted on land, or from the air. Surveyors compile notes and sketches, and make records of data obtained. These data are used to draw maps and to prepare deeds, leases, and other legal documents. Surveys are also used to control the direction and extent of mining.

Drafting is to draw detailed plans or patterns to guide manufacturing, construction, and craft workers. These plans give definite dimensions. Workers use rough or detailed notes to make their drawings. They make a final sketch and check the sizes and materials to be used. They also check how one part

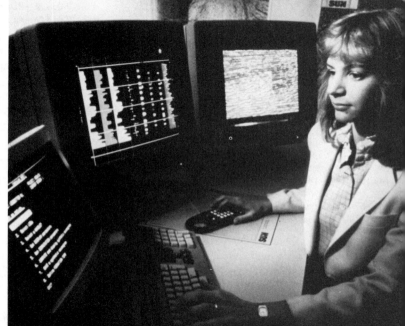

This geodetic surveyor is using a computer to analyze field data.

144

relates to another and how all parts relate to the whole structure or project. They make changes or adjustments and draw finished designs from their sketches. Some workers draw maps or technical illustrations. Others use plans and patterns to prepare materials lists or cost estimates.

Expediting and Coordinating involves the on-time supply of materials to meet production schedules. Workers develop and study lists of raw materials, purchased parts, and equipment needed. They estimate the total amounts needed from engineering drawings and blueprints. Other workers put together and record production data and write reports. They also compile inventory records and prepare requests for supplies.

Expediting and Coordinating also involves the control of aircraft to meet flight schedules. Workers chart and control the movement of aircraft. They may direct the flow of air traffic between altitude sectors and control centers. Some workers may receive and give out flight plans and weather information for pilots. They maintain written records of messages given and received. They issue landing, take off, and taxiing orders. They operate radios and monitor radarscopes.

Petroleum work involves prospecting (looking) for oil or gas. Some workers plan and direct the duties of those who collect seismic data (shockwaves that vibrate the earth) used to find oil and gas. They set off explosives underground and measure and record the shockwaves. They study the earth's strata (layers) to locate oil and gas. Other workers chart the pressure and temperature of oil and gas well boreholes (drilled holes). They measure, record, and interpret data to determine further drilling or production procedures.

Electrical/Electronic involves sending and receiving radio and TV signals. Workers operate radio and video equipment. Some workers use portable equipment to broadcast from the field. Others monitor and control signals. They also keep a log of programs transmitted (sent). Some workers use electronic radiograph signals to X-ray industrial or construction materials for flaws or cracks.

Industrial and Safety involves the quality control of materials and the efficiency of production and personnel. Workers direct the inspection of material to make sure it meets standards. Some workers study and record time, motion, methods, and speed in work performed. Industrial and Safety also involves the inspection of construction work to enforce safety and health standards. Workers inspect new and existing buildings, electrical installations, aircraft, or waste disposal facilities. If regulations have not been met, they issue notices of corrections. Other workers conduct studies of factors that affect vehicle traffic. They do this at congested (crowded) areas or where accidents are frequent.

Mechanical is to produce, send, and use heat or mechanical power. Workers also design and install solar (sun) hot water and space heating systems for new or existing structures.

Environmental Control involves protecting soil, water, and air from pollutants (impurities). Workers conduct surveys and tests to detect pollution. They record data and prepare reports for review. Some workers test personnel, plant facilities, and the work environment to detect radioactive contamination (unsafe conditions caused by radiation).

Jobs in this group may be found with factories, construction companies, architectural and engineering firms, research labs, and airports.

What Skills and Abilities Would Help You Succeed in This Kind of Work?

The most important skills are listed below. All of those listed do not apply to each occupation. As you explore occupations you should identify the specific ones needed.

Conceptualization – to convert technical ideas into working drawings.

Numerical – to use advanced mathematics in making computations and analyzing test data.

Dexterity – to move the arms, hands, and fingers together to use drafting tools or measuring instruments.

Physical Stamina – to walk long distances while carrying instruments or equipment.

Accuracy – to work within precise limits using standards that can be measured or checked.

This surveyor is using a laser transit at a mine site.

Communication – to write clearly and with technical accuracy.

Comprehension – to understand technical language and symbols.

Critical Thinking – to use knowledge, personal experience, and judgment to make decisions and solve problems.

Spatial Perception – to form a mental image (picture) of how shapes and forms can be combined in three dimensions height, width, and depth.

Form Perception – to observe detail in objects or drawings and notice differences in shapes or shadings.

Do You Have or Can You Develop an Interest in This Kind of Work?

Review the following questions. Your answers can give you clues as to your interest in Engineering Technology.

Have you made sketches in three dimensions height, width, depth? How real did your sketches look?

Have you read mechanical or automotive design magazines? Did you understand the drawings and terms used?

Have you collected rocks or minerals? Can you distinguish between them?

Have you used instruments to take measurements? Were you accurate?

Have you taken courses in mechanical drawing? Can you form a mental image of objects from drawings? Do you enjoy this type of activity?

Have you made models of airplanes or cars following detailed plans? Can you follow written instructions easily?

Have you used a compass? Can you read maps correctly?

Have you taken courses in advanced math, physics, or chemistry? Did you like these subjects? How were your grades?

Have you drawn a map for a school subject? Was it neat and accurate?

What Else Should You Know About This Group of Occupations?

Many jobs in this group require workers to stand for long periods of time. Some workers are under a lot of pressure to meet deadlines. Some of these jobs are stressful because they deal with emergency situations. Although most jobs have regular working hours, some require night or evening work. Some workers are subject to changing work schedules, sometimes with little or no notice. Surveyors do most of their work outdoors. They may work long hours when weather conditions are suitable. They are exposed to hazards of machinery on construction projects or cars when surveying near highways. Some surveyors travel to distant job sites or camp out.

Most drafting work takes place in an office, but visits to work sites and factories may be required. Some drafters do specialized tasks, but others do a variety of tasks.

Technicians are often the link between engineers and skilled workers. With experience, technicians may move into more skilled jobs or to supervisory positions.

The military services offer training and experience related to some occupations in this group. These occupations are included in the list at the end of this group description. They are identified by an (M) following the occupational title. More information about the military training and experience opportunities may be found in Appendix A.

A drafter works on a machine drawing – many industries now use computers to prepare drawings.

How Can You Prepare for This Kind of Work?

Most occupations in this group require two to four years of education and training. Some jobs require special training and work experience. Employers usually provide on-the-job training to prepare workers for specific tasks.

Technical and vocational schools offer surveying programs of one to three years. Many colleges offer degrees in surveying. People with some classroom instruction can start as instrument workers. They may become party chiefs or registered surveyors after getting enough experience. Written tests may be required for advancement. People without formal training in surveying start by helping instrument workers. They must get experience and formal training to operate instruments. They become party chiefs only after extensive experience. All fifty states require land surveyors to be licensed. License requirements usually include four to eight years of experience.

For drafting jobs, high school courses in math, science, industrial arts, and mechanical drawing are important. Post high school technical courses are needed for advanced drafting jobs. Workers usually start as assistant drafters and advance as skills develop. Three- and four-year apprenticeship programs in drafting are sometimes offered. Apprentices earn money while getting classroom and on-the-job training.

Technicians usually need specialized training. Credits earned in technical and vocational schools can often be transferred to colleges. These credits can then be applied toward engineering and other degrees.

As you plan your high school program you should include courses related to Engineering Technology. Next, you should include courses needed to enter college or technical school. The following list of courses and skills can help you plan your education. The specific courses you select will depend on your field of specialization.

Electrical/Electronic – courses in electricity, radio-TV, electronics, radiography, radiation safety, and telecommunications.

Business/Industrial – courses in accounting, cost control, inventory control, production control, microcomputer, and word processing.

Communications – courses in report and technical writing and speech.

Mathematics – courses in algebra, geometry, and advanced math.

Drafting – courses in sketching, blueprint reading, mechanical drawing, technical illustration, detail drafting, specialty drafting, topographic drafting, cartography (designing and drafting maps), architectural design and construction, and electronic drafting.

Physical Science – courses in physical geography, astronomy, geology, physics, and chemistry.

Surveying Technology – surveying and mapping, electronic surveying, remote sensing, photogrammetry (aerial photography), topographic mapping, and imaging radar.

Qualifications Profile

This section is a summary of the worker traits and work factors related to successful job performance and worker satisfaction. Try to relate your interests, abilities, aptitudes, and preferences to these traits and factors. An asterisk (*) marks those traits and factors that are related to more than 60% of the occupations listed at the end of this group. The other traits and factors listed are as important, but relate to fewer occupations. See Appendices

B-G for information about all of the worker traits and work factors.

Work Activities

The most important activities related to this group involve:

1. Things and objects.
* 7. Tasks of a scientific and technical nature.
* 9. Processes, methods, or machines.

Working Conditions

These are the physical surroundings in which work is done. In occupations belonging to this group, work is performed:

*I – Inside — workers spend most of their time inside protected from weather conditions but not always from temperature changes.

B – Both inside and outside — workers spend about equal time in each setting.

Work Situations

Workers must be willing to:

1. Perform duties which change frequently.
3. Plan and direct an entire activity.
4. Deal with people.
7. Make decisions using personal judgment.
* 8. Make decisions using standards that can be measured or checked.
*10. Work within precise limits or standards of accuracy.

Data-People-Things

This chart shows the levels for these three basic elements of work as related to this group. Level means the degree of difficulty of job tasks rather than the amount of time involved. The terms low, average, and high indicate the highest level at which occupations are involved. Compare your interests and abilities with the levels checked.

Difficulty Level of Job Tasks

	Levels		
	Low	Avg.	High
Data			*✓
People	*✓		
Things	✓		*✓

Physical Demands

Workers in this group of occupations must be able to do:

S – Sedentary work
L – Light work

Educational Skills

This chart shows the levels of reasoning, math, and language skills related to this group. These skills are usually developed in an educational setting. There are six levels ranging from the simple (1) to the most complex (6).

Skill Levels

Simple ←————————→ Complex

	1	2	3	4	5	6
Reasoning				✓	*✓	
Math				✓	✓	
Language				*✓	✓	

An inspector of industrial waste is resealing a container.

Aptitudes

This chart presents the most important aptitudes related to this group. The levels checked compare aptitudes needed for success in this group to aptitudes of the general working population in all occupations. For example, level 5 is low and represents the bottom 10% of the working population. Level 1 is high and represents the top 10%.

Related Aptitudes (Ability to Learn)		Lower 1/3		Middle 1/3	Upper 1/3	
		Level 5	Level 4	Level 3	Level 2	Level 1
Code	Title	10%	23%	34%	23%	10%
G	General Learning Ability				* ✔	
N	Numerical			✔	* ✔	
S	Spatial			✔	* ✔	
P	Form Perception			✔	* ✔	
Q	Clerical Perception			* ✔	✔	
K	Motor Coordination		✔	✔	✔	

APTITUDE LEVELS COMPARED TO ALL WORKERS

Common Occupations

A full listing of all occupations belonging to this group may be found in the Guide for Occupational Exploration.

The following occupations have been selected to represent this group. They provide the major employment opportunities. However, specific job opportunities will vary according to locations of industry, geographical region, and other factors.

Information may be found in common sources of occupational information, state career information systems, and computerized guidance systems.

An (M) follows the occupational title where the military services offer training and experience.

Surveying

018.167-010 Chief of Party (M)
018.167-014 Geodetic Computer (M)
018.167-026 Photogrammetric Engineer (M)
018.167-034 Surveyor Assistant, Instruments (M)
018.167-038 Surveyor, Geodetic (M)
018.167-042 Surveyor, Geophysical Prospecting
018.167-046 Surveyor, Marine (M)
018.167-050 Surveyor, Mine
184.167-026 Director, Photogrammetry Flight
              Operations (M)
196.167-014 Navigator (M)

Drafting

001.261-010 Drafter, Architectural
001.261-014 Drafter, Landscape
002.261-010 Drafter, Aeronautical
003.261-014 Controls Designer
003.261-018 Integrated Circuit Layout Designer
003.261-022 Printed Circuit Designer
003.281-010 Drafter, Electrical
003.281-014 Drafter, Electronic
003.362-010 Design Technician, Computer-Aided
005.261-014 Civil Engineering Technician
005.281-010 Drafter, Civil (M)
005.281-014 Drafter, Structural (M)
007.161-018 Engineering Assistant,
             Mechanical Equipment
007.261-014 Drafter, Castings
007.281-010 Drafter, Mechanical
010.281-010 Drafter, Directional Survey
010.281-014 Drafter, Geological
010.281-018 Drafter, Geophysical
014.281-010 Drafter, Marine
017.261-014 Design Drafter, Electromechanisms
017.261-026 Drafter, Commercial
017.261-034 Drafter, Heating and Ventilating
017.261-042 Drafter, Computer-Assisted
017.281-022 Drafter, Automotive Design
017.281-030 Drafter, Oil and Gas
017.281-034 Technical Illustrator
018.131-010 Supervisor, Cartography (M)
018.261-010 Drafter, Cartographic (M)
018.261-014 Drafter, Topographical (M)
018.261-018 Editor, Map (M)
018.261-022 Mosaicist (M)
018.261-026 Photogrammetrist (M)
018.281-010 Stereo-Plotter Operator (M)
019.267-010 Specification Writer
160.267-018 Estimator
735.381-018 Sample Maker 2
781.381-022 Pattern Grader-Cutter
781.381-026 Patternmaker

Expediting and Coordinating

012.187-010 Material Scheduler
193.162-010 Air-Traffic Coordinator
193.162-014 Air-Traffic-Control Specialist, Station
193.162-018 Air-Traffic-Control Specialist, Tower (M)
193.167-010 Chief Controller (M)
221.382-018 Production Clerk
912.167-010 Dispatcher (M)

Petroleum

010.161-018 Observer, Seismic Prospecting
930.167-010 Technical Operator

Electrical-Electronic

193.262-018 Field Engineer
193.262-034 Radiotelephone Operator (M)
193.262-038 Transmitter Operator
193.362-014 Radio-Intelligence Operator (M)
194.282-010 Video Operator (M)
199.361-010 Radiographer (M)

Industrial and Safety

012.167-062 Supervisor, Vendor Quality (M)
012.267-010 Industrial Engineering Technician
168.167-030 Inspector, Building
168.167-034 Inspector, Electrical
168.267-010 Building Inspector
168.267-054 Inspector, Industrial Waste (M)
182.267-010 Construction Inspector
199.261-014 Parking Analyst
199.267-030 Traffic Technician
621.261-018 Flight Engineer (M)

Mechanical

007.161-038 Solar-Energy-Systems Designer

Environmental Control

005.261-010 Engineering Technician
029.261-014 Pollution-Control Technician
199.167-010 Radiation Monitor

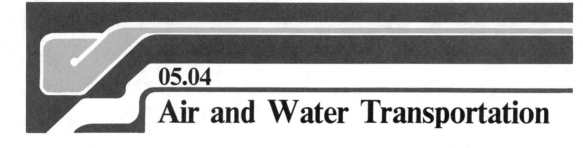
Air and Water Transportation

Air and Water Transportation is to move people or cargo by plane or ship. Workers pilot or help pilot airplanes or ships or supervise others who do. They use their knowledge of complex instruments to get from one place to another. Knowledge of weather and navigation are also important skills. Some workers instruct others on the operation of air and water vehicles. Others test or inspect aircraft or ships. This group includes the subgroups of:

Air
Water

Air transportation is to pilot an aircraft. Some workers instruct and test student pilots in flight methods. They may train new and experienced company pilots in policy and in the use of equipment. Some pilot planes or helicopters to seed fields or to dust or spray them with fertilizers or pesticides. Others fly airplanes to transport people, mail, or freight. Some fly aircraft to test and evaluate their performance. Others observe and evaluate a pilot's knowledge and skills.

Water transportation includes workers who supervise work on or command a ship. It also includes those who command special types of boats such as fishing vessels. Workers interview, hire, and instruct crew members. Some pilot (guide) ships into and out of har-

An airline crew goes over the checklist as part of pre-flight procedure.

bors, straits, sounds, and on rivers, lakes, and bays. They use their knowledge of local winds, weather, tides, and currents. Others command tugboats to pull or push barges and ships. Some operate ferryboats to transport people, motor vehicles, and freight across bays, lakes, and in coastal waters. Some workers set the course of ships using navigational aids. They may maintain the ship's log, examine gear and equipment, and inspect the ship to ensure crew and passenger safety.

Jobs may be found with shipping companies and commercial airlines. Companies and people who have their own boats or airplanes also hire these workers.

What Skills and Abilities Would Help You Succeed in This Kind of Work?

The most important skills are listed below. All of those listed do not apply to each occupation. As you explore occupations you should identify the specific ones needed.

Concentration – to focus on detailed tasks and remain alert for a long period of time.

Composure – to be calm and self-confident in critical or emergency situations.

Critical Thinking – to form opinions and make decisions based on knowledge, judgment, and experience.

Leadership – to plan and direct the work of others.

Motor Coordination – to move hands and fingers together to handle sensitive and delicate instruments.

Numerical – to use math to solve navigation problems.

Accuracy – to follow procedures and work without error.

Interpretation – to understand and express complex and technical information.

Rapport – to deal with people in an effective way and maintain harmony among workers.

Depth Perception – to judge distances and relationships of objects in space.

Communication – to give and exchange information to teach or demonstrate procedures and techniques.

Do You Have or Can You Develop an Interest in This Kind of Work?

Review the following questions. Your answers can give you clues as to your interest in Air and Water Transportation.

Have you read airplane or boat magazines? Do you subscribe to such magazines?

Have you built or operated a model airplane? Did you have any trouble reading and following the instructions?

Have you owned or operated a pleasure boat? Have you completed Coast Guard safety and navigation training? Can you read a compass?

Have you been a member of a Civil Air Patrol Unit? Did it include flight or ground training?

Have you operated a CB radio? Do you understand the rules for its use? Do you know the common code words?

Have you driven in a bike rodeo, car rally, or other vehicle obstacle course? Did you receive a good score?

This ship's pilot is using a computer simulation to review procedures for approaching a port.

What Else Should You Know About This Group of Occupations?

Most workers in this group work under mental stress. They must keep alert and be ready to make quick, accurate decisions. Some face hazards such as severe weather conditions, fires, collisions, and other disasters. Workers in this group are often away from home for a period of time.

The military services offer training and experience related to some occupations in this group. These occupations are included in the list at the end of this group description. They are identified by an (M) following the occupational title. More information about the military training and experience opportunities may be found in Appendix A.

How Can You Prepare for This Kind of Work?

Most occupations in this group require two to ten years of education and training. Flight training is available in the military and in civilian flight schools approved by the Federal Aviation Administration (FAA). A high school education or equal is required for acceptance. Most major airlines have their own advanced pilot training schools. All aircraft pilots must be licensed by the FAA. They are rated for the number of engines and type of airplanes they may fly.

People become ship captains by advancing through lower officer ranks. Most workers earn the lowest rank of command, third mate, by completing a training course at a marine

154

academy. Some marine trade unions offer programs to train seamen. Applicants must be U.S. citizens. Their vision and general health must be approved by the U.S. Public Health Service. They must also pass Coast Guard tests on navigation, freight handling, and deck operations.

As you plan your high school education you should include courses related to Air and Water Transportation. Next, you should include courses needed to enter college, flight school, or marine academy. The following list of courses and skills can help you plan your education.

Mathematics – courses in algebra, geometry, and advanced math.

Physical Science – courses in geography, earth and space science, and meteorology.

Piloting and Navigation – courses in aircraft structure and operation, radio communications, navigation, safety and traffic regulations, and flight training.

Barge and Boat Operation – courses in navigation, electrical systems, main engine and auxiliary steam, cargo handling, safety and firefighting, boat operation, marine administration, and marine law.

Qualifications Profile

This section is a summary of the worker traits and work factors related to successful job performance and worker satisfaction. Try to relate your interests, abilities, aptitudes, and preferences to these traits and factors. An asterisk (*) marks those traits and factors that are related to more than 60% of the occupations listed at the end of this group. The other traits and factors listed are as important, but relate to fewer occupations. See Appendices B-G for information about all of the worker traits and work factors.

Work Activities

The most important activities related to this group involve:

1. Things and objects.
5. Recognition or appreciation from others.
6. Communication of ideas and information.
* 9. Processes, methods, or machines.

Work Situations

Workers must be willing to:

1. Perform duties which change frequently.
3. Plan and direct an entire activity.
4. Deal with people.
* 6. Work under pressure.
* 7. Make decisions using personal judgment.
* 8. Make decisions using standards that can be measured or checked.
*10. Work within precise limits or standards of accuracy.

Physical Demands

Workers in this group of occupations must be able to do:

*L – Light work

Data-People-Things

This chart shows the levels for these three basic elements of work as related to this group. Level means the degree of difficulty of job tasks rather than the amount of time involved. The terms low, average, and high indicate the highest level at which occupations are involved. Compare your interests and abilities with the levels checked.

Difficulty Level of Job Tasks

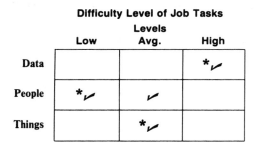

	Low	Avg.	High
Data			*✔
People	*✔	✔	
Things		*✔	

Working Conditions

These are the physical surroundings in which work is done. In occupations belonging to this group, work is performed:

I – Inside — workers spend most of their time inside protected from weather conditions but not always from temperature changes.

B – Both inside and outside — workers spend about equal time in each setting.

Educational Skills

This chart shows the levels of reasoning, math, and language skills related to this group. These skills are usually developed in an educational setting. There are six levels ranging from the simple (1) to the most complex (6).

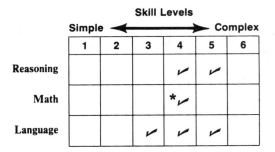

Skill Levels

	Simple ⟵ ⟶ Complex					
	1	2	3	4	5	6
Reasoning				✔	✔	
Math				*✔		
Language			✔	✔	✔	

A tugboat captain at his work station.

Aptitudes

This chart presents the most important aptitudes related to this group. The levels checked compare aptitudes needed for success in this group to aptitudes of the general working population in all occupations. For example, level 5 is low and represents the bottom 10% of the working population. Level 1 is high and represents the top 10%.

APTITUDE LEVELS COMPARED TO ALL WORKERS						
Related Aptitudes (Ability to Learn)		Lower 1/3		Middle 1/3	Upper 1/3	
		Level **5**	Level **4**	Level **3**	Level **2**	Level **1**
Code	Title	10%	23%	34%	23%	10%
G	General Learning Ability			✓	* ✓	
N	Numerical			✓	✓	
S	Spatial			✓	* ✓	
K	Motor Coordination			* ✓	✓	

Common Occupations

A full listing of all occupations belonging to this group may be found in the Guide for Occupational Exploration.

The following occupations have been selected to represent this group. They provide the major employment opportunities. However, specific job opportunities will vary according to locations of industry, geographical region, and other factors.

Information may be found in common sources of occupational information, state career information systems, and computerized guidance systems.

An (M) follows the occupational title where the military services offer training and experience.

Air

196.223-010 Instructor, Flying 1 (M)
196.223-014 Instructor, Pilot (M)
196.263-010 Airplane Pilot
196.263-014 Airplane Pilot, Commercial (M)
196.263-022 Check Pilot
196.263-038 Helicopter Pilot (M)
196.263-042 Test Pilot (M)

Water

197.133-010 Captain, Fishing Vessel
197.133-022 Mate, Ship
197.133-026 Pilot, Ship (M)
197.133-030 Tugboat Captain (M)
197.167-010 Master, Ship (M)
911.363-010 Ferryboat Operator
911.363-014 Quartermaster (M)

05.05
Craft Technology

Craft Technology is highly skilled custom hand and machine work. This requires special training and experience to acquire an in-depth knowledge of the processes and techniques used. Workers select and use tools, materials, and methods needed to make, repair, install, or construct something. This work is usually in nonfactory settings. This group includes the subgroups of:

Construction and Maintenance
Electrical/Electronic
Fine Fabrication and Repair
Food Preparation
Metal Fabrication and Machine Work
Mechanical
Woodworking
Printing

Construction and Maintenance involves craft work on such things as buildings, homes, roads, and dams. Workers build and keep them in good condition. There is a wide range of construction work. Workers may set stone, lay brick or tile, build forms, erect framework, install cabinets, or finish woodwork. They also may hang wallpaper, paint, install drywall, or plaster walls. Some may be pipefitters who assemble and install gas, steam, and related plumbing fixtures, pipes, and fittings in structures.

Electrical/Electronic involves assembling, installing, and repairing electrical or electronic products, components, and equipment. Workers also conduct tests to locate trouble. They work with communication, utility, and transportation equipment.

This rough carpenter is installing roof trusses.

158

Fine Fabrication and Repair involves the building and fixing of delicate products, instruments, and equipment. This includes medical and dental devices; optical, radiological, and electromedical equipment; and musical instruments. It also includes cameras and work with gemstones such as diamonds.

Food Preparation is to plan menus, estimate amounts of food needed, and to prepare it. Some workers supervise others involved in food preparation. And, some are concerned with nutrition. They may prepare special diets as prescribed by doctors or advise others on good eating habits. Some workers design and prepare decorated foods and artistic food arrangements.

Metal Fabrication and Machine Work involves the use of tools, machines, and equipment. These are used to make, assemble, repair, rebuild, and maintain metal products, machinery, and equipment. Workers follow blueprints, drawings, layouts, and templates as they cut, shape, bore, and mill metal parts. They fit, assemble, bolt, and weld metal to make products and structures such as buildings and bridges. They also make heavy metal structural parts for ships, railroad cars, and trucks.

Mechanical involves machines. Workers may assemble, install, repair, and maintain machines, machine parts, or equipment. Some work on vehicles such as cars, tractors, motorcycles, airplanes, and boats. Others may be concerned with engines — airplane, diesel, rocket, automobile, or lawn mower. Many work on heating and air-conditioning units. Photographic devices and farm equipment are other fields. Some workers repair dairy, oil-well drilling, and office machines.

High voltage linemen often work in crane buckets.

Woodworking is to shape wood into objects. Workers may set up and operate woodworking machines to surface, cut, and shape lumber to create products. Some may finish or refinish new or used furniture. Others plan, lay out, and construct wooden forms to make sand molds.

Printing is to produce printed copy with the use of an inked surface and a printing press. Some workers set up and operate cylinder-type, platen-type, web-fed rotary, or offset printing presses. Others assemble and set type by hand or machine. Still others fabricate and finish duplicate electrotype printing plates. These workers usually follow written instructions.

159

Jobs may be found with industries such as construction and printing and in settings such as shipyards, foundries, woodworking shops, machine shops, automotive garages, and restaurants. Some craft workers have their own businesses such as cabinet shops or car repair garages. A few become construction contractors.

What Skills and Abilities Would Help You Succeed in This Kind of Work?

The most important skills are listed below. All of those listed do not apply to each occupation. As you explore occupations you should identify the specific ones needed.

Dexterity – to move the hands and fingers to work skillfully with hand tools, operate machines, or do fine handiwork.

Spatial – to form mental images (pictures) of objects in three dimensions height, width, and depth.

Form Perception – to see slight differences in shapes or surfaces to detect flaws.

Numerical – to use arithmetic quickly to figure dimensions accurately.

Accuracy – to perform tasks within set standards.

Comprehension – to understand and know the uses of tools, materials, and methods for a trade or craft.

Leadership – to plan and oversee the work of others.

Do You Have or Can You Develop an Interest in This Kind of Work?

Review the following questions. Your answers can give you clues as to your interest in Craft Technology.

Have you read magazines or trade papers about mechanics? Did you understand the terms used?

Have you helped to construct stage sets for a school or community play? Can you use hand tools with ease?

Have you built or put together a complicated toy or bicycle which required assembling parts in a certain manner? Were you able to follow the instructions? Do you like doing tasks that require careful attention and accuracy?

Have you taken courses in machine shop or woodworking? Do you like these types of work?

Have you repaired a lamp or extension cord? Can you figure out how things work without looking at directions? Do you like working with electrical equipment?

Have you helped build or repair a house or barn? Do you enjoy working with your hands?

Have you planned and prepared a meal for a group? Do you like to cook?

Have you customized or repaired a car or other vehicle? Do you like mechanical work?

What Else Should You Know About This Group of Occupations?

Some construction workers are employed for years by a single contractor. Others must seek new employment after each project is completed. Many people prefer construction work because they like to be outdoors. However, the weather and the season affect these jobs.

Many craft workers must join a union to be hired. Some are required to furnish their own hand tools. They are usually required to wear safety glasses, hard hats, and other protective devices. Many jobs require evening or night work and workers are often asked to stay overtime.

The military services offer training and experience related to some occupations in this group. These occupations are included in the list at the end of this group description. They are identified by an (M) following the occupational title. More information about the military training and experience opportunities may be found in Appendix A.

How Can You Prepare for This Kind of Work?

Most occupations in this group require two to four years of training and experience. A few may require up to ten years. High school courses in math, general science, home economics, and industrial arts can serve as exploratory courses and can help develop entry level skills. Vocational and technical programs offer the training needed for many jobs in this group. Apprenticeships and on-the-job training are also available.

Many people develop job skills by starting as helpers and working with experienced workers. Some employers train workers to install or repair equipment. Federal and state agencies also sponsor training for some jobs in this group.

Many chefs learn the trade by working as cooks. Apprenticeship programs, technical schools, and large restaurants sometimes offer formal training for these jobs.

As you plan your high school program you should include courses related to Craft Technology. The following list of courses and skills can help you plan your education. Specific courses and programs should be selected for the craft you prefer.

Precision Work – courses in machine shop, sheet metal, welding, woodworking, foundry work, masonry, stonecutting and surfacing, plumbing, heating, air-conditioning, painting, paperhanging, radio-TV, carpentry, cabinetmaking, photography, printing, and dental laboratory.

Industrial Arts – courses in construction, manufacturing, electricity, electronics, upholstering, woodworking, ceramics, and graphic arts.

This central office repairer is searching for a malfunction.

Maintenance and Repair – courses in automotive mechanics, small engines, diesel engines, power mechanics, auto body repair, agriculture mechanics, refrigeration, and hydraulics.

General Mathematics – courses in shop math.

Drafting – courses in mechanical drawing and blueprint reading.

Home Economics – courses in cooking, baking, dietetics, food service, sewing, clothing and textiles, patternmaking, and custom tailoring.

Qualifications Profile

This section is a summary of the worker traits and work factors related to successful job performance and worker satisfaction. Try to relate your interests, abilities, aptitudes, and preferences to these traits and factors. An asterisk (*) marks those traits and factors that are related to more than 60% of the occupations listed at the end of this group. The other traits and factors listed are as important, but relate to fewer occupations. See Appendices B-G for information about all of the worker traits and work factors.

Working Conditions

These are the physical surroundings in which work is done. In occupations belonging to this group, work is performed:

*I – Inside — workers spend most of their time inside protected from weather conditions but not always from temperature changes.

B – Both inside and outside — workers spend about equal time in each setting.

Work Activities

The most important activities related to this group involve:

* 1. Things and objects.
* 9. Processes, methods, or machines.
*10. Working on or producing things.

Work Situations

Workers must be willing to:

1. Perform duties which change frequently.
* 8. Make decisions using standards that can be measured or checked.
*10. Work within precise limits or standards of accuracy.

Physical Demands

Workers in this group of occupations must be able to do:

L – Light work
*M – Medium work

This machinist is turning a part on a metal-cutting lathe.

Data-People-Things

This chart shows the levels for these three basic elements of work as related to this group. Level means the degree of difficulty of job tasks rather than the amount of time involved. The terms low, average, and high indicate the highest level at which occupations are involved. Compare your interests and abilities with the levels checked.

Educational Skills

This chart shows the levels of reasoning, math, and language skills related to this group. These skills are usually developed in an educational setting. There are six levels ranging from the simple (1) to the most complex (6).

Difficulty Level of Job Tasks

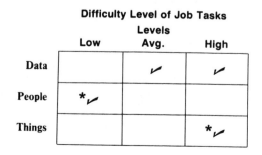

	Low	Levels Avg.	High
Data		✓	✓
People	*✓		
Things			*✓

Skill Levels

Simple ⟵——————⟶ Complex

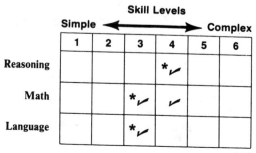

	1	2	3	4	5	6
Reasoning				*✓		
Math			*✓	✓		
Language			*✓			

Aptitudes

This chart presents the most important aptitudes related to this group. The levels checked compare aptitudes needed for success in this group to aptitudes of the general working population in all occupations. For example, level 5 is low and represents the bottom 10% of the working population. Level 1 is high and represents the top 10%.

		Lower 1/3		Middle 1/3	Upper 1/3	
Related Aptitudes (Ability to Learn)		Level **5**	Level **4**	Level **3**	Level **2**	Level **1**
Code	**Title**	10%	23%	34%	23%	10%
G	General Learning Ability			* ✔		
N	Numerical			* ✔		
S	Spatial			✔	✔	
P	Form Perception			* ✔	✔	
K	Motor Coordination			* ✔		
F	Finger Dexterity			* ✔		
M	Manual Dexterity			* ✔	✔	

APTITUDE LEVELS COMPARED TO ALL WORKERS

Common Occupations

A full listing of all occupations belonging to this group may be found in the Guide for Occupational Exploration.

The following occupations have been selected to represent this group. They provide the major employment opportunities. However, specific job opportunities will vary according to locations of industry, geographical region, and other factors.

Information may be found in common sources of occupational information, state career information systems, and computerized guidance systems.

An (M) follows the occupational title where the military services offer training and experience.

Construction and Maintenance

189.167-046 Superintendent, Maintenance
771.381-014 Stonecutter, Hand
806.261-026 Marine-Services Technician (M)
841.381-010 Paperhanger
842.361-018 Plasterer
842.381-010 Dry-Wall Applicator
842.381-014 Stucco Mason
844.364-010 Cement Mason (M)
844.461-010 Concrete-Stone Finisher
860.281-010 Carpenter, Maintenance
860.281-014 Carpenter, Ship
860.381-010 Acoustical Carpenter
860.381-018 Boatbuilder, Wood
860.381-022 Carpenter (M)
860.381-038 Carpenter, Railcar
860.381-042 Carpenter, Rough
860.381-046 Form Builder
860.381-050 Joiner

Checking a proof at the control panel
of a multi-color newspaper press.

860.381-058 Shipwright
860.381-074 Custom Van Installer
861.361-014 Monument Setter
861.381-014 Bricklayer
861.381-018 Bricklayer (M)
861.381-026 Bricklayer, Firebrick and Refractory Tile
861.381-030 Marble Setter
861.381-038 Stonemason
861.381-046 Terrazzo Worker
861.381-054 Tile Setter
861.664-014 Terrazzo Finisher
862.261-010 Pipe Fitter (M)
862.281-018 Oil-Burner-Servicer-And-Installer
862.281-022 Pipe Fitter
862.361-014 Gas-Main Fitter
862.361-018 Pipe Fitter, Diesel Engine 1
862.381-018 Pipe Fitter (M)
862.381-030 Plumber (M)
869.281-014 House Builder

Electrical/Electronic

632.261-010 Aircraft-Armament Mechanic (M)
710.281-026 Instrument Mechanic (M)
721.281-018 Electric-Motor Repairer (M)
722.281-010 Instrument Repairer
726.261-010 Electronics Assembler, Developmental
729.281-010 Audio-Video Repairer (M)
729.281-014 Electric-Meter Repairer
729.281-026 Electrical-Instrument Repairer (M)
820.261-014 Electrician, Powerhouse (M)
821.261-010 Community-Antenna-Television Line
            Technician

821.261-014 Line Maintainer (M)
821.261-026 Trouble Shooter 2
821.361-010 Cable Installer-Repairer (M)
821.361-014 Electric-Meter Installer 1
821.361-018 Line Erector (M)
821.361-026 Line Repairer (M)
821.381-010 Electric-Meter Tester
822.261-010 Electrician, Office
822.261-022 Station Installer-And-Repairer (M)
822.281-010 Automatic-Equipment Technician (M)
822.281-014 Central-Office Repairer (M)
822.281-018 Maintenance Mechanic, Telephone (M)
822.281-022 Private-Branch-Exchange Repairer (M)
822.281-026 Signal Maintainer
822.281-030 Technician, Plant And Maintenance
822.361-010 Cable Tester (M)
822.361-014 Central-Office Installer (M)
822.381-014 Line Installer-Repairer (M)
822.381-018 Private-Branch-Exchange Installer (M)
823.261-010 Public-Address Servicer
823.261-018 Radio Mechanic (M)
823.261-022 Antenna Installer, Satellite
            Communications
823.281-010 Avionics Technician (M)
823.281-014 Electrician, Radio (M)
823.281-018 Meteorological-Equipment Repairer (M)
824.261-010 Electrician (M)
824.281-018 Neon-Sign Servicer
824.381-010 Street-Light Servicer
825.281-014 Electrician (M)
825.281-018 Electrician, Airplane (M)
825.281-026 Electrician, Locomotive

825.281-030 Elevator Repairer
825.381-030 Electrician
827.261-010 Electrical-Appliance Servicer
828.161-010 Supervisor, Electronics Systems
           Maintenance
828.261-014 Field Engineer
828.281-010 Electronics Mechanic (M)
829.261-018 Electrician, Maintenance
829.281-014 Electrical Repairer (M)
829.281-022 Sound Technician (M)
829.361-010 Cable Splicer (M)
829.381-010 Pinsetter Adjuster, Automatic
862.361-010 Furnace Installer

Fine Fabrication and Repair

078.261-018 Orthotist (M)
078.261-022 Prosthetist
078.361-022 Orthotics Assistant (M)
078.361-026 Prosthetics Assistant
199.281-010 Gemologist
364.361-010 Dyer
365.361-014 Shoe Repairer
600.280-010 Instrument Maker
632.261-014 Fire-Control Mechanic (M)
710.281-030 Instrument Technician (M)
711.281-014 Instrument Mechanic, Weapons
           System (M)
712.381-018 Dental-Laboratory Technician (M)
712.381-030 Orthodontic Technician
712.381-034 Orthotics Technician (M)
712.381-038 Prosthetics Technician
713.361-014 Optician, Dispensing 1 (M)
714.281-014 Camera Repairer (M)
714.281-022 Photographic Equipment Technician (M)
714.281-030 Service Technician, Computerized-
           Photofinishing Equipment
715.281-010 Watch Repairer (M)
716.280-008 Optician
716.280-014 Optician (M)
719.261-010 Biomedical Equipment Technician (M)
719.261-014 Radiological-Equipment Specialist (M)
729.281-030 Electromedical-Equipment Repairer (M)
730.281-038 Piano Technician
730.281-054 Wind-Instrument Repairer
730.361-010 Piano Tuner
730.361-014 Pipe-Organ Tuner And Repairer
730.381-018 Brass-Wind-Instrument Maker
770.261-010 Brilliandeer-Lopper
770.261-014 Girdler
770.281-010 Diamond Selector
770.281-014 Gem Cutter
770.381-014 Diamond Cleaver
780.381-010 Automobile Upholsterer

780.381-018 Furniture Upholsterer
780.384-010 Automobile-Seat-Cover-And-Convertible-
           Top Installer
780.684-122 Upholstery Repairer
783.261-010 Furrier
785.261-010 Alteration Tailor (M)
785.261-014 Custom Tailor
785.361-010 Dressmaker
785.361-014 Garment Fitter (M)
785.361-018 Sample Stitcher
785.361-022 Shop Tailor (M)
788.381-014 Shoemaker, Custom
828.261-010 Electronic-Organ Technician
977.381-010 Bookbinder

Food Preparation

077.121-010 Dietetic Technician
077.127-014 Dietitian, Clinical (M)
077.127-018 Dietitian, Consultant (M)
313.131-014 Chef (M)
313.281-010 Chef De Froid
313.361-014 Cook (M)
315.137-014 Sous Chef
524.381-010 Cake Decorator

Metal Fabrication and Machine Work

600.280-022 Machinist (M)
600.280-034 Machinist, Automotive
600.280-038 Machinist, Experimental
600.280-042 Maintenance Machinist (M)
600.280-050 Patternmaker, Metal
600.281-018 Lay-Out Worker
601.280-010 Die Maker, Stamping
601.280-014 Die Maker, Trim
601.280-018 Die Maker, Wire Drawing
601.280-022 Die Sinker
601.280-030 Mold Maker, Die-Casting And Plastic
           Molding
601.280-042 Tool Maker
601.280-046 Tool-And-Die Maker
601.280-054 Tool-Machine Set-Up Operator
601.281-010 Die Maker, Bench, Stamping
601.281-026 Tool Maker, Bench
610.381-010 Blacksmith
619.260-008 Ornamental-Metal Worker
619.360-014 Metal Fabricator
619.361-010 Former, Hand
622.381-014 Car Repairer
632.281-010 Gunsmith (M)
638.281-018 Millwright
693.280-010 Form Builder
693.281-018 Patternmaker, Metal, Bench
701.381-014 Saw Filer
701.381-018 Tool Grinder 1

754.381-014 Patternmaker, Plastics
801.361-014 Structural-Steel Worker (M)
801.381-010 Assembler, Metal Building
801.684-026 Reinforcing-Metal Worker (M)
804.281-010 Sheet-Metal Worker (M)
805.261-014 Boilermaker 1 (M)
805.361-010 Boilerhouse Mechanic (M)
806.261-014 Rigger
806.381-046 Shipfitter (M)
807.261-010 Aircraft Body Repairer (M)
807.281-010 Truck-Body Builder
807.381-010 Automobile-Body Repairer (M)
809.281-010 Lay-Out Worker 1
809.381-022 Ornamental-Iron Worker
810.384-014 Welder, Arc (M)
811.684-014 Welder, Gas
816.364-010 Arc Cutter
819.361-010 Welder-Fitter (M)
819.381-010 Welder-Assembler
819.384-010 Welder, Combination (M)
823.281-022 Rigger (M)
825.361-010 Elevator Constructor
869.261-014 Mechanical-Test Technician
869.361-010 Conduit Mechanic
869.381-026 Sign Erector 1
869.381-030 Steeple Jack

Mechanical

600.281-022 Machine Builder
601.281-014 Die-Try-Out Worker, Stamping
620.261-010 Automobile Mechanic (M)
620.261-022 Construction-Equipment Mechanic (M)
620.261-030 Automobile-Service-Station Mechanic
620.261-034 Automotive-Cooling-System Technician
620.281-010 Air-Conditioning Mechanic (M)
620.281-014 Automotive Technician, Exhaust
             Emissions
620.281-018 Automotive-Maintenance-Equipment
             Servicer
620.281-050 Mechanic, Industrial Truck (M)
620.281-054 Motorcycle Repairer
620.281-058 Tractor Mechanic (M)
620.281-066 Tune-Up Mechanic
620.381-014 Mechanic, Endless Track Vehicle (M)
621.281-014 Airframe-And-Power-Plant Mechanic (M)
621.281-030 Rocket-Engine-Component Mechanic
623.281-026 Machinist, Marine Engine (M)
623.281-034 Maintenance Mechanic, Engine (M)
623.281-038 Motorboat Mechanic (M)
624.281-010 Farm-Equipment Mechanic 1
624.381-018 Farm-Machinery Set-Up Mechanic
625.281-010 Diesel Mechanic (M)
625.281-022 Fuel-Injection Servicer

625.281-026 Gas-Engine Repairer (M)
625.281-034 Small-Engine Mechanic
626.281-010 Machine Repairer, Maintenance
627.281-010 Press Maintainer
629.281-018 Dairy-Equipment Repairer
629.381-014 Oil-Field Equipment Mechanic
630.281-018 Pump Servicer
630.281-034 Service Mechanic, Compressed-Gas
             Equipment (M)
631.261-014 Powerhouse Mechanic (M)
633.281-018 Office-Machine Servicer (M)
633.281-030 Statistical-Machine Servicer (M)
637.261-010 Air-Conditioning Installer-Servicer,
             Window Unit
637.261-014 Environmental-Control-System Installer-
             Servicer (M)
637.261-026 Refrigeration Mechanic (M)
637.261-030 Solar-Energy-System Installer
637.261-034 Air And Hydronic Balancing Technician
638.261-018 Manufacturers Service Representative
638.261-026 Field Service Technician
638.261-030 Machine Repairer, Maintenance
638.281-014 Maintenance Mechanic
638.281-026 Parts Salvager
638.281-034 Hydraulic Repairer
638.381-010 Fuel-System-Maintenance Worker (M)
709.281-010 Locksmith
714.281-018 Machinist, Motion-Picture
             Equipment (M)
714.281-026 Photographic-Equipment-Maintenance
             Technician (M)
827.361-014 Refrigeration Mechanic
869.281-010 Furnace Installer-And-Repairer,
             Hot Air (M)

Woodworking

660.280-010 Cabinetmaker
661.280-010 Patternmaker
661.281-022 Patternmaker, Wood
667.682-086 Variety-Saw Operator
669.380-014 Machinist, Wood
763.381-010 Furniture Finisher

Printing

651.362-010 Cylinder-Press Operator
651.362-018 Platen-Press Operator
651.362-030 Web-Press Operator
651.482-010 Offset-Press Operator 1 (M)
651.582-010 Proof-Press Operator
651.585-010 Assistant-Press Operator
973.381-010 Compositor
973.381-018 Job Printer
974.381-010 Electrotyper
974.382-014 Stereotyper

167

Systems Operation

Systems Operation is the control and care of equipment in a mechanical system. The system transports a product or provides a utility such as fuel, water, or power. This group includes the subgroups of:

Electricity Generation and Transmission
Stationary Engineering
Oil, Gas, and Water Distribution
Processing

Electricity Generation and Transmission systems produce, distribute, and maintain power to industries and homes. Workers control, operate, and maintain equipment. Natural gas, diesel, water, or steam power is used to generate electricity. Some workers control nuclear reactors to generate power. Others control the flow of electricity through power lines to consumers.

Stationary Engineering is to operate and maintain engines, turbines, air compressors, generators, motors, and boilers. This equipment may supply light, heat, refrigeration, ventilation, air conditioning, or mechanical or electrical power. Workers run and maintain equipment for buildings, industries, mines, oilfields, or ships.

Oil, Gas, and Water Distribution is to transport oil, gas, and water. Workers may run power-driven pumps that move these products through pipes. They may control the flow in the system or pipes to ensure volume and pressure for consumer needs. Some workers run compressors to maintain pressure while moving gas from storage to users.

Others gauge and test amounts of oil in storage tanks and control the flow of oil and other oil products in pipelines. Some operate pumps to move water to treatment plants and then to users.

Processing is to operate and control equipment that transports petrochemicals (products made from oil or gas) and wastewater for treatment. Workers run pumps to load trucks, barges, and tank cars. Some operate sewage treatment, sludge processing, and disposal equipment in a wastewater plant. Others control machines and equipment to purify water.

Jobs may be found with utility companies, refineries, in oil fields, construction projects, large buildings, and city and county governments.

What Skills and Abilities Would Help You Succeed in This Kind of Work?

The most important skills are listed below. All of those listed do not apply to each occupation. As you explore occupations you should identify the specific ones needed.

Dexterity – to move hands and fingers to adjust or repair equipment.

Numerical – to use math skills to read and interpret information from meters and gauges.

Composure – to be calm and self-confident in emergency situations.

Judgment – to use knowledge and experience to make decisions and solve problems.

Accuracy – to work within precise limits using standards that can be measured or checked.

Diligence – to adjust or cope with tasks that are repetitive or routine.

Do You Have or Can You Develop an Interest in This Kind of Work?

Review the following questions. Your answers can give you clues as to your interest in Systems Operation.

Have you taken shop courses? Did you like working with machines? How were your grades?

Have you taken courses that require you to solve problems using math formulas? Do you understand the principles of electricity?

Have you built or repaired equipment? Can you spot and correct malfunctions?

Have you set up and operated a model train? Can you find and correct problems?

What Else Should You Know About This Group of Occupations?

Many systems operate twenty-four hours a day and require one or more operators to be on duty at all times. Workers may have to work evening and night shifts. Weekend and holiday duties are also common.

Operators are sometimes exposed to high temperatures, dust, dirt, and fumes. Most workers must be able to think and act quickly in case of emergencies.

The military services offer training and experience related to some occupations in this group. These occupations are included in the list at the end of this group description. They are identified by an (M) following the occupational title. More information about the military training and experience opportunities may be found in Appendix A.

This switchboard distributes the output of a biomass electric generator.

How Can You Prepare for This Kind of Work?

Most occupations in this group require six months to four years of education and training. A few require ten years. Most operators start as helpers and develop the skills needed.

Boiler operators usually serve an apprenticeship which lasts up to four years. A license is required in some states for stationary engineering occupations. Workers in atomic powered plants must have special training.

As you plan your high school program you should include courses related to Systems Operation. The following list of courses and skills can help you plan your education.

Mathematics – courses in shop math, algebra, and geometry.

Science – courses in physics, chemistry, and physical science.

Electric/Electronic – courses in electricity and electronics.

Mechanics – courses in engine mechanics, power technology, diesel, hydraulics, plumbing, and machine shop.

Stationary Engineering – courses in stationary energy sources, power generation, pumping equipment operation, boiler operation, instrumentation and control, hydro-turbine, and emergency safety procedures.

Qualifications Profile

This section is a summary of the worker traits and work factors related to successful job performance and worker satisfaction. Try to relate your interests, abilities, aptitudes, and preferences to these traits and factors. An asterisk (*) marks those traits and factors that are related to more than 60% of the occupations listed at the end of this group. The other traits and factors listed are as important, but relate to fewer occupations. See Appendices B-G for information about all of the worker traits and work factors.

Work Situations

Workers must be willing to:

1. Perform duties which change frequently.
* 8. Make decisions using standards that can be measured or checked.
*10. Work within precise limits or standards of accuracy.

Work Activities

The most important activities related to this group involve:

* 1. Things and objects.
   3. Tasks of a routine, definite nature.
* 9. Processes, methods, or machines.

Working Conditions

These are the physical surroundings in which work is done. In occupations belonging to this group, work is performed:

*I – Inside — workers spend most of their time inside protected from weather conditions but not always from temperature changes.

O – Outside — workers spend most of their time outside with little protection from weather conditions.

B – Both inside and outside — workers spend about equal time in each setting.

Educational Skills

This chart shows the levels of reasoning, math, and language skills related to this group. These skills are usually developed in an educational setting. There are six levels ranging from the simple (1) to the most complex (6).

Skill Levels

Simple ⟵⟶ Complex

	1	2	3	4	5	6
Reasoning			✓	*✓		
Math			*✓			
Language			*✓			

Physical Demands

Workers in this group of occupations must be able to do:

L – Light work
M – Medium work

Data-People-Things

This chart shows the levels for these three basic elements of work as related to this group. Level means the degree of difficulty of job tasks rather than the amount of time involved. The terms low, average, and high indicate the highest level at which occupations are involved. Compare your interests and abilities with the levels checked.

Difficulty Level of Job Tasks

Levels

	Low	Avg.	High
Data		*✓	
People	*✓		
Things		*✓	

An oil pumper is regulating the flow of oil from a well into a collection pipeline.

Aptitudes

This chart presents the most important aptitudes related to this group. The levels checked compare aptitudes needed for success in this group to aptitudes of the general working population in all occupations. For example, level 5 is low and represents the bottom 10% of the working population. Level 1 is high and represents the top 10%.

APTITUDE LEVELS COMPARED TO ALL WORKERS						
Related Aptitudes **(Ability to Learn)**		Lower 1/3		Middle 1/3	Upper 1/3	
		Level **5**	Level **4**	Level **3**	Level **2**	Level **1**
Code	Title	10%	23%	34%	23%	10%
G	General Learning Ability			* ✔		
S	Spatial		✔	* ✔		
Q	Clerical Perception		✔	* ✔		
M	Manual Dexterity			* ✔		

A stationary engineer sets a control on a steam boiler.

Common Occupations

A full listing of all occupations belonging to this group may be found in the Guide for Occupational Exploration.

The following occupations have been selected to represent this group. They provide the major employment opportunities. However, specific job opportunities will vary according to locations of industry, geographical region, and other factors.

Information may be found in common sources of occupational information, state career information systems, and computerized guidance systems.

An (M) follows the occupational title where the military services offer training and experience.

Electricity Generation and Transmission

822.361-030 Trouble Locator, Test Desk
950.382-018 Gas-Engine Operator (M)
952.167-014 Load Dispatcher
952.362-010 Auxiliary-Equipment Opeartor (M)
952.362-018 Hydroelectric-Station Operator
952.362-022 Power-Reactor Operator (M)
952.362-026 Substation Operator
952.362-034 Switchboard Operator
952.362-038 Switchboard Operator
952.362-042 Turbine Operator
952.382-010 Diesel-Plant Operator (M)
952.382-018 Power-Plant Operator

Stationary Engineering

197.130-010 Engineer (M)
950.362-014 Refrigerating Engineer
950.382-010 Boiler Operator (M)
950.382-022 Rotary-Rig Engine Operator
950.382-026 Stationary Engineer (M)
950.685-010 Air-Compressor Operator
951.685-010 Firer, High Pressure
951.685-014 Firer, Low Pressure
951.685-018 Firer, Marine

Oil, Gas, and Water Distribution

914.382-010 Pumper
914.382-022 Pumper, Head
914.384-010 Gager (M)
914.682-010 Pumper
953.167-010 Gas Dispatcher
953.382-010 Gas-Pumping-Station Operator
954.382-010 Pump-Station Operator, Waterworks (M)

Processing

914.382-014 Pumper-Gager (M)
950.362-010 Engineer, Exhauster
954.382-014 Water-Treatment-Plant Operator (M)
955.362-010 Wastewater-Treatment-Plant Operator (M)

Quality Control

Quality Control is to inspect and test equipment, tools, structures, and raw materials. Most of the work takes place in settings other than factories. Workers perform duties that are very much alike. They inspect for defects and damage. Their work ensures that quality standards or legal requirements for operation and safety are met. They may prepare items for testing, mark defects they find, and record data. They may write up repair orders and inspect the final work. This group includes the subgroups of:

Structural
Mechanical
Electrical
Petroleum
Logging and Lumber

Workers in the five subgroups of Quality Control perform duties that are very much alike. They differ in the knowledge and skills needed for the type of inspecting they do.

Structural workers look for defects and examine damage in the structures of equipment, tools, and vehicles. Workers may test metal parts at a commercial lab, or inspect the work in a machine shop. Some inspect railroad cars, roadbeds, and equipment. Others inspect airplane or missile parts for hardness, precision (exact size), or other standards. Some workers examine damaged car or truck bodies, compute repair costs, and write-up repair orders.

A shop estimator points out the extent of damage to a customer.

Mechanical workers inspect engines and other operating parts of cars, trucks, and buses. Some inspect and test vehicles to make sure they meet safety standards. Others check for repairs needed or for quality of repair work done. Some drive experimental models to obtain data on how they operate. Other workers test airplane engines and other equipment after repair to certify that it is safe to operate.

Electrical workers inspect motors and mechanical parts of elevators and escalators. They make adjustments to meet factory standards and safety codes.

Petroleum workers inspect samples of crude or refined oil to certify that shipments conform to quality standards or contract terms. They also may check valves at terminals or ship tanks for leaks.

Logging and Lumber workers inspect logs and pulpwood for rot, knots, or other defects. They measure each log or load, deduct estimated waste, and record the results.

Jobs in this group may be found with construction companies, sawmills, airlines, auto repair shops, machine shops, and railroads. Oil companies and laboratories also hire these workers.

What Skills and Abilities Would Help You Succeed in This Kind of Work?

The most important skills are listed below. All of those listed do not apply to each occupation. As you explore occupations you should identify the specific ones needed.

Communication – to write clearly in order to report findings, make recommendations, or order materials and repairs.

Clerical – to record data to keep records.

Dexterity – to use the hands and fingers to handle measuring and testing instruments or tools.

Analyzation – to use data about a product, process, or material to determine if it meets quality or safety standards.

Comprehension – to understand data obtained from blueprints, diagrams, or standards.

Numerical – to do math quickly and correctly.

Form Perception – to see slight differences in the shape or texture of items being tested or inspected.

Spatial Perception – to form a mental image (picture) of how shapes and forms are combined in three dimensions height, width, and depth.

Accuracy – to make exact measurements or calculations.

Critical Thinking – to use personal judgment to make decisions and solve problems.

Do You Have or Can You Develop an Interest in This Kind of Work?

Review the following questions. Your answers can give you clues as to your interest in Quality Control.

Have you read mechanical or automotive magazines? Did you understand the drawings and terms used?

Have you noticed a change in sound when a car or household appliance was not working right? Did you check to see what was wrong? Did you enjoy this type of activity?

Have you had courses in drafting? Can you read blueprints and diagrams?

This service manager is pointing out an item that needs attention to his customer.

An elevator inspector checks the cables carefully.

Have you put models together? Did you have to measure and fit small parts together? Can you follow detailed directions?

Have you taken woodworking, metalworking, sewing, or cooking? Do you notice small differences in sizes, shapes, or textures?

Have you used gauges, scales, micrometers, or other measuring devices? Are you able to make exact measurements?

Have you checked clothes, cars, appliances, or furniture for defects before buying? Do you notice small details?

Have you repaired a friend's or the family car? Did you estimate the cost of repairs? Was your estimate close or correct?

How Can You Prepare for This Kind of Work?

Most occupations in this group require six months to four years of training and experience. A few require as little as three months or as much as ten years. Many jobs require the ability to read blueprints. High school or vocational courses in shop or mechanical drawing are helpful in developing this skill. Jobs usually require experience in related work. This provides the background needed to judge the quality or the defects of the products or materials involved. Most workers receive on-the-job training in order to learn specific inspection tasks.

As you plan your high school program you should include courses related to Quality Control. The following list of courses and skills can help you plan your education.

176

What Else Should You Know About This Group of Occupations?

Quality Control involves work in a variety of settings. Working conditions may include dust, noise, and some risk of personal injury, although jobs in this group are not considered hazardous. Some jobs may require travel or long and irregular work hours. Most workers gain employment through promotion from jobs in the same field since background knowledge and experience is very important.

The military services offer training and experience related to some occupations in this group. These occupations are included in the list at the end of this group description. They are identified by an (M) following the occupational title. More information about the military training and experience opportunities may be found in Appendix A.

Vehicle and Equipment Mechanics – courses in automotive repair, automotive body repair, diesel engine mechanics, aircraft mechanics (airframe and powerplant), and general equipment mechanics.

Precision Work – courses in metalwork, machine tool operation, machine shop, metal fabrication, and tool and die making.

Industrial Arts – courses in metals and mechanical drawing/blueprint reading.

Electrical/Electronics – courses in industrial electronics and motor repair.

Mathematics – general mathematics and shop math.

Qualifications Profile

This section is a summary of the worker traits and work factors related to successful job performance and worker satisfaction. Try to relate your interests, abilities, aptitudes, and preferences to these traits and factors. An asterisk (*) marks those traits and factors that are related to more than 60% of the occupations listed at the end of this group. The other traits and factors listed are as important, but relate to fewer occupations. See Appendices B-G for information about all of the worker traits and work factors.

Work Situations

Workers must be willing to:

  1. Perform duties which change frequently.
  7. Make decisions using personal judgment.
* 8. Make decisions using standards that can be measured or checked.
*10. Work within precise limits or standards of accuracy.

Work Activities

The most important activities related to this group involve:

* 1. Things and objects.
  3. Tasks of a routine, definite nature.
* 9. Processes, methods, or machines.
  10. Working on or producing things.

Working Conditions

These are the physical surroundings in which work is done. In occupations belonging to this group, work is performed:

*I – Inside — workers spend most of their time inside protected from weather conditions but not always from temperature changes.
B – Both inside and outside — workers spend about equal time in each setting.

Physical Demands

Workers in this group of occupations must be able to do:

*L – Light work

Educational Skills

This chart shows the levels of reasoning, math, and language skills related to this group. These skills are usually developed in an educational setting. There are six levels ranging from the simple (1) to the most complex (6).

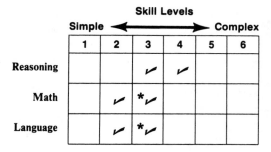

Aptitudes

This chart presents the most important aptitudes related to this group. The levels checked compare aptitudes needed for success in this group to aptitudes of the general working population in all occupations. For example, level 5 is low and represents the bottom 10% of the working population. Level 1 is high and represents the top 10%.

APTITUDE LEVELS COMPARED TO ALL WORKERS						
Related Aptitudes (Ability to Learn)		Lower 1/3		Middle 1/3	Upper 1/3	
		Level 5	Level 4	Level 3	Level 2	Level 1
Code	Title	10%	23%	34%	23%	10%
G	General Learning Ability			*✔	✔	
N	Numerical		✔	*✔		
S	Spatial		✔	✔	✔	
P	Form Perception			✔	✔	

Data-People-Things

This chart shows the levels for these three basic elements of work as related to this group. Level means the degree of difficulty of job tasks rather than the amount of time involved. The terms low, average, and high indicate the highest level at which occupations are involved. Compare your interests and abilities with the levels checked.

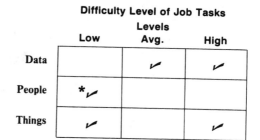

Difficulty Level of Job Tasks

	Low	Avg.	High
Data		✔	✔
People	*✔		
Things	✔		✔

Common Occupations

A full listing of all occupations belonging to this group may be found in the Guide for Occupational Exploration.

The following occupations have been selected to represent this group. They provide the major employment opportunities. However, specific job opportunities will vary according to locations of industry, geographical region, and other factors.

Information may be found in common sources of occupational information, state career information systems, and computerized guidance systems.

An (M) follows the occupational title where the military services offer training and experience.

Structural

011.261-018 Nondestructive Tester (M)
601.281-022 Inspector, Tool
609.361-010 Inspector, Floor

805.667-010 Boilerhouse Inspector
806.281-046 Outside Production Inspector
807.267-010 Shop Estimator
910.367-030 Way Inspector
910.387-014 Railroad-Car Inspector
910.667-010 Car Inspector

Mechanical

379.364-010 Automobile Tester
620.261-014 Automobile Tester
620.261-018 Automobile-Repair-Service Estimator
621.261-010 Airplane Inspector (M)
721.261-010 Electric-Motor Analyst
806.283-010 Test Driver 2

Electrical

825.261-014 Elevator Examiner-And-Adjuster

Petroleum

222.367-046 Petroleum Inspector
549.387-010 Cargo Inspector (M)

Logging and Lumber

455.487-010 Log Scaler

Land and Water Vehicle Operation

Land and Water Vehicle Operation is to drive or operate vehicles to move freight or people or to make deliveries. Land vehicles include trains, trucks, vans, and ambulances. Water vehicles are powered boats. Truck drivers operate on highways and also within mining, construction, and industrial sites. Freight includes both raw materials and finished products. Delivery services include driving an ambulance to move sick or injured people. This group includes the subgroups of:

Truck/Services Delivery
Rail Vehicle Operation
Boat Operation

Truck/Services Delivery includes light and heavy trucks and vans. Drivers often load and unload their vehicles. Some drivers also are responsible for keeping them in good running order. Some drivers operate locally and others make long trips. Some drive on established routes making regular deliveries. Delivery companies provide service to individuals as well as businesses.

Rail Vehicle Operation is to operate trains to transport freight and people. Also included are subway and elevated suburban trains. Engineers are responsible for driving the locomotive. They must follow train orders, time schedules, and safety regulations. Workers who switch cars in railroad yards, industrial plants, and other work sites are also included in this group. So are the workers who assist the engineer operate the train or supervise yard switching crews.

Boat Operation is to transport people or cargo by powered boats. Boat operators use their boats to tow, push, or guide other boats. Boats may be used to ferry passengers from one ship to another or from ship to shore. They also may be involved in patrolling a harbor or beach area. Some operators also clean and service the boat motor. However, they may be assisted by deckhands in these duties. Deckhands may steer the boat while underway. They also handle lines, sweep and wash decks, lower and man lifeboats, and stand lookout watches. They load or unload materials, paint lifeboats, decks, and structures of vessels. They also may oil machinery and equipment and splice and repair cables and ropes.

Jobs may be found with railroads, trucking firms, and water transportation companies. Mining, construction, and industrial companies also provide jobs. Wholesale and retail companies and delivery services hire drivers. Ambulance drivers are hired by hospitals, fire departments, and other establishments. Some workers are self-employed. They contract for local or long-distance hauling or deliveries.

What Skills and Abilities Would Help You Succeed in This Kind of Work?

The most important skills are listed below. All of those listed do not apply to each occupation. As you explore occupations you should identify the specific ones needed.

Comprehension – to understand and follow federal, state, and local traffic rules to qualify for a chauffeur's license or secure other required credentials.

Depth Perception – to judge distances and relationships of objects in space.

Dexterity – to move hands and feet to operate levers, push pedals, and steer the vehicle.

Clerical – to keep records and prepare reports.

Judgment – to make decisions to meet traffic, weather, and other driving conditions.

Stamina – to withstand the physical strain of sitting for long hours while driving.

Numerical – to collect money, make change, and add receipts.

Diligence – to adapt to repetitive tasks or those that are performed frequently.

Do You Have or Can You Develop an Interest in This Kind of Work?

Review the following questions. Your answers can give you clues as to your interest in Land and Water Vehicle Operation.

Have you completed a course in driver's education? Do you have a driver's or chauffeur's license?

Have you driven midget or stock cars? Do you enjoy this type of activity?

Have you driven in a bicycle rodeo, car rally, or over a vehicle obstacle course? Did you receive a good score? Did you stand the pressure?

Have you driven a car pulling a trailer? Did you hook or unhook the trailer from the car? Could you back it safely into a narrow space?

Have you driven much in heavy traffic? Have you driven for long periods of time? Did it bother you?

Have you repaired or customized an automobile? Do you like working with or operating motor vehicles?

Do you often read automotive or trucking magazines? Do you enjoy reading this type of material?

Have you operated a motorboat? Are you able to dock safely?

Have you owned or operated a model train layout? Do you like to read about trains and railroads?

Have you filled out forms to order something from a mail order catalog? Can you understand and complete such forms correctly?

This concrete-mixing-truck driver is placing the mix to a customer's specification.

This tow truck driver must be sure he does not damage the towed vehicle.

What Else Should You Know About This Group of Occupations?

The operation of larger boats and ships is included in Worker Trait Group 05.04, Air and Water Transportation. The operation of taxis and buses to transport people is included in Worker Trait Group 09.03, Passenger Services.

Companies sometimes require a physical exam before hiring a worker and once each year after that. Long-distance truck drivers may spend days or even weeks at a time away from home. The noise, rough ride, and heavy traffic may cause physical or nervous strain. They often drive at night because the roads are less crowded. Local truck drivers who handle food may drive at night or very early in the morning to make deliveries.

The U.S. Department of Transportation sets standards for truck drivers traveling from state to state. They must have good hearing, 20/40 vision with or without glasses, and normal blood pressure. Although some exceptions are made for handicapped workers, drivers usually must have full use of arms and legs. Truck drivers must take a written test on the motor carrier safety rules of the U.S. Department of Transportation. They must also pass a driving test using the type of truck they will drive on the job. A good driving record is also required. Some firms hire only drivers with several years of long-distance trucking experience.

Advancement in truck driving is limited. Some drivers become dispatchers or managers. Others with business ability may buy and operate their own trucks.

Experience as a deckhand provides opportunities to develop skills and maybe to advance to boat operation.

The military services offer training and experience related to some occupations in this group. These occupations are included in the list at the end of this group description. They are identified by an (M) following the occupational title. More information about the military training and experience opportunities may be found in Appendix A.

How Can You Prepare for This Kind of Work?

Most occupations in this group require 30 days to one year of education and training. A few require two to four years. Most states require all truck drivers to have chauffeur licenses. Specific requirements vary from state to state. These licenses usually require applicants to pass physical, written, and driving tests. Knowledge of traffic laws and some truck driving experience helps prepare workers for these jobs. Some training may be taken in high school and vocational schools.

Requirements for local drivers vary with the type of truck driven and the employer's business. The physical requirements are similar to those set for long haul truck drivers. Most firms want workers with good driving records. New workers may learn by riding with a veteran driver. Some firms have classes on general duties, operating and loading trucks, and company rules, forms, and records.

Locomotive engineers usually have experience as helpers (locomotive firers). Promotion is made according to seniority. Helpers ride with engineers and learn to inspect locomotives and check the gages. They also learn to watch for signals and track obstructions. Applicants must have good hearing, vision, and color perception.

As you plan your high school program you should include courses related to Land and Water Vehicle Operation. The following list of courses and skills can help you plan your education.

Vehicle Operation – courses in driver education, road safety, first-aid, truck and bus driving, materials handling, barge and boat operation, and marina operation.

Mechanics – courses in auto and diesel engine mechanics, outboard and inboard marine motors, equipment maintenance, and marine maintenance.

Mathematics – courses in general math and business math.

Clerical – courses that provide training in keeping records and general sales or delivery reports.

Qualifications Profile

This section is a summary of the worker traits and work factors related to successful job performance and worker satisfaction. Try to relate your interests, abilities, aptitudes, and preferences to these traits and factors. An asterisk (*) marks those traits and factors that are related to more than 60% of the occupations listed at the end of this group. The other traits and factors listed are as important, but relate to fewer occupations. See Appendices B-G for information about all of the worker traits and work factors.

Work Activities

The most important activities related to this group involve:

* 1. Things and objects.
* 3. Tasks of a routine, definite nature.
* 9. Processes, methods, or machines.

Work Situations

Workers must be willing to:

1. Perform duties which change frequently.
* 2. Perform routine tasks.
* 8. Make decisions using standards that can be measured or checked.

Working Conditions

These are the physical surroundings in which work is done. In occupations belonging to this group, work is performed:

I – Inside — workers spend most of their time inside protected from weather conditions but not always from temperature changes.

*B – Both inside and outside — workers spend about equal time in each setting.

Data-People-Things

This chart shows the levels for these three basic elements of work as related to this group. Level means the degree of difficulty of job tasks rather than the amount of time involved. The terms low, average, and high indicate the highest level at which occupations are involved. Compare your interests and abilities with the levels checked.

Difficulty Level of Job Tasks

	Low	Avg.	High
Data	*✓	✓	
People	*✓		
Things		*✓	

Levels

Educational Skills

This chart shows the levels of reasoning, math, and language skills related to this group. These skills are usually developed in an educational setting. There are six levels ranging from the simple (1) to the most complex (6).

Skill Levels

Simple ⟵⟶ Complex

	1	2	3	4	5	6
Reasoning			*✓			
Math	✓	*✓				
Language	✓	✓	✓			

Physical Demands

Workers in this group of occupations must be able to do:

L – Light work
*M – Medium work

This yard engineer makes up and breaks up trains and spots cars on customers' sidings.

Aptitudes

This chart presents the most important aptitudes related to this group. The levels checked compare aptitudes needed for success in this group to aptitudes of the general working population in all occupations. For example, level 5 is low and represents the bottom 10% of the working population. Level 1 is high and represents the top 10%.

APTITUDE LEVELS COMPARED TO ALL WORKERS							
Related Aptitudes (Ability to Learn)		Lower 1/3		Middle 1/3	Upper 1/3		
		Level 5	Level 4	Level 3	Level 2	Level 1	
Code	Title	10%	23%	34%	23%	10%	
G	General Learning Ability			*✔			
S	Spatial			*✔	✔		
K	Motor Coordination			*✔			
M	Manual Dexterity			*✔			

Common Occupations

A full listing of all occupations belonging to this group may be found in the Guide for Occupational Exploration.

The following occupations have been selected to represent this group. They provide the major employment opportunities. However, specific job opportunities will vary according to locations of industry, geographical region, and other factors.

Information may be found in common sources of occupational information, state career information systems, and computerized guidance systems.

An (M) follows the occupational title where the military services offer training and experience.

Truck/Services Delivery

292.363-010 Newspaper-Delivery Driver
292.483-010 Coin Collector
900.683-010 Concrete-Mixing-Truck Driver
902.683-010 Dump-Truck Driver

903.683-010 Explosives-Truck Driver
903.683-018 Tank-Truck Driver (M)
904.383-010 Tractor-Trailer-Truck Driver (M)
904.683-010 Log-Truck Driver
905.483-010 Milk Driver
905.663-010 Garbage Collector Driver
905.663-014 Truck Driver, Heavy (M)
905.663-018 Van Driver
905.683-010 Water-Truck Driver 2
906.683-014 Liquid-Fertilizer Servicer
906.683-022 Truck Driver, Light (M)
909.663-010 Hostler
913.683-010 Ambulance Driver
919.663-026 Tow-Truck Operator

Rail Vehicle Operation

910.137-022 Conductor, Yard
910.363-010 Firer, Locomotive
910.363-014 Locomotive Engineer
910.363-018 Yard Engineer
910.683-014 Motor Operator

Boat Operation

911.663-010 Motorboat Operator (M)
911.687-022 Deckhand (M)

Material Control

Material Control is to handle, keep records on, and direct the flow of materials and products. Workers place orders, receive and check in shipments, and store materials. They issue them to other workers as they are needed. This group includes the subgroups of:

Shipping, Receiving, and
  Stock Checking
Estimating, Scheduling, and
  Record Keeping
Verifying, Recording, and Marking

Shipping, Receiving, and Stock Checking involves the control of supplies, equipment, and merchandise. This may be in a stockroom, tool crib, receiving or shipping room, freight yard, or warehouse. Workers have direct contact with the materials involved. Workers sort and place items on racks, shelves, or in bins by size, type, style, color, or product code. They may count the items and post totals. They confirm the count of the stock and adjust errors. They may route inbound and outbound freight. Some workers fill customer's orders. Others receive, store, and issue things such as hand tools, machine tools, dies, and equipment.

Estimating, Scheduling, and Record Keeping involves finding and checking on the progress of job orders. Workers prepare reports used by scheduling and production personnel. Some compile data to make special products for customers. They estimate the amount of materials and labor required to produce such products as jewelry, drapes, upholstery, or printed materials. Workers may schedule and direct the flow of work within or between departments of a manufacturing plant. They also may check on products produced and materials used.

This inventory clerk is counting rolls of sheet aluminum.

Verifying, Recording, and Marking involves the records concerned with quantity, cost, and type of materials received, stored, or issued. Workers may compare material received against an order placed. They may examine items for defects and sort them according to the extent of the defect. Some read electric, gas, water, or other meters and record the figures. Some workers compile records of the amount, kind, and condition of cargo loaded or unloaded from a ship. Others record data from recording instruments or change charts on them. They may compare the data and compute and record average readings. Some workers collect samples of products or raw materials for lab analysis.

Jobs may be found with firms which make, sell, distribute, or receive large amounts of materials or products. Examples are: industrial plants, government agencies, factories, department stores, hotels, restaurants, and hospitals.

What Skills and Abilities Would Help You Succeed in This Kind of Work?

The most important skills are listed below. All of those listed do not apply to each occupation. As you explore occupations you should identify the specific ones needed.

Numerical – to do math quickly and correctly to check invoices, orders, or inventory records.

Comprehension – to understand terms describing material received to make reports.

Physical Stamina – to be on one's feet for a long period of time or lift, move, or handle heavy or bulky materials.

Accuracy – to follow rules and work without error.

Dexterity – to move the fingers and hands to pack, unpack, or sort materials for products.

Concentration – to focus attention on tasks and remain alert for a period of time.

Clerical Perception – to spot errors in orders or records.

Diligence – to adapt to repeating set tasks, following a set plan, method, or sequence.

Do You Have or Can You Develop an Interest in This Kind of Work?

Review the following questions. Your answers can give you clues as to your interest in Material Control.

Have you taken industrial arts or vocational courses? Did you learn to issue, store, and care for tools?

Have you worked as a stock clerk in a store? Did you unpack cartons and place items on shelves? Did you count items or keep records?

Have you been an equipment manager for a sports team? Were you responsible for issuing and maintaining the equipment? Did you like to to this?

Have you taken bookkeeping or general clerical courses? Did you like and do well in them?

What Else Should You Know About This Group of Occupations?

Many jobs in this group require workers to be on their feet most of the workday. Most of the work is done indoors. However, some jobs involve working on loading platforms, in storage yards or in cold storage rooms. A few workers must lift or move heavy objects. Some workers must learn to operate equipment to move items.

A stock clerk selects the proper item to fill an order.

The military services offer training and experience related to some occupations in this group. These occupations are included in the list at the end of this group description. They are identified by an (M) following the occupational title. More information about the military training and experience opportunities may be found in Appendix A.

How Can You Prepare for This Kind of Work?

Most occupations in this group require a few days to two years of education and training, depending upon the specific kind of work. Basic reading, writing, and math skills are required for jobs in this group. Most workers learn specific tasks and procedures through on-the-job training. As workers gain ex-

perience, they are assigned more difficult tasks and duties. Jobs involving tools and machines require knowledge about the care and use of such equipment.

As you plan your high school program you should include courses related to Material Control. The following list of courses and skills can help you plan your education.

Clerical/Business – courses in data processing, bookkeeping, accounting, stock control, record keeping, and typing.

Mathematics – courses in general math and business math. (A few occupations require advanced math.)

Industrial Arts – courses involving tools and machines may be helpful for some jobs.

This meter reader uses a digital recording device that provides input for a billing computer.

Qualifications Profile

This section is a summary of the worker traits and work factors related to successful job performance and worker satisfaction. Try to relate your interests, abilities, aptitudes, and preferences to these traits and factors. An asterisk (*) marks those traits and factors that are related to more than 60% of the occupations listed at the end of this group. The other traits and factors listed are as important, but relate to fewer occupations. See Appendices B-G for information about all of the worker traits and work factors.

Work Activities

The most important activities related to this group involve:

* 1. Things and objects.
  2. Business contact.
* 3. Tasks of a routine, definite nature.
  9. Processes, methods, or machines.

Work Situations

Workers must be willing to:

  2. Perform routine tasks.
  4. Deal with people.
* 8. Make decisions using standards that can be measured or checked.
*10. Work within precise limits or standards of accuracy.

Working Conditions

These are the physical surroundings in which work is done. In occupations belonging to this group, work is performed:

*I – Inside — workers spend most of their time inside protected from weather conditions but not always from temperature changes.

189

Physical Demands

Workers in this group of occupations must be able to do:

*L – Light work
M – Medium work

Data-People-Things

This chart shows the levels for these three basic elements of work as related to this group. Level means the degree of difficulty of job tasks rather than the amount of time involved. The terms low, average, and high indicate the highest level at which occupations are involved. Compare your interests and abilities with the levels checked.

Difficulty Level of Job Tasks

	Levels		
	Low	Avg.	High
Data	✔	*✔	
People	*✔		
Things	*✔		

Educational Skills

This chart shows the levels of reasoning, math, and language skills related to this group. These skills are usually developed in an educational setting. There are six levels ranging from the simple (1) to the most complex (6).

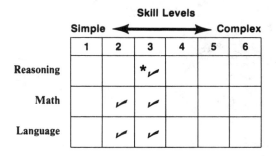

Skill Levels

Simple ⟷ Complex

	1	2	3	4	5	6
Reasoning			*✔			
Math		✔	✔			
Language		✔	✔			

Aptitudes

This chart presents the most important aptitudes related to this group. The levels checked compare aptitudes needed for success in this group to aptitudes of the general working population in all occupations. For example, level 5 is low and represents the bottom 10% of the working population. Level 1 is high and represents the top 10%.

APTITUDE LEVELS COMPARED TO ALL WORKERS						
Related Aptitudes (Ability to Learn)		Lower 1/3		Middle 1/3	Upper 1/3	
		Level **5**	Level **4**	Level **3**	Level **2**	Level **1**
Code	Title	10%	23%	34%	23%	10%
G	General Learning Ability		✔	*✔	✔	
N	Numerical		✔	*✔		
Q	Clerical Perception		✔	*✔	✔	
M	Manual Dexterity		✔	*✔		

Common Occupations

A full listing of all occupations belonging to this group may be found in the Guide for Occupational Exploration.

The following occupations have been selected to represent this group. They provide the major employment opportunities. However, specific job opportunities will vary according to locations of industry, geographical region, and other factors.

Information may be found in common sources of occupational information, state career information systems, and computerized guidance systems.

An (M) follows the occupational title where the military services offer training and experience.

Shipping, Receiving, and Stock Checking

074.387-010	Pharmacy Helper (M)
221.587-030	Tallier
222.137-030	Shipping-And-Receiving Supervisor (M)
222.367-042	Parts Clerk (M)
222.367-062	Tool-Crib Attendant
222.387-026	Inventory Clerk (M)
222.387-030	Linen-Room Attendant
222.387-050	Shipping and Receiving Clerk (M)
222.387-062	Storekeeper (M)
222.487-014	Order Filler

222.587-030	Mailer
222.684-010	Meat Clerk
222.687-030	Shipping Checker
248.367-018	Cargo Agent (M)
299.367-014	Stock Clerk, Self-Service Store (M)
369.687-026	Marker
922.687-058	Laborer, Stores

Estimating, Scheduling, and Record Keeping

221.167-014	Material Coordinator
221.167-018	Production Coordinator
221.367-014	Estimator, Printing
221.367-042	Material Expediter
221.367-062	Sales Correspondent
221.387-014	Complaint Clerk
221.387-022	Estimator, Jewelry
221.387-034	Job Tracer
222.367-038	Magazine Keeper (M)
222.367-050	Prescription Clerk, Lens-And-Frames
222.387-058	Stock Clerk (M)
299.364-010	Drapery And Upholstery Measurer
299.387-010	Drapery And Upholstery Estimator
726.361-010	Electronics Utility Worker

Verifying, Recording, and Marking

209.567-010	Meter Reader
221.584-010	Chart Changer
222.367-010	Cargo Checker
222.387-034	Material Clerk (M)
222.687-018	Receiving Checker
922.687-054	Laboratory-Sample Carrier

Skilled Hand and Machine Work
(Crafts)

Skilled Hand and Machine Work is to construct, process, install, and repair materials, products, or structural parts. Workers use their hands and hand tools skillfully. They are required to have some knowledge of established processes and methods. This group includes the subgroups of:

Structural – Mechanical – Electrical –
  Electronic
Reproduction
Blasting
Painting, Dyeing, and Coating
Food Preparation
Environmental

Structural – Mechanical – Electrical – Electronic is to install, maintain, adjust, and repair products. Workers must use tools and equipment skillfully. They do such construction work as install drywall, insulation, siding, floors, windows, roofs, swimming pools and fences. They may clean stone, brick, and metal exteriors of buildings. Others repair, adjust, and service automobiles, large home appliances, and machines. They install and repair electrical-electronic products such as radios, TVs, and small electrical appliances and hand tools. Workers do a variety of other precise work. This ranges from fitting customers with eyeglass frames and contact lenses to deep-sea or scuba diving in construction work or ship repair work.

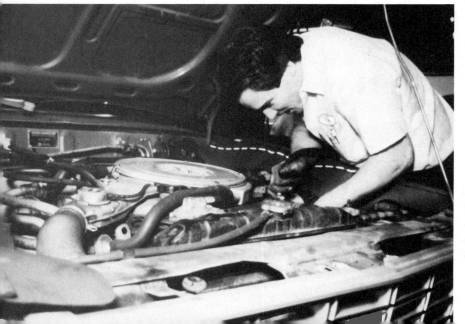

This carburetor mechanic is checking part of the pollution control system.

Reproduction is to operate and control equipment that reproduces sound, materials, or photographic prints and negatives. Some workers decide where to place mikes to record sound. They monitor the audio signals and adjust the tone and volume controls. Other workers operate machines to reproduce typewritten matter, drawings, and graphs or to engrave designs or letters on products. Some workers operate machines that produce photographic prints, videotapes, or motion-picture films. Others operate cameras to film documents.

Blasting is to use explosives to blow up things. Some workers detonate (set off) explosives to loosen earth, rock, stumps, or to demolish structures. Others use them in mines, pits, or quarries to break the material so it can be handled. And, some use explosives to start or renew the flow of oil in wells. These workers inspect the site of the explosion and decide the size, number, and location of charges needed. They connect wires from the charge to the firing device. Then they push the plunger, turn the dial, or press the button to set it off.

Painting, Dyeing, and Coating is to apply paint, varnish, stain, enamel, or lacquer to a surface. Workers use brushes, spray guns, and rollers. They prepare the surface for painting by cleaning and sanding it. They also fill cracks and holes with plaster or putty. They mix and match the colors of paint, varnish, stain, or shellac. They often sand the surface between coats of finish.

Food Preparation is to plan, prepare, and cook food in a private home, hotel, or restaurant. Some workers plan the menus and order the food to prepare. Cooks sometime specialize and prepare only one type of food. They may prepare bread, rolls, muffins, and biscuits. Or, they may prepare only pizza. Some prepare salads and others prepare cold dishes such as sandwiches. Some chefs supervise workers who prepare desserts. Butchers and Meat Cutters also are included in this subgroup. They cut, trim, bone, tie, and grind meats. They also clean and cut fish and poultry.

Environmental is to be concerned with the control of pests. Exterminators spray chemicals or toxic gases and set traps to kill pests that infest buildings and surroundings areas.

Jobs may be found with firms that repair, install, and maintain products. The construction and mining industries also employ these workers. Examples of other employment sites are repair shops, garages, hotels, and wholesale or retail stores. The printing and publishing industry is another example.

An appliance repairer reassembles the oven after adjusting the pilot light.

What Skills and Abilities Would Help You Succeed in This Kind of Work?

The most important skills are listed below. All of those listed do not apply to each occupation. As you explore occupations you should identify the specific ones needed.

Analytical – to identify mechanical and electrical problems and potential solutions.

Spatial Perception – to form a mental image (picture) of how shapes and forms appear in three dimensions height, width, and depth.

Dexterity – to move hands and fingers to use hand tools or operate machines.

Comprehension – to read and understand repair manuals, prescriptions, recipes and other cooking instructions, and equipment operating instructions.

Numerical – to do math accurately, to measure ingredients, or estimate quantities.

Physical Stamina – to lift heavy items such as ladders and pots; withstand heat, cold, and humidity; and stand for long periods of time.

Form Perception – to see slight differences in form or texture of substances.

Accuracy – to follow directions and make measurements exactly.

Do You Have or Can You Develop an Interest in This Kind of Work?

Review the following questions. Your answers can give you clues as to your interest in Skilled Hand and Machine Work.

Have you helped paint your bedroom? Did you select the color? Did you help prepare the walls for the paint?

Have you planned and prepared a meal? Did you order the food? Did you measure and mix ingredients according to recipes?

Have you repaired a lamp, extension cord, or other broken items? Did you locate the defective part? Do you like to work with electrical equipment?

Have you customized or repaired a car or other vehicle? Can you work skillfully with hand tools? Do you like mechanical work?

Have you taken pictures with a camera? Did you develop your own film?

Have you built or put together a complicated model which required assembling parts in a certain manner? Do you like doing tasks that require accuracy?

Have you taken courses in machine shop or woodworking? Do you like this kind of work? How were your grades?

Have you helped build or repair a house or barn? Do you like this kind of work?

Have you assembled a bicycle or tricycle? Did you understand the terms and drawings used in the instructions?

What Else Should You Know About This Group of Occupations?

Workers who repair equipment often work in narrow spaces and uncomfortable positions. They also may be exposed to unpleasant conditions. They often work in dirt, dust, and grease. These workers must keep up with rapidly changing technology in their field.

Working conditions for cooks depend on the size of the restaurant and the kinds of food served. Many kitchens are well-lighted, well-equipped, and properly ventilated. However, heavy lifting, oven and range heat, and long hours of standing and walking are common. Many of these jobs require rotating shift work and some cooks and chefs may be required to work late into the night.

194

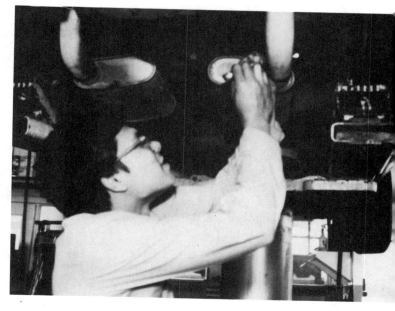

Finishing the installation of a new muffler.

The military services offer training and experience related to some occupations in this group. These occupations are included in the list at the end of this group description. They are identified by an (M) following the occupational title. More information about the military training and experience opportunities may be found in Appendix A.

How Can You Prepare for This Kind of Work?

Most occupations in this group require from three months to four years of education and training. A few jobs require only on-the-job training. Most jobs require training offered at vocational and technical schools in programs lasting up to two years. High schools, private vocational schools, or correspondence schools also offer some training programs. A few companies provide their own extensive training for specific types of repair work.

Many cooks begin as kitchen helpers to get the needed experience and training. High school or post high school training in food preparation is helpful. Training programs are offered by the armed forces, some private schools, and some large hotels and restaurants. A few apprenticeships are available.

As you plan your high school program you should include courses related to Skilled Hand and Machine Work. The following list of programs, courses, and skills can help you plan your education. Many of the programs are occupation specific.

Industrial Arts – courses in this area provide background skills for many occupations. There are introductory experiences in the use of handtools and machines, mechanical drawing, electricity, and metals. Some programs in this area offer in-depth training depending upon the school program and number of courses offered. Examples of these programs are construction and electricity/electronics.

Home Economics – courses in this area provide exploratory experiences, background for more specialized courses, and some in-depth training depending upon the school and the number of courses offered. Food production and management services offer programs in baking, chef/cook, dietetic aide, food catering, food service, food testing, school food service, and foods management.

Vocational and Technical – programs and courses in automotive mechanics, carpentry, electrical and electronics equipment repair, communications electronics, major appliance repair, small appliance repair, vending and recreational machine repair, construction trades (roofing, painting and decorating, drywall installation, glazing, floor covering installation, etc.), slaughtering and butchering, and meat cutting.

Graphics and Printing – programs and courses in graphic and printing communications, commercial photography, photographic laboratory and darkroom, printing press operation, photoengraving, lithography, and platemaking.

Mathematics – courses in general math, shop math, and other mathematics specifically applied to trade or occupations.

Qualifications Profile

This section is a summary of the worker traits and work factors related to successful job performance and worker satisfaction. Try to relate your interests, abilities, aptitudes, and preferences to these traits and factors. An asterisk (*) marks those traits and factors that are related to more than 60% of the occupations listed at the end of this group. The other traits and factors listed are as important, but relate to fewer occupations. See Appendices B-G for information about all of the worker traits and work factors.

Work Situations

Workers must be willing to:

1. Perform duties which change frequently.
2. Perform routine tasks.
7. Make decisions using personal judgment.
* 8. Make decisions using standards that can be measured or checked.
*10. Work within precise limits or standards of accuracy.

This aircraft mechanic works on the hydraulics system.

Work Activities

The most important activities related to this group involve:

* 1. Things and objects.
  3. Tasks of a routine, definite nature.
* 9. Processes, methods, or machines.
  10. Working on or producing things.

Educational Skills

This chart shows the levels of reasoning, math, and language skills related to this group. These skills are usually developed in an educational setting. There are six levels ranging from the simple (1) to the most complex (6).

Skill Levels

	Simple ⟷ Complex					
	1	2	3	4	5	6
Reasoning			*✔	✔		
Math		✔	✔			
Language		✔	✔			

Data-People-Things

This chart shows the levels for these three basic elements of work as related to this group. Level means the degree of difficulty of job tasks rather than the amount of time involved. The terms low, average, and high indicate the highest level at which occupations are involved. Compare your interests and abilities with the levels checked.

Difficulty Level of Job Tasks

	Levels		
	Low	Avg.	High
Data	✔	✔	✔
People	✔		
Things		✔	✔

Physical Demands

Workers in this group of occupations must be able to do:

L – Light work
M – Medium work
H – Heavy work

Working Conditions

These are the physical surroundings in which work is done. In occupations belonging to this group, work is performed:

*I – Inside — workers spend most of their time inside protected from weather conditions but not always from temperature changes.
B – Both inside and outside — workers spend about equal time in each setting.

Aptitudes

This chart presents the most important aptitudes related to this group. The levels checked compare aptitudes needed for success in this group to aptitudes of the general working population in all occupations. For example, level 5 is low and represents the bottom 10% of the working population. Level 1 is high and represents the top 10%.

APTITUDE LEVELS COMPARED TO ALL WORKERS						
Related Aptitudes (Ability to Learn)		Lower 1/3		Middle 1/3	Upper 1/3	
		Level 5	Level 4	Level 3	Level 2	Level 1
Code	Title	10%	23%	34%	23%	10%
G	General Learning Ability			*✔		
S	Spatial		✔	*✔		
P	Form Perception		✔	*✔		
K	Motor Coordination		✔	*✔		
M	Manual Dexterity			*✔	✔	

Common Occupations

A full listing of all occupations belonging to this group may be found in the Guide for Occupational Exploration.

The following occupations have been selected to represent this group. They provide the major employment opportunities. However, specific job opportunities will vary according to locations of industry, geographical region, and other factors.

Information may be found in common sources of occupational information, state career information systems, and computerized guidance systems.

An (M) follows the occupational title where the military services offer training and experience.

Structural-Mechanical-Electrical-Electronic

299.474-010 Optician, Dispensing 2
379.384-010 Scuba Diver (M)
620.281-026 Brake Repairer
620.281-034 Carburetor Mechanic (M)
620.281-038 Front-End Mechanic
620.281-062 Transmission Mechanic
620.381-010 Automobile-Radiator Mechanic (M)
621.381-014 Mechanic, Aircraft Accessories
629.261-010 Laundry-Machine Mechanic
632.261-018 Ordnance Artificer (M)
637.261-018 Gas-Appliance Servicer
638.261-022 Pinsetter Mechanic, Automatic
639.281-014 Coin-Machine-Service Repairer
639.281-018 Sewing-Machine Repairer
639.281-022 Medical-Equipment Repairer
639.681-010 Bicycle Repairer
709.364-014 Towel-Cabinet Repairer
710.381-022 Gas-Meter Mechanic 1

720.281-010   Radio Repairer
720.281-018   Television-And-Radio Repairer (M)
723.381-010   Electrical-Appliance Repairer
723.584-010   Appliance Repairer
729.281-022   Electric-Tool Repairer (M)
739.381-054   Survival-Equipment Repairer (M)
763.684-034   Finish Patcher
789.684-038   Parachute Mender (M)
800.684-010   Riveter
800.684-014   Riveter, Pneumatic
806.464-010   Boat Rigger
806.684-038   Automobile-Accessories Installer
807.664-010   Muffler Installer
816.464-010   Thermal Cutter, Hand 1
821.281-010   Television-Cable Installer
827.464-010   Air-Conditioning Installer, Domestic
827.661-010   Household-Appliance Installer
829.261-014   Dental-Equipment Installer
              And Servicer(M)
842.681-010   Dry-Wall Applicator
860.664-010   Carpenter 1
862.381-010   Aircraft Mechanic, Plumbing
              And Hydraulics (M)
863.364-014   Insulation Worker
863.684-014   Sider
864.381-010   Carpet Layer
864.481-010   Floor Layer
865.381-010   Glazier
865.684-010   Glass Installer
866.381-010   Roofer
869.381-010   House Repairer
869.463-010   Swimming Pool Installer-And-Servicer
869.664-014   Construction Worker 1
869.684-022   Fence Erector
869.684-046   Roustabout
891.684-018   Swimming-Pool Servicer
891.684-022   Building Cleaner
899.261-010   Diver (M)
899.281-014   Maintenance Repairer, Factory Or Mill
899.381-010   Maintenance Repairer, Building
899.484-010   Mobile-Home-Lot Utility Worker
899.684-026   Pipeliner
910.384-010   Tank-Car Inspector (M)
915.467-010   Automobile-Service-Station Attendant
952.364-010   Trouble Shooter 1
959.361-010   Customer Service Representative
962.261-014   Stage Technician
962.362-014   Light Technician

Reproduction

194.262-010   Audio Operator (M)
194.262-018   Sound Mixer (M)
194.362-010   Recording Engineer (M)

651.362-038   Offset-Duplicating-Machine Operator,
              Instant Print
651.682-014   Offset-Duplicating-Machine Operator
704.382-010   Engraver, Pantograph 1
704.682-010   Engraver, Machine 1
960.362-010   Motion-Picture Projectionist
960.382-010   Audiovisual Technician
962.382-010   Recordist (M)
972.282-014   Laser-Beam-Color-Scanner Operator
976.267-010   Quality-Control Technician (M)
976.380-010   Computer-Controlled-Color-Photograph
             -Printer Operator
976.382-014   Color-Printer Operator (M)
976.382-018   Film Developer (M)
976.487-010   Photograph Finisher
976.681-010   Developer (M)
976.682-014   Printer Operator, Black-And-White
976.682-022   Microfilm-Camera Operator
979.682-014   Blueprinting-Machine Operator

Blasting

859.261-010   Blaster (M)
931.261-010   Blaster (M)
931.361-014   Shooter

Painting, Dyeing, and Coating

741.684-026   Painter, Spray 1
840.381-010   Painter
840.381-018   Painter, Shipyard
845.381-014   Painter, Transportation Equipment (M)
864.684-010   Floor And Wall Applier, Liquid

Food Preparation

305.281-010   Cook
313.131-022   Pastry Chef
313.361-022   Cook, Short Order 1
313.361-026   Cook, Specialty
313.381-010   Baker (M)
313.381-014   Baker, Pizza
313.381-026   Cook, Pastry
313.381-030   Cook, School Cafeteria (M)
315.361-010   Cook (M)
315.371-010   Cook, Mess
315.381-018   Cook, Railroad
316.661-010   Carver
316.681-010   Butcher, Meat (M)
316.684-018   Meat Cutter (M)
317.384-010   Salad Maker
317.684-014   Pantry Goods Maker

Environmental

389.684-010   Exterminator

05.11

Equipment Operation

Equipment Operation involves the use of machines to excavate, drill, mine, hoist, dredge, pave, or move materials. Workers control the machines and equipment by using levers, pedals, and wheels. Some workers operate heavy equipment to move, haul, and grade the earth. Others operate machines that lay concrete and asphalt to build highways and parking lots. Still others operate machines that lift, move, stack, and dump materials. Some workers tend equipment to drill wells or undercut coal seams. This group includes the subgroups of:

Construction
Mining and Quarrying
Drilling and Oil Exploration
Materials Handling

Workers in the four subgroups of Equipment Operation perform duties that are very much alike. They differ in the knowledge and skills needed for the type of work they do or the specific equipment they operate. *Construction* workers run machines for excavating, grading, and paving. They also use equipment for building and repairing structures. *Mining and Quarrying* workers extract minerals or process materials at or near a mining site. They may work in an underground mine or at a strip mine.

Workers in *Drilling and Oil Exploration* operate drilling rigs and control hoisting equipment. They drill boreholes for oil or gas wells. *Materials Handling* workers operate cranes, tractors, winches, lift trucks, hoists, and conveyors. They move materials, machines, or products.

This bulldozer operator is intent on the problem at hand.

A long-wall mining machine utilizes a water spray which reduces the possibility of an explosion.

Jobs may be found at mines and construction sites, factories, warehouses, and on docks. Some workers are self-employed. They purchase their own equipment and do contract work.

What Skills and Abilities Would Help You Succeed in This Kind of Work?

The most important skills are listed below. All of those listed do not apply to each occupation. As you explore occupations you should identify the specific ones needed.

Comprehension – to understand and follow instructions on blueprints, sketches, or work orders.

Diligence – to repeat the same tasks day after day.

Dexterity – to move the arms, hands, and feet to use levers, pedals, and other controls.

Physical Stamina – to stand or ride for long periods of time.

Depth Perception – to judge distance and relationships of objects.

Adaptability – to adapt to and tolerate the vibration and noise of heavy equipment.

Do You Have or Can You Develop an Interest in This Kind of Work?

Review the following questions. Your answers can give you clues as to your interest in Equipment Operation.

Have you read mechanical or automotive design magazines? Did you understand the terms and drawings?

Have you driven a van, truck, tractor, or other large motor vehicle? Can you react quickly and safely to sudden dangerous situations?

Have you taken industrial arts classes or had a home workshop where you operated machines? Did you enjoy this type of activity?

Have you had a summer or part-time job in road construction? Did you mind the vibration and noise of heavy equipment? Did you enjoy the work?

Have you visited a mine, quarry, or oil drilling site? Do you like this type of work setting?

Have you watched heavy equipment in operation at a construction site? Do you think you would like to operate such equipment?

Have you taken driver education? Do you like to drive?

201

What Else Should You Know About This Group of Occupations?

Many jobs in this group require union membership. Some unions assign workers to jobs with contractors. Work hours and pay rates depend upon local union scales. Most jobs in this group involve outdoor work. People work in rain, snow, heat, and cold. Work in the construction industry is seasonal in some regions of the country. Workers are subjected to noisy and dusty conditions. They must be alert to keep machines under control. Those who drive equipment on public streets and roads must have state operator licenses.

Some equipment operators are employed for years by a single contractor. Others must seek new employment after each project is completed. Workers who can operate a variety of equipment usually can find jobs more easily.

Some workers with highway construction, oil production, and pipeline crews travel long distances from their homes to work sites. They may live in trailers at the project site.

The military services offer training and experience related to some occupations in this group. These occupations are included in the list at the end of this group description. They are identified by an (M) following the occupational title. More information about the military training and experience opportunities may be found in Appendix A.

How Can You Prepare for This Kind of Work?

Most occupations in this group require three months to one year of education and training. Most operators learn their jobs through apprenticeship programs. These programs teach them to operate and maintain a variety of machines. Some private schools offer short courses in heavy equipment operation. Other workers learn to operate equipment through on-the-job training. Some experienced operators advance to become supervisors.

Some machine operators are promoted from manual labor jobs in the same company. Jobs in Worker Trait Group 05.12, Elemental Work: Mechanical, provide this related work experience. Some of these workers help equipment operators.

As you plan your high school program you should include courses related to Equipment Operation. The following list of courses and skills can help you plan your education.

Industrial Arts – drafting, blueprint reading, metals, and construction.

Equipment Operation – courses in vehicle and equipment operation, mining equipment operation, material handling, truck driving, and construction equipment operation.

Vehicle and Equipment Mechanics – courses in equipment mechanics, gasoline and diesel engine mechanics, and power mechanics. (Some operators maintain their equipment and make small repairs and adjustments.)

A tractor crane operator needs good depth perception and a light touch on sensitive controls.

Qualifications Profile

This section is a summary of the worker traits and work factors related to successful job performance and worker satisfaction. Try to relate your interests, abilities, aptitudes, and preferences to these traits and factors. An asterisk (*) marks those traits and factors that are related to more than 60% of the occupations listed at the end of this group. The other traits and factors listed are as important, but relate to fewer occupations. See Appendices B-G for information about all of the worker traits and work factors.

Work Situations

Workers must be willing to:

* 2. Perform routine tasks.
  8. Make decisions using standards that can be measured or checked.
*10. Work within precise limits or standards of accuracy.

Physical Demands

Workers in this group of occupations must be able to do:

  L – Light work
*M – Medium work

Work Activities

The most important activities related to this group involve:

* 1. Things and objects.
* 3. Tasks of a routine, definite nature.
* 9. Processes, methods, or machines.

Data-People-Things

This chart shows the levels for these three basic elements of work as related to this group. Level means the degree of difficulty of job tasks rather than the amount of time involved. The terms low, average, and high indicate the highest level at which occupations are involved. Compare your interests and abilities with the levels checked.

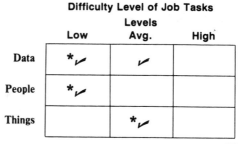

Difficulty Level of Job Tasks

	Levels		
	Low	Avg.	High
Data	*✓	✓	
People	*✓		
Things		*✓	

Working Conditions

These are the physical surroundings in which work is done. In occupations belonging to this group, work is performed:

I – Inside — workers spend most of their time inside protected from weather conditions but not always from temperature changes.

O – Outside — workers spend most of their time outside with little protection from weather conditions.

B – Both inside and outside — workers spend about equal time in each setting.

Aptitudes

This chart presents the most important aptitudes related to this group. The levels checked compare aptitudes needed for success in this group to aptitudes of the general working population in all occupations. For example, level 5 is low and represents the bottom 10% of the working population. Level 1 is high and represents the top 10%.

Educational Skills

This chart shows the levels of reasoning, math, and language skills related to this group. These skills are usually developed in an educational setting. There are six levels ranging from the simple (1) to the most complex (6).

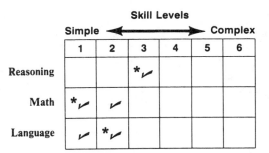

		Skill Levels				
	Simple ⟵⟶ Complex					
	1	2	3	4	5	6
Reasoning			*✓			
Math	*✓	✓				
Language	✓	*✓				

APTITUDE LEVELS COMPARED TO ALL WORKERS						
Related Aptitudes (Ability to Learn)		Lower 1/3		Middle 1/3	Upper 1/3	
		Level 5	Level 4	Level 3	Level 2	Level 1
Code	Title	10%	23%	34%	23%	10%
G	General Learning Ability			*✓		
S	Spatial			*✓		
P	Form Perception		✓	✓		
K	Motor Coordination			*✓		
M	Manual Dexterity			*✓		

Common Occupations

A full listing of all occupations belonging to this group may be found in the Guide for Occupational Exploration.

The following occupations have been selected to represent this group. They provide the major employment opportunities. However, specific job opportunities will vary according to locations of industry, geographical region, and other factors.

Information may be found in common sources of occupational information, state career information systems, and computerized guidance systems.

An (M) follows the occupational title where the military services offer training and experience.

Construction

850.381-010	Miner
850.663-022	Motor-Grader Operator
850.683-010	Bulldozer Operator 1 (M)
850.683-030	Power-Shovel Operator (M)
850.683-038	Scraper Operator (M)
850.683-046	Utility-Tractor Operator (M)
853.663-010	Asphalt-Paving-Machine Operator (M)
853.663-014	Concrete-Paving-Machine Operator (M)
859.682-010	Earth-Boring-Machine Operator (M)
859.682-018	Pile-Driver Operator
859.683-010	Operating Engineer (M)
859.683-030	Road-Roller Operator (M)
869.683-014	Rigger (M)
919.683-022	Street-Sweeper Operator
921.663-054	Tower-Crane Operator
955.463-010	Sanitary Landfill Operator

Mining and Quarrying

921.663-050	Scraper-Loader Operator
930.482-010	Drilling-Machine Operator
930.665-010	Long-Wall-Mining-Machine Tender
930.683-010	Continuous-Mining-Machine Operator
930.683-014	Cutter Operator
930.683-026	Roof Bolter
932.363-010	Hoist Operator
932.683-014	Loading-Machine Operator
932.683-022	Shuttle-Car Operator
939.281-010	Miner 1

Drilling and Oil Exploration

859.362-010	Well-Drill Operator (M)
930.382-018	Prospecting Driller
930.382-022	Rotary Derrick Operator
930.382-026	Rotary Driller
930.382-030	Well Puller

Materials Handling

850.683-018	Dragline Operator
850.683-042	Tower-Excavator Operator
911.663-014	Stevedore 1 (M)
921.260-010	Rigger (M)
921.563-010	Coke Loader
921.663-010	Bridge-Or-Gantry-Crane Operator
921.663-022	Derrick Operator
921.663-030	Hoisting Engineer
921.663-038	Locomotive-Crane Operator
921.663-058	Tractor-Crane Operator (M)
921.663-062	Truck-Crane Operator (M)
921.683-018	Cantilever-Crane Operator
921.683-026	Conveyor Operator
921.683-042	Front-End Loader Operator
921.683-058	Log Loader
921.683-078	Transfer-Car Operator
921.683-082	Winch Driver (M)
929.583-010	Yard Worker
929.683-014	Tractor Operator

Elemental Work: Mechanical

Elemental Work: Mechanical involves the use of physical strength and skills to perform work tasks. These tasks are done with the aid of tools, equipment, and machines. Some workers carry, lift, move, or handle materials. Others tend or operate simple machines or equipment to aid them in their physical work. Workers usually clean and maintain their work areas and equipment, or those of more skilled workers they may help. This group includes the subgroups of:

Services
Materials Movement
Fabrication and Structural Work

Services involve cleaning and maintenance work in homes and business settings. Also in this group is the use of machines to copy, sort, and fold mail and other print materials. Workers use hand tools, power tools, and light machines. Cleaning and maintenance services take care of building interiors. This may be in homes, hotels, restaurants, hospitals, or businesses. Manual work is involved in keeping equipment, work areas, and building interiors clean. Workers also may carry, arrange, and store materials or supplies. In addition to cleaning duties some workers in homes and restaurants help clean and prepare food. Experienced workers supervise others, instruct them in work methods and routines, and inspect their work.

Materials Movement is to extract, process, transport, or store raw materials and products. Workers do manual tasks and help others operate machines and equipment. Some are involved in mining, quarrying, or drilling. They extract raw materials such as coal, ore, and oil from the earth. Many workers are involved in a variety of manual work jobs to transport freight by railroad, water, air, and motor vehicles. Some load and unload the freight by using hoists, hand trucks, and conveyors. Some workers clean and oil the equipment they use.

Hospital cleaner at work in a corridor.

Fabrication and Structural Work is to make, assemble, and repair equipment and products. Workers help the more skilled workers who operate equipment and use tools in their work. Some are involved in mechanical work or machinery repair. Others are involved in welding and forging work. Some do a variety of manual work such as painting, oiling, and other maintenance tasks.

Jobs are found in a variety of nonfactory settings such as mining, transportation (freight), construction, and repair shops. Also included are restaurants and cleaning and maintenance services. Businesses providing photocopying and other general reproduction services are other job sites.

What Skills and Abilities Would Help You Succeed in This Kind of Work?

The most important skills are listed below. All of those listed do not apply to each occupation. As you explore occupations you should identify the specific ones needed.

Strength – to lift, carry, and move materials, tools, and equipment.

Physical Stamina – to do physical tasks as a major part of each day's work.

Physical Movement – to bend, stoop, crouch, climb, and to balance the body.

Dexterity – to use the hands and fingers to use tools, and to tend or operate machines and equipment.

Comprehension – to understand and follow simple instructions.

Diligence – to perform routine work or to repeat the same task over and over again.

Coping – to cope with work that involves unpleasant tasks or working conditions such as bad weather.

This truck driver's helper is ready to lash down the load.

Do You Have or Can You Develop an Interest in This Kind of Work?

Review the following questions. Your answers can give you clues as to your interest in Elemental Mechanical Work.

Have you cleaned a house or garage? Do you like cleaning work? Do you take pride in keeping things clean?

Have you helped move furniture or other heavy objects? Do you have the physical strength to do this easily?

Have you shoveled snow, raked leaves, or mowed lawns? Do you like work that keeps you physically active?

Have you bagged groceries? Do you like work that requires little decision-making?

Do you enjoy physical education, sports, or recreation activities that require physical skills? Can you do them easily?

A suveryor's helper carrying the transit.

What Else Should You Know
About This Group of Occupations?

Weather or other factors such as economic conditions can cause periods of unemployment. Most work involves a 40-hour week. Sometimes overtime work may be needed to complete a job on schedule. Evening or night shift work is required with some jobs.

Many of the jobs in this group are open to beginners or to workers with few job skills. Some workers use their jobs to get experience related to a trade and to learn job skills from skilled workers that they help. Also, satisfactory performance in a job can lead to advancement in machine tending and operating jobs. (See Worker Trait Group 05.11)

Working conditions vary according to th work setting. Many jobs require work ou doors. These workers may be exposed to a kinds of weather. Some jobs involve hazar and workers are often required to wear safe clothing. These work sites involve strict safe precautions and working conditions are i spected routinely.

Worker Trait Group 06.04, Element Work: Industrial, includes similar kinds work but jobs are found in industrial setting

The military services offer training and e perience related to some occupations in th group. These occupations are included in th list at the end of this group description. Th are identified by an (M) following the occup tional title. More information about th military training and experience opportuniti may be found in Appendix A.

How Can You Prepare for This Kind of Work?

Occupations in this group usually require training extending from a short demonstration to three months. Specific work tasks are usually learned on the job with only a brief explanation of job duties. Being able to understand instructions and having the physical ability to perform manual work is important. Training or experience in using basic tools and equipment is helpful. Also, good work attitudes are needed to keep a job. Some of these jobs are obtained through union hiring halls.

As you plan your high school program you should take courses related to mechanical work. You should plan courses leading to graduation from high school since a high school diploma, or its equal, is important to qualify for apprenticeship programs leading to more advanced job skills. This is especially important in the construction industry. The following list of courses and skills can help you plan your education.

General Studies – courses in basic math, communication skills, and other courses leading to a high school diploma.

Practical and Vocational – courses in industrial arts, trade and industrial education, home economics, or other courses where skills in using tools and equipment may be developed along with good job attitudes.

Physical Education – courses that contribute to the development of physical strength, stamina, and body coordination.

Qualifications Profile

This section is a summary of the worker traits and work factors related to successful job performance and worker satisfaction. Try to relate your interests, abilities, aptitudes, and preferences to these traits and factors. An asterisk (*) marks those traits and factors that are related to more than 60% of the occupations listed at the end of this group. The other traits and factors listed are as important, but relate to fewer occupations. See Appendices B-G for information about all of the worker traits and work factors.

Work Situations

Workers must be willing to:

1. Perform duties which change frequently.
* 2. Perform routine tasks.
8. Make decisions using standards that can be measured or checked.
10. Work within precise limits or standards of accuracy.

Work Activities

The most important activities related to this group involve:

* 1. Things and objects.
* 3. Tasks of a routine, definite nature.
  9. Processes, methods, or machines.

Working Conditions

These are the physical surroundings in which work is done. In occupations belonging to this group, work is performed:

I – Inside — workers spend most of their time inside protected from weather conditions but not always from temperature changes.
O – Outside — workers spend most of their time outside with little protection from weather conditions.
B – Both inside and outside — workers spend about equal time in each setting.

Physical Demands

Workers in this group of occupations must be able to do:

L – Light work
M – Medium work
H – Heavy work

Data-People-Things

This chart shows the levels for these three basic elements of work as related to this group. Level means the degree of difficulty of job tasks rather than the amount of time involved. The terms low, average, and high indicate the highest level at which occupations are involved. Compare your interests and abilities with the levels checked.

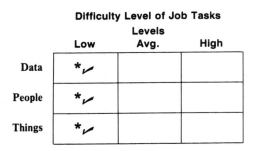

Difficulty Level of Job Tasks

	Low	Avg.	High
Data	* ✓		
People	* ✓		
Things	* ✓		

Educational Skills

This chart shows the levels of reasoning, math, and language skills related to this group. These skills are usually developed in an educational setting. There are six levels ranging from the simple (1) to the most complex (6).

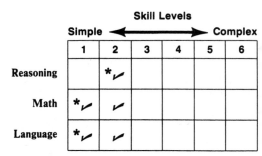

Skill Levels
Simple ⟵⟶ Complex

	1	2	3	4	5	6
Reasoning		* ✓				
Math	* ✓	✓				
Language	* ✓	✓				

Aptitudes

This chart presents the most important aptitudes related to this group. The levels checked compare aptitudes needed for success in this group to aptitudes of the general working population in all occupations. For example, level 5 is low and represents the bottom 10% of the working population. Level 1 is high and represents the top 10%.

		APTITUDE LEVELS COMPARED TO ALL WORKERS				
Related Aptitudes (Ability to Learn)		Lower 1/3		Middle 1/3	Upper 1/3	
Code	Title	Level 5 10%	Level 4 23%	Level 3 34%	Level 2 23%	Level 1 10%
K	Motor Coordination		✔	✔		
M	Manual Dexterity		✔	*✔		

Common Occupations

A full listing of all occupations belonging to this group may be found in the Guide for Occupational Exploration.

The following occupations have been selected to represent this group. They provide the major employment opportunities. However, specific job opportunities will vary according to locations of industry, geographical region, and other factors.

Information may be found in common sources of occupational information, state career information systems, and computerized guidance systems.

An (M) follows the occupational title where the military services offer training and experience.

Services

079.164.010 Supervisor, Central Supply (M)
207.685-010 Braille-Duplicating-Machine Operator
207.685-014 Photocopying-Machine Operator
207.685-018 Photographic-Machine Operator
208.685-030 Sorting-Machine Operator
208.685-034 Wing-Mailer-Machine Operator
301.137-010 Housekeeper, Home
301.474-010 House Worker, General
301.687-010 Caretaker
301.687-014 Day Worker
310.137-018 Steward/Stewardess
313.684-010 Baker Helper
317.687-010 Cook Helper
318.137-010 Kitchen Steward/Stewardess
318.687-010 Kitchen Helper
319.484-010 Food Assembler, Kitchen
321.137-010 Housekeeper
323.687-010 Cleaner, Hospital

This construction worker is helping to set large sewer tile.

323.687-014	Cleaner, Housekeeping
323.687-018	Housecleaner
364.684-014	Shoe Dyer
372.667-022	Flagger
381.687-010	Central-Supply Worker (M)
381.687-014	Cleaner, Commercial Or Institutional
381.687-018	Cleaner, Industrial
381.687-022	Cleaner, Laboratory Equipment
381.687-026	Cleaner, Wall
381.687-034	Waxer, Floor
382.664-010	Janitor
389.683-010	Sweeper-Cleaner, Industrial
389.687-014	Cleaner, Window

Materials Movement

503.687-010	Sandblaster
549.687-018	Laborer, Petroleum Refinery
579.665-014	Laborer, Concrete-Mixing Plant
905.687-010	Truck-Driver Helper
905.687-014	Van-Driver Helper
909.687-010	Garbage Collector
909.687-014	Laborer, General
910.367-010	Brake Coupler, Road Freight
910.664-010	Yard Coupler
910.667-026	Switch Tender
910.682-010	Track Repairer

910.687-010	Baggage Handler
911.131-010	Boatswain (M)
911.137-018	Header
911.364-010	Able Seaman (M)
911.364-014	Boat Loader 1 (M)
911.584-010	Marine Oiler
911.687-030	Ordinary Seaman (M)
912.687-010	Line-Service Attendant
914.687-010	Laborer, Pipe-Lines
914.687-014	Loader Helper
915.684-010	Tire Repairer
915.687-014	Garage Servicer, Industrial
915.687-018	Lubrication Servicer
915.687-022	Porter, Used-Car Lot
921.133-018	Material-Handling Supervisor
921.667-022	Laborer, Hoisting
921.667-026	Wharf Worker
921.683-014	Boom-Conveyor Operator
921.683-038	Elevator Operator, Freight
921.685-014	Bull-Chain Operator
921.685-046	Fruit Distributor
921.686-022	Pond Worker
921.687-014	Choke Setter
921.687-022	Log Loader Helper
922.687-070	Lumber Handler
922.687-090	Stevedore 2 (M)

922.687-102 Yard Laborer
929.687-030 Material Handler (M)
930.666-010 Driller Helper
930.684-026 Rotary-Driller Helper
931.361-010 Sample-Taker Operator
932.667-010 Bottomer 1
939.667-014 Quarry Worker
939.685-014 Washer-And-Crusher Tender
939.686-010 Loading-Machine-Operator Helper
939.687-014 Company Laborer
939.687-018 Laborer
939.687-026 Rock-Dust Sprayer
952.665-010 Laborer, Powerhouse
955.585-010 Wastewater-Treatment-Plant Attendant
955.687-018 Street Cleaner
962.687-022 Grip

Fabrication and Structural Work

610.684-010 Blacksmith Helper
620.684-014 Automobile-Mechanic Helper
623.684-010 Motorboat-Mechanic Helper
623.687-010 Machinist Helper, Outside
637.687-014 Refrigeration-Mechanic Helper
638.684-018 Maintenance-Mechanic Helper

699.687-018 Oiler
709.684-050 Key Cutter
741.687-014 Painter Helper, Spray
750.684-022 Tire Builder
806.687-050 Shipfitter Helper
807.687-010 Automobile-Body-Repairer Helper
809.687-022 Laborer, Shipyard
819.687-014 Welder Helper
822.684-018 Signal Maintainer Helper
829.684-018 Cable Puller
829.684-022 Electrician Helper
829.684-026 Electrician Helper
843.684-014 Undercoater
845.684-014 Painter Helper, Automotive
861.684-018 Tile Setter
862.684-014 Laborer, Construction Or Leak Gang
862.684-022 Pipe-Fitter Helper
869.567-010 Surveyor Helper
869.687-026 Construction Worker 2 (M)
891.684-010 Dock Hand
891.687-022 Tank Cleaner (M)
899.131-010 Labor-Crew Supervisor
899.684-014 Highway-Maintenance Worker
899.687-014 Laborer, Airport Maintenance

06 INDUSTRIAL

People with an industrial interest enjoy work that involves the mass production of products. This type of production uses several workers to produce a product. Each worker performs only part of the process. It is skilled hand and machine work that is highly organized and repetitive. Workers are more involved in the process and work tasks they perform than with the product they produce. This plan of work results in products being made faster, in greater numbers, and for less money. Work usually takes place in a factory setting where safe habits are important.

The Industrial area includes about half of the occupations in the world of work. However, employment in this area is on the decline as the country is moving toward a more service oriented economy.

The Industrial area is divided into two clusters: Production Work and Production Quality.

Production Work

The Production Work cluster includes both skilled and semiskilled workers. Skilled workers use their knowledge of a product and production process to set up and run machines. They make products or process materials according to set standards. The semiskilled workers tend, control, and monitor machines and equipment. They also may use simple hand and power tools to perform some tasks. Their work is routine and very little decision-making is involved.

Production Quality

Production Quality workers inspect products and materials for quality control. They test, weigh, sort, and grade items to make sure standards are being met. These standards can be measured or checked. The standards may be (1) set by engineers who design the product, (2) set by the company that makes it, or (3) those required by law.

The following Worker Trait Groups and Subgroups are related to the Production Work and Production Quality clusters.

Industrial: an interest in working on or producing things in a factory setting.

Production Work

06.01 Production Technology
Machine Set-Up and
Operation
Precision Hand Work
Inspection

06.02 Production Work
Machine Work
Equipment Operation
Manual Work

06.04 Elemental Work: Industrial
Machine Work
Equipment Operation
Manual Work

Production Quality

6.03 Production Control
Inspecting, Testing, and
Repairing
Inspecting, Grading, Sorting,
Weighing, and Recording

Production Technology

Production Technology is the set up and operation of production machines. It involves a knowledge of a complex product or process. Workers in this group do tasks requiring strict attention to standards. Some workers inspect products to make sure they conform exactly to a blueprint or work order. Others do very precise (exact) hand work as they assemble, adjust, or test products. This group includes the subgroups of:

Machine Set-Up and Operation
Precision Hand Work
Inspection

This refinery operator monitors a computer which controls operations.

Machine Set-Up and Operation involves preparing a machine to manufacture a product or one of its parts. Some workers set up machines for others to operate. Other workers set up as well as operate their machines. Workers read blueprints or job orders to get the data to set up the machines. They load, position, level, and align parts. They adjust machines to run smoothly. Some workers repair or replace defective parts. Workers who operate machines watch gauges and signals to detect trouble. They also watch the product as it is being made.

Precision Hand Work is to use the hands or hand tools to do detailed and precise work. Some workers fabricate (make or construct), repair, or assemble instruments, equipment, or small products. Some workers form molds or cores that are used to make metal castings. Others blow glass to shape glassware. Some workers are involved with larger products that require precision hand work. For example, they may assemble and install parts for aircraft and space vehicles.

Inspection is to check or test products against standards. Workers look for defects and make sure the products are of the desired quality. They perform tests, review and interpret the results, and record the inspection data. They mark the defects and suggest corrections. They also write reports on their findings.

Jobs may be found with various industries involved in manufacturing products and processing materials.

This machine set-up operator is making an adjustment on the tool holder.

What Skills and Abilities Would Help You Succeed in This Kind of Work?

The most important skills are listed below. All of those listed do not apply to each occupation. As you explore occupations you should identify the specific ones needed.

Comprehension – to understand and follow blueprints and wiring diagrams.

Dexterity – to use the hands and fingers to do precise hand work.

Accuracy – to do very precise or exact work.

Numerical – to use math skills, to set machines to operate within precise limits or tolerances, or to calibrate (adjust) instruments.

Form Perception – to detect small differences in shape, size, and texture.

Do You Have or Can You Develop an Interest in This Kind of Work?

Review the following questions. Your answers can give you clues as to your interest in Production Technology.

Have you helped to construct stage sets for school or community plays? Did you like measuring, making, and putting parts together? Did they fit as you expected?

Have you had a summer or part-time job where mechanical equipment was used? Did you enjoy working in this type of setting?

Have you taken a course in mechanical drawing? Can you read blueprints?

Have you assembled a bicycle, model, or toy by following drawings or written instructions? Was it easy for you to do?

Have you belonged to Junior Achievement or been involved in doing production work as a class project?

Have you taken a machine shop course? Can you use micrometers, gauges, and other measuring devices?

Have you operated a sewing machine? Did you have any difficulty?

Have you repaired or modified a car or motorcycle? Do you like working with hand tools and machines?

Can you follow directions very precisely? Have you followed a recipe to bake or cook something? How did it turn out?

Have you taken an industrial arts course? Are you interested in this type of work?

Can you use your fingers for fine detail work? Can you thread a needle easily?

What Else Should You Know About This Group of Occupations?

Workers in this group are exposed to different types of factory conditions. Working around machinery may be noisy and can be hazardous. Safe work habits are important.

Work may require overtime or night and evening shifts. Some workers receive hourly wages and others are paid according to the number of pieces they produce. Job promotions within a plant are often based on seniority as well as skill.

The military services offer training and experience related to some occupations in this group. These occupations are included in the list at the end of this group description. They are identified by an (M) following the occupational title. More information about the military training and experience opportunities may be found in Appendix A.

This man operates a programmable paper cutter.

How Can You Prepare
for This Kind of Work?

Most occupations in this group require one to four years of education and training, depending upon the specific kind of work. There are many ways to enter this field. One way is through an apprenticeship program. Another method of entry is through supervised on-the-job experience. Many workers start as helpers or machine hands. These workers may be promoted after they increase their knowledge and skill through experience.

As you plan your high school program you should include courses related to Production Technology. The following list of courses and skills can help you plan your education.

Precision Work – courses in precision metal and foundry work; machine tool operation/machine shop; metal fabrication and patternmaking; sheet metal; tool and die making; welding; jewelry design, fabrication, and repair; plastics; and optical goods work.

Industrial Arts – courses in manufacturing/materials processing, mechanical drawing, and blueprint reading. Skills in machine operation and tools can be helpful.

Mathematics – courses in general mathematics, shop math, algebra, and geometry. Many jobs now utilize advanced mathematics.

Qualifications Profile

This section is a summary of the worker traits and work factors related to successful job performance and worker satisfaction. Try to relate your interests, abilities, aptitudes, and preferences to these traits and factors. An asterisk (*) marks those traits and factors that are related to more than 60% of the occupations listed at the end of this group. The other traits and factors listed are as important, but relate to fewer occupations. See Appendices B-G for information about all of the worker traits and work factors.

Work Situations

Workers must be willing to:

1. Perform duties which change frequently.
3. Plan and direct an entire activity.
4. Deal with people.
* 8. Make decisions using standards that can be measured or checked.
*10. Work within precise limits or standards of accuracy.

A solderer assembles links to make a gold chain.

Work Activities

The most important activities related to this group involve:

* * 1. Things and objects.
*   2. Business contact.
*   5. Recognition or appreciation from others.
* * 9. Processes, methods, or machines.
* 10. Working on or producing things.

Educational Skills

This chart shows the levels of reasoning, math, and language skills related to this group. These skills are usually developed in an educational setting. There are six levels ranging from the simple (1) to the most complex (6).

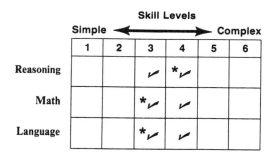

	Skill Levels					
	Simple ⟷ Complex					
	1	2	3	4	5	6
Reasoning			✔	*✔		
Math			*✔	✔		
Language			*✔	✔		

Data-People-Things

This chart shows the levels for these three basic elements of work as related to this group. Level means the degree of difficulty of job tasks rather than the amount of time involved. The terms low, average, and high indicate the highest level at which occupations are involved. Compare your interests and abilities with the levels checked.

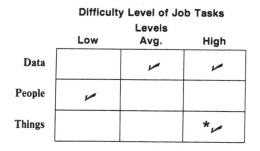

Difficulty Level of Job Tasks

	Levels		
	Low	Avg.	High
Data		✔	✔
People	✔		
Things			*✔

Physical Demands

Workers in this group of occupations must be able to do:

L – Light work
M – Medium work

Aptitudes

This chart presents the most important aptitudes related to this group. The levels checked compare aptitudes needed for success in this group to aptitudes of the general working population in all occupations. For example, level 5 is low and represents the bottom 10% of the working population. Level 1 is high and represents the top 10%.

Working Conditions

These are the physical surroundings in which work is done. In occupations belonging to this group, work is performed:

*I – Inside — workers spend most of their time inside protected from weather conditions but not always from temperature changes.

APTITUDE LEVELS COMPARED TO ALL WORKERS							
Related Aptitudes (Ability to Learn)		Lower 1/3		Middle 1/3	Upper 1/3		
		Level **5**	Level **4**	Level **3**	Level **2**	Level **1**	
Code	Title	10%	23%	34%	23%	10%	
G	General Learning Ability			*✓	✓		
N	Numerical		✓	*✓			
S	Spatial			*✓	✓		
P	Form Perception			*✓	✓		
K	Motor Coordination		✓	*✓			
F	Finger Dexterity		✓	*✓			
M	Manual Dexterity			*✓			

This assembler is working in an aircraft factory.

Common Occupations

A full listing of all occupations belonging to this group may be found in the Guide for Occupational Exploration.

The following occupations have been selected to represent this group. They provide the major employment opportunities. However, specific job opportunities will vary according to locations of industry, geographical region, and other factors.

Information may be found in common sources of occupational information, state career information systems, and computerized guidance systems.

An (M) follows the occupational title where the military services offer training and experience.

Machine Set-Up and Operation

549.260-010 Refinery Operator
559.382-018 Chemical Operator 3
600.380-014 Job Setter
600.380-018 Machine Set-Up Operator (M)
603.240-010 Grinder Set-Up Operator, Thread Tool
603.280-010 Grinder Operator, External, Tool
603.280-018 Grinder Operator, Tool
603.280-022 Grinder Set-Up Opertor, Internal 1
603.280-026 Grinder Set-Up Operator, Jig
603.280-038 Tool-Grinder Operator
604.280-022 Turret-Lathe Set-Up Operator, Tool
604.360-010 Setter, Automatic-Spinning Lathe
604.362-010 Lathe Operator, Numerical Control
604.380-010 Chucking-Machine Set-Up Operator
604.380-018 Engine-Lathe Set-Up Operator
604.380-022 Screw-Machine Set-Up Operator, Production
604.380-026 Turret-Lathe Set-Up Operator

605.360-010 Router Set-Up Operator,
                    Numerical Control
605.380-010 Milling-Machine Operator,
                    Numerical Control
606.280-014 Boring-Mill Set-Up Operator, Horizontal
606.380-014 Drill-Press Set-Up Operator, Radial
612.360-010 Die Setter
612.462-010 Multi-Operation-Machine Operator
613.462-018 Rolling-Mill Operator
616.260-014 Multi-Operation-Forming-Machine Setter
616.360-018 Machine Operator 1
616.380-014 Job Setter
616.460-010 Nail-Making-Machine Setter
651.380-010 Printer 2 (M)
669.280-010 Machine Setter
683.260-018 Loom Fixer
689.260-010 Machine Fixer
689.280-014 Knitting-Machine Fixer
689.360-010 Needle-Loom Setter
690.680-010 Rubber-Goods Cutter-Finisher
976.360-010 Print Controller (M)

Precision Hand Work

518.361-010 Molder
518.381-014 Coremaker
700.381-010 Chain Maker, Hand
700.381-050 Solderer
710.381-042 Instrument Mechanic (M)
710.681-014 Calibrator 1 (M)
711.381-010 Optical-Instrument Assembler
715.381-094 Watch Assembler
716.681-018 Lens Polisher, Hand

722.381-010 Assembler
735.381-010 Bench Hand
770.381-030 Jewel-Bearing Maker
772.681-010 Glass Blower
806.381-014 Aircraft Mechanic, Heat And Vent (M)
806.381-026 Assembler, Aircraft, Structures
                    And Surfaces
806.381-054 Skin Fitter (M)
820.381-014 Transformer Assembler

Inspection

529.281-010 Taster
601.281-018 Inspector, Gage And Instrument
612.261-010 Inspector
619.261-010 Inspector, Metal Fabricating
621.261-014 Engine Tester (M)
621.281-010 Air-Conditioning Check-Out Mechanic (M)
709.261-010 Inspector, Aircraft Accessories
710.381-014 Balancer, Scale
710.381-038 Inspector, Mechanical And Electrical
711.281-010 Inspector, Optical Instrument (M)
721.281-030 Tester, Motors And Controls
721.361-010 Inspector, Motors And Generators
726.130-010 Supervisor, Electronics (M)
726.281-014 Electronics Tester 1 (M)
736.381-018 Process Inspector
806.261-010 Internal-Combustion-Engine Inspector (M)
806.281-022 Inspector, Assemblies And Installations
806.281-030 Inspector, Missile (M)
806.281-054 Tester, Plumbing Systems (M)
806.361-022 Inspector, Fabrication
819.281-018 Weld Inspector 1 (M)

06.02

Production Work

Production Work is to manufacture goods with hand tools or machines. Workers in this group make or repair products or process materials. They also perform a general inspection of products. Some may need a great deal of knowledge about the products or materials they work with. Workers in this group are highly skilled and develop their skills through training and experience. This type of work takes place in a factory setting. This group includes the subgroups of:

Machine Work
Equipment Operation
Manual Work

Machine Work is to set-up, operate, or tend various production machines. Workers use such materials as metal, wood, and paper to produce products. Others work with textile and leather products. They work from blueprints or written instructions. Some workers tend one or more machines.

Equipment Operation involves the use of equipment and machines to prepare basic materials for the manufacturing process. Workers process such materials as metals, chemicals, petroleum, glass, food, textiles, clay, and coke. Workers may control furnaces to heat and pour metals. Some weld, braze, and solder. Others are involved in coating or plating materials. Still others operate equipment to clean clothes or carpets. Some workers assemble wood products, parts for aircraft, and appliances.

Manual Work is the use of the hands or physical skills to produce or process materials. Workers may use hand and power tools. Some workers assemble products or product parts. Some prepare or process materials to be used in making products. This may be to layout, mark, and cut materials for assembly by other workers. Jobs in this group are considered routine. Workers are not required to make many decisions.

Jobs may be found with manufacturing and processing plants.

Drilling a hole with one of a bank of drill presses.

224

This woman is inspecting the output of a box printing machine.

What Skills and Abilities Would Help You Succeed in This Kind of Work?

The most important skills are listed below. All of those listed do not apply to each occupation. As you explore occupations you should identify the specific ones needed.

Dexterity – to use hands and fingers to adjust machine controls.

Form Perception – to detect differences in shape, size, and texture.

Numerical – to use arithmetic correctly for measuring, computing, or record keeping.

Accuracy – to follow instructions to meet standards for product or materials quality.

Physical Stamina – to be able to stand, reach, and bend for long periods of time.

Do You Have or Can You Develop an Interest in This Kind of Work?

Review the following questions. Your answers can give you clues as to your interest in Production Work.

Have you taken industrial arts or machine shop courses? Did you like operating machines?

Have you built a model airplane, car, or bridge? Did you follow written instructions or drawings? Was it fairly easy for you to do?

Have you assembled jigsaw puzzles? Do you have problems matching shapes and forms or colors?

Have you repaired a radio, TV, or amplifier? Do you like to work with small tools? Have you built such items, using a commercial kit?

Have you made belts, billfolds, or other leather items? Could you use the tools easily? Were you accurate in cutting the leather?

Have you taken courses in math or applied math courses? Did you like these classes? Do you like projects that use math skills?

Have you worked with others to build or assemble something? Did it bother you to not be able to control the quality of all the work?

What Else Should You Know About This Group of Occupations?

A related Worker Trait Group is 06.04, Elemental Work: Industrial. The work is similar but requires only semiskilled workers.

Good safety habits are important to people in these jobs. Although modern equipment and safety programs have reduced the number of accidents, workers can still be exposed to unpleasant conditions such as a high noise level.

Tasks in these jobs change little from day to day because workers must follow set procedures. Their jobs can be tedious and boring. They may be required to stand for long periods of time and do a large amount of reaching and bending. Evening or overtime work may be required for some jobs.

The military services offer training and experience related to some occupations in this group. These occupations are included in the list at the end of this group description. The are identified by an (M) following the occupational title. More information about the military training and experience opportunities may be found in Appendix A.

How Can You Prepare For This Kind of Work?

Most occupations in this group require three months to two years of education and training depending upon the specific kind of work. A few jobs require four or more years. The common method of preparation is through on-the-job training. Apprenticeship programs are available for some jobs. Many workers start as helpers and work up to more responsible jobs as they gain experience and seniority. Machine shop or other similar vocational courses provide good background for jobs in this group.

As you plan your high school program you should include courses related to Production Work. The following list of courses and skills will help you plan your education.

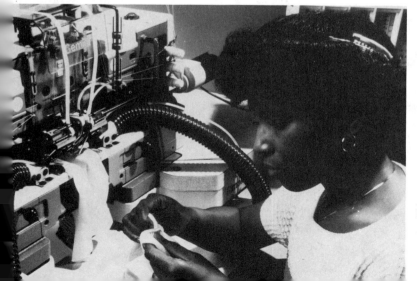

A sewing machine operator inspects a hem.

Mathematics – courses in shop math, algebra, geometry, and math computation.

Industrial Arts – courses involving use of hand and power tools and machines. Working with wood, metal, and other materials is also helpful.

Home Economics – courses in textiles, cooking, sewing, and food services can provide related experiences.

Precision Work – courses in food production, meatcutting, metal work, foundry work, machine shop, metal fabrication, patternmaking, industrial ceramics, plastics, woodworking, furniture making, and upholstering.

Qualifications Profile

This section is a summary of the worker traits and work factors related to successful job performance and worker satisfaction. Try to relate your interests, abilities, aptitudes, and preferences to these traits and factors. An asterisk (*) marks those traits and factors that are related to more than 60% of the occupations listed at the end of this group. The other traits and factors listed are as important, but relate to fewer occupations. See Appendices B-G for information about all of the worker traits and work factors.

Work Activities

The most important activities related to this group involve:

* 1. Things and objects.
  3. Tasks of a routine, definite nature.
* 9. Processes, methods, or machines.

Work Situations

Workers must be willing to:

  2. Perform routine tasks.
* 8. Make decisions using standards that can be measured or checked.
*10. Work within precise limits or standards of accuracy.

Working Conditions

These are the physical surroundings in which work is done. In occupations belonging to this group, work is performed:

*I – Inside — workers spend most of their time inside protected from weather conditions but not always from temperature changes.

Physical Demands

Workers in this group of occupations must be able to do:

L – Light work
M – Medium work

Educational Skills

This chart shows the levels of reasoning, math, and language skills related to this group. These skills are usually developed in an educational setting. There are six levels ranging from the simple (1) to the most complex (6).

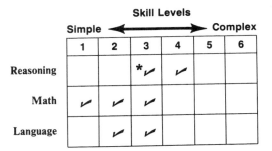

	Skill Levels					
	Simple ←			→ Complex		
	1	2	3	4	5	6
Reasoning			*✔	✔		
Math	✔	✔	✔			
Language		✔	✔			

Data-People-Things

This chart shows the levels for these three basic elements of work as related to this group. Level means the degree of difficulty of job tasks rather than the amount of time involved. The terms low, average, and high indicate the highest level at which occupations are involved. Compare your interests and abilities with the levels checked.

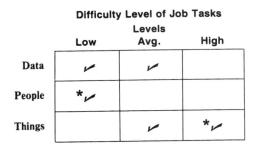

Difficulty Level of Job Tasks

	Levels		
	Low	Avg.	High
Data	✔	✔	
People	*✔		
Things		✔	*✔

A pharmaceutical operator watches a pill-making machine.

Aptitudes

This chart presents the most important aptitudes related to this group. The levels checked compare aptitudes needed for success in this group to aptitudes of the general working population in all occupations. For example, level 5 is low and represents the bottom 10% of the working population. Level 1 is high and represents the top 10%.

APTITUDE LEVELS COMPARED TO ALL WORKERS							
Related Aptitudes (Ability to Learn)		Lower 1/3		Middle 1/3	Upper 1/3		
		Level 5	Level 4	Level 3	Level 2	Level 1	
Code	Title	10%	23%	34%	23%	10%	
G	General Learning Ability			* ✔			
P	Form Perception		✔	* ✔			
K	Motor Coordination		✔	* ✔			
F	Finger Dexterity		✔	✔			
M	Manual Dexterity			* ✔			

Common Occupations

A full listing of all occupations belonging to this group may be found in the Guide for Occupational Exploration.

The following occupations have been selected to represent this group. They provide the major employment opportunities. However, specific job opportunities will vary according to locations of industry, geographical region, and other factors.

Information may be found in common sources of occupational information, state career information systems, and computerized guidance systems.

An (M) follows the occupational title where the military services offer training and experience.

Machine Work

208.582-014	Embossing-Machine Operator 1
222.137-018	Magazine Supervisor (M)
515.382-010	Grinding-Mill Operator
575.682-018	Press Operator
575.685-038	Forming-Machine Tender
602.382-022	Gear-Milling-Machine Set-Up Operator
603.382-010	Buffing-Machine Operator
603.382-018	Honing-Machine Set-Up Operator
603.482-022	Grinder Set-Up Operator, Surface
603.682-026	Polishing-Machine Operator
603.685-062	Grinder Operator, Production
605.280-014	Profiling-Machine Set-Up Operator 1
605.282-018	Planer-Type-Milling-Machine Set-Up Operator
606.362-010	Drill-Press Operator, Numerical Control
606.382-014	Jig-Boring Machine Operator, Numerical Control
606.682-014	Drill-Press Operator

606.682-022 Tapper Operator
606.685-030 Drilling-Machine Operator, Automatic
607.382-010 Contour-Band-Saw Operator, Vertical
609.662-010 Numerical-Control-Machine Operator
610.462-010 Drop-Hammer Operator
611.482-010 Forging-Press Operator 1
612.361-010 Heavy Forger
613.382-014 Finisher
613.482-010 Mill Operator, Rolls
614.382-014 Wire Drawer
614.482-014 Extruder Operator
614.682-014 Fancy-Wire Drawer
615.482-010 Angle Shear Operator
615.482-014 Duplicator-Punch Operator
615.482-018 Ironworker-Machine Operator
615.482-026 Punch-Press Operator, Automatic
615.482-034 Shear Operator 1
616.682-034 Stranding-Machine Operator
617.260-010 Press Operator, Heavy Duty
619.682-022 Heater
640.682-018 Cutting-Machine Operator
649.685-046 Folding-Machine Operator
649.685-070 Machine Operator, General
652.382-010 Cloth Printer
652.662-014 Wallpaper Printer 1
652.682-010 Box Printer
652.682-022 Stamper, Machine
653.662-010 Saddle-Stitching-Machine Operator
659.682-026 Sign Writer, Machine
665.382-018 Wood-Carving-Machine Operator
665.482-018 Timber-Sizer Operator
665.682-026 Profile-Shaper Operator, Automatic
667.662-010 Head Sawyer
667.682-022 Cut-Off-Saw Operator
667.682-030 Gang Sawyer
667.682-054 Radial-Arm-Saw Operator
667.682-062 Rip-And-Groove-Machine Operator
667.682-066 Ripsaw Operator
669.682-058 Nailing-Machine Operator
673.382-018 Stone Polisher, Machine
674.382-010 Glass-Lathe Operator
677.682-022 Stonecutter, Machine
683.662-010 Jacquard-Loom Weaver
683.665-010 Weaver, Needle Loom
683.682-010 Carpet Weaver
683.682-018 Drawing-In-Machine Tender
683.682-030 Plush Weaver
683.682-034 Weaver
683.682-038 Weaver
689.682-010 Looper

690.662-014 Tuber-Machine Operator
690.682-086 Trimmer, Machine 2
699.482-010 Riveting-Machine Operator 1
699.682-014 Cutter
699.682-018 Cutter Operator
699.682-022 Die Cutter
716.382-018 Precision-Lens Grinder
716.462-010 Precision-Lens Centerer And Edger
770.382-010 Lathe Operator
774.382-010 Pottery-Machine Operator
780.682-018 Upholstery Sewer
783.682-014 Sewing-Machine Operator
786.682-170 Lockstitch-Machine Operator
787.682-010 Binder
787.682-022 Embroidery-Machine Operator
787.682-030 Mender (M)
787.682-046 Sewing-Machine Operator
787.682-066 Sewing-Machine Operator
787.682-078 Shirring-Machine Operator

Equipment Operation
362.382-014 Dry Cleaner
500.362-014 Plater, Barrel
500.380-010 Plater
500.682-010 Anodizer
502.482-010 Caster
502.482-018 Rotor Casting-Machine Operator
504.682-010 Annealer
504.682-022 Heat-Treating Bluer
512.362-014 Furnace Operator
512.362-018 Furnace Operator
512.483-010 Furnace Charger
514.662-010 Casting Operator
520.582-010 Dough Mixer
520.685-186 Press Tender
521.662-010 Miller, Wet Process
521.682-022 Flake Miller, Wheat And Oats
521.682-026 Grinder Operator
521.682-038 Shrimp-Peeling-Machine Operator
522.382-014 Fermentation Operator
522.382-026 Still Operator
523.382-010 Gunner
523.682-014 Coffee Roaster
526.381-010 Baker
526.382-014 Confectionery Cooker
526.682-022 Doughnut-Machine Operator
526.682-030 Oven Operator, Automatic
529.362-010 Buttermaker
529.382-018 Dairy-Processing-Equipment Operator
530.382-010 Pulp-Refiner Operator

532.362-010 Digester Operator
533.362-010 Bleacher, Pulp
534.662-010 Back Tender, Paper Machine
539.362-010 Cylinder-Machine Operator
539.362-014 Fourdrinier-Machine Tender
540.462-010 Blender
541.382-010 Coal Washer
542.362-010 Heater
546.382-010 Control-Panel Operator
549.360-010 Pumper
549.382-010 Natural-Gas-Treating-Unit Operator
550.382-022 Mixing-Machine Operator
550.485-010 Chemical Mixer
552.362-014 Oxygen-Plant Operator (M)
554.362-010 Calender Operator
554.682-018 Roll Operator
556.382-010 Compressor
556.382-014 Injection-Molding-Machine Operator
556.682-014 Compression-Molding-Machine Operator
557.382-010 Extruder Operator
558.382-014 Burner Operator
558.482-010 Furnace Operator
559.382-042 Pharmaceutical Operator
559.682-066 Utility Operator 1
569.682-014 Press Operator, Hardboard
570.382-010 Mill Operator
573.362-010 Dry-Kiln Operator
573.382-010 Rotary-Kiln Operator
573.662-010 Firer, Kiln
575.382-010 Brick-And-Tile-Making-Machine Operator
575.382-014 Forming-Machine Operator
575.662-010 Dry-Press Operator
582.482-018 Tanning-Drum Operator
582.582-010 Dye-Range Operator, Cloth
590.682-014 Impregnator
599.382-010 Paint-Sprayer Operator, Automatic
613.362-010 Heater
613.362-014 Roller, Primary Mill
613.462-010 Cold-Mill Operator
613.462-014 Furnace Operator
641.682-014 Gluing-Machine Operator, Automatic
689.687-066 Rug Cleaner
810.382-010 Welding-Machine Operator, Arc
811.482-010 Welding-Machine Operator, Gas
815.682-010 Laser-Beam-Machine Operator
819.685-010 Welding-Machine Tender
939.362-014 Panelboard Operator

Manual Work

362.381-010 Spotter
363.684-010 Blocker

369.384-014 Rug Cleaner, Hand
502.381-010 Caster
502.664-014 Steel Pourer
519.684-010 Ladle Liner
520.384-010 Bench Hand
525.381-014 Butcher, All-Round
529.361-014 Candy Maker
575.461-010 Concrete-Stone Fabricator
624.381-010 Assembly Repairer
685.680-010 Threader
705.684-070 Polisher, Sand
706.681-010 Precision Assembler, Bench
706.684-070 Lock Assembler
706.684-098 Valve Grinder
709.684-090 Tube Bender, Hand 1
721.484-010 Electric-Motor Winder (M)
724.684-018 Armature Winder, Repair (M)
725.684-022 Tube Assembler, Cathode Ray
726.684-018 Electronics Assembler
726.684-034 Assembler, Semiconductor
730.381-022 Electric-Organ Assembler And Checker
730.684-010 Assembler, Musical Instruments
735.681-010 Bracelet And Brooch Maker
750.384-010 Tire Builder, Automobile
762.684-014 Assembler, Component
763.684-038 Furniture Assembler
771.384-010 Coper, Hand
772.687-010 Glass-Worker, Pressed Or Blown
774.684-014 Dipper
775.684-022 Glass Cutter
777.381-034 Plaster Molder 1
780.681-010 Upholsterer, Inside
780.684-034 Chair Upholsterer
781.384-010 Cutter, Fabrics And Materials
781.684-014 Cutter, Machine 1
782.684-042 Mender
783.684-010 Assembler, Leather Goods 1
788.381-010 Cobbler
806.361-014 Assembler-Installer, General
806.381-022 Assembler, Aircraft Power Plant
806.481-014 Assembler, Internal Combustion Engine
809.381-010 Fabricator-Assembler, Metal Products
825.381-010 Aircraft Mechanic, Electrical And Radio
827.684-010 Appliance Assembler, Line
865.684-018 Glazier, Metal Furniture
865.684-022 Refrigerator Glazier
869.684-026 Installer
979.684-030 Screen Printer

06.03

Production Control
(Quality Control)

Production Control is inspecting products and materials to see that product standards are being met. Some standards are set by law. They provide for the safety and protect the health of users. Quality standards may be set to make a better product than produced by competitors and to get a higher price. Standards may state the maximum number of products that may be produced with flaws. Those products with flaws need to be repaired, sold at a lower cost as "seconds," or scrapped (not sold). Standards may be set by engineers that design the product or process. These standards describe what needs to be done to make the product or material work.

Workers usually inspect each product. They measure or check such things as color, size, fit, and weight. They compare it to a set standard. Inspection may occur as part of the production process or as the product is being packaged. This group includes the subgroups of:

Inspecting, Testing, and Repairing
Inspecting, Grading, Sorting,
    Weighing, and Recording

Inspecting refrigerator compressors.

Inspecting, Testing, and Repairing is a level of inspecting where workers compile (record) and analyze (determine the meaning of) data. These data are used to make production quality decisions. Correcting a problem might mean only a simple adjustment on a machine or in the process. It could involve more complex decisions made by others. These might be a redesign of the product or process, or more training for the workers involved. Some workers make adjustments or repairs on the products they inspect.

Inspecting, Grading, Sorting, Weighing, and Recording is a level of inspecting where workers compare (look at differences between) products and standards. They sort out products with defects. They also grade (sort) products by size, color, weight, or quality standards.

Jobs may be found in factories and other large plants that process materials or manufacture products.

What Skills and Abilities Would Help You Succeed in This Kind of Work?

The most important skills are listed below. All of those listed do not apply to each occupation. As you explore occupations you should identify the specific ones needed.

Diligence – to repeat the same tasks over and over according to set procedures.

Dexterity – to use the hands and fingers to handle gauges, measuring tools, and products.

Numerical – to use math skills to count, measure, or keep inspection records.

Decisiveness – to make decisions based on standards that can be measured or checked.

Analysis – to examine defects or flaws and determine what caused them.

Form Perception – to see slight differences in form or texture of substances being tested.

Do You Have or Can You Develop an Interest in This Kind of Work?

Review the following questions. Your answers can give you clues as to your interest in Production Control.

Have you sorted paper, metal, or glass for recycling? Were you able to tell the difference between similar types of materials?

Have you had general or applied mathematics courses? Do you like to keep tallies or other simple records?

Have you taken a machine shop course? Can you use micrometers, gauges, and other measuring devices?

Have you taken a course in drafting? Can you read blueprints?

Have you repaired a car or motorcycle? Do you like working with hand tools and machines?

Have you taken an industrial arts course? Are you interested in this type of work?

Do you notice things that appear to be different? Do you spot pictures that are not hanging straight?

What Else Should You Know About This Group of Occupations?

Although jobs in this group may not require working near machines, workers are exposed to different types of factory conditions. Therefore, safe work habits are very important. A few jobs in this group require overtime and night shift work.

Many of these jobs are open to persons without training. Job promotions within a plant are often based on seniority as well as skill.

The military services offer training and experience related to some occupations in this group. These occupations are included in the list at the end of this group description. They are identified by an (M) following the occupational title. More information about the military training and experience opportunities may be found in Appendix A.

Inspecting printed circuit boards.

Final inspection of the interior finish of an automobile.

How Can You Prepare for This Kind of Work?

Occupations in this group require thirty days to one year of education and training depending upon the specific kind of work. Some jobs can be learned in a few days or with a short demonstration. The common way to start is through on-the-job training. Many workers start as helpers and work up to more responsible jobs as they gain experience and seniority.

As you plan your high school program you should select courses leading toward graduation. Next, you should include courses related to Production Control. The following list of courses and skills can help you plan your education.

Industrial Arts – courses involving operating machines and equipment and using hand and power tools.

General Studies – basic skills in math and communications can be helpful.

Qualifications Profile

This section is a summary of the worker traits and work factors related to successful job performance and worker satisfaction. Try to relate your interests, abilities, aptitudes, and preferences to these traits and factors. An asterisk (*) marks those traits and factors that are related to more than 60% of the occupations listed at the end of this group. The other traits and factors listed are as important, but relate to fewer occupations. See Appendices B-G for information about all of the worker traits and work factors.

Work Activities

The most important activities related to this group involve:

* 1. Things and objects.
* 3. Tasks of a routine, definite nature.
* 9. Processes, methods, or machines.

Work Situations

Workers must be willing to:

  2. Perform routine tasks.
  7. Make decisions using personal judgment.
* 8. Make decisions using standards that can be measured or checked.
*10. Work within precise limits or standards of accuracy.

Working Conditions

These are the physical surroundings in which work is done. In occupations belonging to this group, work is performed:

*I – Inside — workers spend most of their time inside protected from weather conditions but not always from temperature changes.

Educational Skills

This chart shows the levels of reasoning, math, and language skills related to this group. These skills are usually developed in an educational setting. There are six levels ranging from the simple (1) to the most complex (6).

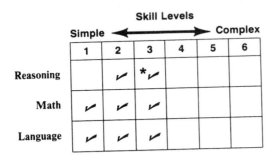

Skill Levels

Simple ←——————→ Complex

	1	2	3	4	5	6
Reasoning		✔	* ✔			
Math	✔	✔	✔			
Language	✔	✔	✔			

Aptitudes

This chart presents the most important aptitudes related to this group. The levels checked compare aptitudes needed for success in this group to aptitudes of the general working population in all occupations. For example, level 5 is low and represents the bottom 10% of the working population. Level 1 is high and represents the top 10%.

Data-People-Things

This chart shows the levels for these three basic elements of work as related to this group. Level means the degree of difficulty of job tasks rather than the amount of time involved. The terms low, average, and high indicate the highest level at which occupations are involved. Compare your interests and abilities with the levels checked.

Difficulty Level of Job Tasks

Levels

	Low	Avg.	High
Data	* ✔	✔	
People	* ✔		
Things	* ✔	✔	

Physical Demands

Workers in this group of occupations must be able to do:

*L – Light work

APTITUDE LEVELS COMPARED TO ALL WORKERS						
Related Aptitudes **(Ability to Learn)**		Lower 1/3		Middle 1/3	Upper 1/3	
		Level **5**	Level **4**	Level **3**	Level **2**	Level **1**
		10%	23%	34%	23%	10%
Code	**Title**					
G	General Learning Ability		✔	* ✔		
P	Form Perception			* ✔		
K	Motor Coordination		* ✔	✔		
M	Manual Dexterity		✔	* ✔		

Common Occupations

A full listing of all occupations belonging to this group may be found in the Guide for Occupational Exploration.

The following occupations have been selected to represent this group. They provide the major employment opportunities. However, specific job opportunities will vary according to locations of industry, geographical region, and other factors.

Information may be found in common sources of occupational information, state career information systems, and computerized guidance systems.

An (M) follows the occupational title where the military services offer training and experience.

Inspecting, Testing, and Repairing

502.382-014	Fluoroscope Operator
525.387-010	Grader, Meat
529.387-030	Quality-Control Technician
529.687-074	Egg Candler
539.364-010	Pulp-And-Paper Tester
549.364-010	Tester, Compressed Gases (M)
559.367-010	Quality-Control Tester
559.381-010	Inspector
589.387-010	Inspector And Sorter
649.367-010	Inspector, Paper Products
689.384-010	Cloth Tester, Quality
689.384-014	Laboratory Tester
706.387-014	Machine Tester
709.367-010	Inspector, Metal Can
710.384-014	Inspector
729.387-022	Inspector 1
730.367-010	Final Inspector
732.364-010	Inspector
788.384-010	Inspector
806.281-050	Test Driver 1
806.384-026	Tester, Motor

Inspecting, Grading, Sorting, Weighing, and Recording

361.687-014	Classifier
369.687-010	Assembler
369.687-022	Inspector
521.687-086	Nut Sorter
529.687-102	Grader, Dressed Poultry
559.387-014	Inspector
569.587-010	Veneer Grader
579.687-022	Glass Inspector
579.687-030	Selector
609.684-010	Inspector, General
649.687-010	Paper Sorter And Counter
669.587-010	Grader
689.684-010	Burler
689.685-038	Cloth Examiner, Machine
689.687-086	Yarn Sorter
725.687-026	Quality-Control Inspector
726.684-062	Inspector, Printed Circuit Boards
726.684-102	Tester, Semiconductor Wafers
739.687-082	Examiner
741.687-010	Paint-Spray Inspector
763.687-026	Finished-Stock Inspector
781.687-014	Cloth Examiner, Hand
789.587-014	Inspector, Fabric
789.687-070	Grament Inspector
789.687-114	Parachute Inspector (M)
806.684-134	Transmission Tester
806.687-018	Final Inspector
869.687-038	Inspector
922.687-074	Lumber Sorter
976.687-014	Photo Checker And Assembler

06.04

Elemental Work: Industrial

Elemental Work: Industrial is semiskilled manual work using tools and machines. Workers process materials and assemble products. They tend, control, and monitor machines. Also, they may use simple hand and power tools to perform some job tasks. Some workers feed and offbear (load and unload) the machines they tend. They may assist other workers who set up the machines. The work is routine and very little decision-making is involved. Some may work on an assembly line where the pace of the work is controlled by a machine or a conveyor. Workers must be able to repeat the same tasks over and over and follow set procedures. They are more involved with the process they do than with the end product. This group includes the subgroups of:

Machine Work
Equipment Operation
Manual Work

Machine Work is the use of machines to perform work tasks in the manufacturing process. Workers use machines to bend, cut, shape, and join materials. Some may fold, bag, box, or bind the completed products or materials. Workers may regulate their machines and do minor adjustments. Some oil and do other light maintenance work on their machines. Workers also may handle the materials used or the products made.

Equipment Operation is the use of machines in the manufacturing process. Workers process materials such as ore, wood,

A binder worker operates a gathering-stitching machine.

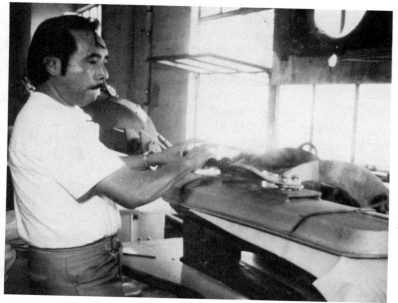

This all-round presser works in a small dry-cleaning shop.

paper, and food. They operate equipment to mix, heat, pump, grind, slice, and wind. They also rivet, nail, staple, and mount. Some workers coat or plate materials (put on a thin layer of other material). And, some workers use tools and equipment to assemble large products such as automobiles.

Manual Work involves assembly of small products, commercial food processing, and installing glass and stone products. Workers also do a variety of bench jobs. They grind, polish, buff, rub, and sand to finish products. Some workers weld or solder on a production line. Workers also do physical labor as they handle the products and materials. For example, some workers fold, pack, and weigh products. Although workers may use equipment and tools, their major work tasks involve physical labor.

Jobs are found in industrial settings. This includes factories and plants where materials are processed or products are mass produced.

What Skills and Abilities Would Help You Succeed in This Kind of Work?

The most important skills are listed below. All of those listed do not apply to each occupation. As you explore occupations you should identify the specific ones needed.

Physical Stamina – to perform physical tasks continuously during a work shift.

Dexterity – to use hands and fingers to load, unload, and tend machines or assemble products.

Diligence – to concentrate and perform the same tasks over and over again and follow safety rules.

Physical Strength – to move or lift heavy materials or products.

239

Do You Have or Can You Develop an Interest in This Kind of Work?

Review the following questions. Your answers can give you clues as to your interest in Elemental Industrial Work.

Have you helped install, repair, or build something? Can you follow directions?

Have you taken an industrial arts course? Did you like working with tools, machines, and your hands?

Are you able to participate in physical activities without becoming overtired? Do you enjoy physical education classes? Do you enjoy a leisure time activity that involves physical exercise?

Do you enjoy working with tools, machines, or equipment? Would you enjoy a job where you did?

Do you have a hobby that involves building things? Have you made belts or other things out of leather?

Have you assembled models or toys? Can you do fine finger work such as carving or needlework?

Have you helped can or preserve food? Can you bake or decorate cakes?

What Else Should You Know About This Group of Occupations?

Jobs in factories and plants may involve night work, shifts, or overtime work. Most jobs in this group are open to inexperienced workers and do not require much training. Many employers provide training on the specific machine or piece of equipment to be operated. Work activities in most jobs change very little each day. With experience and good job performance some workers may advance to supervisory jobs or to more specialized jobs.

Occupations in Worker Trait Group 06.02, Production Work, provide some advancement opportunity. Also, some similar jobs are found in Worker Trait Group 05.12, Elemental Work: Mechanical, but are in non-factory settings.

The military services offer training and experience related to some occupations in this group. These occupations are included in the list at the end of this group description. They are identified by an (M) following the occupational title. More information about the military training and experience opportunities may be found in Appendix A.

How Can You Prepare For This Kind of Work?

Most jobs require little or no training or experience. A short demonstration on-the-job or up to three months of training is all that is usually needed. However, this is different when many people are looking for work. Then, those with training and experience using machines, equipment, and tools may be selected over less skilled applicants. A high school diploma or its equivalent may be required by most employers.

As you plan your high school program you should select courses leading toward graduation. Next you should include courses that offer some basic skills related to occupations in this group. The following list of courses and skills will help you plan your education.

Industrial Arts – courses involving operating machines and equipment and using hand and power tools.

General Studies – basic skills in math and communications can be helpful.

Physical Education – courses and activities relating to the development of physical stamina and coordination.

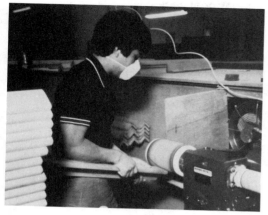

This woodworking shop hand is using a spindle sanding machine.

Qualifications Profile

This section is a summary of the worker traits and work factors related to successful job performance and worker satisfaction. Try to relate your interests, abilities, aptitudes, and preferences to these traits and factors. An asterisk (*) marks those traits and factors that are related to more than 60% of the occupations listed at the end of this group. The other traits and factors listed are as important, but relate to fewer occupations. See Appendices B-G for information about all of the worker traits and work factors.

Work Activities

The most important activities related to this group involve:

* 1. Things and objects.
* 3. Tasks of a routine, definite nature.
* 9. Processes, methods, or machines.

Work Situations

Workers must be willing to:

1. Perform duties which change frequently.
* 2. Perform routine tasks.
*10. Work within precise limits or standards of accuracy.

Working Conditions

These are the physical surroundings in which work is done. In occupations belonging to this group, work is performed:

*I – Inside — workers spend most of their time inside protected from weather conditions but not always from temperature changes.

241

Physical Demands

Workers in this group of occupations must be able to do:

L – Light work
M – Medium work
H – Heavy work

Data-People-Things

This chart shows the levels for these three basic elements of work as related to this group. Level means the degree of difficulty of job tasks rather than the amount of time involved. The terms low, average, and high indicate the highest level at which occupations are involved. Compare your interests and abilities with the levels checked.

Difficulty Level of Job Tasks

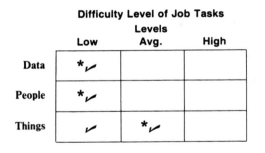

	Low	Levels Avg.	High
Data	*✔		
People	*✔		
Things	✔	*✔	

Educational Skills

This chart shows the levels of reasoning, math, and language skills related to this group. These skills are usually developed in an educational setting. There are six levels ranging from the simple (1) to the most complex (6).

Skill Levels

Simple ◄──────► Complex

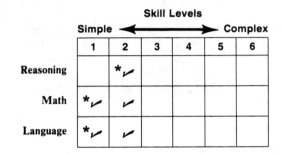

	1	2	3	4	5	6
Reasoning		*✔				
Math	*✔	✔				
Language	*✔	✔				

Aptitudes

This chart presents the most important aptitudes related to this group. The levels checked compare aptitudes needed for success in this group to aptitudes of the general working population in all occupations. For example, level 5 is low and represents the bottom 10% of the working population. Level 1 is high and represents the top 10%.

APTITUDE LEVELS COMPARED TO ALL WORKERS							
Related Aptitudes (Ability to Learn)		Lower 1/3		Middle 1/3	Upper 1/3		
		Level **5**	Level **4**	Level **3**	Level **2**	Level **1**	
Code	Title	10%	23%	34%	23%	10%	
K	Motor Coordination		✔	✔			
F	Finger Dexterity		*✔	✔			
M	Manual Dexterity			*✔			

Common Occupations

A full listing of all occupations belonging to this group may be found in the Guide for Occupational Exploration.

The following occupations have been selected to represent this group. They provide the major employment opportunities. However, specific job opportunities will vary according to locations of industry, geographical region, and other factors.

Information may be found in common sources of occupational information, state career information systems, and computerized guidance systems.

An (M) follows the occupational title where the military services offer training and experience.

Machine Work

363.682-018	Presser, Machine
518.685-014	Coremaker, Machine 1
569.685-046	Gluing-Machine Operator
569.686-026	Laborer, Hot-Plate Plywood Press
570.685-046	Miller
583.685-030	Embosser
583.685-042	Folding-Machine Operator
585.685-102	Shearing-Machine Operator
599.685-110	Tumbler Operator
603.665-010	Buffing-Machine Tender
604.685-026	Lathe Operator, Production
605.685-030	Milling-Machine Operator, Production
606.685-010	Boring-Machine Operator, Production
609.685-018	Production-Machine Tender
612.685-010	Lever Tender
615.685-042	Turret-Punch-Press Operator, Tape-Control
619.685-062	Machine Operator 2

641.685-022	Carton-Forming-Machine Operator
641.685-098	Wrapping-Machine Operator
649.685-014	Bag-Machine Operator
649.685-018	Bindery Worker
649.685-042	Envelope-Machine Operator
651.685-022	Platen-Press Feeder
652.586-010	Utility Worker, Cloth Printing
652.685-030	Embossing-Press Operator
653.685-010	Bindery Worker (M)
653.685-030	Spiral Binder
653.686-014	Folding-Machine Feeder
664.682-014	Barrel-Lathe Operator, Outside
667.685-054	Slasher Operator
669.686-018	Chain Offbearer
669.686-030	Woodworking-Machine Feeder
669.686-034	Woodworking-Machine Offbearer
679.685-010	Machine Operator, Ceramics
679.685-022	Tile Grinder
680.685-014	Card Stripper
680.685-070	Opener Tender
680.685-074	Picker Tender
680.685-098	Slubber Tender
681.585-014	Bobbin Winder, Machine
681.685-126	Twister
681.685-138	Uptwister Tender
681.685-150	Winder Operator, Automatic
681.685-154	Yarn Winder
681.686-018	Spooler Operator, Automatic
685.665-014	Knitting-Machine Operator
689.586-010	Cloth Doffer
689.686-022	Doffer
689.687-030	Creeler
690.385-010	Platen Grinder
690.485-010	Band-Sawing-Machine Operator
690.685-122	Cutting-Machine Tender
690.685-154	Electric-Sealing-Machine Operator
690.685-162	Fastener, Machine
690.685-226	Heel-Nailing-Machine Operator
690.685-378	Skiver, Machine

690.686-018 Cementer, Machine Applicator
692.686-038 Dynamite-Packing-Machine Feeder
716.685-022 Lens-Fabricating-Machine Tender
779.684-038 Mirror Specialist
786.685-014 Buttonhole-Machine Operator
786.685-030 Sewing-Machine Operator, Semi-Automatic
787.685-038 Shirring-Machine Operator, Automatic
787.685-042 Tacking-Machine Operator
979.665-010 Silk-Screen Printer, Machine

Equipment Operation

359.685-010 Cremator
500.665-010 Plater, Production
501.685-010 Plater, Hot Dip
502.664-010 Blast-Furnace Keeper
504.685-014 Flame-Hardening-Machine Operator
504.687-010 Annealer
512.685-010 Furnace Tender
514.664-014 Tapper
514.684-022 Pourer, Metal
518.685-026 Shell Molder
520.685-010 Batter Mixer
520.685-086 Dividing-Machine Operator
520.685-098 Feed Mixer
520.685-210 Stuffer
521.685-122 Feed Grinder
521.685-146 Fruit-Press Operator
521.685-166 Grinder Operator
521.685-210 Meal-Grinder Tender
521.685-214 Meat Grinder
521.685-306 Slicing-Machine Operator
521.685-370 Winery Worker
523.585-034 Roaster, Grain
524.685-034 Icer, Machine
526.685-014 Cook, Fry, Deep Fat
526.685-030 Oven Tender
526.685-046 Potato-Chip Frier
529.665-010 Fruit-Grader Operator
529.685-054 Chocolate Molder, Machine
529.685-106 Expeller Operator
529.686-014 Cannery Worker
530.685-010 Coating-Mixer Tender
533.685-022 Screen Tender
539.685-034 Winder Helper
549.684-010 Pumper Helper
550.485-014 Mixing-Machine Operator
550.485-018 Paint Mixer, Machine
550.685-078 Mixer
550.685-082 Mixer Operator
553.685-102 Tire Molder
556.685-070 Record-Press Tender
557.685-026 Spinner
559.665-026 Mixer

559.665-030 Press Operator (M)
559.685-018 Ampoule Filler
559.685-110 Laborer, General
561.585-010 Stain Applicator
570.685-010 Auxiliary-Equipment Tender
571.685-010 Burner Tender
573.682-010 Kiln Burner
574.585-010 Paperhanger
575.685-014 Block-Making-Machine Operator
583.686-030 Press Feeder
589.686-014 Cloth Feeder
590.685-030 Etcher, Printed Circuits
590.685-090 Oven Curing Attendant
599.685-026 Dipper
599.685-066 Paint-Line Operator
599.685-074 Painting-Machine Operator
616.685-058 Riveting-Machine Operator
669.685-042 Corrugated-Fastener Driver
669.685-050 Doweling-Machine Operator
669.685-066 Nailing-Machine Operator, Automatic
690.685-014 Assembly-Press Operator
690,685-090 Contact-Lens Molder
692.685-162 Sealing-Machine Operator
692.685-202 Stapling-Machine Operator
914.585-010 Gas-Transfer Operator
976.685-022 Mounter, Automatic
976.685-026 Print Developer, Automatic (M)

Manual Work

208.462-010 Mailing-Machine Operator
361.665-010 Washer, Machine
361.684-010 Launderer, Hand
361.687-018 Laundry Laborer
362.684-010 Dry Cleaner, Hand
363.682-010 Leather Finisher
363.682-014 Presser, All-Around
363.684-018 Presser, Hand
363.685-010 Press Operator
363.685-014 Presser, Automatic
363.685-018 Presser, Form
363.685-026 Shirt Presser
363.686-010 Flatwork Finisher
369.684-014 Laundry Operator
369.687-018 Folder
500.684-010 Electroformer
503.685-030 Metal-Cleaner, Immersion
509.684-010 Enameler
509.686-010 Laborer, General
518.682-010 Machine Molder
518.684-010 Core Setter
519.683-014 Larry Operator
519.687-022 Foundry Worker, General
520.587-010 Pretzel Twister

521.687-122	Shellfish Shucker
524.684-022	Icer, Hand
525.587-014	Smoked Meat Preparer
525.684-010	Boner, Meat
525.684-014	Butcher, Fish
525.687-070	Poultry Dresser
525.687-082	Poultry-Dressing Worker
529.685-074	Container Washer, Machine
529.686-050	Laborer, Cheesemaking
529.687-066	Distillery Worker, General
529.687-130	Laborer
549.587-010	Compressed-Gas-Plant Worker (M)
556.684-018	Mold-Filling Operator
559.687-050	Laborer, Chemical Processing
562.687-010	Dyer
573.686-022	Hacker
579.667-010	Laborer, General
579.686-010	Laborer, Concrete Plant
579.687-018	Floor Attendant
589.686-026	Laborer, General
599.687-030	Washer
659.686-010	Jogger
667.686-014	Sawmill Worker
677.687-010	Log Roller
699.687-014	Machine Cleaner
700.684-030	Earring Maker
700.687-058	Polisher
705.684-010	Bench Grinder
705.684-014	Buffer 1
705.684-026	Grinder 1
705.684-034	Metal Finisher
705.684-058	Polisher
705.687-014	Laborer, Grinding And Polishing
706.684-022	Assembler, Small Parts
706.684-078	Lock Installer
706.687-010	Assembler, Production
709.684-066	Riveter, Hand
709.687-010	Cleaner And Polisher
715.684-058	Clock Assembler
721.684-022	Electric-Motor Assembler
724.684-026	Coil Winder
726.687-018	Silk-Screen Printer
728.684-022	Wireworker
729.687-010	Assembler, Electrical Accessories 1
731.684-010	Coin-Machine Assembler
731.687-034	Toy Assembler
735.687-034	Stone Setter
739.664-010	Candlemaker
739.687-030	Assembler, Small Products
740.684-022	Painter, Brush
742.684-010	Rubber
742.684-014	Stainer
749.684-042	Putty Glazer
754.684-010	Assembler
754.684-030	Finisher, Hand
760.684-010	Bench Carpenter
761.687-010	Sander, Hand
762.684-010	Assembler
762.687-026	Crossband Layer
763.684-074	Table-Top Tile Setter
769.684-054	Weaver
769.687-054	Woodworking-Shop Hand
780.684-062	Fabricator, Foam Rubber
780.684-118	Upholsterer, Outside
780.684-134	Upholsterer, Assembly Line
780.685-014	Stuffing-Machine Operator
781.684-018	Cutter, Rotary Shear
781.687-066	Stenciler
781.687-070	Trimmer, Hand
782.684-010	Canvas Repairer (M)
782.684-058	Sewer, Hand
782.687-014	Buttoner
788.684-054	Hand Sewer, Shoes
788.687-066	Laborer, Boot And Shoe
789.684-034	Parachute Folder (M)
789.687-066	Garment Folder
794.684-014	Box Maker, Paperboard
795.687-014	Gluer
806.684-010	Assembler, Automobile
810.664-010	Welder, Gun
813.684-022	Solderer, Production Line
819.684-010	Welder, Production Line
865.484-010	Safety-Glass Installer
865.684-014	Glass Installer
912.684-010	Parachute Rigger (M)
914.667-010	Loader 1 (M)
920.484-010	Crater (M)
920.585-010	Bundle Tier And Labeler
920.587-018	Packager, Hand (M)
920.685-010	Baling-Machine Tender
920.685-026	Bottle Packer
920.685-058	Feed Weigher
920.685-074	Package Sealer, Machine
920.685-078	Packager, Machine (M)
920.687-018	Bagger
920.687-166	Shoe Packer
920.687-178	Stenciler
921.565-010	Cement Loader
921.682-014	Palletizer Operator 1
921.683-050	Industrial-Truck Operator (M)
921.683-070	Straddle-Truck Operator
921.686-014	Conveyor Feeder-Offbearer
929.686-010	Bakery Worker
929.687-022	Laborer, Salvage
977.687-010	Collator, Hand
979.684-034	Screen Printer

07 BUSINESS DETAIL

People with an interest in the many details of a business operation enjoy work in this area. The office setting of their work could be in an industry, a bank, or in a doctor's or lawyer's office. Workers perform business services that have a direct effect on people's lives. This work may be as simple as providing information to answer a question or as complex as computing cost and production records. Workers must be well organized and their work must be accurate. Their work is clearly defined and they must pay attention to details. Some workers are involved with the computing and recording of business data. They need clerical and numerical skills and must know how to operate business machines. Other workers deal with people. Those who work directly with people need to use tact (be sensitive to the feelings and needs of people) and be courteous.

The Business Detail area is divided into two clusters: Business Machine Operation and Communication of Ideas/Information.

Business Machine Operation

The Business Machine Operation cluster includes workers who use machines to record or process data and those who do general office tasks. Many workers gather, organize, compute, and record numerical data. They use adding or calculating machines or computers. Some workers receive and disburse money. These workers are responsible for the money they handle. Some workers in this cluster use machines that type, print, sort, compute, or send and receive data. Others perform general office duties that require little training. They file, sort, copy, and route materials. They also deliver items such as letters, packages, or messages.

Communication of Ideas/Information

The Communication of Ideas/Information cluster includes administrative detail, oral communications, and records processing. Some workers need special skills and knowledge to perform management duties. They often make minor decisions related to running an office. Others are directly involved with the public. They give and receive information verbally and keep records. They communicate with people in person or by telephone or radio. However, some workers do not deal with people directly. They may coordinate the activities of others or schedule the delivery of equipment and materials.

The following Worker Trait Groups and Subgroups are related to the Business Machine Operation and Communication of Ideas/Information clusters.

Business Detail: an interest in organized, clearly defined activities requiring accuracy and attention to details, primarily in an office setting.

Business Machine Operation

07.02 Mathematical Detail
Bookkeeping and Auditing
Accounting
Statistical Reporting and
Analysis
Billing and Rate Computation
Payroll and Timekeeping

07.03 Financial Detail
Paying and Receiving

07.06 Clerical Machine Operation
Computer Operation
Keyboard Machine Operation

07.07 Clerical Handling
Filing
Sorting and Distribution
General Clerical Work

Communication of Ideas/Information

07.01 Administrative Detail
Interviewing
Administration
Secretarial Work
Financial Work
Certifying
Investigating
Test Administration

07.04 Oral Communications
Interviewing
Order, Complaint, and Claims
Handling
Registration
Reception and Information
Giving
Information Transmitting and
Receiving
Switchboard Services

07.05 Records Processing
Coordinating and Scheduling
Record Verification and
Proofing
Record Preparation and
Maintenance
Routing and Distribution

07.01
Administrative Detail

Administrative Detail involves clerical work (office) that requires special skills and knowledge. Workers perform management duties following set methods. They make minor decisions related to running an office. They use a variety of office machines. This group includes the subgroups of:

Interviewing
Administration
Secretarial Work
Financial Work
Certifying
Investigating
Test Administration

Interviewing is to talk with people to obtain facts. This is usually done face to face. Some workers talk with people to find out if they are eligible for low rent housing or public aid. Others analyze loan contracts and try to collect overdue payments. Still others talk with students seeking loans for college. Some workers are involved with people placed on probation. They conduct pretrial hearings, interpret findings, and suggest treatment. They also follow-up to rate the probationer's progress and recommend remedial (corrective) action when needed.

Administration is to manage the clerical work of an office. These workers compile and maintain records. They copy data and prepare and send out letters. Some compile data to prepare reports or purchase orders. Others assist professional workers such as teachers. And, some manage the duties of people in other types of office settings such as train stations.

Secretarial Work is made up of a variety of office duties such as typing and word processing. Workers also may use computers and other office machines. They may arrange social and business functions for their bosses. They schedule meetings, greet people, answer phones, and keep files. They may take shorthand and transcribe the notes. They read and route incoming mail and compose and type routine letters.

Financial Work is to compile, compute, and record financial data. Some workers hold funds, legal papers or other items, in escrow (not available to either party) until contracts are fulfilled. They prepare the escrow contracts and carry out the terms. Other workers prepare budgets. To do this, they review sales records and expenses. They prepare charts

A counselor talks with a student seeking a loan to attend college.

and graphs based upon financial data obtained. And, some workers maintain records on the rental or sale of real estate. They compute interest owed and the amounts paid on the principal and taxes in each payment. Other workers record security transactions. They receive money, issue receipts, and compute dividends.

Certifying is to review records or contracts to prove they are valid (true) as written. Workers may research contracts to make sure they comply with company standards. Others may search public records and study transfers of titles to prove the legal status of property. They may assess data to find out who is eligible for government programs. Some workers review and approve passport requests. Others explain hospital and medical insurance and instruct clerical staff on admitting and billing methods.

Investigating is to study and examine any of a variety of conditions. Some workers look into the reasons students miss school. They find out if the reasons are lawful and known to parents. Other workers collect evidence at the scene of a crime or fatal accident. They "lift" fingerprints using a special tape. They also take pictures of the scene of a crime and develop the film. Some people work for Members of Congress. They research laws and procedures of Federal agencies. They also work to resolve problems or complaints of constituents (voters).

Test Administration is to give written or performance tests to determine knowledge or skill. Some workers test people applying for drivers' licenses. They rate the drivers' abilities, collect fees, and issue licenses. They also lecture school and community groups on safe driving. Other workers give civil service exams. They maintain order, keep time, and answer questions from people taking exams.

This school secretary needs to be able to relate with students, staff, and parents.

Jobs may be found with businesses, industries, courts, and government agencies. Doctors, lawyers, and other professionals also hire these workers.

What Skills and Abilities Would Help You Succeed in This Kind of Work?

The most important skills are listed below. All of those listed do not apply to each occupation. As you explore occupations you should identify the specific ones needed.

Communication – to speak and write clearly and with accuracy.

Comprehension – to understand and carry out instructions without close supervision.

Critical Thinking – to make decisions based on set policy.

Leadership – to plan work schedules for yourself and others.

Dexterity – to use the hands and fingers to type, write shorthand, or record data.

249

Form Perception – to recognize small differences in forms and shapes to record or read shorthand symbols.

Clerical – to recognize errors in spelling, grammar, and punctuation to proof copy.

Numerical – to do arithmetic quickly and accurately.

Rapport – to relate with people in an understanding way and maintain harmony among workers.

Do You Have or Can You Develop an Interest in This Kind of Work?

Review the following questions. Your answers can give you clues as to your interest in Administrative Detail.

Have you had a checking account? Did you balance your monthly bank statements with your checkbook? Were you accurate?

Have you served as a secretary for a group or club? Did you keep minutes of the meetings? Do you enjoy this type of activity?

Have you taken courses in typing and shorthand? Did you build your speed and accuracy? How were your grades?

Have you worked in a school office or held other part-time clerical jobs? Did you work with records? Could you answer the questions of students and visitors?

Have you written a business letter? Did you use proper grammar and punctuation? Can you write correctly and to the point?

Have you been responsible for the work of others? Do you work well with others?

What Else Should You Know About This Group of Occupations?

Some of the jobs in this group require evening and weekend work. Working conditions are usually pleasant and most offices are modern and well-lighted. Workers in small offices often do a variety of tasks. They may serve as bookkeeper, clerk, and receptionist.

Many of these jobs require workers who can be trusted to handle confidential information.

The military services offer training and experience related to some occupations in this group. These occupations are included in the list at the end of this group description. They are identified by an (M) following the occupational title. More information about the military training and experience opportunities may be found in Appendix A.

A title examiner reviews deed records to update the title before property can be bought or sold.

How Can You Prepare for This Kind of Work?

Most occupations in this group require six months to four years of education and training. Most jobs require training in typing. Many require shorthand or the use of dictation transcribing equipment. Training is offered by high schools and technical schools. Business and community colleges offer one- and two-year training programs. Workers may be promoted to these jobs from other clerical jobs. People with above average vocabulary, grammar, and spelling skills can enter some of these jobs and receive on-the-job training. Applicants usually need to take a civil service test to enter government jobs.

As you plan your high school program you should includes courses related to Administrative Detail. The following list of courses and skills can help you plan your high school program.

Secretarial and Clerical – courses in executive, legal, and medical secretarial work; stenography; typing; word processing; and general office work.

Supervision and Management – courses in office supervision and personnel and training programs.

General Business – courses in bookkeeping or accounting.

General Studies – courses in general English, speech, business writing, psychology, civics, and sociology also may be helpful for some occupations in this group.

Qualifications Profile

This section is a summary of the worker traits and work factors related to successful job performance and worker satisfaction. Try to relate your interests, abilities, aptitudes, and preferences to these traits and factors. An asterisk (*) marks those traits and factors that are related to more than 60% of the occupations listed at the end of this group. The other traits and factors listed are as important, but relate to fewer occupations. See Appendices B-G for information about all of the worker traits and work factors.

Work Activities

The most important activities related to this group involve:

* * 2. Business contact.
  5. Recognition or appreciation from others.
* * 6. Communication of ideas and information.

Work Situations

Workers must be willing to:

1. Perform duties which change frequently.
* * 4. Deal with people.
* * 7. Make decisions using personal judgment.
  8. Make decisions using standards that can be measured or checked.
  10. Work within precise limits or standards of accuracy.

Aptitudes

This chart presents the most important aptitudes related to this group. The levels checked compare aptitudes needed for success in this group to aptitudes of the general working population in all occupations. For example, level 5 is low and represents the bottom 10% of the working population. Level 1 is high and represents the top 10%.

APTITUDE LEVELS COMPARED TO ALL WORKERS						
Related Aptitudes (Ability to Learn)		Lower 1/3		Middle 1/3	Upper 1/3	
		Level 5	Level 4	Level 3	Level 2	Level 1
Code	Title	10%	23%	34%	23%	10%
G	General Learning Ability			✔	✔	
V	Verbal			✔	✔	
N	Numerical			* ✔	✔	
Q	Clerical Perception			✔	* ✔	

Physical Demands

Workers in this group of occupations must be able to do:

*S – Sedentary work
L – Light work

Educational Skills

This chart shows the levels of reasoning, math, and language skills related to this group. These skills are usually developed in an educational setting. There are six levels ranging from the simple (1) to the most complex (6).

Skill Levels

Simple ← → Complex

	1	2	3	4	5	6
Reasoning				* ✔	✔	
Math		✔	* ✔	✔		
Language				✔	* ✔	

Working Conditions

These are the physical surroundings in which work is done. In occupations belonging to this group, work is performed:

*I – Inside — workers spend most of their time inside protected from weather conditions but not always from temperature changes.

A driver's license examiner checks an applicant's papers.

Data-People-Things

This chart shows the levels for these three basic elements of work as related to this group. Level means the degree of difficulty of job tasks rather than the amount of time involved. The terms low, average, and high indicate the highest level at which occupations are involved. Compare your interests and abilities with the levels checked.

Difficulty Level of Job Tasks

	Low	Avg.	High
Data		✔	✔
People	* ✔		
Things	* ✔	✔	

Common Occupations

A full listing of all occupations belonging to this group may be found in the Guide for Occupational Exploration.

The following occupations have been selected to represent this group. They provide the major employment opportunities. However, specific job opportunities will vary according to locations of industry, geographical region, and other factors.

Information may be found in common sources of occupational information, state career information systems, and computerized guidance systems.

An (M) follows the occupational title where the military services offer training and experience.

Interviewing
168.267-038 Eligibility-And-Occupancy Interviewer
169.267-018 Financial-Aid Counselor
186.267-014 Loan Counselor
195.167-034 Probation Officer
195.267-010 Eligibility Worker
195.367-014 Management Aide

Administration
161.167-034 Manager, Office (M)
201.362-018 Membership Secretary
219.362-010 Administrative Clerk (M)
243.362-010 Court Clerk (M)

249.367-066 Procurement Clerk (M)
249.367-074 Teacher Aide 2
910.137-038 Station Agent 1

Secretarial Work
201.162-010 Social Secretary
201.362-010 Legal Secretary (M)
201.362-014 Medical Secretary
201.362-022 School Secretary
201.362-030 Secretary (M)

Financial Work
119.367-010 Escrow Officer
216.382-022 Budget Clerk (M)
219.362-046 Real-Estate Clerk
219.362-054 Securities Clerk
249.137-030 Supervisor, Real-Estate Office

Certifying
119.267-018 Contract Clerk
119.287-010 Title Examiner
166.267-014 Hospital-Insurance Representative
169.267-014 Examiner
169.267-030 Passport-Application Examiner

Investigating
168.367-010 Attendance Officer
169.262-010 Caseworker
375.384-010 Police Officer, Identification And Records

Test Administration
168.267-034 Drivers License Examiner
199.267-018 Examination Proctor

07.02

Mathematical Detail

Mathematical Detail is to use math skills to process numerical data related to running a business. Workers figure and keep records of quantities (amounts), costs, and charges. Most of these workers use adding or calculating machines or computers. Some operate bookkeeping machines and typewriters. This group includes the subgroups of:

Bookkeeping and Auditing
Accounting
Statistical Reporting and Analysis
Billing and Rate Computation
Payroll and Timekeeping

Bookkeeping and Auditing are to compute, classify, and record numerical data to keep records. Verifying the accuracy of recorded data is also included. Audit Clerks figure percentages and totals and compare the results with the recorded entries. They also correct errors or list discrepancies (differences). Bookkeepers keep a complete set of financial records for a business. They enter amounts in ledger accounts and cash journals. They balance books and compile reports. They also figure wages and prepare checks to meet payrolls.

Accounting is the system used to record, classify, and summarize money transactions of a business. Workers compile data to compute charges and prepare invoices. They receive monies, issue receipts, and record payments. They verify and balance data entries. They keep records and prepare reports. Some workers prepare income tax forms.

Statistical Reporting and Analysis are to collect, analyze, interpret, and present financial information or other data. Some workers read, measure, plot, and record flight test data. Others review insurance claims that have been settled. They make sure payments conform with company practices. Still others are concerned with ships' cargoes. They prepare reports of labor and equipment costs for loading and unloading the cargo. Some workers compile data and use formulas to prepare statistical summaries. Other workers compare the cost and volume of advertising with their competition (rivals). They also compare items sold with or without advertising. And, some workers keep records on how much fuel was bought, received, stored, and used in steam-electric generating plants.

Billing and Rate Computation is to figure out the cost of items bought or services rendered and then prepare and send a bill for that amount. Workers prepare or verify such things as bills, invoices, rates, and tariffs.

Payroll and Timekeeping is to compute and record time worked. These data are used to prepare payrolls. Workers compute wages and post the amount to payroll records. They also verify and correct errors on computer printouts to maintain these records. Some workers also may use calculators.

Jobs may be found with businesses, industries, and government agencies. Banks, finance companies, and accounting firms also offer employment.

What Skills and Abilities Would Help You Succeed in This Kind of Work?

The most important skills are listed below. All of those listed do not apply to each occupation. As you explore occupations you should identify the specific ones needed.

Numerical – to compute and record numerical data correctly.

Dexterity – to move hands and fingers to use computing machines or to enter figures in a ledger.

Leadership – to plan and oversee the work of others.

Accuracy – to read and copy long columns or large numbers without errors.

Clerical – to do detailed office work.

Organization – to organize information into standard systems and procedures for keeping records.

Communication – to give or exchange information.

Do You Have or Can You Develop an Interest in This Kind of Work?

Review the following questions. Your answers can give you clues as to your interest in Mathematical Detail.

Do you use a pocket calculator? Are you accurate?

Have you served as treasurer for a school or local group? Did your records balance at the end of your term of office? Did you prepare summaries or statements?

Have you balanced a checkbook? Are you quick to spot errors?

Have you had business or general math courses? How were your grades? Do you like working with numbers?

Have you taken bookkeeping or accounting courses? Are you interested in these fields?

This accounting clerk is totaling some journal sheets.

Have you held a summer or part-time office job that involved working with numbers? Do you like routine work of this kind?

Have you filled out an income tax form? Did you understand the terms used? Do you enjoy this type of activity?

What Else Should You Know About This Group of Occupations?

Bookkeeping requires sitting for long periods of time and may be tiring. Working closely with numbers may cause eyestrain and stress. Workers in small offices do a variety of computing tasks.

They may keep all numerical records for a business or agency. Prior training and experience is usually needed for these jobs. Large offices may divide the duties among many workers. Workers in these settings may do the same thing every day. People with little or no experience may be hired for some of these jobs.

The military services offer training and experience related to some occupations in this group. These occupations are included in the list at the end of this group description. They are identified by an (M) following the occupational title. More information about the military training and experience opportunities may be found in Appendix A.

How Can You Prepare for This Kind of Work?

Most occupations in this group require thirty days to one year of education and training. People able to do basic arithmetic accurately can enter some of these jobs where they receive on-the-job training. However, some jobs require prior training in bookkeeping, accounting, or business math. High schools and business schools offer this type of training. Some programs give business

A billing typist must first be accurate – and then fast.

students an opportunity to learn on the job through work-study programs. The ability to use bookkeeping machines and computers is an asset. A knowledge of typing also is useful. Federal government jobs usually require entrance tests.

As you plan your high school program you should includes courses related to Mathematical Detail. The following list of courses and skills can help you plan your education.

Accounting – courses in accounting, computing, and bookkeeping.

Business Machines – courses in typing and in using calculating, adding, billing, bookkeeping, and accounting machines.

Math – courses in algebra, geometry, statistics, statistical methods, and calculus.

General Business – courses in data processing and office practice are helpful for occupations in this group.

Qualifications Profile

This section is a summary of the worker traits and work factors related to successful job performance and worker satisfaction. Try to relate your interests, abilities, aptitudes, and preferences to these traits and factors. An asterisk (*) marks those traits and factors that are related to more than 60% of the occupations listed at the end of this group. The other traits and factors listed are as important, but relate to fewer occupations. See Appendices B-G for information about all of the worker traits and work factors.

Work Situations

Workers must be willing to:

* 2. Perform routine tasks.
   8. Make decisions using standards that can be measured or checked.
*10. Work within precise limits or standards of accuracy.

Work Activities

The most important activities related to this group involve:

* 1. Things and objects.
   2. Business contact.
* 3. Tasks of a routine, definite nature.
   9. Processes, methods, or machines.

Working Conditions

These are the physical surroundings in which work is done. In occupations belonging to this group, work is performed:

*I – Inside — workers spend most of their time inside protected from weather conditions but not always from temperature changes.

Aptitudes

This chart presents the most important aptitudes related to this group. The levels checked compare aptitudes needed for success in this group to aptitudes of the general working population in all occupations. For example, level 5 is low and represents the bottom 10% of the working population. Level 1 is high and represents the top 10%.

APTITUDE LEVELS COMPARED TO ALL WORKERS						
Related Aptitudes (Ability to Learn)		Lower 1/3		Middle 1/3	Upper 1/3	
		Level 5	Level 4	Level 3	Level 2	Level 1
Code	Title	10%	23%	34%	23%	10%
G	General Learning Ability			*✔	✔	
N	Numerical			*✔	✔	
Q	Clerical Perception			✔	*✔	

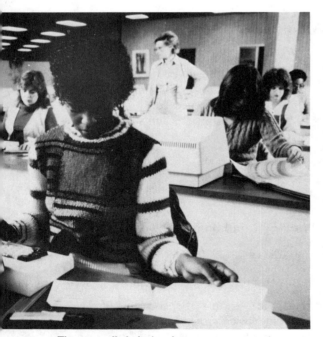

These payroll clerks in a large company are using keyboards to enter data in a computer.

Physical Demands

Workers in this group of occupations must be able to do:

*S – Sedentary work

Educational Skills

This chart shows the levels of reasoning, math, and language skills related to this group. These skills are usually developed in an educational setting. There are six levels ranging from the simple (1) to the most complex (6).

	Skill Levels					
	Simple ←				→ Complex	
	1	2	3	4	5	6
Reasoning			✔	✔		
Math			*✔	✔		
Language		✔	*✔	✔		

Data-People-Things

This chart shows the levels for these three basic elements of work as related to this group. Level means the degree of difficulty of job tasks rather than the amount of time involved. The terms low, average, and high indicate the highest level at which occupations are involved. Compare your interests and abilities with the levels checked.

Difficulty Level of Job Tasks

	Low	Avg.	High
Data		*✓	
People	*✓		
Things	✓	*✓	

Common Occupations

A full listing of all occupations belonging to this group may be found in the Guide for Occupational Exploration.

The following occupations have been selected to represent this group. They provide the major employment opportunities. However, specific job opportunities will vary according to locations of industry, geographical region, and other factors.

Information may be found in common sources of occupational information, state career information systems, and computerized guidance systems.

An (M) follows the occupational title where the military services offer training and experience.

Bookkeeping and Auditing
210.382-010 Audit Clerk (M)
210.382-014 Bookkeeper 1 (M)

Accounting
210.382-038 Credit-Card Clerk
210.382-054 Night Auditor
211.362-022 Teller, Collection And Exchange
211.462-030 Drivers-Cash Clerk
214.382-010 Account Analyst
216.362-014 Collection Clerk
216.362-022 Food-And-Beverage Controller
216.362-030 Probate Clerk

216.382-010 Accounting Clerk, Data Processing (M)
216.382-034 Cost Clerk (M)
216.482-010 Accounting Clerk (M)
216.587-014 Posting Clerk
219.362-058 Statement Clerk
219.362-070 Tax Preparer
219.482-010 Brokerage Clerk 1

Statistical Reporting and Analysis
002.281-010 Flight-Test-Data Transcriber
168.267-014 Claim Examiner
216.382-054 Receipt-And-Report Clerk
216.382-062 Statistical Clerk (M)
216.382-066 Statistical Clerk, Advertising
222.387-018 Fuel-Oil Clerk

Billing and Rate Computation
214.362-010 Demurrage Clerk
214.362-014 Documentation-Billing Clerk
214.362-022 Insurance Clerk
214.362-026 Invoice-Control Clerk
214.362-038 Traffic-Rate Clerk
214.382-014 Billing Typist
214.387-010 Billing-Control Clerk
214.467-010 Foreign Clerk
214.482-022 Rater
214.587-014 Traffic Clerk
248.382-010 Ticketing Clerk

Payroll and Timekeeping
215.137-014 Payroll Clerk, Chief
215.367-022 Timekeeper
215.382-010 Payroll Clerk, Data Processing
215.482-010 Payroll Clerk (M)

07.03

Financial Detail

Financial Detail is work that requires math skills and the ability to deal with the public. Workers receive and disburse (pay out) money. They also keep records of transactions (business dealings). They are responsible for the money they handle. At the end of their work period, they must balance the money on hand with the transactions that were made. This group includes the subgroup of:

Paying and Receiving

Paying and Receiving involves the exchange of money or other financial transactions. Workers receive cash, checks, or credit cards. They count the money given them and give change and receipts. They also answer questions. These workers perform various duties depending upon their place of employment. Some may operate a cash register to get a total of purchases. Others may accept and pay off bets placed by patrons. And, still others collect tolls for the use of bridges, highways, or tunnels. Some workers receive money for deposits or payment on loans or utility bills. They also cash checks after they verify the customer's signature.

Some workers sell tickets for public transportation or for admission to places where the public is entertained. Others serve as clerks and sell postage stamps and issue money orders. Some may redeem books of trading stamps in exchange for items. Workers may store, receive payment for, and release layaways. Some clerks record amounts of final bids at auctions and receive the money from the highest bidders.

Jobs in this group may be found where money is paid to or received from the public. Banks and other financial institutions also offer employment.

What Skills and Abilities Would Help You Succeed in This Kind of Work?

The most important skills are listed below. All of those listed do not apply to each occupation. As you explore occupations you should identify the specific ones needed.

Numerical – to use arithmetic skills to compute costs and make change.

Clerical – to keep records according to a set system.

Dexterity – to use the hands and fingers to operate an adding machine or cash register.

Social Skills – to use tact and courtesy in dealing with the public.

Diligence – to do routine work each day following set procedures.

Leadership – to plan and oversee the work of others.

Communication – to give and exchange information.

Accuracy – to work without error.

Do You Have or Can You Develop an Interest in This Kind of Work?

Review the following questions. Your answers can give you clues as to your interest in Financial Detail.

Have you helped work out a budget? Do you like working with numbers?

Have you sold anything to the public? Can you make change rapidly and correctly? Did you enjoy the public contact?

Have you used a calculator or adding machine? Do you like operating this type of equipment?

Have you balanced a personal checking account? Did your figures agree with the bank statement?

Have you taken a course in bookkeeping or business math? How were your grades?

Have you served as treasurer for a school, church, or club? Did your records balance at the end of your term of office?

Have you kept records on your personal financial transactions? Do you enjoy this type of activity?

What Else Should You Know About This Group of Occupations?

Workers in this group must be friendly and attentive to the public. They may have to stand for long periods of time. Some jobs require evening and weekend work. Workers often stay after a firm closes to the public. They must make their cash and records

This restaurant cashier needs to be pleasant, accurate, and well groomed.

balance each day. Workers who handle money may have to be bonded to insure their employers against losses.

The military services offer training and experience related to one occupation in this group - Post-Office Clerk. This occupation is included in the list at the end of this group description. It is identified by an (M) following the occupational title. More information about the military training and experience opportunities may be found in Appendix A.

How Can You Prepare for This Kind of Work?

Many occupations in this group require only a short demonstration; others, up to one year of education and training. Basic math skills are required for entering many of these jobs. Workers receive on-the-job training for specific tasks. Applicants usually need to take a civil service test to enter government jobs.

As you plan your high school program you should include courses related to Financial Detail. The following list of courses and skills can help you to plan your education.

Business Education – courses involving keyboarding, business math, and record keeping.

Distributive Education – courses involving cashiering and use of other sales related business machines, customer relations, records, telephone etiquette, and financial transactions.

Financial Record Processing – courses involving banking transactions and procedures, data entry and retrieval, and operation of related business machines.

General Studies – courses in general math, general English, and speech are important for occupations in this group.

Qualifications Profile

This section is a summary of the worker traits and work factors related to successful job performance and worker satisfaction. Try to relate your interests, abilities, aptitudes, and preferences to these traits and factors. An asterisk (*) marks those traits and factors that are related to more than 60% of the occupations listed at the end of this group. The other traits and factors listed are as important, but relate to fewer occupations. See Appendices B-G for information about all of the worker traits and work factors.

Work Activities

The most important activities related to this group involve:

1. Things and objects.
* 2. Business contact.
* 3. Tasks of a routine, definite nature.

Physical Demands

Workers in this group of occupations must be able to do:

S – Sedentary work
*L – Light work

Bank tellers have many brief public contacts and need to be very accurate.

Work Situations

Workers must be willing to:

1. Perform duties which change frequently.
2. Perform routine tasks.
* 4. Deal with people.
*10. Work within precise limits or standards of accuracy.

Working Conditions

These are the physical surroundings in which work is done. In occupations belonging to this group, work is performed:

*I – Inside — workers spend most of their time inside protected from weather conditions but not always from temperature changes.

Data-People-Things

This chart shows the levels for these three basic elements of work as related to this group. Level means the degree of difficulty of job tasks rather than the amount of time involved. The terms low, average, and high indicate the highest level at which occupations are involved. Compare your interests and abilities with the levels checked.

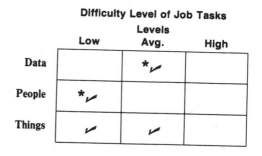

Difficulty Level of Job Tasks

	Low	Levels Avg.	High
Data		* ✔	
People	* ✔		
Things	✔	✔	

Aptitudes

This chart presents the most important aptitudes related to this group. The levels checked compare aptitudes needed for success in this group to aptitudes of the general working population in all occupations. For example, level 5 is low and represents the bottom 10% of the working population. Level 1 is high and represents the top 10%.

APTITUDE LEVELS COMPARED TO ALL WORKERS						
Related Aptitudes **(Ability to Learn)**		Lower 1/3		Middle 1/3	Upper 1/3	
		Level **5**	Level **4**	Level **3**	Level **2**	Level **1**
Code	Title	10%	23%	34%	23%	10%
G	General Learning Ability			* ✔	✔	
N	Numerical			* ✔	✔	
Q	Clerical Perception			* ✔	✔	
F	Finger Dexterity		✔	✔	✔	

Selling tickets in this bus station calls for bilingual skills.

Educational Skills

This chart shows the levels of reasoning, math, and language skills related to this group. These skills are usually developed in an educational setting. There are six levels ranging from the simple (1) to the most complex (6).

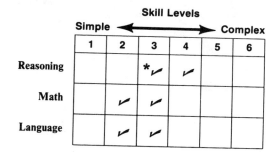

		Skill Levels				
	Simple ←			→ Complex		
	1	**2**	**3**	**4**	**5**	**6**
Reasoning			*✓	✓		
Math		✓	✓			
Language		✓	✓			

Common Occupations

A full listing of all occupations belonging to this group may be found in the Guide for Occupational Exploration.

The following occupations have been selected to represent this group. They provide the major employment opportunities. However, specific job opportunities will vary according to locations of industry, geographical region, and other factors.

Information may be found in common sources of occupational information, state career information systems, and computerized guidance systems.

An (M) follows the occupational title where the military services offer training and experience.

Paying and Receiving

211.362-010 Cashier 1
211.362-018 Teller
211.362-026 Teller, Note
211.462-014 Cashier-Checker
211.462-022 Cashier, Gambling
211.462-034 Teller
211.462-038 Toll Collector
211.467-030 Ticket Seller
211.467-034 Change Person
238.367-026 Ticket Agent
243.367-014 Post-Office Clerk (M)
290.477-010 Coupon-Redemption Clerk
294.567-010 Auction Clerk
299.467-010 Layaway Clerk

Oral Communications

Oral Communications involves speaking with people to give or receive information. Workers may deal with people in person or by telephone or radio. Many of these workers keep records of the information they receive. This group includes the subgroups of:

Interviewing
Order, Complaint, and Claims Handling
Registration
Reception and Information Giving
Information Transmitting and Receiving
Switchboard Services

Interviewing is to talk with people to obtain personal and financial data. Workers make up personal records or compile legal or statistical (numerical) data. The people they interview may be asking for loans, utility service, jobs, or credit. Or, the worker may be finding out if they are eligible for bonding or admission to a hospital. Some workers trace (look for) people who move without paying their bills or letting their creditors know.

Order, Complaint, and Claims Handling involve receiving orders or customers' complaints. Some workers read incoming letters and gather data to answer them. Other workers take food and beverage orders over a telephone or intercom system. They record the orders on tickets. Still others receive ads for newspapers or magazines over the phone or in person. They figure the total charge for the customer. And, some workers notify customers of past-due accounts and try to secure payment.

Registration is to record data on forms or in books. Some workers obtain personal information such as names and addresses. They may register visitors to public places such as state parks. Or, they may register and assign people to hotel rooms. Other workers make flight reservations or schedule the use of recreation facilities. Some workers record personal data on forms to issue licenses or permits. Others work during an election. They obtain signatures and record the names of voters. Still others assist the public to adopt animals. They also compile records of impounded animals. And, some workers record births and deaths and issue certificates. Others record reports of communicable diseases.

A utility company employee interviews a man applying for residential gas service.

Reception and Information Giving is to receive people or telephone calls and to answer requests for information. Some workers handle only telephone inquiries. This may be for automobile clubs, travel agents, or stock brokers. Other workers give information to people in person. They may provide them with bus, train, or airline time schedules or just answer general questions. Some workers assist the public. They greet them when they come in and direct them to the proper place. Other workers keep records of the selection and assignment of people recruited for civil service jobs.

Information Transmitting and Receiving involves the use of radios or telephones to receive and send information. Most workers use radios. They may dispatch (send out) buses, trolleys, or taxicabs, or work crews. Some use the radio to transmit and receive messages between ground stations and airplanes. Others report forest fires and weather conditions.

Switchboard Services involve receiving and placing telephone calls. These workers use switchboards to direct incoming or interoffice calls and to connect inside phones with outside lines. They also may supply information or provide an answering service for clients.

Jobs may be found with private businesses, institutions, and government agencies.

What Skills and Abilities Would Help You Succeed in This Kind of Work?

The most important skills are listed below. All of those listed do not apply to each occupation. As you explore occupations you should identify the specific ones needed.

Communication – to speak clearly to give or exchange information.

Rapport – to be sensitive to people's feelings and use tact and courtesy in dealing with the public.

Dexterity – to move the hands and fingers skillfully to type and use communication equipment.

Numerical – to do arithmetic quickly and correctly.

Versatile –to change often from one type of task to another.

Leadership – to plan and oversee the work of others.

Clerical – to recognize errors when recording information.

This woman makes price quotes over the telephone, using a computer terminal to provide data.

Do You Have or Can You Develop an Interest in This Kind of Work?

Review the following questions. Your answers can give you clues as to your interest in Oral Communications.

Have you given directions to others for finding your home? Were they able to follow your directions?

Have you taken speech courses? Do you have a clear speaking voice? Do you use good grammar?

Have you worked in a school or community survey? Were you courteous when asking questions? Did you enjoy meeting and interviewing people?

Have you operated a CB radio? Do you like to use this equipment?

Have you registered people for a meeting or event? Did you answer their questions? Do you enjoy this type of activity?

Have you taken business courses? Did you like them? How were your grades?

What Else Should You Know About This Group of Occupations?

Some workers in this group are required to work rotating shifts and weekends. They are often required to ask for confidential or personal information. People may become hostile when this occurs.

Workers in small offices may be assigned a variety of tasks. Jobs in large offices are often specialized. They may involve only one or a few limited tasks.

The military services offer training and experience related to some occupations in this group. These occupations are included in the list at the end of this group description. They are identified by an (M) following the occupational title. More information about the military training and experience opportunities may be found in Appendix A.

How Can You Prepare for This Kind of Work?

Occupations in this group vary widely in the education and training needed. Some only require a short demonstration. Others may require four years of education and training. Some employers frequently provide on-the-job training. This may range from one month to two years. People who enter these jobs usually have a good vocabulary and like contact with people. High school courses in typing or sales are helpful. General education or business training beyond high school

This congressional district aide is making a constituent feel welcome.

improves chances for promotion. Applicants usually need to take a civil service test to enter government jobs.

As you plan your high school program you should include courses related to Oral Communications. The following list of courses and skills will help you plan your education.

Secretarial and Clerical – courses in typing, record keeping, general office, and related programs; and receptionist and communication systems operation.

General Studies – courses in general English, speech, psychology, and sociology are important for occupations in this group.

Qualifications Profile

This section is a summary of the worker traits and work factors related to successful job performance and worker satisfaction. Try to relate your interests, abilities, aptitudes, and preferences to these traits and factors. An asterisk (*) marks those traits and factors that are related to more than 60% of the occupations listed at the end of this group. The other traits and factors listed are as important, but relate to fewer occupations. See Appendices B-G for information about all of the worker traits and work factors.

Work Activities

The most important activities related to this group involve:

* 2. Business contact.
  3. Tasks of a routine, definite nature.
  6. Communication of ideas and information.
  9. Processes, methods, or machines.

Work Situations

Workers must be willing to:

1. Perform duties which change frequently.
2. Perform routine tasks.

* 4. Deal with people.
  8. Make decisions using standards that can be measured or checked.
  10. Work within precise limits or standards of accuracy.

Data-People-Things

This chart shows the levels for these three basic elements of work as related to this group. Level means the degree of difficulty of job tasks rather than the amount of time involved. The terms low, average, and high indicate the highest level at which occupations are involved. Compare your interests and abilities with the levels checked.

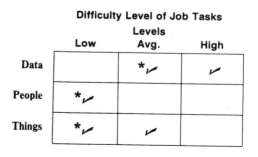

Difficulty Level of Job Tasks

	Low	Avg.	High
Data		*✓	✓
People	*✓		
Things	*✓	✓	

Levels

Aptitudes

This chart presents the most important aptitudes related to this group. The levels checked compare aptitudes needed for success in this group to aptitudes of the general working population in all occupations. For example, level 5 is low and represents the bottom 10% of the working population. Level 1 is high and represents the top 10%.

APTITUDE LEVELS COMPARED TO ALL WORKERS							
Related Aptitudes **(Ability to Learn)**		Lower 1/3		Middle 1/3	Upper 1/3		
		Level 5	Level 4	Level 3	Level 2	Level 1	
Code	Title	10%	23%	34%	23%	10%	
G	General Learning Ability			*✔			
V	Verbal			*✔	✔		
Q	Clerical Perception			*✔	✔		

Physical Demands

Workers in this group of occupations must be able to do:

*S – Sedentary work
L – Light work

Educational Skills

This chart shows the levels of reasoning, math, and language skills related to this group. These skills are usually developed in an educational setting. There are six levels ranging from the simple (1) to the most complex (6).

Skill Levels

Simple ←——→ Complex

	1	2	3	4	5	6
Reasoning			✔	✔		
Math		*✔	✔			
Language			*✔	✔		

Working Conditions

These are the physical surroundings in which work is done. In occupations belonging to this group, work is performed:

*I – Inside — workers spend most of their time inside protected from weather conditions but not always from temperature changes.

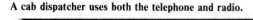

A cab dispatcher uses both the telephone and radio.

Common Occupations

A full listing of all occupations belonging to this group may be found in the Guide for Occupational Exploration.

The following occupations have been selected to represent this group. They provide the major employment opportunities. However, specific job opportunities will vary according to locations of industry, geographical region, and other factors.

Information may be found in common sources of occupational information, state career information systems, and computerized guidance systems.

An (M) follows the occupational title where the military services offer training and experience.

Interviewing

186.267-010 Bonding Agent
205.137-010 Admitting Officer
205.362-014 Employment Clerk (M)
205.362-018 Hospital-Admitting Clerk (M)
205.362-030 Outpatient-Admitting Clerk (M)
205.367-014 Charge-Account Clerk
205.367-022 Credit Clerk
205.367-042 Registration Clerk
205.367-054 Survey Worker
239.367-010 Customer-Service Representative
241.367-018 Loan Interviewer
241.367-026 Skip Tracer

Order, Complaint, and Claims Handling

209.262-010 Correspondence Clerk
209.567-014 Order Clerk, Food And Beverage
241.357-010 Collection Clerk
247.367-010 Classified-Ad Clerk 1

Registration

169.167-046 Public Health Registrar
205.367-030 Election Clerk
205.367-034 License Clerk
205.367-038 Registrar
238.362-010 Hotel Clerk (M)
238.367-018 Reservations Agent
249.367-010 Animal-Shelter Clerk
249.367-082 Park Aide
341.367-010 Recreation-Facility Attendant

Reception and Information Giving

205.362-010 Civil-Service Clerk (M)
209.362-030 Congressional-District Aide
237.267-010 Information Clerk, Automobile Club
237.367-018 Information Clerk
237.367-022 Information Clerk
237.367-038 Receptionist
237.367-046 Telephone-Quotation Clerk
238.367-030 Travel Clerk

Information Transmitting and Receiving

193.262-010 Airline-Radio Operator
193.262-022 Radio Officer (M)
193.262-030 Radiotelegraph Operator (M)
235.662-014 Communication-Center Operator
236.562-010 Telegrapher
239.367-014 Dispatcher, Maintenance Service
243.362-014 Police Aide
379.362-010 Dispatcher, Radio
452.367-010 Fire Lookout
912.367-010 Flight-Information Expediter (M)
913.167-010 Bus Dispatcher, Interstate
913.167-014 Dispatcher, Bus and Trolley
913.367-010 Taxicab Starter
919.162-010 Dispatcher, Traffic Or System
939.362-010 Dispatcher, Oil Well Services
959.167-010 Dispatcher, Service

Switchboard Services

235.462-010 Central-Office Operator (M)
235.662-018 Directory-Assistance Operator
235.662-022 Telephone Operator (M)
235.662-026 Telephone-Answering-Service Operator

Records Processing

Records Processing is to enter, review, maintain, or summarize data. Workers in this group check records to make sure they are correct. They coordinate and schedule activities of people. They also schedule the delivery or use of equipment and materials. This group includes the subgroups of:

Coordinating and Scheduling
Record Verification and Proofing
Record Preparation and Maintenance
Routing and Distribution

Coordinating and Scheduling involves directing the flow of materials and people to meet time schedules. Some workers contact vendors and shippers to be sure that items are sent out on a certain date. Others oversee the movement of freight, mail, baggage, and people through airline terminals. Some set schedules for workers such as flight crews. They may schedule freight shipments to meet customer requirements. Others make reservations for travelers. Some workers make daily and advance program schedules for TV.

Record Verification and Proofing involves reviewing written materials to prove they are correct. Some workers read radio or TV scripts to detect errors. They also view video or sound tapes to beep (delete) vulgar words or curses before the tape is aired. Some workers compare and proof newspaper ads and other typesetting with original copy. Others search legal papers or recorded data to make sure they are correct. Some review applications or other forms to make sure all questions are

Using public records in a title search may require lots of standing and lifting heavy books.

answered. Some examine bills, records, or computer displays or printouts to respond to customers.

Record Preparation and Maintenance involves gathering and entering data to form records and keeping them updated. Workers gather and place these data in folders and files. They also search the files for specific data to compile directories, reports, or other documents. Some workers classify data by assigning codes before filing. Some work with special files or records such as in a hospital. Others may take notes by shorthand or machine in a law office, court, or public stenographic service.

Routing and Distribution involves sorting mail or freight for proper delivery. Some workers read, sort, and route incoming and outgoing mail. Other workers deliver it on foot or in motor vehicles. Some workers contact and schedule freight carriers to ship orders. Others prepare itemized delivery sheets for the freight being shipped.

Jobs may be found with large business offices, government agencies, and institutions such as banks and hospitals.

What Skills and Abilities Would Help You Succeed in This Kind of Work?

The most important skills are listed below. All of those listed do not apply to each occupation. As you explore occupations you should identify the specific ones needed.

Analytical – to analyze and classify data according to set procedures.

Clerical Perception – to recognize errors in punctuation, grammar, and spelling.

Accuracy – to gather and record numerical data correctly.

Diligence – to do routine work which is repeated daily.

Leadership – to plan and oversee the work of others.

Do You Have or Can You Develop an Interest in This Kind of Work?

Review the following questions. Your answers can give you clues as to your interest in Records Processing.

Have you read proof for a school newspaper or yearbook? Can you spot errors in spelling and punctuation easily?

This medical records technician has a lot of information at her fingertips.

Have you taken business courses? How were your grades? Do you like to classify and file materials?

Have you been an officer in a school, church, or social group? Did you record the minutes? Did you keep a file of minutes or correspondence?

Have you used the library card catalog to compile a report? Can you locate the information you need quickly and easily?

Have you collected stamps or coins? Do you have them classified and arranged according to a plan?

What Else Should You Know About This Group of Occupations?

Some jobs in this group require workers to be on their feet for long periods of time. The work is routine and may become boring for some jobs. However, many of these jobs offer advancement possibilities. Part-time or temporary work is usually available. Workers in small offices may be assigned a variety of tasks. Jobs in large offices are often specialized with only one or a few tasks assigned. Some jobs require evening, night-shift, or weekend work.

The military services offer training and experience related to some occupations in this group. These occupations are included in the list at the end of this group description. They are identified by an (M) following the occupational title. More information about the military training and experience opportunities may be found in Appendix A.

How Can You Prepare for This Type of Work?

Most occupations in this group require from thirty days to two years of education and training. Some employers prefer workers who have completed business courses. Training for entry into many of these jobs is provided by federal or state programs for unemployed and low-skilled workers. Some jobs, such as in law offices, courts, and hospitals, require a knowledge of special terms used.

Filing demands quick fingers as well as accuracy. (left)

Carrying the mail is a breeze – on nice days. (right)

On-the-job training ranges from a short demonstration to a one-year program. Some employers test an applicant's ability to perform or to learn job duties.

As you plan your high school program you should include courses related to records processing. The following list of courses and skills can help you plan your education.

Business – courses in data processing, scheduling, and marketing.

Secretarial and Clerical – courses in typing, business machine operation, and general office work (filing, coding, etc.).

General Studies – courses in general English, composition, speech, civics, and geography are important for occupations in this group.

Qualifications Profile

This section is a summary of the worker traits and work factors related to successful job performance and worker satisfaction. Try to relate your interests, abilities, aptitudes, and preferences to these traits and factors. An asterisk (*) marks those traits and factors that are related to more than 60% of the occupations listed at the end of this group. The other traits and factors listed are as important, but relate to fewer occupations. See Appendices B-G for information about all of the worker traits and work factors.

Physical Demands

Workers in this group of occupations must be able to do:

*S – Sedentary work
L – Light work

Work Situations

Workers must be willing to:

1. Perform duties which change frequently.
2. Perform routine tasks.
4. Deal with people.
8. Make decisions using standards that can be measured or checked.
10. Work within precise limits or standards of accuracy.

Work Activities

The most important activities related to this group involve:

1. Things and objects.
2. Business contact.
* 3. Tasks of a routine, definite nature.
* 6. Communication of ideas and information.

Aptitudes

This chart presents the most important aptitudes related to this group. The levels checked compare aptitudes needed for success in this group to aptitudes of the general working population in all occupations. For example, level 5 is low and represents the bottom 10% of the working population. Level 1 is high and represents the top 10%.

APTITUDE LEVELS COMPARED TO ALL WORKERS						
Related Aptitudes (Ability to Learn)		Lower 1/3		Middle 1/3	Upper 1/3	
		Level **5**	Level **4**	Level **3**	Level **2**	Level **1**
Code	Title	10%	23%	34%	23%	10%
G	General Learning Ability			*✓		
V	Verbal			*✓		
Q	Clerical Perception			*✓	✓	

Educational Skills

This chart shows the levels of reasoning, math, and language skills related to this group. These skills are usually developed in an educational setting. There are six levels ranging from the simple (1) to the most complex (6).

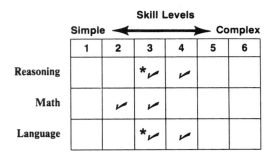

Skill Levels

Simple ⟵⟶ Complex

	1	2	3	4	5	6
Reasoning			*✓	✓		
Math		✓	✓			
Language			*✓	✓		

Data-People-Things

This chart shows the levels for these three basic elements of work as related to this group. Level means the degree of difficulty of job tasks rather than the amount of time involved. The terms low, average, and high indicate the highest level at which occupations are involved. Compare your interests and abilities with the levels checked.

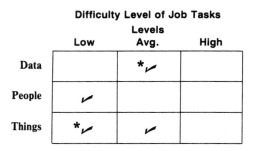

Difficulty Level of Job Tasks

Levels

	Low	Avg.	High
Data		*✓	
People	✓		
Things	*✓	✓	

Working Conditions

These are the physical surroundings in which work is done. In occupations belonging to this group, work is performed:

*I – Inside — workers spend most of their time inside protected from weather conditions but not always from temperature changes.

Common Occupations

A full listing of all occupations belonging to this group may be found in the Guide for Occupational Exploration.

The following occupations have been selected to represent this group. They provide the major employment opportunities. However, specific job opportunities will vary according to locations of industry, geographical region, and other factors.

Information may be found in common sources of occupational information, state career information systems, and computerized guidance systems.

An (M) follows the occupational title where the military services offer training and experience.

Coordinating and Scheduling

199.387-010	Television-Schedule Coordinator
215.362-010	Crew Scheduler
221.367-066	Scheduler, Maintenance (M)
221.367-078	Traffic Clerk
222.367-018	Expediter
238.137-010	Manager, Reservations
238.167-010	Travel Clerk (M)
238.167-014	Travel Counselor, Automobile Club
238.362-014	Reservation Clerk (M)
238.367-014	Reservation Clerk
248.367-014	Booking Clerk
249.167-014	Dispatcher, Motor Vehicle (M)
353.167-010	Guide, Travel
912.367-014	Transportation Agent (M)

Record Verification and Proofing

131.267-022	Script Reader
209.367-046	Title Searcher
209.387-030	Proofreader
209.687-010	Checker 2
209.687-018	Reviewer

219.482-014	Insurance Checker
241.267-034	Investigator, Utility-Bill Complaints
241.362-010	Claims Clerk 1
241.367-014	Customer-Complaint Clerk
241.367-042	Property-Assessment Monitor
247.387-022	Classified-Ad Clerk 2
247.667-010	Production Proofreader
249.387-022	Reader

Record Preparation and Maintenance

079.367-014	Medical Record Technician (M)
202.362-010	Shorthand Reporter (M)
202.362-014	Stenographer (M)
202.362-022	Stenotype Operator (M)
206.367-014	File Clerk 2
206.387-010	Classification Clerk
206.387-014	Fingerprint Clerk 2
206.387-018	Librarian, Morgue
206.387-026	Records Custodian
206.387-030	Tape Librarian
209.362-010	Circulation Clerk
209.362-026	Personnel Clerk (M)
209.367-038	News Assistant
209.367-054	Yard Clerk
209.387-010	Coding Clerk
209.387-014	Compiler
219.367-034	Stock-Control Clerk (M)
219.387-014	Insurance Clerk 1
221.362-010	Aircraft-Log Clerk (M)
222.137-038	Stock-Control Supervisor (M)
245.362-010	Medical-Record Clerk (M)
245.362-014	Ward Clerk (M)
248.367-010	Airplane-Dispatch Clerk (M)
249.367-054	Order Clerk

Routing and Distribution

209.367-018	Correspondence-Review Clerk
209.587-026	Mail Clerk
209.687-014	Mail Handler
219.367-030	Shipping-Order Clerk
222.587-034	Route-Delviery Clerk
230.363-010	Rural-Mail Carrier
230.367-010	Mail Carrier
230.367-014	Messenger, Bank

Clerical Machine Operation

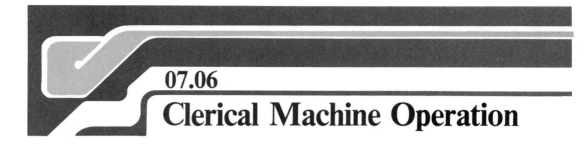

Clerical Machine Operation is to use business machines to record or process data. Workers use machines that type, print, sort, compute, or send and receive data. This group includes the subgroups of:

Computer Operation
Keyboard Machine Operation

Computer Operation is to control the input and output of data. Workers follow written orders to determine computer operations needed. They set the controls and load the equipment with paper and tapes or disks. They type in commands or monitor the computer and respond to messages. If errors occur they may correct them or end the program. Some workers operate peripheral (related) equipment such as printers. They prepare printouts as copy for business, scientific, or technical reports or publications.

Word processors are now common office machines.

Keyboard Machine Operation is to press keys to type, send or receive messages, or add figures. It also includes setting type matter for printing. Workers compile and prepare data to type reports, letters, or other materials. Some workers code, transmit, and decode secret messages. Others transcribe data onto magnetic tapes or punchcards. Some workers operate billing machines to compute bills. Others operate proof machines to sort, record, and prove bank records. Still others operate machines that prepare type for printing or printing plates.

Jobs may be found wherever large amounts of data are processed, sent, or received. Businesses, industries, and government agencies employ most of the workers in this group.

What Skills and Abilities Would Help You Succeed in This Kind of Work?

The most important skills are listed below. All of those listed do not apply to each occupation. As you explore occupations you should identify the specific ones needed.

Dexterity –to move the hands and fingers to operate a typewriter or other keyboard.

Accuracy – to operate a keyboard with speed and maintain a very high degree of accuracy.

Clerical – to observe details and recognize errors in numbers, spelling, and punctuation in written materials, charts, and tables.

Diligence – to do routine work and set tasks.

Leadership – to plan and oversee the work of others.

This man is using a proof machine in a financial office.

Do You Have or Can You Develop an Interest in This Kind of Work?

Review the following questions. Your answers can give you clues as to your interest in Clerical Machine Operation.

Have you played computer games? Did you have any trouble? Do you enjoy this type of activity?

Have you worked as an office helper at school or somewhere else? Did you type or operate any office machines? Was your work accurate?

Have you used a calculator? Can you use it rapidly and accurately?

Have you taken courses in typing? Was the typewriter keyboard easy to use? Were your speed test scores average or above? Do you enjoy typing?

What Else Should You Know About This Group of Occupations?

Workers in this group may sit for long periods of time. They may be exposed to noise caused by various office machines. They may develop eyestrain due to close work and the use of computer screens. Large offices usually have enough work to keep machines operating all the time. In small offices, machine operators may do a variety of other clerical tasks. Some computers are in use 24 hours a day, seven days a week. Therefore, computer operators may work evening and night shifts.

The military services offer training and experience related to some occupations in this group. These occupations are included in the list at the end of this group description. They are identified by an (M) following the occupational title. More information about the military training and experience opportunities may be found in Appendix A.

How Can You Prepare for This Kind of Work?

Jobs in this group require three months to two years of education and training. Spelling and grammar skills are important in some jobs in this group. Basic math skills may also be important. Employers may prefer workers who can operate several machines.

Some employers provide machine instruction and on-the-job training. However, applicants with some training usually have better chances for employment. Vocational and technical schools offer courses to prepare operators of computer terminals and keyboard machines.

Experienced workers with leadership ability may become supervisors.

As you plan your high school program you should include courses related to Clerical Machine Operation. The following list of courses and skills will help you plan your education.

Secretarial and Clerical – courses in word processing, typing, stenography, general office work, and related clerical programs.

Business Data Processing – courses in computer and console operation and data processing equipment operation.

General Studies – courses in basic and business math, general English, and composition can be helpful for some occupations in this group.

Qualifications Profile

This section is a summary of the worker traits and work factors related to successful job performance and worker satisfaction. Try to relate your interests, abilities, aptitudes, and preferences to these traits and factors. An asterisk (*) marks those traits and factors that are related to more than 60% of the occupations listed at the end of this group. The other traits and factors listed are as important, but relate to fewer occupations. See Appendices B-G for information about all of the worker traits and work factors.

Work Activities

The most important activities related to this group involve:

1. Things and objects.
* 3. Tasks of a routine, definite nature.
* 9. Processes, methods, or machines.

Work Situations

Workers must be willing to:

2. Perform routine tasks.

8. Make decisions using standards that can be measured or checked.
*10. Work within precise limits or standards of accuracy.

Data-People-Things

This chart shows the levels for these three basic elements of work as related to this group. Level means the degree of difficulty of job tasks rather than the amount of time involved. The terms low, average, and high indicate the highest level at which occupations are involved. Compare your interests and abilities with the levels checked.

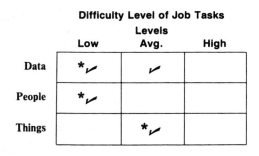

Difficulty Level of Job Tasks

	Levels		
	Low	Avg.	High
Data	*✓	✓	
People	*✓		
Things		*✓	

Aptitudes

This chart presents the most important aptitudes related to this group. The levels checked compare aptitudes needed for success in this group to aptitudes of the general working population in all occupations. For example, level 5 is low and represents the bottom 10% of the working population. Level 1 is high and represents the top 10%.

APTITUDE LEVELS COMPARED TO ALL WORKERS						
Related Aptitudes (Ability to Learn)		Lower 1/3		Middle 1/3	Upper 1/3	
		Level **5**	Level **4**	Level **3**	Level **2**	Level **1**
Code	**Title**	10%	23%	34%	23%	10%
G	General Learning Ability			*⤶		
P	Form Perception		⤶	*⤶		
Q	Clerical Perception				*⤶	
K	Motor Coordination			⤶	⤶	
F	Finger Dexterity			*⤶	⤶	
M	Manual Dexterity		⤶	*⤶		

A telegraphic-typewriter operator uses a special keyboard.

Physical Demands

Workers in this group of occupations must be able to do:

*S – Sedentary work
L – Light work

Working Conditions

These are the physical surroundings in which work is done. In occupations belonging to this group, work is performed:

*I – Inside — workers spend most of their time inside protected from weather conditions but not always from temperature changes.

Educational Skills

This chart shows the levels of reasoning, math, and language skills related to this group. These skills are usually developed in an educational setting. There are six levels ranging from the simple (1) to the most complex (6).

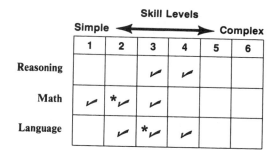

	Skill Levels					
	Simple ← → Complex					
	1	2	3	4	5	6
Reasoning			✔	✔		
Math	✔	*✔	✔			
Language		✔	*✔	✔		

Common Occupations

A full listing of all occupations belonging to this group may be found in the Guide for Occupational Exploration.

The following occupations have been selected to represent this group. They provide the major employment opportunities. However, specific job opportunities will vary according to locations of industry, geographical region, and other factors.

Information may be found in common sources of occupational information, state career information systems, and computerized guidance systems.

An (M) follows the occupational title where the military services offer training and experience.

Computer Operation

203.362-018 Terminal-System Operator
203.582-054 Terminal Operator
208.382-010 Terminal-Makeup Operator
213.132-010 Supervisor, Computer Operations (M)
213.362-010 Computer Operator (M)

213.382-010 Computer-Peripheral-Equipment Operator (M)
214.582-010 Invoicing Systems Operator

Keyboard Machine Operation

203.362-010 Clerk-Typist (M)
203.362-022 Word-Processing-Machine Operator (M)
203.582-018 Cryptographic-Machine Operator (M)
203.582-022 Data Typist
203.582-026 Data-Coder Operator (M)
203.582-030 Keypunch Operator (M)
203.582-034 Magnetic-Tape-Typewriter Operator
203.582-042 Photocomposing-Perforator-Machine Operator
203.582-050 Telegraphic-Typewriter Operator (M)
203.582-058 Transcribing-Machine Operator
203.582-062 Typesetter-Perforator Operator
203.582-066 Typist
203.582-070 Verifier Operator (M)
203.582-074 Electronic-Typesetting-Machine Operator
203.582-078 Notereader (M)
211.482-014 Food Checker
214.482-010 Billing-Machine Operator
217.382-010 Proof-Machine Operator
217.382-014 Transit Clerk
650.582-010 Linotype Operator
650.582-014 Monotype-Keyboard Operator
650.582-022 Phototypesetter Operator

07.07

Clerical Handling

Clerical Handling is to perform routine office tasks. Workers file, sort, copy, route, or deliver data. These tasks require little specific training or skill. This group includes the subgroups of:

Filing
Sorting and Distribution
General Clerical Work

Filing is to arrange materials in a certain order. Materials or records are filed in numerical order, by subject matter, or other system. Workers stamp and read incoming materials and sort them for filing. They may record index codes on materials for reference before placing them in folders, cabinets, drawers, or boxes. They also locate and remove materials from the files. They keep records of materials removed and trace (find) missing folders.

Sorting and Distribution involves giving out materials or arranging them into a certain sequence or grouping. Workers sort data to be mailed, copied, filed, or delivered. They may keep records of where these materials were sent or how they were processed. Some workers distribute (give out) samples, handbills, and coupons to advertise a product or service. Still others deliver messages, documents, or packages to homes or businesses.

General Clerical Work involves a variety of duties. Workers open, sort, and distribute incoming mail. They collect, address, seal, and stamp outgoing mail. They type, copy, and file materials, and answer the telephone. Some workers do not work in offices. They deliver messages and run errands. Others collect coins or coin boxes from parking meters or telephone pay stations.

Jobs in this group may be found with large businesses, industries, and government agencies.

What Skills and Abilities Would Help You Succeed in This Kind of Work?

The most important skills are listed below. All of those listed do not apply to each occupation. As you explore occupations you should identify the specific ones needed.

Accuracy – to keep records and copy numbers without error.

Diligence – to do routine work daily.

Congenial – to get along with others and work as a member of a team.

Comprehension – to understand and follow directions and set procedures.

Clerical – to perform office tasks that do not require special skills.

This distributing clerk is checking the accuracy of materials to be delivered.

Do You Have or Can You Develop an Interest in This Kind of Work?

Review the following questions. Your answers can give you clues as to your interest in Clerical Handling.

Have you helped to address and stamp newsletters? Did you enjoy this routine type of work?

Have you collected stamps or coins? Did you arrange them in a book or album?

Do you have a photo album? Have you arranged the pictures in a certain order?

Have you worked as an office helper at school or somewhere else? Did you run errands?

Have you kept records of something for yourself or for a club or group? Were you able to keep the record accurately?

Have you helped put papers or cards in order according to the alphabet? Could you follow set filing procedures? Could you adjust to routine work?

Have you kept attendance records for a class or club? Do you enjoy this type of work?

What Else Should You Know
About This Group of Occupations?

Some jobs in this group may be part-time. Although the pay is low, the experience gained can be valuable for advancement. The chances of getting a job are higher if you can type. Most workers in this group are on their feet for long periods of time. Some jobs may require evening or night-shift work.

The military services offer training and experience related to some occupations in this group. These occupations are included in the list at the end of this group description. They are identified by an (M) following the occupational title. More information about the military training and experience opportunities may be found in Appendix A.

How Can You Prepare
For This Kind of Work?

Most occupations in this group require little preparation. Thirty days to three months of education and training is all that is usually needed. Most employers provide on-the-job training. However, high school level commercial courses are helpful in getting these jobs. Federal government jobs usually require applicants to take a civil service exam.

Employers sometimes hire workers who have clerical training but no experience. Workers are then selected from these entry jobs to fill openings in higher level jobs as they gain experience and demonstrate good job attitudes. As a result, jobs in this group are often a starting place for promotion to other types of office jobs.

As you plan your high school program you should include courses related to Clerical Handling. The following list of courses and skills can help you plan your education.

Secretarial and Clerical – courses in business such as record keeping, typing, and filing.

General Studies – courses in general English, composition, spelling, math, and other courses leading to a high school diploma can be helpful for most occupations in this group.

Qualifications Profile

This section is a summary of the worker traits and work factors related to successful job performance and worker satisfaction. Try to relate your interests, abilities, aptitudes, and preferences to these traits and factors. An asterisk (*) marks those traits and factors that are related to more than 60% of the occupations listed at the end of this group. The other traits and factors listed are as important, but relate to fewer occupations. See Appendices B-G for information about all of the worker traits and work factors.

Work Situations

Workers must be willing to:

   1. Perform duties which change frequently.
* 2. Perform routine tasks.
  10. Work within precise limits or standards of accuracy.

Some clerical workers have outside jobs, as this man making deliveries.

Work Activities

The most important activities related to this group involve:

1. Things and objects.
2. Business contact.
* 3. Tasks of a routine, definite nature.

Working Conditions

These are the physical surroundings in which work is done. In occupations belonging to this group, work is performed:

*I – Inside — workers spend most of their time inside protected from weather conditions but not always from temperature changes.

O – Outside — workers spend most of their time outside with little protection from weather conditions.

Data-People-Things

This chart shows the levels for these three basic elements of work as related to this group. Level means the degree of difficulty of job tasks rather than the amount of time involved. The terms low, average, and high indicate the highest level at which occupations are involved. Compare your interests and abilities with the levels checked.

Difficulty Level of Job Tasks

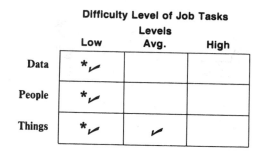

	Levels		
	Low	Avg.	High
Data	*✓		
People	*✓		
Things	*✓	✓	

This general clerk works in the mailroom of a well-equipped center.

Aptitudes

This chart presents the most important aptitudes related to this group. The levels checked compare aptitudes needed for success in this group to aptitudes of the general working population in all occupations. For example, level 5 is low and represents the bottom 10% of the working population. Level 1 is high and represents the top 10%.

Physical Demands

Workers in this group of occupations must be able to do:

*L – Light work

APTITUDE LEVELS COMPARED TO ALL WORKERS						
Related Aptitudes **(Ability to Learn)**		Lower 1/3		Middle 1/3	Upper 1/3	
		Level 5	Level 4	Level 3	Level 2	Level 1
Code	Title	10%	23%	34%	23%	10%
G	General Learning Ability		✔	✔		
Q	Clerical Perception		✔	✔		
M	Manual Dexterity		✔	*✔		

288

Educational Skills

This chart shows the levels of reasoning, math, and language skills related to this group. These skills are usually developed in an educational setting. There are six levels ranging from the simple (1) to the most complex (6).

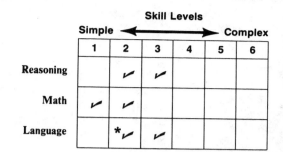

	Simple					**Complex**
	Skill Levels					
	1	**2**	**3**	**4**	**5**	**6**
Reasoning		✔	✔			
Math	✔	✔				
Language		*✔	✔			

Common Occupations

A full listing of all occupations belonging to this group may be found in the Guide for Occupational Exploration.

The following occupations have been selected to represent this group. They provide the major employment opportunities. However, specific job opportunities will vary according to locations of industry, geographical region, and other factors.

Information may be found in common sources of occupational information, state career information systems, and computerized guidance systems.

An (M) follows the occupational title where the military services offer training and experience.

Filing
206.362-010 File Clerk 1

Sorting and Distribution
209.587-010 Addresser
209.687-022 Sorter
222.587-018 Distributing Clerk
222.687-022 Routing Clerk
230.667-010 Deliverer, Outside
230.687-010 Advertising-Material Distributor
239.677-010 Messenger, Copy

General Clerical Work
209.562-010 Clerk, General (M)
209.567-022 Office Clerk
239.567-010 Office Helper
248.362-014 Weather Clerk (M)
292.687-010 Coin-Machine Collector

08 PERSUASIVE
(Selling)

People with an interest in persuading others to a point of view can satisfy this interest through selling. Workers explain, demonstrate, and sell products or services. Many different methods of selling are used. Workers may travel a set route, work in a single location, or go door-to-door. Some may sell through home demonstration parties or at entertainment events. Sales workers need to have background knowledge of the products or services they sell. The more complex the product or service, the more background needed. Customers need to feel confident that what they are buying will meet their needs. Sales work provides an opportunity to combine an interest in sales with another interest or ability. For example, a person with an interest in sports can sell sporting goods and equipment.

Workers in selling need to be able to express themselves well. They need to be enthusiastic about what they are selling. Some sales work involves an aggressive sales pitch to get the potential customers' attention. For example, vendors call out to crowds what they are selling. And, an auctioneer excites a crowd into a competitive mood for sales. All sales workers need to treat customers with respect and courtesy. Workers need basic math skills. Some need skills to add sales and make change. Others need more skills to compute costs and prepare sales contracts.

The Persuasive area is divided into two clusters: Technical Sales and General Sales.

Technical Sales

The Technical Sales cluster requires a broad background knowledge of the products or services being sold. Workers must be able to provide technical data for buyers and help them select products or services to meet their needs. Other workers need a knowledge of products to buy for resale. Some workers seek out prospects in industry, business, or professional clients. Some are paid a commission on sales. They get a percentage of the price of products sold.

General Sales

The General Sales cluster involves routine sales. Workers only need to answer general questions and point out the good features of a product or service. Some sell inexpensive items such as novelties and snacks. Most of the jobs in this cluster are found in retail and wholesale stores. Workers greet customers, answer questions, prepare sales slips, and receive payment or secure credit approval. Some workers take telephone orders from customers. Others solicit (seek) customers for a product or service by making phone calls to people in an area.

The following Worker Trait Groups and Subgroups are related to the Technical Sales and General Sales clusters.

Persuasive: an interest in influencing others through sales and promotional techniques.

Technical Sales

08.01 Sales Technology
Technical Sales
Intangible Sales
Purchasing and Sales

General Sales

08.02 General Sales
Wholesale
Retail
Special Sales

08.03 Vending
Peddling and Hawking

08.01

Sales Technology

Sales Technology is to seek out prospects and sell major products and services to industry, business, and professional clients. Workers need to have extensive knowledge of their products and of the field. They must take care of the customers they have and find new ones in the area or region to which they are assigned. They make decisions as they prepare bids on projects, write sales contracts, compute costs, and advise their clients. They may write sales proposals and reports. All workers in this group perform similar tasks but differ in the knowledge and skills needed for the type of products or services sold. This group includes the subgroups of:

Technical Sales
Intangible Sales
Purchasing and Sales

Technical Sales involves contact with managers and owners of businesses and industries. Workers sell such products as machinery, raw and processed materials, computer and electronic systems, and medical equipment and supplies. They must be able to determine customer needs and show how their products can increase a customer's production, sales, or quality of services.

Intangible Sales involve services. This may be in the form of insurance and financial services. It includes services of utilities such as gas, electric, and telephone. Also included are travel, freight, printing, and other business services such as space for advertising in publications and radio and TV time.

Purchasing and Sales involves buying for resale. Workers must be able to judge the quality and value of what they buy and estimate the number that will be sold, so that a profit can be made. They must keep up with the market, trends, and fashions. What they deal in ranges from business enterprises to livestock or articles sold in pawnshops.

Jobs may be found with manufacturers, wholesalers, and with financial, insurance, and business service firms.

A construction machinery salesman listens intently as his prospect raises a question.

Insurance sales approaches today include stations like this in a department store.

What Skills and Abilities Would Help You Succeed in This Kind of Work?

The most important skills are listed below. All of those listed do not apply to each occupation. As you explore occupations you should identify the specific ones needed.

Comprehension – to learn and understand technical information about products or services bought and sold.

Verbalization – to express yourself well and explain technical information in a clear and concise manner.

Social Skills – to gain the trust of others through attitude and behavior.

Clerical – to note errors in figures or wording in contracts or purchase orders.

Numerical – to do math quickly and correctly.

Persuasiveness – to use words to influence the thinking and actions of others to sell products and services.

Organizational – to plan and manage time and work.

Analytical – to know credit rules and when it is best to buy or sell.

Do You Have or Can You Develop an Interest in This Kind of Work?

Review the following questions. Your answers can give you clues as to your interest in Sales Technology.

Have you sold advertising space in the school yearbook, newspaper, or magazine? Did you find people easy to persuade?

Have you read business magazines or newspapers? Do you enjoy this type of reading?

Have you attended auctions? Can you judge, in advance, the prices at which items will sell? Do you like to estimate the cost of items?

Have you taken business or sales related subjects in school? Did you like the courses?

Have you bought and resold items? Did you make a good profit? Do you enjoy selling?

Have you made speeches or been in debates? Did you enjoy presenting ideas to people?

What Else Should You Know
About This Group of Occupations?

Most workers in this group work alone much of the time. They set their hours to conform to travel and client schedules. Their pay may depend on their performance. They often work long and irregular hours. They may spend their evenings writing reports or filling out orders. Some workers travel a lot in the region they cover. They may be on their feet for long periods of time and may carry heavy catalogs or sample cases.

Many workers are under pressure. They must make important decisions. These decisions affect sales or investments involving large sums of money. Some workers receive a salary. Others work on a commission. This commission is usually a percent of the price of the goods or services sold. Some workers own their businesses. Usually these owners receive little more than living expenses until the businesses show a profit.

How Can You Prepare
for This Kind of Work?

Most occupations in this group require one to four years of education and training. The most common way to prepare for this work is to obtain a two or four-year degree. A major in business administration, marketing, or a related field would help prepare workers for these jobs. A degree in engineering, chemistry, or physics may help workers sell technical products. Workers with related work experience and a high school education or its equal may be advanced to these jobs.

Most employers give new workers formal and informal training. This training helps workers learn the policies, methods, and details of their work. The training period may last up to one year. Jobs in insurance often require the worker to have a state or local license. These licenses are usually obtained by passing a written test.

As you plan your high school education you should include courses related to Sales

This financial planner is employed by a bank – his other duties include helping savers open accounts.

Technology. Also, you should include courses needed to enter college. The following list of courses and skills will help you plan your education.

General Merchandising and Sales – courses in financial services marketing, general marketing, insurance marketing, and entrepreneurship (starting and running a business).

Marketing Services – courses in business and personal services marketing.

Engineering Sales – courses in chemistry, physics, drafting, advanced math, industrial and machine technology, and industrial safety.

Technical Sales – courses in subjects related to the products sold.

General Studies – courses in general English, speech, math, data processing, and technical writing can be helpful for occupations in this group.

Qualifications Profile

This section is a summary of the worker traits and work factors related to successful job performance and worker satisfaction. Try to relate your interests, abilities, aptitudes, and preferences to these traits and factors. An asterisk (*) marks those traits and factors that are related to more than 60% of the occupations listed at the end of this group. The other traits and factors listed are as important, but relate to fewer occupations. See Appendices B-G for information about all of the worker traits and work factors.

Work Activities

The most important activities related to this group involve:

* * 2. Business contact.
  5. Recognition or appreciation from others.
* * 6. Communication of ideas and information.

Work Situations

Workers must be willing to:

* * 4. Deal with people.
* * 5. Influence people's opinions, attitudes, and judgments.
* * 7. Make decisions using personal judgment.
  8. Make decisions using standards that can be measured or checked.

Working Conditions

These are the physical surroundings in which work is done. In occupations belonging to this group, work is performed:

* *I – Inside — workers spend most of their time inside protected from weather conditions but not always from temperature changes.

Aptitudes

This chart presents the most important aptitudes related to this group. The levels checked compare aptitudes needed for success in this group to aptitudes of the general working population in all occupations. For example, level 5 is low and represents the bottom 10% of the working population. Level 1 is high and represents the top 10%.

APTITUDE LEVELS COMPARED TO ALL WORKERS						
Related Aptitudes (Ability to Learn)		Lower 1/3		Middle 1/3	Upper 1/3	
		Level **5**	Level **4**	Level **3**	Level **2**	Level **1**
Code	Title	10%	23%	34%	23%	10%
G	General Learning Ability			✔	* ✔	
V	Verbal			✔	* ✔	
N	Numerical			* ✔	✔	
Q	Clerical Perception			* ✔	✔	

Physical Demands

Workers in this group of occupations must be able to do:

*L – Light work

Educational Skills

This chart shows the levels of reasoning, math, and language skills related to this group. These skills are usually developed in an educational setting. There are six levels ranging from the simple (1) to the most complex (6).

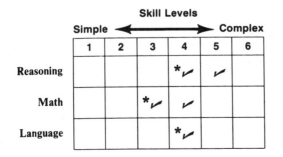

Skill Levels

Simple ⟵⟶ Complex

	1	2	3	4	5	6
Reasoning				* ✔	✔	
Math			* ✔	✔		
Language				* ✔		

Buyers, such as this man in a sporting goods store, must know inventories and sales levels.

Data-People-Things

This chart shows the levels for these three basic elements of work as related to this group. Level means the degree of difficulty of job tasks rather than the amount of time involved. The terms low, average, and high indicate the highest level at which occupations are involved. Compare your interests and abilities with the levels checked.

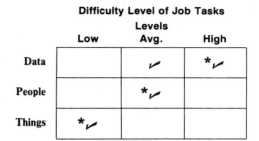

Difficulty Level of Job Tasks

	Levels		
	Low	Avg.	High
Data		✔	*✔
People		*✔	
Things	*✔		

Common Occupations

A full listing of all occupations belonging to this group may be found in the Guide for Occupational Exploration.

The following occupations have been selected to represent this group. They provide the major employment opportunities. However, specific job opportunities will vary according to locations of industry, geographical region, and other factors.

Information may be found in common sources of occupational information, state career information systems, and computerized guidance systems.

An (M) follows the occupational title where the military services offer training and experience.

08.01 SALES TECHNOLOGY

Technical Sales

254.257-010	Sales Representative, Signs and Displays
262.357-010	Chemicals and Drugs
271.357-010	Electronics Parts
274.257-010	Foundry And Machine Shop Products
274.357-022	Construction Machinery
274.357-038	Industrial Machinery
274.357-058	Oilfield Supplies And Equipment
275.257-010	Computers And EDP Systems
276.257-010	Dental And Medical Equipment

Intangible Sales

250.257-010	Sales Agent, Insurance
251.257-010	Sales Agent, Financial Services
251.257-014	Sales Agent, Psychological Tests And Industrial Relations
251.257-022	Financial Planner
252.257-010	Traffic Agent
253.257-010	Sales Representative, Telephone Services
253.357-010	Public Utilities
254.357-014	Advertising
254.357-018	Printing
259.157-014	Hotel Services
259.257-010	Education Courses
259.357-018	Radio And Television Time

Purchasing and Sales

162.157-018	Buyer
162.157-022	Buyer, Assistant
162.157-026	Commission Agent, Livestock
189.157-010	Business-Opportunity-And-Property -Investment Broker
191.157-010	Pawnbroker
260.257-010	Sales Representative, Livestock
296.367-014	Comparison Shopper

08.02

General Sales

General Sales is to explain, demonstrate, and sell consumer products and services. Some workers call on businesses or individual customers. They may have a set route they cover. Others work in a single location such as a music or clothing store. Some who sell complex products or services need more background knowledge. This group includes the subgroups of:

Wholesale
Retail
Special Sales

Wholesale is to sell large amounts of products to retail merchants for resale. Workers compile lists of prospective (possible) buyers and solicit (seek) their orders in person or by phone. They display or use the products and explain the features. They quote prices and credit terms and prepare sales orders. They estimate delivery dates, write reports, and keep expense accounts. They also advise their customers on ways to display products and how to increase their sales.

Retail is to sell products in small amounts directly to the consumer. Workers greet customers and find out what needs or interests they have. They suggest products that meet the customers' needs and may help them make their selections. They answer questions and stress the good features of articles, such as quality, durability, or style. They prepare sales slips and receive payment or secure credit approval. They also place new products on display.

Special Sales involve selling products, land, or services in a unique way. In most of these jobs, the customer makes the first contact. Special Sales include selling or renting property, pest control, travel arrangements, furniture upholstery, and business services. Workers in this group use different methods of selling. Some drive regular routes to deliver and sell products or services. Others sell by demonstrating products in a home or place of business. Still others sell over the phone or from door-to-door. And, some sell items to the highest bidder at auctions.

Jobs in this group are found wherever there is contact with people for the purpose of selling. This includes retail and wholesale stores and businesses. Some workers are self-employed.

What Skills and Abilities Would Help You Succeed in This Kind of Work?

The most important skills are listed below. All of those listed do not apply to each occupation. As you explore occupations you should identify the specific ones needed.

Verbalization – to speak clearly and hold the attention of others.

Social Skills – to gain the trust of others through your attitude and behavior.

Numerical – to complete order blanks, enter prices, figure costs, and make change.

Physical Stamina – to stay alert all day and be physically active as needed.

Clerical – to keep records of sales, customers contacted, and personal expenses.

Comprehension – to understand and explain company policies.

Persuasiveness – to use words to influence the thinking and action of others for the sale of products or services.

Do You Have or Can You Develop an Interest in This Kind of Work?

Review the following questions. Your answers can give you clues as to your interest in General Sales.

Have you sold advertising space in a school yearbook, newspaper, or magazine? Did you find people easy to talk with and persuade?

Have you worked in a grocery or other store? Do you like sales work? Can you figure prices and make change correctly?

Have you given oral reports in front of a group? Can you express your ideas easily?

Have you solicited clothes, food, and other supplies for needy people? Were you successful? Did you mind asking people to donate?

Have you had courses in sales, bookkeeping, or business math? Did you like these courses? Can you work with numbers?

Have you sold items door-to-door for a class or civic group? Do you like to meet people this way?

What Else Should You Know About This Group of Occupations?

Some sales work provides flexible hours or part-time work. Many workers in this group, such as Sales Representatives, set their own schedules. They make calls when it is convenient for the customer. Therefore, they may have to travel evenings or weekends. Some of these workers are under pressure to meet sales quotas.

Some workers may have to stand on their feet for long periods of time. Working hours vary in many retail jobs. Many stores stay open evenings, Sundays, and holidays.

Some workers are paid by the hour. Others are paid according to how much they sell. Some pay scales may combine both of these ways. Workers with sales experience are sometimes promoted to managers.

Other sales occupations are included in WTG 08.01, Sales Technology. Those occupations require more training and experience and some offer chances for advancement from occupations in General Sales.

A women's apparel salesperson displays for a buyer in a hotel's sample room.

This retail salesperson of athletic shoes has many styles of special-purpose shoes.

How Can You Prepare
for This Kind of Work?

Most occupations in this group require three months to two years of education and training. Most of the jobs in this group require a high school education or its equal. Many high schools, junior colleges, and community colleges offer helpful courses in selling or retailing. Some schools provide work study

programs in which students work part-time as well as attend classes. Selling experience during vacations would also help prepare for this type of work.

Employers usually provide some on-the-job training. New workers learn about the company policies and the products or services to be sold. These training programs may last from one week to three months. Some jobs may require workers to have an extra skill such as driving a truck or using a keyboard such as a cash register/computer. Other jobs may require workers to make minor repairs or adjustments on the equipment they sell.

As you plan your high school program you should include courses related to General Sales. The following list of courses and skills can help you plan your education.

General Merchandising and Sales – courses in apparel and accessories marketing; entrepreneurship; flowers, plants, farm pro-

Travel agents sell dreams as well as tickets and reservations for business trips.

duce and garden supplies marketing; hospitality and recreation marketing; insurance marketing; and transportation and travel marketing.

General Studies – courses in English, general math, speech, and distributive education can be helpful for occupations in this group.

Qualifications Profile

This section is a summary of the worker traits and work factors related to successful job performance and worker satisfaction. Try to relate your interests, abilities, aptitudes, and preferences to these traits and factors. An asterisk (*) marks those traits and factors that are related to more than 60% of the occupations listed at the end of this group. The other traits and factors listed are as important, but relate to fewer occupations. See Appendices B-G for information about all of the worker traits and work factors.

Work Activities

The most important activities related to this group involve:

* 2. Business contact.
  3. Tasks of a routine, definite nature.
* 6. Communication of ideas and information.

Work Situations

Workers must be willing to:

* 4. Deal with people.
* 5. Influence people's opinions, attitudes, and judgments.
* 7. Make decisions using personal judgment.

Working Conditions

These are the physical surroundings in which work is done. In occupations belonging to this group, work is performed:

*I – Inside — workers spend most of their time inside protected from weather conditions but not always from temperature changes.

Data-People-Things

This chart shows the levels for these three basic elements of work as related to this group. Level means the degree of difficulty of job tasks rather than the amount of time involved. The terms low, average, and high indicate the highest level at which occupations are involved. Compare your interests and abilities with the levels checked.

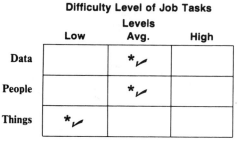

Difficulty Level of Job Tasks

	Low	Avg.	High
Data		*✓	
People		*✓	
Things	*✓		

Aptitudes

This chart presents the most important aptitudes related to this group. The levels checked compare aptitudes needed for success in this group to aptitudes of the general working population in all occupations. For example, level 5 is low and represents the bottom 10% of the working population. Level 1 is high and represents the top 10%.

APTITUDE LEVELS COMPARED TO ALL WORKERS						
Related Aptitudes (Ability to Learn)		Lower 1/3		Middle 1/3	Upper 1/3	
		Level **5**	Level **4**	Level **3**	Level **2**	Level **1**
Code	Title	10%	23%	34%	23%	10%
G	General Learning Ability			*✔		
V	Verbal			*✔	✔	
N	Numerical			*✔		
Q	Clerical Perception		✔	*✔		

This route salesman is a retail worker – many products have wholesale routes.

Physical Demands

Workers in this group of occupations must be able to do:

*L – Light work

Educational Skills

This chart shows the levels of reasoning, math, and language skills related to this group. These skills are usually developed in an educational setting. There are six levels ranging from the simple (1) to the most complex (6).

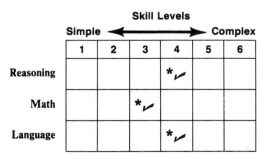

	Skill Levels Simple ← → Complex					
	1	2	3	4	5	6
Reasoning				*✔		
Math			*✔			
Language				*✔		

Common Occupations

A full listing of all occupations belonging to this group may be found in the Guide for Occupational Exploration.

The following occupations have been selected to represent this group. They provide the major employment opportunities. However, specific job opportunities will vary according to locations of industry, geographical region, and other factors.

Information may be found in common sources of occupational information, state career information systems, and computerized guidance systems.

An (M) follows the occupational title where the military services offer training and experience.

Wholesale

260.357-014	Sales Representative, Food Products
261.357-018	Sales Representative, Footwear
261.357-022	Mens And Boys Apparel
261.357-038	Womens And Girls Apparel
262.357-014	Toilet Preparations
269.357-018	Sales-Promotion Representative
270.357-010	Sales Representative, Home Furnishings
270.357-014	Household Appliances
272.357-014	Farm And Garden Equipment And Supplies
273.357-018	Boats And Marine Supplies
273.357-022	Motor Vehicles And Supplies
274.357-034	Hardware Supplies
275.357-010	Barber And Beauty Equipment
275.357-018	Commercial Equipment And Supplies
275.357-026	Hotel And Restaurant Equipment
275.357-034	Office Machines
277.357-022	Publications
277.357-026	Recreation And Sporting Goods
279.157-010	Manufacturers Representative
279.357-014	Sales Representative, General Merchandise
279.357-018	Jewelry
279.357-026	Paper And Paper Products
279.357-030	Plastic Products

Retail

260.357-026	Salesperson, Flowers
261.357-050	Mens And Boys Clothing
261.357-054	Mens Furnishings
261.357-062	Shoes
261.357-066	Womens Apparel And Accessories
261.357-070	Yard Goods
262.357-018	Cosmetics And Toiletries
270.357-022	Curtains And Draperies
270.357-026	Floor Coverings
270.357-030	Furniture
270.357-034	Household Appliances
270.357-038	Stereo Equipment
272.357-022	Horticultural And Nursery Products
273.353-010	Automobiles
273.357-030	Automobile Accessories
276.354-010	Hearing Aids
277.357-034	Books
277.357-038	Musical Instruments And Accessories
277.357-042	Pets And Pet Supplies
277.357-050	Photographic Supplies And Equipment
277.357-058	Sporting Goods
279.357-042	Burial Needs
279.357-050	General Hardware
279.357-054	General Merchandise
279.357-058	Jewelry
279.357-062	Parts
294.257-010	Auctioneer

Special Sales

250.157-010	Superintendent, Sales
250.357-010	Building Consultant
250.357-018	Sales Agent, Real Estate
251.357-010	Sales Agent, Business Services
251.357-018	Sales Agent, Pest Control Service
252.157-010	Travel Agent
259.357-026	Sales Representative, Upholstery And Furniture Rep
279.357-038	Salesperson-Demonstrator, Party Plan
291.357-010	Sales Representative, Door-To-Door
292.353-010	Driver, Sales Route
292.667-010	Driver Helper, Sales Route
297.354-010	Demonstrator
297.454-010	Demonstrator, Sewing Techniques
299.357-014	Telephone Solicitor

Vending

Vending is to sell low-priced items in public places. Workers may shout, gesture, sing, or ring bells to draw attention to what they are selling. They make many quick sales. They have to add the total cost of items in their heads and make correct change quickly. This subgroup includes the subgroup of:

Peddling and Hawking

Peddling and Hawking is to travel from place to place with goods for sale. Some workers sell food, drinks, vegetables, or flowers from a pushcart or truck. Others take pictures of people and try to persuade them to buy additional prints. Still others move through stands during a public event and sell programs, novelties, or food items.

Jobs may be found with restaurants, clubs, and sports arenas. Some workers are self-employed.

What Skills and Abilities Would Help You Succeed in This Kind of Work?

The most important skills are listed below. All of those listed do not apply to each occupation. As you explore occupations you should identify the specific ones needed.

Verbalization – to express words and speak clearly.

Persuasiveness – to influence the thinking of others for the sale of products.

Numerical – to add numbers mentally and make correct change.

Physical Stamina – to walk and carry the products being sold or to stand for long periods of time.

Dexterity – to move the hands and fingers in coordination with the eyes.

This vendor sets up at fairs, in malls, and other locations where people congregate.

Vendors carry food and beverages through crowds at many sporting events.

Do You Have or Can You Develop an Interest in This Kind of Work?

Review the following questions. Your answers can give you clues as to your interest in Vending.

Have you sold advertising space in a school yearbook, newspaper, or magazine? Did you find people easy to talk with and to persuade?

Have you worked at a garage or rummage sale or the refreshment stand at a game? Can you figure the cost of several items rapidly and make change correctly?

Have you sold magazines or candy door-to-door? Do you like to approach people?

Have you tried to sell products to raise money for a school or civic project? Did you sell the number of products assigned to you?

Have you sold programs or food at a community carnival or fair? Did you enjoy shouting or gesturing to get the attention of a crowd?

What Else Should You Know About This Group of Occupations?

Some jobs in this group are seasonal. Workers who sell on the streets or at outdoor public events usually cannot work during cold weather. The work can be tiring for those who carry heavy loads of items around or up and down steps. Most of the jobs offer part-time employment. However, the experience gained can be applied to other saleswork.

How Can You Prepare for This Kind of Work?

Occupations in this group require a few days to three months of training depending upon the specific kind of work. Workers may only receive short instructions from their employers. These instructions usually include the selling price of items. Most jobs in this group are open to anyone.

As you plan your high school program you should include courses related to Vending. The following list of courses and skills will help you plan your education.

General Studies – courses in math, general merchandising and sales, speech, English, and distributive education are important for occupations in this group.

Sidewalk vendors are licensed in many of the major cities.

Qualifications Profile

This section is a summary of the worker traits and work factors related to successful job performance and worker satisfaction. Try to relate your interests, abilities, aptitudes, and preferences to these traits and factors. An asterisk (*) marks those traits and factors that are related to more than 60% of the occupations listed at the end of this group. The other traits and factors listed are as important, but relate to fewer occupations. See Appendices B-G for information about all of the worker traits and work factors.

Work Activities

The most important activities related to this group involve:

1. Things and objects.
* 2. Business contact.
3. Tasks of a routine, definite nature.
6. Communication of ideas and information.

Physical Demands

Workers in this group of occupations must be able to do:

  L – Light work
* M – Medium work

Work Situations

Workers must be willing to:

2. Perform routine tasks.
* 4. Deal with people.
5. Influence people's opinions, attitudes, and judgments.

Data-People-Things

This chart shows the levels for these three basic elements of work as related to this group. Level means the degree of difficulty of job tasks rather than the amount of time involved. The terms low, average, and high indicate the highest level at which occupations are involved. Compare your interests and abilities with the levels checked.

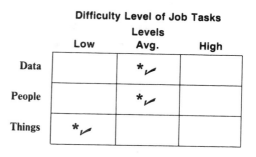

Difficulty Level of Job Tasks

	Low	Avg.	High
Data		* ✓	
People		* ✓	
Things	* ✓		

Aptitudes

This chart presents the most important aptitudes related to this group. The levels checked compare aptitudes needed for success in this group to aptitudes of the general working population in all occupations. For example, level 5 is low and represents the bottom 10% of the working population. Level 1 is high and represents the top 10%.

		APTITUDE LEVELS COMPARED TO ALL WORKERS				
Related Aptitudes (Ability to Learn)		Lower 1/3		Middle 1/3	Upper 1/3	
		Level 5	Level 4	Level 3	Level 2	Level 1
Code	Title	10%	23%	34%	23%	10%
N	Numerical		✔	✔		
F	Finger Dexterity		*✔	✔		
M	Manual Dexterity		*✔	✔		

Educational Skills

This chart shows the levels of reasoning, math, and language skills related to this group. These skills are usually developed in an educational setting. There are six levels ranging from the simple (1) to the most complex (6).

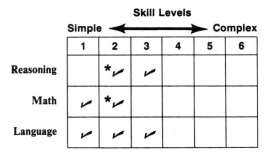

Skill Levels

Simple ←————————→ Complex

	1	2	3	4	5	6
Reasoning		*✔	✔			
Math	✔	*✔				
Language	✔	✔	✔			

Working Conditions

These are the physical surroundings in which work is done. In occupations belonging to this group, work is performed:

I – Inside — workers spend most of their time inside protected from weather conditions but not always from temperature changes.

O – Outside — workers spend most of their time outside with little protection from weather conditions.

B – Both inside and outside — workers spend about equal time in each setting.

Common Occupations

A full listing of all occupations belonging to this group may be found in the Guide for Occupational Exploration.

The following occupations have been selected to represent this group. They provide the major employment opportunities. However, specific job opportunities will vary according to locations of industry, geographical region, and other factors.

Information may be found in common sources of occupational information, state career information systems, and computerized guidance systems.

An (M) follows the occupational title where the military services offer training and experience.

Peddling and Hawking

143.457-010 Photographer
291.457-014 Lounge-Car Attendant
291.457-018 Peddler
291.457-022 Vendor

ACCOMMODATING

People with an interest in catering (providing people with services they need or desire) enjoy work in this area. Workers serve and assist people usually on a one-to-one basis. They need the ability to meet and get along with all kinds of people. And, they must deal with the different moods customers may be in. Workers should have poise, good dress and personal grooming habits, and pleasant dispositions (attitudes and moods). Workers must have a feeling of concern for the people they serve. This may be for their safety. Or, it may be to make them feel at ease and enjoy themselves.

The Accommodating area is divided into two clusters: Hospitality/Customer Services and Barber/Beauty Services.

Hospitality/Customer Services

The Hospitality/Customer Services cluster includes travel, lodging, food, passenger, customer, and attendant services. Some workers perform duties to make people feel at ease in a social setting or while traveling. Other workers transport people by bus, taxi, limousine, or other vehicle. They follow directions given by passengers or follow a set route each day. Their work involves more than driving. They answer questions and provide information to help make their customers feel welcome. They may provide a special service such as holding an umbrella to keep a customer dry while entering or leaving. Other workers assist people who pay for purchases or services. Jobs range from delivering newspapers to serving food. Some workers provide direct services such as carrying luggage for hotel guests. Others perform indirect services such as cleaning and setting tables in a restaurant.

Barber/Beauty Services

The Barber/Beauty Services cluster involves helping people to improve or change their personal appearances. Workers are involved with treatment of the skin, hair, and nails. They cut, wash, and style hair. They also advise their patrons on how to care for their hair. They may give facial massages and clean, shape, and polish fingernails and toenails. They need good finger and manual dexterity (the ability to move their hands and fingers with ease) and the ability to see the difference between closely related colors. These workers need to be good listeners and gain their customers' trust. They need to make new customers feel at ease and want to return as well as to keep their regular customers.

The following Worker Trait Groups and Subgroups are related to the Hospitality/Customer Services and Barber/Beauty Services.

Accommodating: an interest in providing personal and customer services to meet the needs of people.

Hospitality/Customer Services

09.01 Hospitality Services
Social and Recreational
Activities
Guide Services
Food Services
Safety and Comfort Services

09.03 Passenger Services
Group Transportation
Individual Transportation
Instruction and Supervision

09.04 Customer Services
Food Services
Sales Services

09.05 Attendant Services
Physical Conditioning
Miscellaneous Personal
Services

Barber/Beauty Services

09.02 Barbering and Beauty Services
Cosmetology
Barbering

09.01
Hospitality Services

Hospitality Services involve doing things for others to make them feel at ease and enjoy themselves. Workers may plan and direct social events or serve as escorts or guides. They also may be concerned with the safety and needs of people who are traveling or on vacation. This group includes the subgroups of:

Social and Recreational Activities
Guide Services
Food Services
Safety and Comfort Services

Social and Recreational Activities involve helping people of all ages enjoy themselves in a variety of activities. Workers may organize senior citizen's or children's groups. They plan and direct cultural, recreational, arts and crafts, and social activities. Some workers may plan and organize activities for guests in hotels or passengers on board ships. They greet new arrivals, introduce them to other guests, and encourage them to take part in group activities. Other workers greet guests arriving at social functions. They may instruct those who serve the food and drinks. They also may plan and take part in social activities. Other workers may serve as guides for people who hunt or fish. They may plan trips and arrange for the transportation. They also may explain hunting and fishing laws and give instructions on how to use the gear (equipment).

Guide Services involve escorting visitors and giving them information. Workers may talk about points of interest in a city. Some take groups through museums or other public places. They lecture on interesting features and answer questions. Some may need to speak a foreign language. Some workers may collect fees or help with the luggage or equipment.

Food Services include workers who supervise and coordinate food service activities. They may greet and seat customers and supervise the duties of other workers. They also may schedule work hours, keep time records, and assist in planning menus. Some workers are concerned with duties in and around a private household. They may oversee the serving of meals and supervise other household workers in cooking, cleaning, and other duties.

Safety and Comfort Services involve attending to the personal needs of passengers. This may be on a ship, train, or airplane. Workers may greet passengers and collect or verify their tickets. They may need to assist some as they board or leave. Some may serve drinks and snacks. They must be concerned with the passengers' comfort and safety. They may explain the use of safety equipment. They also may prepare reports on passenger problems, money collected, or food and drink supplies.

Jobs may be found with airline, railroad, ship, and escort companies. Resorts and hotels also employ these workers. Jobs also may be found with social clubs, museums, retirement homes, and private households.

What Skills and Abilities Would Help You Succeed in This Kind of Work?

The most important skills are listed below. All of those listed do not apply to each occupation. As you explore occupations you should identify the specific ones needed.

Communication – to give or exchange information clearly and accurately.

Composure – to be calm and self-confident in emergency situations.

Versatile – to do a variety of tasks that may change often.

Leadership – to plan and direct the work of others.

Judgment – to make decisions about how to assist people with information or services they need.

Vocabulary – to use a variety of words to speak clearly.

Social – to meet and talk with all kinds of people and put them at ease.

Do You Have or Can You Develop an Interest in This Kind of Work?

Review the following questions. Your answers can give you clues as to your interest in the Hospitality Services field.

Do you feel comfortable in a group situation? Do you meet people easily?

Have you helped in planning a family picnic or other social activity? Did you lead others in games or group activities?

Have you announced a program? Have you had courses in speech? Do you like to speak to groups?

Have you waited tables at a school or club function? Did you enjoy the work involved?

Have you served as a volunteer at a youth camp or center? Was there an emergency? Did you remain calm?

Have you been a member of a school or civic group? Do you like to socialize?

Camp counselors enjoy children and have a special relationship with them.

Restaurant hostesses welcome guests, assign tables, and usually supervise workers.

Have you helped others learn to dance? Did they seem to enjoy the lessons?

Have you been treasurer or secretary for a social group? Can you keep accurate records?

What Else Should You Know About This Group of Occupations?

Most jobs in this group require workers to walk or stand most of the time. These workers also must remain pleasant and efficient regardless of how tired they are. Some have to travel often or live in hotels or resorts. However, this type of work provides an opportunity to meet interesting people and see new places. Night or holiday work may be required and some workers must wear uniforms.

The military services offer training and experience related to some occupations in this group. These occupations are included in the list at the end of this group description. They are identified by an (M) following the occupational title. More information about the military training and experience opportunities may be found in Appendix A.

How Can You Prepare for This Kind of Work?

Occupations in this group require from thirty days to over two years of education and training. Employers provide on-the-job training for most jobs in this group. Airplane flight attendants need formal training before being assigned a job. This training covers subjects such as personal grooming, in-flight service, and first aid. Most commercial airlines provide training programs. Some community colleges offer related courses. Some jobs require experience in related work to advance to supervising the work of others.

As you plan your high school education you should include courses related to

Hospitality Services. The courses and skills listed below will help you plan your education.

General Merchandising and Sales – courses in distributive education, food and related services, and tourism.

Speech – courses to gain competencies in speaking and listening.

Physical Education and Recreation – courses in outdoor recreation, leisure and recreational activities, crafts, games, and hobbies.

Courses in health and safety can be helpful to occupations in this group.

Courses in industrial arts and home economics also provide skills and can help you determine an interest in the Hospitality Services field.

Qualifications Profile

This section is a summary of the worker traits and work factors related to successful job performance and worker satisfaction. Try to relate your interests, abilities, aptitudes, and preferences to these traits and factors. An asterisk (*) marks those traits and factors that are related to more than 60% of the occupations listed at the end of this group. The other traits and factors listed are as important, but relate to fewer occupations. See Appendices B-G for information about all of the worker traits and work factors.

Work Activities

The most important activities related to this group involve:

* 2. Business contact.
  4. Direct personal contact to help or instruct others.
  5. Recognition or appreciation from others.
  6. Communication of ideas and information.

Work Situations

Workers must be willing to:

* 1. Perform duties which change frequently.
  3. Plan and direct an entire activity.
* 4. Deal with people.

Educational Skills

This chart shows the levels of reasoning, math, and language skills related to this group. These skills are usually developed in an educational setting. There are six levels ranging from the simple (1) to the most complex (6).

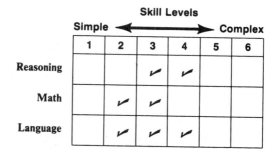

Physical Demands

Workers in this group of occupations must be able to do:

*L – Light work
M – Medium work

Working Conditions

These are the physical surroundings in which work is done. In occupations belonging to this group, work is performed:

*I – Inside — workers spend most of their time inside protected from weather conditions but not always from temperature changes.
B – Both inside and outside — workers spend about equal time in each setting.

Data-People-Things

This chart shows the levels for these three basic elements of work as related to this group. Level means the degree of difficulty of job tasks rather than the amount of time involved. The terms low, average, and high indicate the highest level at which occupations are involved. Compare your interests and abilities with the levels checked.

Difficulty Level of Job Tasks

	Levels		
	Low	Avg.	High
Data	✔	✔	✔
People	*✔		
Things	*✔		

Flight attendants demonstrate safety features, serve passengers, and help children and handicapped persons.

Aptitudes

This chart presents the most important aptitudes related to this group. The levels checked compare aptitudes needed for success in this group to aptitudes of the general working population in all occupations. For example, level 5 is low and represents the bottom 10% of the working population. Level 1 is high and represents the top 10%.

APTITUDE LEVELS COMPARED TO ALL WORKERS						
Related Aptitudes (Ability to Learn)		Lower 1/3		Middle 1/3	Upper 1/3	
		Level 5	Level 4	Level 3	Level 2	Level 1
Code	Title	10%	23%	34%	23%	10%
G	General Learning Ability			* ✔	✔	
V	Verbal			* ✔	✔	
Q	Clerical Perception		* ✔	✔		

Common Occupations

A full listing of all occupations belonging to this group may be found in the Guide for Occupational Exploration.

The following occupations have been selected to represent this group. They provide the major employment opportunities. However, specific job opportunities will vary according to locations of industry, geographical region, and other factors.

Information may be found in common sources of occupational information, state career information systems, and computerized guidance systems.

An (M) follows the occupational title where the military services offer training and experience.

Social and Recreational Activities

159.124-010 Counselor, Camp
195.164-010 Group Worker
195.227-014 Recreation Leader (M)
195.367-030 Recreation Aide
352.167-010 Director, Social
352.667-010 Host/Hostess
353.161-010 Guide, Hunting And Fishing

Guide Services

353.367-010 Guide
353.367-014 Guide, Establishment

Food Services

309.137-010 Butler
310.137-010 Host/Hostess, Restaurant
311.137-022 Waiter/Waitress, Head

Safety and Comfort Services

198.167-014 Conductor, Pullman
350.677-022 Steward/Stewardess
351.677-010 Service Attendant, Sleeping Car
352.367-010 Airplane-Flight Attendant (M)
352.377-010 Host/Hostess, Ground (M)
359.677-014 Funeral Attendant
359.677-022 Passenger Service Representative
910.364-010 Braker, Passenger Train

317

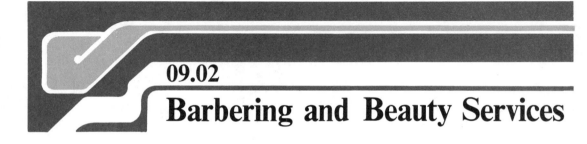

Barbering and Beauty Services

Barbering and Beauty Services are given to help change or improve personal appearance. Workers are concerned with the care of the hair, skin, scalp, and nails. This group includes the subgroups of:

Cosmetology
Barbering

Cosmetology is the practice of cosmetic treatment to the skin, hair, and nails. Workers provide many types of beauty services for their customers. They may study the hair to determine its condition. They wash, cut, and style it. They also may bleach, dye, or tint hair. Some workers may massage and treat the scalp. They may fit and service wigs or hairpieces. They also clean, shape, and polish fingernails and toenails. These workers advise their customers on how to care for their hair. They may keep records of treatments used on customers. They also keep their work area clean and their tools sanitized.

Barbering is a service that provides haircuts, facial massages, scalp treatments, and shaves. Barbers cut, trim, wash, and style hair. They may cut and shape mustaches and trim beards. They give shampoos and scalp treatments. They also may give facial treatments and massages. Some may fit hairpieces for their customers.

Jobs may be found with barber and beauty shops. Department stores, hotels, and nursing and retirement homes also employ these workers. A few workers may find jobs on passenger ships. Some workers own and operate their own businesses.

What Skills and Abilities Would Help You Succeed in This Kind of Work?

The most important skills are listed below. All of those listed do not apply to each occupation. As you explore occupations you should identify the specific ones needed.

Color Discrimination – to recognize different shades and tones of color.

Comprehension – to understand instructions for applying hair color and permanent waving solutions.

Dexterity – to move the hands and fingers in coordination with the eyes.

Esthetic Perception – to know quality or beauty to enhance the personal appearance of others.

Form Perception – to see differences in shapes, widths, and lengths of lines when cutting hair and shaping eyebrows.

Imagination – to form a mental image (picture) of a hair style to enhance the facial features of a patron.

Physical Stamina – to stand for long periods of time.

Rapport – to establish a relationship with people and to deal with them in an effective way and handle them with tact and courtesy.

Verbalization – to converse with patrons on a variety of topics.

Stylists must know fashions and help clients select becoming arrangements.

Do You Have or Can You Develop an Interest in This Kind of Work?

Review the following questions. Your answers can give you clues as to your interest in Barbering and Beauty Services.

Have you applied makeup to others for a school or community play? Did you enjoy improving or changing their appearance?

Have you trimmed or cut another person's hair? Do you style your own hair? Do you like to try new and different hairstyles?

Have you read health or beauty magazines? Do you like to keep informed of new grooming techniques? Can you recognize various skin tones or hair textures?

Have you given a home permanent to yourself or a friend? Did it turn out well?

Have you worked at a health spa or athletic club? Do you enjoy helping others?

What Else Should You Know About This Group of Occupations?

Jobs in this group are in clean, pleasant surroundings with good lighting. However, workers may have to stand for most of the day. They usually work with their hands at shoulder level and this can be very tiring. Also, the odors and fumes from chemicals used in hair care may be a problem. Workers may be required to provide and wear uniforms. Work hours may vary and include evenings and weekends.

Workers' pay usually depends on the number of customers they serve and tips they receive. They rarely receive a straight salary. Most employers set the prices for services offered and the worker receives a portion of what is charged. The worker's share may vary, depending on what supplies and tools the employer provides. Employers who provide all supplies receive a larger share of the money collected. Due to changing hair styles, new products, and new techniques, frequent attendance at training and demonstration classes is necessary.

The military services offer training and experience related to one occupation in this group - Barber. More information about the military training and experience opportunities may be found in Appendix A.

How Can You Prepare
for This Kind of Work?

Occupations in this group require from six months to two years of education and training. They also require a state license. Both public and private schools offer courses that help people fulfill licensing requirements. Sometimes high school seniors are admitted to these schools. Also, cosmetology and other beauty care courses may be offered as a high school vocational education program. Students in these programs receive academic credit as well as vocational training.

Training requirements vary according to the job and state involved. These requirements range between 1,600 and 2,600 hours of training. Courses may include dermatology, physiology, scalp analysis, and hair-cutting techniques.

Trained persons must pass written and oral tests. A license granted by a state board is required in many states. A health certificate is also required to show that the worker is free from contagious diseases.

Beginners often help with permanents.

Trained workers may apply directly to employers for jobs. Schools, employment services, or trade and labor unions may refer workers to employers. Beauty shops, in some areas, may hire people who have not completed training. These trainees may shampoo hair, remove curlers, or stock supplies.

As you plan your high school program, you should included courses related to Barbering and Beauty Services. The courses and skills listed below can help you plan your education.

Personal Services – courses in barbering/hairstyling, cosmetology, electrolysis, massage, and make-up artistry.

Health – courses in promoting the health of individuals.

Courses in personal grooming, art, speech, and life science can be helpful for occupations in this group.

Qualifications Profile

This section is a summary of the worker traits and work factors related to successful job performance and worker satisfaction. Try to relate your interests, abilities, aptitudes, and preferences to these traits and factors. An asterisk (*) marks those traits and factors that are related to more than 60% of the occupations listed at the end of this group. The other traits and factors listed are as important, but relate to fewer occupations. See Appendices B-G for information about all of the worker traits and work factors.

Work Activities

The most important activities related to this group involve:

* 2. Business contact.
* 8. Creative thinking.
  9. Processes, methods, or machines.
  10. Working on or producing things.

Physical Demands

Workers in this group of occupations must be able to do:

*L – Light work

Educational Skills

This chart shows the levels of reasoning, math, and language skills related to this group. These skills are usually developed in an educational setting. There are six levels ranging from the simple (1) to the most complex (6).

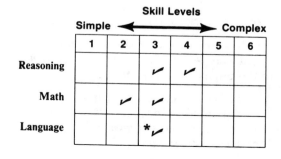

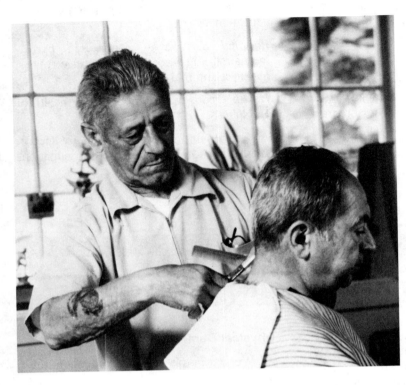

Barbers usually follow the customer's lead in conversation and style of cut.

Work Situations

Workers must be willing to:

* 1. Perform duties which change frequently.
* 4. Deal with people.
* 7. Make decisions using personal judgment.
  10. Work within precise limits or standards of accuracy.

Working Conditions

These are the physical surroundings in which work is done. In occupations belonging to this group, work is performed:

*I – Inside — workers spend most of their time inside protected from weather conditions but not always from temperature changes.

Data-People-Things

This chart shows the levels for these three basic elements of work as related to this group. Level means the degree of difficulty of job tasks rather than the amount of time involved. The terms low, average, and high indicate the highest level at which occupations are involved. Compare your interests and abilities with the levels checked.

Difficulty Level of Job Tasks

	Levels		
	Low	Avg.	High
Data		✓	✓
People	*✓		
Things			*✓

Aptitudes

This chart presents the most important aptitudes related to this group. The levels checked compare aptitudes needed for success in this group to aptitudes of the general working population in all occupations. For example, level 5 is low and represents the bottom 10% of the working population. Level 1 is high and represents the top 10%.

APTITUDE LEVELS COMPARED TO ALL WORKERS							
Related Aptitudes (Ability to Learn)		Lower 1/3		Middle 1/3	Upper 1/3		
		Level **5**	Level **4**	Level **3**	Level **2**	Level **1**	
Code	Title	10%	23%	34%	23%	10%	
G	General Learning Ability			*✔			
S	Spatial			*✔			
P	Form Perception			✔	✔		
K	Motor Coordination			✔	*✔		
F	Finger Dexterity			*✔	✔		
M	Manual Dexterity			*✔			

Common Occupations

A full listing of all occupations belonging to this group may be found in the Guide for Occupational Exploration.

The following occupations have been selected to represent this group. They provide the major employment opportunities. However, specific job opportunities will vary according to locations of industry, geographical region, and other factors.

Information may be found in common sources of occupational information, state career information systems, and computerized guidance systems.

An (M) follows the occupational title where the military services offer training and experience.

Cosmetology

332.271-010 Cosmetologist
332.271-018 Hair Stylist
339.371-014 Scalp-Treatment Operator

Barbering

330.371-010 Barber (M)

09.03

Passenger Services

Passenger Services transport people by bus, taxi, limousine, or other vehicle. Workers drive these vehicles or instruct and supervise those who do. This group includes the subgroups of:

Group Transportation
Individual Transportation
Instruction and Supervision

Group Transportation is to transport groups of people, primarily in buses. Bus Drivers follow exact routes and time schedules. They may help people with luggage and collect tickets or fares. They also may make minor repairs to the bus. Drivers of chartered (hired) buses take groups who stay together for the entire trip. Mobile-Lounge Drivers take airline passengers between the terminal and the plane. Day-Haul or Farm Charter Bus Drivers pick up workers to take them to the fields. In addition to driving the bus, they may decide how many workers are needed. They also may select these workers.

Individual Transportation is to drive people in a taxi or limousine. Taxi Drivers respond to a dispatcher's radio request for service. They may cruise streets for riders or wait at cab stands at hotels, airports, or train and bus depots. They collect fees and record their work on log sheets. Chauffeurs provide private and commercial service. They may be hired by an individual or small group. They may serve office personnel and visitors of businesses. In addition to driving people, they may do errands. Some clean the car and make minor repairs.

Instruction and Supervision involve teaching people how to drive cars or other vehicles. It also involves the supervision of workers who operate buses or cabs. Driving Instructors teach theory as well as driving skills. They show and explain how a vehicle is operated. They watch how their students react to driving situations. They also observe students to judge their progress. They may teach them how to keep records and make accident reports. They also may conduct hearing and vision tests. Supervisors oversee the work of bus and taxi drivers. They may set-up schedules. Some may hire drivers. They may check a driver's honesty and performance. They also may respond to complaints from passengers. They often investigate accidents and robberies and settle claims. The Cab Supervisor may aid drivers in locating difficult addresses.

Jobs in this group may be found with taxi, bus, or street railway companies. Jobs are also found with private driving schools and public schools.

What Skills and Abilities Would Help You Succeed in This Kind of Work?

The most important skills are listed below. All of those listed do not apply to each occupation. As you explore occupations you should identify the specific ones needed.

Communication – to exchange information with passengers or to instruct or supervise drivers.

Composure – to be calm and self-confident to cope with all types of traffic situations.

Comprehension – to understand federal, state, and local traffic rules.

Dexterity – to move the eyes, hands, and feet together to start, stop, and steer a vehicle.

Memorization – to learn routes and established passenger pick-up locations.

Physical Stamina – to withstand the strain of long hours of sitting.

Congenial – to use courtesy and tact in dealing with people.

Spatial Perception – to distinguish height, width, and depth to judge distance and speeds.

Color Discrimination – to recognize different colors of traffic signals and road signs.

Do You Have or Can You Develop an Interest in This Kind of Work?

Review the following questions. Your answers can give you clues as to your interest in the Passenger Services field.

Can you drive? Do you have a driver's or chauffeur's license?

Have you driven a vehicle loaded with passengers? Did the noise distract you?

Have you completed a driver education course? Was your grade satisfactory or better?

Have you driven a vehicle in heavy traffic? Did you stay calm?

Have you taken care of your own car or one owned by your family? Can you do minor service or repair work?

Have you driven in a bicycle rodeo, car rally, or over a vehicle obstacle course? Did you receive a good score?

Do you often read automotive magazines? Are you interested in work being done to improve car performance and safety?

What Else Should You Know About This Group of Occupations?

Work is often tiresome or stressful for many jobs in this group. Heavy traffic and long trips can cause nervous tension. Operating large vehicles requires free shoulder movements and more strength than driving a small car. Physical exams are required. This is to make sure that drivers have not developed a medical condition that might affect their work.

Workers in these jobs may have night and weekend duty. They also may have to report for work on short notice. Chances for promotion in all of these jobs are limited. Experienced bus drivers may obtain preferred routes

A school bus driver often has a special place in the hearts of her charges.

and more pay. A few may become dispatchers, supervisors, or terminal managers. Some taxi drivers buy and drive their own cabs.

The military services offer training and experience related to one occupation in this group - Bus Driver. More information about the military training and experience opportunities may be found in Appendix A.

How Can You Prepare for This Kind of Work?

Occupations in this group require thirty days to three months of education and training. Many employers require workers to have a high school education or its equal. Intercity bus drivers must meet requirements set by the U.S. Department of Transportation. They must be able to talk with passengers and read and write to complete reports. They also must have good hearing, 20/40 vision with or without glasses, and full use of their arms and legs. Bus drivers also must take a written test on federal and state motor vehicle rules. If hired, they must pass a driving test in the type of bus they will drive. Many intercity bus lines prefer workers with bus or truck driving experience. Most of these firms have their own training programs for new drivers.

Local bus drivers are required to have a state chauffeur's license. They also need to be of normal adult height and weight and have good eyesight and health. They are usually required to have one or two years of experience driving a large vehicle. Most local transit companies test all applicants for driving positions. These companies frequently provide training courses with both classroom and driving sessions. State departments of education set special rules for drivers of school buses.

Taxi drivers must have a state chauffeur's license. They also may need a special taxi operator's license. In most large cities, the license is issued after passing a written test on traffic laws and street locations. Many cities

A cab driver must know the area and may be asked about area attractions and where to eat.

also require that workers have good driving records and no criminal history.

As you plan your high school program, you should includes courses related to Passenger Services. The courses and skills listed below will help you plan your education.

Driver Education – courses in driving theory, safety and driving skills.

Transportation and Materials Moving – courses in vehicle and equipment operation and truck and bus driving.

Consumer and Personal Services – courses in consumer, personal, and miscellaneous services.

Courses in speech and auto mechanics can be helpful for occupations in this group.

Qualifications Profile

This section is a summary of the worker traits and work factors related to successful job performance and worker satisfaction. Try to relate your interests, abilities, aptitudes, and preferences to these traits and factors. An asterisk (*) marks those traits and factors that are related to more than 60% of the occupations listed at the end of this group. The other traits and factors listed are as important, but relate to fewer occupations. See Appendices B-G for information about all of the worker traits and work factors.

Work Activities

The most important activities related to this group involve:

  1. Things and objects.
* 2. Business contact.
  3. Tasks of a routine, definite nature.
  5. Recognition or appreciation from others.
* 9. Processes, methods, or machines.

Physical Demands

Workers in this group of occupations must be able to do:

*L – Light work
M – Medium work

Educational Skills

This chart shows the levels of reasoning, math, and language skills related to this group. These skills are usually developed in an educational setting. There are six levels ranging from the simple (1) to the most complex (6).

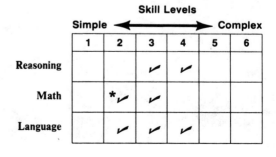

Work Situations

Workers must be willing to:

   3. Plan and direct an entire activity.
* 4. Deal with people.
* 7. Make decisions using personal judgment.
* 8. Make decisions using standards that can
     be measured or checked.

Working Conditions

These are the physical surroundings in which work is done. In occupations belonging to this group, work is performed:

*I – Inside — workers spend most of their time inside protected from weather conditions but not always from temperature changes.

Data-People-Things

This chart shows the levels for these three basic elements of work as related to this group. Level means the degree of difficulty of job tasks rather than the amount of time involved. The terms low, average, and high indicate the highest level at which occupations are involved. Compare your interests and abilities with the levels checked.

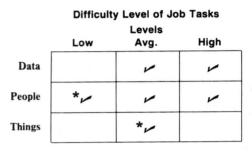

Difficulty Level of Job Tasks

	Low	Levels Avg.	High
Data		✔	✔
People	* ✔	✔	✔
Things		* ✔	

Calmness and nerves of steel help a driver instructor through his day.

Aptitudes

This chart presents the most important aptitudes related to this group. The levels checked compare aptitudes needed for success in this group to aptitudes of the general working population in all occupations. For example, level 5 is low and represents the bottom 10% of the working population. Level 1 is high and represents the top 10%.

APTITUDE LEVELS COMPARED TO ALL WORKERS							
Related Aptitudes (Ability to Learn)		Lower 1/3		Middle 1/3	Upper 1/3		
		Level 5	Level 4	Level 3	Level 2	Level 1	
Code	Title	10%	23%	34%	23%	10%	
G	General Learning Ability			* ✔			
N	Numerical		✔	✔			
S	Spatial			* ✔			
K	Motor Coordination			* ✔			
M	Manual Dexterity			* ✔			

Common Occupations

A full listing of all occupations belonging to this group may be found in the Guide for Occupational Exploration.

The following occupations have been selected to represent this group. They provide the major employment opportunities. However, specific job opportunities will vary according to locations of industry, geographical region, and other factors.

Information may be found in common sources of occupational information, state career information systems, and computerized guidance systems.

An (M) follows the occupational title where the military services offer training and experience.

Group Transportation

913.363-010 Bus Driver, Day-Haul or Farm Charter
913.463-010 Bus Driver (M)
913.663-014 Mobile-Lounge Driver

Individual Transportation

913.463-018 Taxi Driver
913.663-010 Chauffeur

Instruction and Supervision

099.223-010 Instructor, Driving
913.133-010 Road Supervisor
913.133-014 Supervisor, Cab
919.223-010 Instructor, Bus, Trolley, And Taxi

09.04
Customer Services

Customer Services involve assisting people who pay for purchases or services. This sales and service assistance includes a wide range of jobs from delivering newspapers to serving food. Tasks usually include accepting payment and making change. This group includes the subgroups of:

Food Services
Sales Services

Food Services involve providing food and beverages to people for pay. Workers may serve food in a formal or informal setting. These workers take or memorize orders and answer questions. They also compute the bill and accept payment. They may remove dishes and place clean linens on the tables. Some workers mix and serve drinks. Some manage refreshment stands. They inventory and purchase food and direct its storage, preparation, and how it is served. They may assign vendors to different locations. They also may tabulate receipts and balance accounts.

Some workers may drive lunch trucks over scheduled routes to sell food. They load and unload their trucks and may prepare and wrap sandwiches. Other workers may stock machines where food is dispensed from coin-operated machines. They place food or drink items on shelves and change labels as required. They also may make change for customers and answer their questions. They collect money from the machines and keep records of receipts.

Sales Services is to assist customers with services or sell and rent them products.

Welcoming smile, pleasant attention, and thoughtful service mean repeat customers.

A lunch truck driver must find the business.

Workers include sales and rental clerks, attendants, and cashiers. Most workers provide services or sell products that do not require sales knowledge other than the price involved. In addition to delivering a product or service they usually must prepare a bill and receive payment. Some operate cash registers. They must be able to make change so that sales and payments received are in balance (agree). They may verify credit cards and fill out charge slips. They also may keep records and inventory stock. Some workers may need to clean and maintain their sales or work area.

Jobs in this group may be found with hotels, restaurants, resorts, and stores. Places that rent equipment or where gambling is legal also employ these workers. Some jobs may be found on trains, airplanes, and ships.

What Skills and Abilities Would Help You Succeed in This Kind of Work?

The most important skills are listed below. All of those listed do not apply to each occupation. As you explore occupations you should identify the specific ones needed.

Communication – to give or exchange information.

Dexterity – to move eyes, hands, and fingers to handle or wrap products and count money.

Physical Stamina – to lift and carry things and to stand and walk for long periods of time.

Numerical – to do math quickly and correctly.

Congenial – to deal with people in an effective way.

Do You Have or Can You Develop an Interest in This Kind of Work?

Review the following questions. Your answers can give you clues as to your interest in the Customer Services field.

Have you given a party? Did you prepare and serve snacks and beverages? Were you able to do so without spilling anything?

Have you waited on tables at a school or community dinner? Were you able to carry trays and be on your feet for a long period of time?

Have you given directions to anyone? Did the person understand your directions?

Have you sold things to raise money for clubs or local groups? Did you collect payment, make change, and keep records of sales?

Have you had a job where you did the same tasks each day? Did this bother you?

Sales service people should know products, store policies, and remain pleasant even under trying conditions.

What Else Should You Know About This Group of Occupations?

Most jobs in this group deal directly with the public. The work is often hectic and tiring. Food and beverage service workers often have changing work hours. They may work at night and during weekends and holidays. They usually must wear uniforms. The income of these workers is often wages and tips combined.

The military services offer training and experience related to one occupation in this group - Sales Clerk. More information about the military training and experience opportunities may be found in Appendix A.

How Can You Prepare for This Kind of Work?

Occupations in this group require a short demonstration or up to six months of education and training. Most workers in this group learn their jobs after being hired. However, some employers hire only persons with experience. Workers may get the training and experience needed by starting in a related job. For example, a person may start as a dining room attendant and become a waiter or waitress.

As you plan your high school program, you should included courses related to the Customer Services field. The following list of courses and skills can help you plan your education.

Mathematics – courses in general mathematics.

General Merchandising and Sales – courses in business and personal services, marketing, and food marketing.

Speech – courses to gain competencies in speaking and listening.

Food Service – courses in food preparation and service.

Distributive Education – courses in sales and customer services.

Some courses in home economics may be helpful.

Qualifications Profile

This section is a summary of the worker traits and work factors related to successful job performance and worker satisfaction. Try to relate your interests, abilities, aptitudes, and preferences to these traits and factors. An asterisk (*) marks those traits and factors that are related to more than 60% of the occupations listed at the end of this group. The other traits and factors listed are as important, but relate to fewer occupations. See Appendices B-G for information about all of the worker traits and work factors.

Educational Skills

This chart shows the levels of reasoning, math, and language skills related to this group. These skills are usually developed in an educational setting. There are six levels ranging from the simple (1) to the most complex (6).

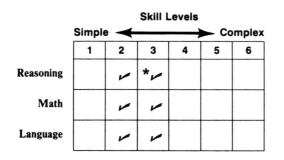

Data-People-Things

This chart shows the levels for these three basic elements of work as related to this group. Level means the degree of difficulty of job tasks rather than the amount of time involved. The terms low, average, and high indicate the highest level at which occupations are involved. Compare your interests and abilities with the levels checked.

Difficulty Level of Job Tasks

	Low	Avg.	High
Data		*✓	
People	*✓		
Things	*✓		

Work Activities

The most important activities related to this group involve:

1. Things and objects.
* 2. Business contact.
* 3. Tasks of a routine, definite nature.

333

A cashier must use a keyboard skill as well as decipher prices.

Aptitudes

This chart presents the most important aptitudes related to this group. The levels checked compare aptitudes needed for success in this group to aptitudes of the general working population in all occupations. For example, level 5 is low and represents the bottom 10% of the working population. Level 1 is high and represents the top 10%.

APTITUDE LEVELS COMPARED TO ALL WORKERS						
Related Aptitudes (Ability to Learn)		Lower 1/3		Middle 1/3	Upper 1/3	
		Level 5	Level 4	Level 3	Level 2	Level 1
Code	Title	10%	23%	34%	23%	10%
G	General Learning Ability		✔	*✔		
V	Verbal		✔	*✔		
N	Numerical		✔	✔		
Q	Clerical Perception		✔	✔		
M	Manual Dexterity		✔	✔		

Work Situations

Workers must be willing to:

2. Perform routine tasks.
3. Plan and direct an entire activity.
* 4. Deal with people.

Physical Demands

Workers in this group of occupations must be able to do:

*L – Light work

Working Conditions

These are the physical surroundings in which work is done. In occupations belonging to this group, work is performed:

*I – Inside — workers spend most of their time inside protected from weather conditions but not always from temperature changes.

Common Occupations

A full listing of all occupations belonging to this group may be found in the Guide for Occupational Exploration.

The following occupations have been selected to represent this group. They provide the major employment opportunities. However, specific job opportunities will vary according to locations of industry, geographical region, and other factors.

Information may be found in common sources of occupational information, state career information systems, and computerized guidance systems.

An (M) follows the occupational title where the military services offer training and experience.

Food Services

185.167-022	Manager, Food Concession
292.463-010	Lunch-Truck Driver
311.472-010	Fast-Foods Worker
311.477-014	Counter Attendant, Lunchroom or Coffee Shop
311.477-018	Waiter/Waitress, Bar
311.477-022	Waiter/Waitress, Dining Car
311.477-026	Waiter/Waitress, Formal
311.477-030	Waiter/Waitress, Informal
311.674-010	Canteen Operator
312.474-010	Bartender
312.477-010	Bar Attendant
319.464-014	Vending-Machine Attendant

Sales Services

211.462-018	Cashier-Wrapper
211.467-010	Cashier, Courtesy Booth
290.477-014	Sales Clerk (M)
290.477-018	Sales Clerk, Food
292.457-010	Newspaper Carrier
295.357-014	Tool-And-Equipment-Rental Clerk
295.467-022	Trailer-Rental Clerk
295.477-010	Automobile-Rental Clerk
299.587-010	Produce Weigher
299.677-010	Sales Attendant
299.677-014	Sales Attendant, Building Materials
340.367-010	Desk Clerk, Bowling Floor
342.457-010	Game Attendant
343.467-018	Gambling Dealer
369.677-010	Self-Service-Laundry-and-Dry-Cleaning Attendant
915.473-010	Parking-Lot Attendant
915.477-010	Automobile-Self-Serve-Service-Station Attendant
915.667-010	Car-Wash Attendant, Automatic

Attendant Services

Attendant Services involve duties performed to assist others. This type of service makes life easier and more pleasant. Some workers provide direct services such as carrying luggage for hotel guests. Others perform indirect services such as cleaning and setting tables in a restaurant. This group includes the subgroups of:

Physical Conditioning
Miscellaneous Personal Services

Physical Conditioning includes services given to enhance beauty and condition the body. Some workers give massages to help condition the body or just to help people relax. Workers who do this use their hands or equipment that vibrates. They also may use steam, dry heat, or whirlpool water treatments. Some workers assist people to plan and carry out a weight loss program. They may weigh and measure clients and keep records of changes. They also may discuss eating habits and explain a diet. Some may help clients learn to work out. Other workers are concerned with the beauty needs of clients. They clean, shape, and polish fingernails and toenails. Some remove unwanted hair from the skin using an electric needle.

Miscellaneous Personal Services include small tasks performed for the comfort of others. Personal services often involve food services. Workers serve food from counters and steam tables. They may carry trays for customers or hospital patients. They also remove dirty dishes and clean and set tables. They may help clean equipment and serving areas. Portering and baggage service is another type of personal service. These workers carry luggage for travelers and do small errands. Some workers provide doorkeeping services. They open doors for guests, give directions, and help them in getting cabs.

Some workers provide individualized service such as a caddie carrying a golf bag for a golfer. Some workers provide locker room or shoe shine services. Others serve as ushers, ticket takers, or elevator operators. Some help customers such as a bagger in a grocery store. These miscellaneous personal services may not seem important, but they make a big difference in the customer's satisfaction.

Jobs may be found with hotels, restaurants, cafeterias, and drive-ins. Athletic clubs, reducing salons, and golf courses also employ these workers. Jobs also may be found with airports and on ships.

What Skills and Abilities Would Help You Succeed in This Kind of Work?

The most important skills are listed below. All of those listed do not apply to each occupation. As you explore occupations you should identify the specific ones needed.

Comprehension – to understand and follow oral and written instructions.

Dexterity – to move the hands and fingers skillfully when performing such tasks as giving rub-downs, manicures, opening oysters, and bagging groceries.

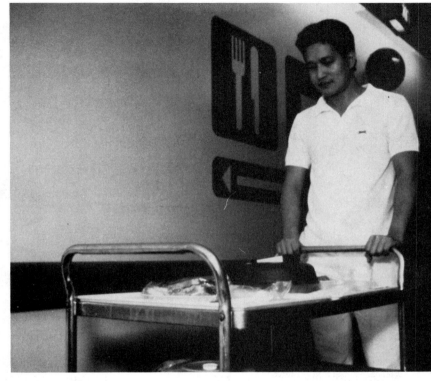

This hospital food service worker delivers a cart of late trays to the patients' floor.

Physical Stamina – to have the strength to carry baggage or packages and to stand or walk most of a work day.

Diligence – to perform the same tasks over and over.

Congenial – to get along with all kinds of people.

Do You Have or Can You Develop an Interest in This Kind of Work?

Review the following questions. Your answers can give you clues as to your interest in the Attendant Services field.

Have you helped with the wardrobe for a school or community play? Did you enjoy assisting others?

Have you served food, set tables, or carried dirty dishes for a school or group dinner? Did it bother you to stand or walk for long periods of time?

Have you been in charge of sports equipment for a team? Did you enjoy providing this type of service for players?

Have you carried baggage or parcels for other people? Have you assisted elderly people? Do you like to help others?

Have you collected tickets or ushered at a school play? Did you remain pleasant and courteous if people were rude?

Have you helped a friend to plan a diet or exercise program to lose weight? Did you keep a record of the weight loss?

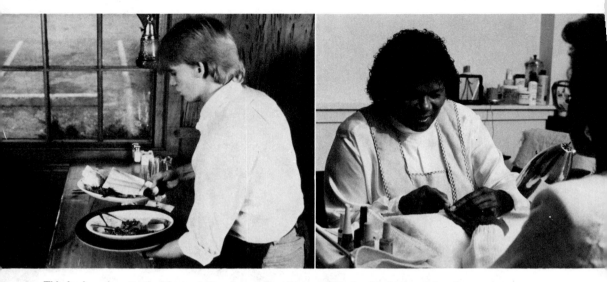

This food service attendant keeps tables clear and ready for customers.

Manicuring is a specialty of many shops.

What Else Should You Know About This Group of Occupations?

Most workers in this group start at low wages, but many receive tips that add to their incomes. Workers may be required to wear uniforms. If food is served, they may need a certificate stating they are in good health. Employers consider personal appearance and attitude very important. Working hours vary for most of these jobs and workers may be required to work weekends, evenings, and holidays.

The military services offer training and experience related to one occupation in this group – Gate Agent. The occupation is included in the list at the end of this group description. It is identified by an (M) following the occupational title. More information about the military training and experience opportunities may be found in Appendix A.

How Can You Prepare For This Kind of Work?

Most jobs in this group require a short demonstration or up to three months of training and experience. Some require two years. These are supervisory jobs where experience is important. Many employers offer on-the-job training. However, some formal training is available. Courses in customer service and food and beverage service are offered in some vocational programs. Some jobs, such as Electrologist, require city or state licenses.

As you plan your high school program you should include courses related to Attendant Services. Next, you should consider courses needed to enter a related vocational program or technical school you are considering. The following list of courses and skills will help you plan your education.

General Merchandising and Sales – courses in business, distributive education, personal services, and marketing.

Personal Services – courses in cosmetology, electrolysis, massage, and consumer, personal, and miscellaneous services.

Consumer and Personal Services – courses in hospitality, recreation, marketing, and food service.

Health – courses in health related activities to promote the health of others.

Speech – courses to gain competencies in speaking and listening.

Some courses in home economics also may be helpful for some occupations in this group.

Qualifications Profile

This section is a summary of the worker traits and work factors related to successful job performance and worker satisfaction. Try to relate your interests, abilities, aptitudes, and preferences to these traits and factors. An asterisk (*) marks those traits and factors that are related to more than 60% of the occupations listed at the end of this group. The other traits and factors listed are as important, but relate to fewer occupations. See Appendices B-G for information about all of the worker traits and work factors.

Work Situations

Workers must be willing to:

* 2. Perform routine tasks.
  3. Plan and direct an entire activity.
* 4. Deal with people.

Physical Demands

Workers in this group of occupations must be able to do:

L – Light work
M – Medium work

Work Activities

The most important activities related to this group involve:

  1. Things and objects.
* 2. Business contact.
* 3. Tasks of a routine, definite nature.

Educational Skills

This chart shows the levels of reasoning, math, and language skills related to this group. These skills are usually developed in an educational setting. There are six levels ranging from the simple (1) to the most complex (6).

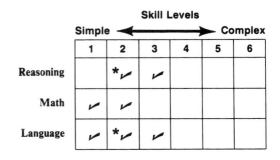

Bellhops perform many special services as well as carry baggage and make sure rooms are in order for guests.

Aptitudes

This chart presents the most important aptitudes related to this group. The levels checked compare aptitudes needed for success in this group to aptitudes of the general working population in all occupations. For example, level 5 is low and represents the bottom 10% of the working population. Level 1 is high and represents the top 10%.

Working Conditions

These are the physical surroundings in which work is done. In occupations belonging to this group, work is performed:

*I – Inside — workers spend most of their time inside protected from weather conditions but not always from temperature changes.

APTITUDE LEVELS COMPARED TO ALL WORKERS							
Related Aptitudes **(Ability to Learn)**		Lower 1/3		Middle 1/3		Upper 1/3	
		Level **5**	Level **4**	Level **3**		Level **2**	Level **1**
Code	Title	10%	23%	34%		23%	10%
G	General Learning Ability		*✔	✔			
V	Verbal		*✔	✔			
K	Motor Coordination		*✔	✔			
M	Manual Dexterity		✔	✔			

Data-People-Things

This chart shows the levels for these three basic elements of work as related to this group. Level means the degree of difficulty of job tasks rather than the amount of time involved. The terms low, average, and high indicate the highest level at which occupations are involved. Compare your interests and abilities with the levels checked.

Difficulty Level of Job Tasks

| | Levels | | |
	Low	Avg.	High
Data	*⟋		
People	*⟋		
Things	*⟋		

Common Occupations

A full listing of all occupations belonging to this group may be found in the Guide for Occupational Exploration.

The following occupations have been selected to represent this group. They provide the major employment opportunities. However, specific job opportunities will vary according to locations of industry, geographical region, and other factors.

Information may be found in common sources of occupational information, state career information systems, and computerized guidance systems.

An (M) follows the occupational title where the military services offer training and experience.

Physical Conditioning

331.674-010 Manicurist
334.374-010 Masseur/Masseuse
339.371-010 Electrologist
359.367-014 Weight-Reduction Specialist
359.567-010 Reducing-Salon Attendant

Miscellaneous Personal Services

238.367-010 Gate Agent (M)
310.357-010 Wine Steward/Stewardess
311.674-014 Raw Shellfish Preparer
311.674-018 Waiter/Waitress, Buffet
311.677-010 Cafeteria Attendant
311.677-014 Counter Attendant, Cafeteria
311.677-018 Dining Room Attendant
319.677-010 Caterer Helper
319.687-010 Counter-Supply Worker
324.137-014 Bell Captain
324.577-010 Room-Service Clerk
324.677-010 Bellhop
324.677-014 Doorkeeper
341.677-010 Caddie
342.677-010 Ride Attendant
344.667-010 Ticket Taker
344.677-014 Usher
350.677-010 Mess Attendant
350.677-014 Passenger Attendant
350.677-030 Waiter/Waitress
355.677-010 Food-Service Worker, Hospital
355.677-014 Hospital Entrance Attendant
357.477-010 Baggage Checker
357.677-010 Porter
358.677-010 Checkroom Attendant
358.677-014 Locker-Room Attendant
366.677-010 Shoe Shiner
388.663-010 Elevator Operator
910.667-014 Conductor
920.687-014 Bagger

341

10 HUMANITARIAN

People with an interest in helping others with personal problems enjoy work in which caring for others is important. In addition to an interest in helping people, workers need special knowledge and skill. Many jobs in this area require graduate degree work and clinical practice is required for some. Workers need very good oral and written communication skills and must be able to make decisions during trying circumstances (events). Many decisions involve personal judgment that requires expert training. Workers need the ability to understand other people's feelings (empathy). They need to care without becoming emotionally involved. They must gain people's trust and confidence and keep information about their clients private.

A few occupations in Child and Adult Care do not require a broad background of training and experience. Also, private organizations (groups) which help clients with such problems as drugs or alcohol sometimes hire people who have a special knowledge of the problem even though they lack formal training. The Humanitarian area is divided into two clusters: Social Services and Nursing-Therapy/Child-Adult Care.

Social Services

The Social Services cluster provides guidance and counseling to people with problems and needs. These may be social, emotional, religious, or vocational needs. Workers counsel with one person at a time and also provide group sessions for people with similar problems. They usually talk with people to help them work through their problems. Workers are usually active in community activities and with professional groups. They often write articles for general publication or professional journals.

Nursing-Therapy/ Child-Adult Care

The Nursing-Therapy/Child-Adult Care cluster involves workers who help sick, injured, or handicapped people. Workers deal with the physical needs and welfare of others. They care for, treat, or train people to help them improve their physical and emotional well-being. Some care for the elderly, the very young, or the disabled. These workers often help people do things they cannot do for themselves. Some workers assist doctors or nurses in treating people and may provide post treatment care.

The following Worker Trait Groups and Subgroups are related to the Social Services and Nursing-Therapy/Child-Adult Care clusters.

Humanitarian: an interest in helping people with their mental, spiritual, social, physical, or vocational concerns.

Social Services

10.01 Social Services
Religious
Counseling and Social Work

Nursing-Therapy/ Child-Adult Care

10.02 Nursing and Therapy Services
Nursing
Therapy and Rehabilitation
Specialized Teaching

10.03 Child and Adult Care
Data Collection
Patient Care
Care of Others

10.01
Social Services

Social Services provide guidance and counseling to people with problems and needs. These needs may be social, personal, vocational, educational, or religious. Some needs of people are met through religious worship. Workers are bound by rules of ethics and must keep information about their clients private. This group includes the subgroups of:

Religious
Counseling and Social Work

Religious is to serve people's spiritual needs. Clergy Members prepare and deliver sermons. They counsel church members and comfort those who have lost loved ones. They conduct weddings and funeral services and visit the sick and shut-ins. They may write articles and be active in the locality. Directors of Religious Activities direct programs for college students. They work with students who have marital, health, money, or religious problems. They also plan and conduct meetings and courses to help explain religion.

Counseling and Social Work involve helping people with problems. Counselors deal with such problems as drug and alcohol abuse. They also provide vocational and educational guidance to clients. They talk with people, help them learn their needs, and then work out a course of action. Psychologists assess and diagnose mental and emotional problems. They give and interpret tests and use the results and other evaluations to develop programs of treatment. They may do research or private consulting.

Social Workers determine clients' needs through interviews and other kinds of investigations. Some may work with people who have troubled human relations or drug or alcohol abuse problems. They may counsel and help them to change their attitudes and behaviors. Others work with children and adults who break the law. They also may work with patients with medical and mental problems. There also are workers who assist Social Workers. Their duties relate to the simpler aspects of cases. Some workers are involved with foreign students and help them to adjust to campus life. They also may direct other kinds of student programs such as the job placement services.

Jobs in this group may be found with churches, schools, guidance and counseling centers, and mental health clinics. Agencies in such areas as welfare, employment, vocational rehabilitation, and the juvenile court also offer jobs in this group.

What Skills and Abilities Would Help You Succeed in This Kind of Work?

The most important skills are listed below. All of those listed do not apply to each occupation. As you explore occupations you should identify the specific ones needed.

General Learning Ability – to understand instructions, facts, and underlying reasoning to complete graduate level college training.

Leadership – to plan and direct programs.

Verbalization – to express ideas through the use of words.

Empathy – to share the feelings of others and have a desire to be of help.

Social Skills – to deal with people in an effective way to gain their trust and confidence.

Critical Thinking – to form opinions and make decisions based upon knowledge, judgment, and experience.

Creative Thinking – to use original ideas to develop programs of treatment.

Versatile – to do a variety of tasks that may change often.

Numerical – to understand concepts in advanced mathematics and statistics related to client test and evaluation results.

Do You Have or Can You Develop an Interest in This Kind of Work?

Review the following questions. Your answers can give you clues as to your interest in Social Services.

Do you enjoy listening to other people's problems? Do you have a strong interest in helping others?

Have you been active in church or civic groups? Do you like to work with other people toward a common goal?

Do you like to study the behavior of people or groups of people? Have you taken courses in psychology, sociology, or other social sciences? How were your grades?

Have your friends come to you for advice or help on their personal problems? Did you enjoy trying to help them? Are you usually helpful? Did you keep their secrets?

Have you helped someone with a learning disability? Were you patient? Did you stay with the task until it was finished?

Have you done volunteer work for a hospital? Did you enjoy helping others? Could you do this type of work every day?

Have you been on a debate team or in a speech contest? Do you enjoy appearing before a group of people?

Counseling is an activity of members of the clergy.

What Else Should You Know About This Group of Occupations?

Most jobs in this group have regular working hours. However, weekend, evening, and overtime work may sometimes be required. Some workers may need to be on call at all hours. Many workers in this group feel that helping others may be more important than the amount of pay received. Local recognition may also be important to them. These workers enjoy a sense of personal satisfaction they gain from helping others.

Most workers in this group must update their knowledge and skills regularly. They read professional journals and study new policies and rules. They also attend seminars, summer school, and workshops.

The military services offer training and experience related to some occupations in this group. These occupations are included in the list at the end of this group description. They are identified by an (M) following the occupational title. More information about the military training and experience opportunities may be found in Appendix A.

How Can You Prepare for This Kind of Work?

Most occupations in this group require two to four years of training and experience. Others may require up to ten years. Education beyond the four-year college level is required for most jobs in this group. Two or more years of additional graduate study is often required for jobs in social work and psychology. School counseling jobs usually require a master's degree and one or two years of teaching experience. Certificates or other credentials are required for many jobs in this group.

Some workers enter this field as social service and case aides. These workers receive on-the-job training. Private agencies that deal with problems of drug addicts, rape victims, or minority groups may accept actual experience and proven human relations skills in place of formal training.

As you plan your high school program you should include courses related to Social Services. Next, you should include courses needed to enter college. The following list of courses and skills can help you plan your education.

Public Affairs – courses in social work and community services.

Psychology – courses in general and clinical counseling, quantitative and social psychology, and psychometrics.

Education – courses in school psychology, social foundations, elementary and secondary education administration, and religious education.

School counselors handle many types of problems.

Sociology and Anthropology – courses in anthropology, sociology, urban studies, and other social sciences.

Speech – courses in speech, debate, and forensics.

Courses in area and ethnic studies, foreign language, philosophy, and biology can be helpful for some occupations in this group. Courses in social studies and health may also be helpful.

Qualifications Profile

This medical social worker must be alert to symptoms.

This section is a summary of the worker traits and work factors related to successful job performance and worker satisfaction. Try to relate your interests, abilities, aptitudes, and preferences to these traits and factors. An asterisk (*) marks those traits and factors that are related to more than 60% of the occupations listed at the end of this group. The other traits and factors listed are as important, but relate to fewer occupations. See Appendices B-G for information about all of the worker traits and work factors.

Work Activities

The most important activities related to this group involve:

* 4. Direct personal contact to help or instruct others.
* 5. Recognition or appreciation from others.
* 6. Communication of ideas and information.

Work Situations

Workers must be willing to:

* 1. Perform duties which change frequently.
* 3. Plan and direct an entire activity.
* 4. Deal with people.
* 5. Influence people's opinions, attitudes, and judgments.
  7. Make decisions using personal judgment.

347

A parole officer has difficult tasks and a varied case load.

Data-People-Things

This chart shows the levels for these three basic elements of work as related to this group. Level means the degree of difficulty of job tasks rather than the amount of time involved. The terms low, average, and high indicate the highest level at which occupations are involved. Compare your interests and abilities with the levels checked.

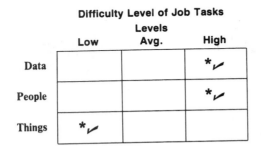

Difficulty Level of Job Tasks

	Levels		
	Low	Avg.	High
Data			*✔
People			*✔
Things	*✔		

Physical Demands

Workers in this group of occupations must be able to do:

*S – Sedentary work
L – Light work

Working Conditions

These are the physical surroundings in which work is done. In occupations belonging to this group, work is performed:

*I – Inside — workers spend most of their time inside protected from weather conditions but not always from temperature changes.

Educational Skills

This chart shows the levels of reasoning, math, and language skills related to this group. These skills are usually developed in an educational setting. There are six levels ranging from the simple (1) to the most complex (6).

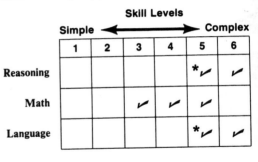

Skill Levels

	Simple					Complex
	1	2	3	4	5	6
Reasoning					*✔	✔
Math			✔	✔	✔	
Language					*✔	✔

Aptitudes

This chart presents the most important aptitudes related to this group. The levels checked compare aptitudes needed for success in this group to aptitudes of the general working population in all occupations. For example, level 5 is low and represents the bottom 10% of the working population. Level 1 is high and represents the top 10%.

		APTITUDE LEVELS COMPARED TO ALL WORKERS				
Related Aptitudes (Ability to Learn)		Lower 1/3		Middle 1/3	Upper 1/3	
		Level **5**	Level **4**	Level **3**	Level **2**	Level **1**
Code	**Title**	10%	23%	34%	23%	10%
G	General Learning Ability				* ✓	✓
V	Verbal				* ✓	✓
N	Numerical			* ✓	✓	
Q	Clerical Perception	* ✓		✓		

Common Occupations

A full listing of all occupations belonging to this group may be found in the Guide for Occupational Exploration.

The following occupations have been selected to represent this group. They provide the major employment opportunities. However, specific job opportunities will vary according to locations of industry, geographical region, and other factors.

Information may be found in common sources of occupational information, state career information systems, and computerized guidance systems.

An (M) follows the occupational title where the military services offer training and experience.

Religious

120.007-010 Clergy Member (M)
129.107-018 Director of Religious Activities (M)

Counseling and Social Work

045.107-010 Counselor
045.107-018 Director of Counseling (M)
045.107-022 Psychologist, Clinical (M)
045.107-026 Psychologist, Counseling (M)
045.107-034 Psychologist, School
045.107-038 Residence Counselor
045.107-042 Vocational-Rehabilitation Counselor
045.107-046 Psychologist, Chief (M)
090.107-010 Foreign-Student Adviser
090.117-018 Dean of Students 1 (M)
166.167-014 Director of Placement
195.107-010 Caseworker (M)
195.107-022 Social Group Worker (M)
195.107-026 Social Worker, Delinquency Prevention
195.107-030 Social Worker, Medical (M)
195.107-034 Social Worker, Psychiatric (M)
195.107-038 Social Worker, School
195.107-046 Probation-And-Parole Officer
195.167-030 Parole Officer
195.267-014 Human Relations or Drug And Alcohol Counselor (M)
195.367-010 Case Aide
195.367-034 Social-Services Aide (M)

349

10.02
Nursing and Therapy Services

(Nursing, Therapy, and Specialized Teaching Services)

Nursing and Therapy Services involve caring for the sick and helping the disabled. They also involve advising people how to maintain and improve their health. This includes both physical and emotional health. Workers in this group may teach or train the handicapped. This group includes the subgroups of:

Nursing
Therapy and Rehabilitation
Specialized Teaching

Nursing is to perform a variety of skilled duties to take care of the ill or injured. The duties performed are determined by the work setting. Nurses may take vital signs such as temperature, pulse, and blood pressure. They observe patients and record their symptoms, reactions, and progress. They give medications prescribed by doctors and keep records of drugs used. Some deliver babies and instruct in prenatal and postnatal health care. Other nurses give anesthetics for surgical or dental work. Nurses are often employed by doctors. They help the doctor care for and treat patients who come into the office. They also may conduct lab tests and clean and sterilize instruments and equipment.

Some nurses may instruct others in health education and disease prevention. School nurses plan and carry out school health programs. They may teach classes such as first aid and child care. Also included in this subgroup are nursing supervisors and instructors. Nurse instructors demonstrate and teach patient

care to nursing students. They also teach other subjects related to nursing. Supervisors plan and direct nursing programs and assign nursing duties.

Therapy and Rehabilitation involve the treatment of people with physical or mental disorders. Therapists review patients' medical records. They perform tests and assess the findings to develop programs of treatment. They give treatments to patients and teach them and their families how to give treatments at home. Therapists usually specialize in one

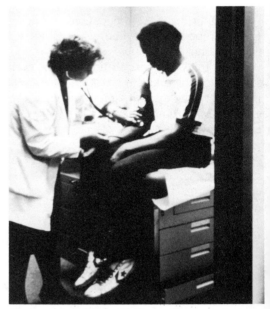

Nurses record vital signs before patients see a doctor.

field. These fields include occupational, physical, recreational, art, and music therapy. Some therapists assist the blind to become independent in their daily living.

This subgroup also includes medical and dental technology jobs. These workers may set up and operate kidney machines (dialysis) or operate X-ray machines. Some workers in this subgroup advise and treat athletes. They help them develop and maintain high levels of physical fitness. Other workers teach calisthenics, gymnastics, or reducing and corrective exercises.

Specialized Teaching is to instruct in schools or programs for the handicapped. Also included are preschool or kindergarten teachers. These teachers use special skills to promote the physical, mental, and social development of their students. Those who instruct deaf students use lip reading, finger spelling, cued speech, and sign language.

Teachers who instruct blind students use the Braille system as well as records and tapes. They may need to prepare some instructional materials in Braille or bold faced type for the partially sighted.

Some teachers work with physically handicapped students. They adapt their teaching methods to meet each person's needs. They devise or use special teaching tools, techniques, and equipment. Other teachers work with students who are mentally retarded. They teach school subjects as well as help with personal skills to prepare students for independent living.

Jobs may be found with hospitals, nursing homes, and rehabilitation centers. Schools, industrial plants, doctors' offices, and private homes offer some employment. Sports organizations also hire workers in this group. Some therapists and athletic trainers open their own facilities.

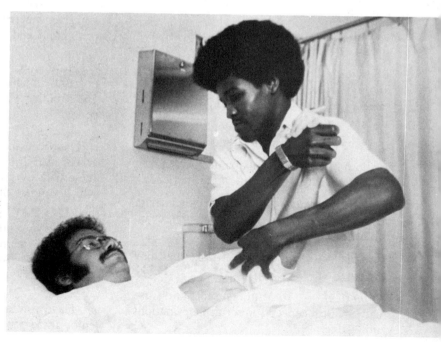

A physical therapist helps a patient recover use of a limb after a cast is removed.

What Skills and Abilities Would Help You Succeed in This Kind of Work?

The most important skills are listed below. All of those listed do not apply to each occupation. As you explore occupations you should identify the specific ones needed.

General Learning Ability – to have reading and listening comprehension to complete nursing or therapy training and read technical journals and reports to maintain skills.

Empathy – to share the feelings of others and have a desire to be of help.

Accuracy – to follow detailed instructions exactly and keep accurate records.

Leadership – to instruct or plan and oversee the work of others.

Verbalization – to speak clearly and to communicate meaningfully with ill or handicapped people.

Dexterity – to move the eyes, hands, and fingers together with skill.

Composure – to remain calm in emergencies and in situations requiring a great deal of patience.

Social Skills – to deal with people in an effective way to gain their trust and confidence.

Critical Thinking – to make decisions based upon knowledge, judgment, and experience.

Creative Thinking – to evaluate patients data and devise individual medical, therapy, or instructional programs.

Versatile – to do a variety of tasks that may change often.

Numerical – to understand and use mathematical concepts in medical evaluations and testing.

Do You Have or Can You Develop an Interest in This Kind of Work?

Review the following questions. Your answers can give you clues as to your interest in Nursing and Therapy Services.

Have you tutored a person in school subjects? Did they understand what you were teaching? Did you enjoy helping them?

Have you taken a science course in which an animal was dissected? Did it bother you?

Have you assembled or studied a plastic model of a human body? Does human anatomy interest you?

Can you use your fingers with skill? Can you use small instruments such as tweezers with skill?

Have you taken a first aid course? Have you given emergency treatment to someone ill or injured? Did you remain calm?

Have you worked as a volunteer in a hospital, nursing home, or such other setting? Did it bother you to be around ill or injured people?

Have you had courses or training in art, crafts, speech, or music? Could you teach these skills to others? Would you like a job in which you use these skills to help others?

Have you cared for a sick or injured friend or family member? Did you take their temperature? Would you like to do this type of work every day?

Have you taken science courses? Did you enjoy these courses? How were your grades?

What Else Should You Know About This Group of Occupations?

Most jobs in this group are physically tiring and sometimes emotionally stressful. Workers are on their feet most of the day. Many of them are required to do shift work that involves evening, night, and weekend work. Some may be on call or have to work overtime. Many older workers can be selective about when they work because of their seniority.

Workers in this group have close contact with people. They learn to adjust to conditions associated with mental, emotional, or physical problems. There is a high demand for workers in this field.

Jobs in nursing and therapy involve direct patient care, supervision, research, or teaching. Some jobs may combine these activities. There are many areas of specialization in this field.

The military services offer training and experience related to some occupations in this group. These occupations are included in the list at the end of this group description. They are identified by an (M) following the occupational title. More information about the military training and experience opportunities may be found in Appendix A.

How Can You Prepare for This Kind of Work?

Most occupations in this group require two to four years of training and experience. Some require one to two years and a few may require up to ten years. There are three types of programs that prepare students to become registered nurses. Graduates of all three programs (diploma, degree, and associate degree) are required to pass a state board test to be licensed as nurses. The diploma program, in general, is three years in length and hospital based. In some cases, students take basic science and liberal arts courses at nearby colleges. In other cases, students receive all instruction at the hospital school. These programs include instruction and clinical experience which prepare students to give nursing care to patients.

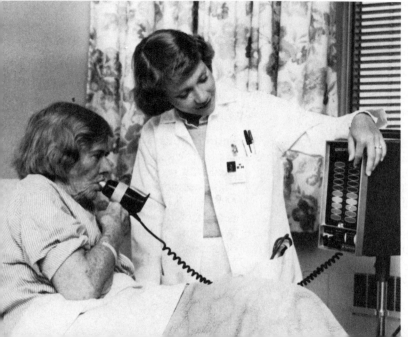

The inhalation test is one measure of a patient's recovery.

Bachelor's degree programs are, in general, four years in length. These programs offer the student a wider variety of courses, clinical experiences, and skills directly related to patient care. Community colleges, technical schools, or universities offer associate degree programs. In general, these programs are two years in length.

A two-year associate degree or a four-year bachelor's degree in a related field is required to enter most therapy jobs. Training includes course work related to the specific kind of therapy as well as supervised clinical experience. Certificate programs are offered in physical therapy, vocational therapy, and other therapy areas. Graduates of therapy programs must pass a test before they can be certified to practice.

As you plan your high school program you should includes courses related to Nursing and Therapy Services. You also should include courses needed to enter college. The following courses and skills can help you plan your education.

Health Science – courses in basic clinical health sciences and nursing such as anatomy and physiology.

Mental Health and Rehab Services – courses in the care and treatment of the mentally ill, aged, drug addicted, and physically handicapped.

Life Science – courses in general biology, biochemistry and biophysics, and anatomy.

Chemistry – courses in general chemistry, analytical chemistry, and physical chemistry.

Courses in psychology, music, art, child care, family development, nutrition, woodworking, and crafts can be helpful for occupations in this group. Courses in health, physical education, and science can help you determine your interest in this group.

Qualifications Profile

This section is a summary of the worker traits and work factors related to successful job performance and worker satisfaction. Try to relate your interests, abilities, aptitudes, and preferences to these traits and factors. An asterisk (*) marks those traits and factors that are related to more than 60% of the occupations listed at the end of this group. The other traits and factors listed are as important, but relate to fewer occupations. See Appendices B-G for information about all of the worker traits and work factors.

Work Situations

Workers must be willing to:

1. Perform duties which change frequently.
3. Plan and direct an entire activity.
* 4. Deal with people.
7. Make decisions using personal judgment.
* 8. Make decisions using standards that can be measured or checked.
10. Work within precise limits or standards of accuracy.

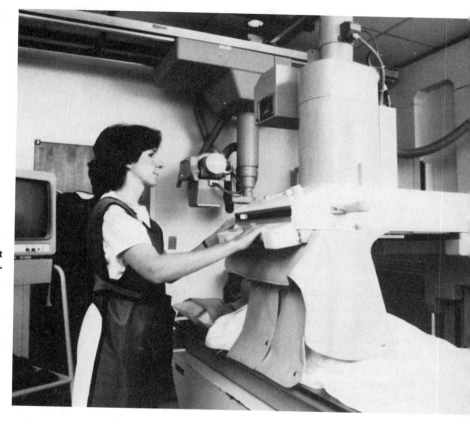

An X-ray technician must observe safety precautions.

Work Activities

The most important activities related to this group involve:

* 4. Direct personal contact to help or instruct others.
  6. Communication of ideas and information.
* 7. Tasks of a scientific and technical nature.

Physical Demands

Workers in this group of occupations must be able to do:

*L – Light work
M – Medium work

Educational Skills

This chart shows the levels of reasoning, math, and language skills related to this group. These skills are usually developed in an educational setting. There are six levels ranging from the simple (1) to the most complex (6).

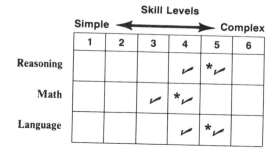

	Skill Levels					
	Simple ⬅ ➡ Complex					
	1	2	3	4	5	6
Reasoning				✔	*✔	
Math			✔	*✔		
Language				✔	*✔	

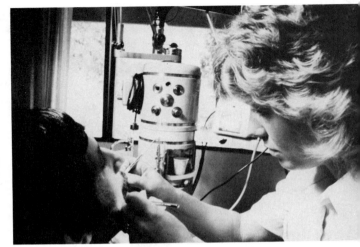

This dental hygienist
is cleaning a client's teeth.

Aptitudes

This chart presents the most important aptitudes related to this group. The levels checked compare aptitudes needed for success in this group to aptitudes of the general working population in all occupations. For example, level 5 is low and represents the bottom 10% of the working population. Level 1 is high and represents the top 10%.

Working Conditions

These are the physical surroundings in which work is done. In occupations belonging to this group, work is performed:

*I – Inside — workers spend most of their time inside protected from weather conditions but not always from temperature changes.

APTITUDE LEVELS COMPARED TO ALL WORKERS						
Related Aptitudes (Ability to Learn)		Lower 1/3		Middle 1/3	Upper 1/3	
		Level 5	Level 4	Level 3	Level 2	Level 1
Code	**Title**	10%	23%	34%	23%	10%
G	General Learning Ability			✔	*✔	
V	Verbal			✔	*✔	
N	Numerical			*✔	✔	
Q	Clerical Perception		✔	*✔	✔	
K	Motor Coordination		✔	*✔	✔	
F	Finger Dexterity		✔	*✔	✔	
M	Manual Dexterity		✔	*✔	✔	

Data-People-Things

This chart shows the levels for these three basic elements of work as related to this group. Level means the degree of difficulty of job tasks rather than the amount of time involved. The terms low, average, and high indicate the highest level at which occupations are involved. Compare your interests and abilities with the levels checked.

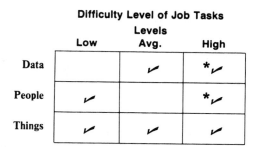

Difficulty Level of Job Tasks

	Low	**Avg.**	**High**
Data		✔	*✔
People	✔		*✔
Things	✔	✔	✔

Common Occupations

A full listing of all occupations belonging to this group may be found in the Guide for Occupational Exploration.

The following occupations have been selected to represent this group. They provide the major employment opportunities. However, specific job opportunities will vary according to locations of industry, geographical region, and other factors.

Information may be found in common sources of occupational information, state career information systems, and computerized guidance systems.

An (M) follows the occupational title where the military services offer training and experience.

Nursing

075.117-018 Director, Educational, Community-Health Nursing (M)
075.121-010 Nurse, Instructor (M)
075.124-010 Nurse, School
075.124-014 Nurse, Staff, Community Health (M)
075.127-018 Nurse, Head (M)
075.127-022 Nurse, Supervisor (M)
075.127-026 Nurse, Supervisor, Community-Health Nursing (M)
075.137-010 Nurse, Supervisor, Occupational Health Nursing (M)
075.264-010 Nurse Practitioner (M)
075.264-014 Nurse-Midwife (M)

075.371-010 Nurse Anesthetist (M)
075.374-010 Nurse, General Duty (M)
075.374-014 Nurse, Office (M)
075.374-022 Nurse, Staff, Occupational Health Nursing (M)
079.364-018 Physician Assistant (M)
079.374-014 Nurse, Licensed Practical (M)

Therapy and Rehabilitation

076.121-010 Occupational Therapist (M)
076.121-014 Physical Therapist (M)
076.124-014 Recreational Therapist
076.127-010 Art Therapist
076.127-014 Music Therapist
076.221-010 Orientation Therapist For The Blind
076.224-010 Physical Therapist Assistant (M)
076.264-010 Physical-Integration Practitioner (M)
076.364-010 Occupational Therapy Assistant (M)
078.361-010 Dental Hygienist (M)
078.361-018 Nuclear Medical Technologist (M)
078.362-014 Dialysis Technician
078.362-026 Radiologic Technologist (M)
079.361-010 Respiratory Therapist (M)
079.374-026 Psychiatric Technician (M)
153.224-010 Athletic Trainer
153.227-014 Instructor, Physical (M)

Specialized Teaching

092.227-014 Teacher, Kindergarten
092.227-018 Teacher, Preschool
094.224-010 Teacher, Deaf
094.227-014 Teacher, Blind
094.227-018 Teacher, Handicapped Students
094.227-022 Teacher, Mentally Retarded

Child and Adult Care

Child and Adult Care involve routine, essential tasks to assist in the physical care or welfare of others. Some workers mainly care for old people or for young children. Other workers care for the sick, injured, or physically handicapped. Many of these jobs involve assisting doctors and nurses in treating the ill or injured. This group includes the subgroups of:

Data Collection
Patient Care
Care of Others

Data Collection involves the use of equipment to collect medical data about people. Technicians set up and operate equipment to test body functions such as breathing and hearing. They also monitor and test heart, brain, cardiovascular (heart and blood vessels) and pulmonary (lungs) functions. These workers are skilled in using test equipment and metering devices. They may analyze and interpret test findings. However, most workers conduct the tests and record results for the doctor to evaluate.

Patient Care involves assisting other medical staff in the care of patients. Some workers obtain and record case histories and prepare patients for exams. They take and record their vital signs such as temperature and pulse. They also may clean and sterilize instruments. Other workers answer emergency calls. They give first-aid and transport sick or injured persons to a medical facility. Some workers assist in operating rooms. They clean the rooms and obtain the needed equipment and supplies. They prepare patients for surgery and keep track of the sponges, needles, and instruments used. Other workers assist in the direct care of patients. They bathe and dress them, change their beds, and clean their rooms. These workers also take and record vital signs. They may serve and collect food trays and feed patients needing help. Some workers install and show people how to use rented medical equipment.

Care of Others involves attending to the physical comfort, safety, and appearance of patients. Some workers care for old, handicapped, or sick people in their homes. They

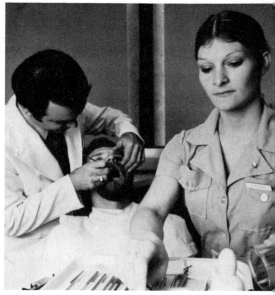

A dental assistant has many tasks in assisting the doctor.

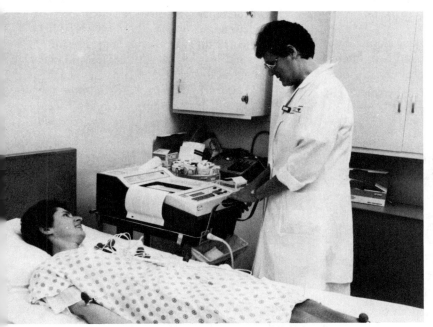

An electrocardiograph technician makes a test in a physician's examining room.

change bed linens and wash and iron the laundry. They purchase, cook, and serve food. They also assist the patients in and out of bed and to dress and undress. Other workers are concerned with young children. They may attend to the personal needs of the handicapped attending school. They may care for groups of children housed in city or county homes. These workers organize and lead activities and direct children in dressing, eating, and resting. They often discipline the children and teach them to pick up and put away toys. Other workers are concerned with the safety of children. They assist children at street crossings during school hours. They report traffic violators to the police.

Jobs in this group may be found with hospitals, clinics, day care centers, and nursery schools. Treatment centers for the handicapped and private homes also offer employment.

What Skills and Abilities Would Help You Succeed in This Kind of Work?

The most important skills are listed below. All of those listed do not apply to each occupation. As you explore occupations you should identify the specific ones needed.

Comprehension – to understand and follow written or spoken instructions exactly.

Dexterity – to move the eyes, hands, and fingers skillfully to use medical instruments.

Verbalization – to talk and communicate with sick or handicapped people.

Tolerance – to work in situations that may involve odors or other conditions.

Physical Stamina – to have the strength to endure long hours of standing on your feet.

Empathy – to share the feelings of others and have a desire to be of help.

Do You Have or Can You Develop an Interest in This Kind of Work?

Review the following questions. Your answers can give you clues as to your interest in Child and Adult Care.

Have you worked as a baby-sitter? Did you read to or play games with the children? Do you enjoy this type of work?

Have you had first-aid training? Have you given emergency treatment to someone ill or injured? Did you react quickly and calmly?

Have you worked as a volunteer in a hospital or nursing home? Are you concerned with the welfare of others? Do you like this kind of work?

Are you good at games? Do you have some talent in art, music, or crafts? Would you enjoy teaching these to young children?

Have you cared for children or sick people? Are you patient? Do you relate to those who cannot care for themselves?

What Else Should You Know About This Group of Occupations?

Workers in this group have close contact with people. The work can be strenuous, due to standing on one's feet and lifting patients in and out of bed. Workers must deal with the emotional stress that comes from taking care of sick, elderly, or handicapped people. However, there is often a great personal satisfaction in assisting others who need help.

Since health care is required 24 hours a day, working hours will be varied for many of these jobs. Room and board may be considered as part of the wages for some jobs. Workers in this group often feel secure because of the growing demand for health care.

The military services offer training and experience related to some occupations in this group. These occupations are included in the list at the end of this group description. They are identified by an (M) following the occupational title. More information about the military training and experience opportunities may be found in Appendix A.

How Can You Prepare for This Kind of Work?

Most of the technician occupations and assistants to doctors require one to two years of education and training beyond high school. Attendants and aides require less formal training. High school graduates have more opportunity for employment. Employers may hire workers with less education for some jobs if the demand is critical. For many jobs in this group, hospitals and clinics offer on-the-job training. This training usually includes classroom instruction, demonstration, and supervised practice. Training for some jobs can be obtained in local health care agencies, junior colleges, and vocational schools.

As you plan your high school education you should include courses related to Child and Adult Care. The following list of courses and skills can help you plan your education.

Health Services – courses in dental services, miscellaneous allied health services, and nursing related services.

This audiometrist is testing a patient's hearing.

Diagnostic and Treatment Services – courses in the use of medical equipment for diagnostic and treatment purposes.

General Mathematics – courses that develop skills in reading charts, graphs, and technical instructions in mathematical or diagram form.

Home Economics – courses in child and adult care, homemaking, and first-aid.

Life Science – courses in biology and anatomy.

Courses in general science, health, physical education, and safety can help you determine an interest in this field.

Qualifications Profile

This section is a summary of the worker traits and work factors related to successful job performance and worker satisfaction. Try to relate your interests, abilities, aptitudes, and preferences to these traits and factors. An asterisk (*) marks those traits and factors that are related to more than 60% of the occupations listed at the end of this group. The other traits and factors listed are as important, but relate to fewer occupations. See Appendices B-G for information about all of the worker traits and work factors.

Work Activities

The most important activities related to this group involve:

  2. Business contact.
* 4. Direct personal contact to help or instruct others.
  7. Tasks of a scientific and technical nature.

Work Situations

Workers must be willing to:

  1. Perform duties which change frequently.
* 4. Deal with people.

  6. Work under pressure.
  7. Make decisions using personal judgment.
  8. Make decisions using standards that can be measured or checked.
10. Work within precise limits or standards of accuracy.

Data-People-Things

This chart shows the levels for these three basic elements of work as related to this group. Level means the degree of difficulty of job tasks rather than the amount of time involved. The terms low, average, and high indicate the highest level at which occupations are involved. Compare your interests and abilities with the levels checked.

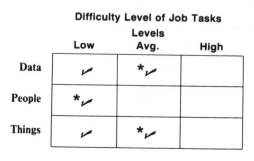

Difficulty Level of Job Tasks

	Low	Avg.	High
Data	✓	*✓	
People	*✓		
Things	✓	*✓	

Levels

Ambulance attendants place an
accident victim on a stretcher.

Aptitudes

This chart presents the most important aptitudes related to this group. The levels checked compare aptitudes needed for success in
this group to aptitudes of the general working
population in all occupations. For example,
level 5 is low and represents the bottom 10%
of the working population. Level 1 is high and
represents the top 10%.

APTITUDE LEVELS COMPARED TO ALL WORKERS							
Related Aptitudes (Ability to Learn)		Lower 1/3		Middle 1/3	Upper 1/3		
		Level **5**	Level **4**	Level **3**	Level **2**	Level **1**	
Code	Title	10%	23%	34%	23%	10%	
G	General Learning Ability		✔	* ✔	✔		
V	Verbal			* ✔			
P	Form Perception		✔	✔	✔		
Q	Clerical Perception		* ✔	✔	✔		
K	Motor Coordination		✔	✔	✔		
M	Manual Dexterity		✔	* ✔			

Working Conditions

These are the physical surroundings in which work is done. In occupations belonging to this group, work is performed:

*I – Inside — workers spend most of their time inside protected from weather conditions but not always from temperature changes.

Physical Demands

Workers in this group of occupations must be able to do:

L – Light work
M – Medium work

Educational Skills

This chart shows the levels of reasoning, math, and language skills related to this group. These skills are usually developed in an educational setting. There are six levels ranging from the simple (1) to the most complex (6).

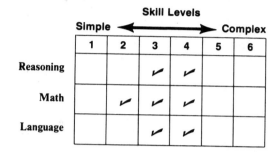

	Skill Levels					
	Simple ←		→		Complex	
	1	2	3	4	5	6
Reasoning			✓	✓		
Math		✓	✓	✓		
Language			✓	✓		

Common Occupations

A full listing of all occupations belonging to this group may be found in the Guide for Occupational Exploration.

The following occupations have been selected to represent this group. They provide the major employment opportunities. However, specific job opportunities will vary according to locations of industry, geographical region, and other factors.

Information may be found in common sources of occupational information, state career information systems, and computerized guidance systems.

An (M) follows the occupational title where the military services offer training and experience.

Data Collection

078.262-010 Pulmonary-Function Technician (M)
078.362-010 Audiometrist (M)
078.362-018 Electrocardiograph Technician (M)
078.362-022 Electroencephalographic Technologist (M)
078.362-030 Cardiopulmonary Technologist (M)

Patient Care

079.364-014 Optometric Assistant (M)
079.367-010 Medical Assistant (M)
079.371-010 Dental Assistant (M)
079.374-010 Emergency Medical Technician (M)
079.374-022 Surgical Technician (M)
354.374-010 Nurse, Practical
355.354-010 Physical Therapy Aide (M)
355.374-010 Ambulance Attendant
355.374-014 Medication Aide (M)
355.377-010 Occupational Therapy Aide (M)
355.377-014 Psychiatric Aide (M)
355.674-014 Nurse Aide (M)
355.674-018 Orderly (M)
359.363-010 Health-Equipment Servicer
712.661-010 Orthopedic Assistant (M)

Care of Others

354.377-014 Home Attendant
355.674-010 Child-Care Attendant, School
359.677-010 Attendant, Childrens Institution
359.677-018 Nursery School Attendant
371.567-010 Guard, School-Crossing

11 SOCIAL/BUSINESS

(Leading-Influencing)

People with an interest in the Social-Business field can satisfy this interest through work in many fields. These include law, education, finance, social research, and business management. Workers need a high level of verbal and numerical skills. They plan, direct, and manage work tasks to organize and deliver programs and services. They must make many decisions. They must analyze and interpret data and use their personal judgment when making decisions. To lead and influence others, they must be able to speak and write clearly (communication skills). These workers enjoy recognition and appreciation for the work they do.

The Social-Business area is divided into four clusters: Communications-Promotion, Business-Numerical, Educational-Social, and Legal.

Communications-Promotion

The Communications-Promotion cluster includes workers who write, edit, report, and translate factual information. They inform the public of what is going on in general news or in a special field. Some workers influence the feelings and action of others. They promote the sales of products and services, raise funds, and conduct membership drives. Workers in this cluster must be able to speak or write clearly and be convincing.

Business-Numerical

The Business-Numerical cluster includes workers who manage business affairs for a company or firm. They may prepare reports, records, and budgets.

They also supervise others to ensure that things run smoothly. This cluster also includes workers who use math skills to design and use record systems, conduct research, and analyze data to solve problems. They must deal with statistics and use skills of logic. Some workers apply accounting and auditing principles to keep or check financial records. Most workers need to know how to apply computer technology to their work.

Educational-Social

The Educational-Social cluster includes workers who do general and special teaching and library work. Some may provide vocational training. It also includes social research workers who study people and the culture in which they live. Some workers manage programs and projects that provide people with services such as health, education, welfare, and recreation.

Legal

The Legal cluster includes workers who advise others and act in their interests in legal matters. They may appear in court to conduct criminal or civil cases. Some prepare legal papers such as wills or handle real estate matters. Most lawyers specialize in one kind of law such as criminal, tax, civil, labor, or patent law. Some workers enforce government or company regulations. Others negotiate contracts and settle claims.

The following Worker Trait Groups and Subgroups are related to the Communications-Promotion, Business-Numerical, Educational-Social, and Legal clusters.

364

Communications-Promotion

11.08 Communications
Editing
Writing
Writing and Broadcasting
Translating and Interpreting

11.09 Promotion
Sales
Fund and Membership Solicitation
Public Relations

Business-Numerical

11.01 Mathematics and Statistics
Data Processing Design
Data Analysis

11.05 Business Administration
Management Services:
    Non-Government
Administrative Specialization
Management Services: Government

11.06 Finance
Accounting and Auditing
Records Systems Analysis
Risk and Profit Analysis
Brokering
Budget and Financial Control

11.11 Business Management
Lodging
Recreation and Amusement
Transportation
Services
Wholesale-Retail

Education-Social

**11.02 Education and Library
    Services**
General Teaching and Instructing
Vocational and Industrial Teaching
Home Economics, Agriculture, and
    Related Teaching
Library Services

11.03 Social Research
Psychological
Sociological
Historical
Occupational
Economic

11.07 Services Administration
Social Services
Health and Safety Services
Education Services
Recreation Services

Social-Business: an interest in leading and influencing others through activities involving the communication of ideas and information.

Legal

11.04 Law
Justice Administration
Legal Practice
Conciliation
Abstracting, Document Preparation

11.10 Regulations Enforcement
Finance
Individual Rights
Health and Safety
Immigration and Customs
Company Policy

11.12 Contracts and Claims
Claims Settlement
Rental and Leasing
Booking
Contract Negotiations

11.01

Mathematics and Statistics

Mathematics and Statistics involve solving problems, conducting research, and using advanced math and data analysis procedures. This may include the use of computers to process data. The results are used to make decisions and plans. Some workers design computer programs to manage business data. Some solve problems in science and engineering. And some conduct research in math theory or develop new methods of using statistics. This group includes the subgroups of:

Data Processing Design
Data Analysis

Data Processing Design involves organizing facts or stating problems in a format for computer processing. This may include the design of sample problems. It could involve the design of a computer program to handle business accounting systems. Most jobs involve managing, storing, and retrieving data using computers.

Data Analysis is the use of math and problem solving methods in a variety of jobs. Some workers use math and statistics to solve engineering and physical science problems. Other workers compute insurance rates, investment risks, or provide data for research.

Jobs may be found in colleges, universities, and research organizations. Large businesses and industries, as well as government agencies, also hire workers in this group.

What Skills and Abilities Would Help You Succeed in This Kind of Work?

The most important skills are listed below. All of those listed do not apply to each occupation. As you explore occupations you should identify the specific ones needed.

Analytical – to use advanced logic and scientific thinking to solve a variety of complex problems.

Numerical – to understand advanced mathematical concepts and statistics.

Critical Thinking – to use personal judgment and facts to make decisions and solve problems.

Technical – to use computer technology in problem solving and information processing.

Communication – to speak and write clearly and correctly.

Conceptual – to form a mental image of the functioning of computer flowcharts.

Accuracy – to work with symbols and numbers without error.

Comprehension – to understand and use technical terms and processes.

Graphic Communication – to develop, understand, and use complex charts, graphs, and symbols.

A business systems programmer checks program functions with a machine operator.

Do You Have or Can You Develop an Interest in This Kind of Work?

Review the following questions. Your answers can give you clues as to your interest in Mathematics and Statistics.

Have you taken advanced math courses? Do you understand the ideas presented in these courses? Do you enjoy working with mathematical concepts?

Do you like to solve math problems? Have you ever played logic games? Can you identify the procedures used to solve such problems and games?

Have you used a pocket calculator? Can you enter long columns of numbers correctly? Do you know how to use all of the function keys?

Have you taken computer science courses? Do you have a knowledge of how computers function? Do you enjoy solving problems with a computer?

Have you prepared charts and graphs to present information for reports? Do you enjoy constructing charts and graphs?

Do you read computer magazines? Are you interested in finding the capabilities and limitations of computers?

This actuary manipulates data in a computer to keep rate tables current.

What Else Should You Know About This Group of Occupations?

Workers in Mathematics and Statistics are expected to keep up with rapid change or new procedures in their specific area. They may attend seminars and workshops or study for advanced degrees. Knowledge of several computer languages may be required. Extensive reading of technical journals and reports is necessary to remain up-to-date. Usually, these workers are hired as trainees, even with the required education. Promotion follows on-the-job work experiences. Sometimes workers in this field take tests to obtain credentials or to use a professional title.

The military services offer training and experience related to some occupations in this group. These occupations are included in the list at the end of this group description. They are identified by an (M) following the occupational title. More information abut the military training and experience opportunities may be found in Appendix A.

How Can You Prepare for This Kind of Work?

Most occupations in this group require two to four years of training and experience. Others may require up to ten years. Coursework in mathematics, economics, and statistics is required to enter this type of work. Some jobs require experience in banking, insurance, accounting, or a related field. Experience and training in a scientific or technical field is required for other jobs. Government agencies usually require applicants to pass a civil service test.

As you plan your high school program, you should include courses related to Mathematics and Statistics. Next you should include courses needed to enter college. The following list of courses and skills will help you plan your education.

Computer Science – courses in general computer and information sciences, computer programming, data processing, systems analysis, and microcomputer applications.

Advanced Mathematics – courses in actuarial sciences, applied mathematics, pure mathematics, and statistics.

Courses in general mathematics, algebra/geometry, and general science can help you determine your interest in this group.

Qualifications Profile

This section is a summary of the worker traits and work factors related to successful job performance and worker satisfaction. Try to relate your interests, abilities, aptitudes, and preferences to these traits and factors. An asterisk (*) marks those traits and factors that are related to more than 60% of the occupations listed at the end of this group. The other traits and factors listed are as important, but relate to fewer occupations. See Appendices B-G for information about all of the worker traits and work factors.

Work Activities

The most important activities related to this group involve:

   5. Recognition or appreciation from others.
   6. Communication of ideas and information.
* 7. Tasks of a scientific and technical nature.
* 9. Processes, methods, or machines.

Data-People-Things

This chart shows the levels for these three basic elements of work as related to this group. Level means the degree of difficulty of job tasks rather than the amount of time involved. The terms low, average, and high indicate the highest level at which occupations are involved. Compare your interests and abilities with the levels checked.

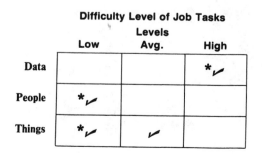

Difficulty Level of Job Tasks

	Low	Avg.	High
Data			*✓
People	*✓		
Things	*✓	✓	

Work Situations

Workers must be willing to:

1. Perform duties which change frequently.
3. Plan and direct an entire activity.
4. Deal with people.
7. Make decisions using personal judgment.
* 8. Make decisions using standards that can be measured or checked.
10. Work within precise limits or standards of accuracy.

Working Conditions

These are the physical surroundings in which work is done. In occupations belonging to this group, work is performed:

*I – Inside — workers spend most of their time inside protected from weather conditions but not always from temperature changes.

Physical Demands

Workers in this group of occupations must be able to do:

*S – Sedentary work

Educational Skills

This chart shows the levels of reasoning, math, and language skills related to this group. These skills are usually developed in an educational setting. There are six levels ranging from the simple (1) to the most complex (6).

	Skill Levels					
	Simple ⟵			⟶ Complex		
	1	2	3	4	5	6
Reasoning				✔	*✔	✔
Math				✔	✔	✔
Language				✔	✔	✔

Keyboarding skills help this financial analyst in his daily work.

Aptitudes

This chart presents the most important aptitudes related to this group. The levels checked compare aptitudes needed for success in this group to aptitudes of the general working population in all occupations. For example, level 5 is low and represents the bottom 10% of the working population. Level 1 is high and represents the top 10%.

APTITUDE LEVELS COMPARED TO ALL WORKERS						
Related Aptitudes (Ability to Learn)		Lower 1/3		Middle 1/3	Upper 1/3	
		Level 5	Level 4	Level 3	Level 2	Level 1
Code	Title	10%	23%	34%	23%	10%
G	General Learning Ability				*✔	✔
V	Verbal				*✔	✔
N	Numerical				✔	✔
S	Spatial		✔	✔	✔	
Q	Clerical Perception			✔	✔	✔

 # Common Occupations

A full listing of all occupations belonging to this group may be found in the Guide for Occupational Exploration.

The following occupations have been selected to represent this group. They provide the major employment opportunities. However, specific job opportunities will vary according to locations of industry, geographical region, and other factors.

Information may be found in common sources of occupational information, state career information systems, and computerized guidance systems.

An (M) follows the occupational title where the military services offer training and experience.

Data Processing Design

012.167-066 Systems Analyst, Electronic Data Processing (M)
020.067-010 Engineering Analyst
020.067-018 Operations-Research Analyst (M)
020.067-022 Statistician, Mathematical
020.162-014 Programer, Business (M)
020.167-018 Programer, Chief, Business
020.167-022 Programer, Engineering and Scientific
020.187-010 Programer, Information System (M)
020.224-010 Customer-Support Specialist
020.262-010 Software Technician
109.067-010 Information Scientist (M)
161.117-014 Director, Records Management (M)
161.267-018 Forms Analyst
169.167-030 Manager, Electronic Data Processing (M)
219.367-026 Programer, Detail (M)

Data Analysis

020.162-010 Mathematical Technician
020.167-010 Actuary
020.167-014 Financial Analyst
020.167-026 Statistician, Applied (M)
189.167-010 Consultant

11.02

Education and Library Services

Education and Library Services include teaching, advising, and library work. Teachers encourage students to explore many interests. They also help them learn to think and make decisions. Some teach basic courses and special subjects. Others teach specific job-related skills. Some workers advise about farm and home management or work with youth and community groups. Library work includes administration of libraries and providing a variety of library services for people. This group includes the subgroups of:

General Teaching and Instructing
Vocational and Industrial Teaching
Home Economics, Agricultural and
    Related Teaching
Library Services

General Teaching and Instructing is to help students gain information and skills they need to function in the world around them. Teaching duties vary depending upon the type of school and level being taught. At the grade school level, teaching may involve all basic subjects. It also includes teaching social and physical skills. At the secondary level, teachers usually teach only one or two subject fields. For example, one person may teach English or math. Teachers at the college level are more specialized. Most teach in only one field, such as physics or art.

Vocational and Industrial Teaching helps prepare students for jobs that do not require a college degree. It also includes the training of workers on the job. These teachers need to be able to demonstrate skills. They

Teaching mathematics involves motivating students as well as explaining principles.

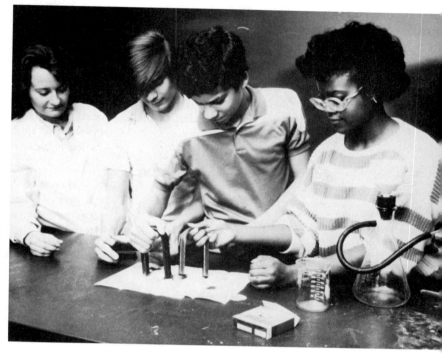

Guided experiments make physics teaching exciting and challenging.

teach the proper use of tools, machines, and equipment. They teach how to use charts, diagrams, and drawings, and how to use technical data. They also lecture on theory, practice, methods, and safety rules. Most teach in only one trade area or job field.

Home Economics, Agricultural and Related Teaching includes jobs that advise and inform homemakers, farmers, and community groups. Duties may involve ways to improve home and family life. Workers in this group lecture on and demonstrate good home and farm management methods. They may teach how to plan a budget or save energy. Or, they may show how to provide good nutrition and child care. They may conduct radio or TV programs. And, some may write articles or reports for newspapers or magazines. Others may organize and direct activities of clubs such as the 4-H club.

Workers duties may also include helping community groups in health care areas.

Library Services include many types of librarians. Some select and acquire materials. Others catalog, classify, or maintain them. Some help people find the books and materials they want to use. Librarians may work with one type of material such as music or media. Some work with one topic such as careers. And, some may work with special groups, such as children.

Jobs may be found in public and private schools. They also may be found in vocational schools, technical and career centers, and colleges. Most librarian jobs are also found in these schools. Some find work in public libraries. Hospitals, prisons, governments, and large businesses also use the services of librarians.

373

What Skills and Abilities Would Help You Succeed in This Kind of Work?

The most important skills are listed below. All of those listed do not apply to each occupation. As you explore occupations, you should identify specific ones needed.

Communication – to give and exchange information.

Creative Thinking – to develop original ideas or ways to present information to groups or individuals.

Empathy – to care about the welfare and needs of others and to have the desire to help.

Interpretation – to explain ideas, information, and feelings.

Leadership – to plan and direct the work of others.

Organization – to arrange ideas, thoughts, and information in a way that can be understood.

Persuasiveness – to use words to influence the thinking and actions of others.

Poise – to be calm and self-confident in front of an audience.

Verbalization – to express ideas through the use of words.

Rapport – to deal with people in an effective way and maintain harmony among them.

Social Skills – to deal with people in an effective manner.

Do You Have or Can You Develop an Interest in This Kind of Work?

Review the following questions. Your answers can give you clues as to your interest in the Education and Library Services field.

Have you been a camp or playground instructor? Do you enjoy working with children? Were you able to explain again and again when a learner was unable to understand the first time?

Have you helped friends or relatives with their homework? Can you explain things and communicate ideas? Can you think of new examples to help them learn?

Have you been a member of Future Teachers of America (FTA) or a similar group? Do you want to teach others?

Have you helped a librarian catalog or shelve books? Do you like to work in libraries?

Have you been a school office worker or teacher's helper? Do you enjoy helping or assisting people?

What Else Should You Know About This Group of Occupations?

Openings for teachers may vary according to the subject area or specialty. Other factors such as enrollment changes and financial support can affect employment. Most teachers are hired for only nine months each year. Some use the summer to further their education or find employment to supplement their teaching income.

Most of these jobs have regular hours. But, many teachers need to put in extra time to plan activities, grade papers, and attend meetings. They also may supervise student activities after school hours. They may receive extra pay for some of these duties.

Job prospects have improved some in recent years. This is due to a sharp drop in the number of new graduates prepared to teach. Science and math teachers are and may remain in short supply. Some schools also fail to find enough teachers qualified in special

education, vocational and bilingual (speak more than one language) education.

The teaching of special groups such as blind, deaf, and retarded students is included in Worker Trait Group 10.01, Social Services.

How Can You Prepare for This Kind of Work?

Most occupations in this group require two to four years of education and training. Some jobs require over ten years. In some cases, the salary depends on the amount of education you have. As a result, getting special training or an advanced degree may be important. School principals and college teachers must have graduate degrees.

Teachers in public schools must have state certificates for the subjects or grade levels they teach. Certificate requirements vary among the states. However, a college degree and student teaching are standard. Vocational

Teaching basic keyboarding skill in a typing class.

teachers usually must have several years of experience in business or industry. Graduates in Library Sciences who participate in internship programs or who work part time may have an employment advantage over other new graduates.

As you plan your high school program you should include courses related to Education and Library Services. Next, you should include courses needed to enter college. The following list of courses and skills can help you plan your education.

Education – courses in teaching methods, educational testing, curriculum, educational media, psychology, social foundations, history of education, special education, and teaching the gifted and talented.

Subject Matter – courses in the subject area to be taught. Depending upon the location of the school, teachers may need to be bilingual.

Library and Archival Science – courses in liberal/general studies, general library and archival sciences, and library science.

Courses in literature, speech, technical/business writing, psychology, and sociology/anthropology are important for some occupations in this group. Courses in general mathematics, general science, and social studies can help you determine your interest in this group.

Courses in agriculture, home economics, or dietetics as related to the specific area of interest in extension services.

Qualifications Profile

This section is a summary of the worker traits and work factors related to successful job performance and worker satisfaction. Try to relate your interests, abilities, aptitudes, and preferences to these traits and factors. An asterisk (*) marks those traits and factors that are related to more than 60% of the occupations listed at the end of this group. The other traits and factors listed are as important, but relate to fewer occupations. See Appendices B-G for information about all of the worker traits and work factors.

Work Activities

The most important activities related to this group involve:

2. Business contact.
4. Direct personal contact to help or instruct others.
5. Recognition or appreciation from others.
* 6. Communication of ideas and information.

Physical Demands

Workers in this group of occupations must be able to do:

S – Sedentary work
*L – Light work

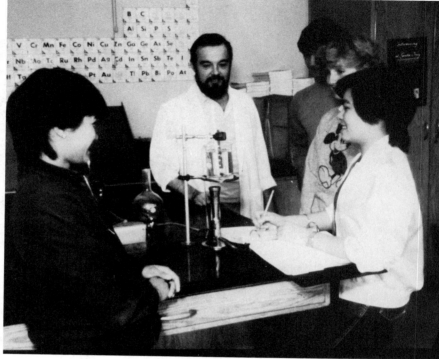

A chemistry teacher observes a student group's experiment.

Work Situations

Workers must be willing to:

1. Perform duties which change frequently.
3. Plan and direct an entire activity.
* 4. Deal with people.
5. Influence people's opinions, attitudes, and judgments.
* 7. Make decisions using personal judgment.

Working Conditions

These are the physical surroundings in which work is done. In occupations belonging to this group, work is performed:

*I – Inside — workers spend most of their time inside protected from weather conditions but not always from temperature changes.

Educational Skills

This chart shows the levels of reasoning, math, and language skills related to this group. These skills are usually developed in an educational setting. There are six levels ranging from the simple (1) to the most complex (6).

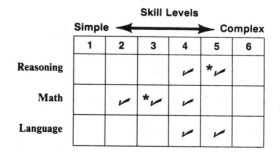

	Skill Levels					
	Simple ←		→		Complex	
	1	2	3	4	5	6
Reasoning				✓	*✓	
Math		✓	*✓	✓		
Language				✓	✓	

Librarians do a lot of teaching, as well as answer many, many questions.

Aptitudes

This chart presents the most important aptitudes related to this group. The levels checked compare aptitudes needed for success in this group to aptitudes of the general working population in all occupations. For example, level 5 is low and represents the bottom 10% of the working population. Level 1 is high and represents the top 10%.

APTITUDE LEVELS COMPARED TO ALL WORKERS						
Related Aptitudes **(Ability to Learn)**		Lower 1/3		Middle 1/3	Upper 1/3	
		Level **5**	Level **4**	Level **3**	Level **2**	Level **1**
Code	Title	10%	23%	34%	23%	10%
G	General Learning Ability			✔	* ✔	
V	Verbal				* ✔	
N	Numerical			* ✔	✔	
Q	Clerical Perception			✔	✔	

Data-People-Things

This chart shows the levels for these three basic elements of work as related to this group. Level means the degree of difficulty of job tasks rather than the amount of time involved. The terms low, average, and high indicate the highest level at which occupations are involved. Compare your interests and abilities with the levels checked.

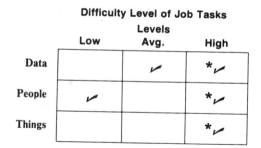

Difficulty Level of Job Tasks

	Low	Avg.	High
Data		✓	* ✓
People	✓		* ✓
Things			* ✓

Common Occupations

A full listing of all occupations belonging to this group may be found in the Guide for Occupational Exploration.

The following occupations have been selected to represent this group. They provide the major employment opportunities. However, specific job opportunities will vary according to locations of industry, geographical region, and other factors.

Information may be found in common sources of occupational information, state career information systems, and computerized guidance systems.

An (M) follows the occupational title where the military services offer training and experience.

Teaching and Instructing, General

090.227-010 Faculty Member, College or University (M)
090.227-018 Instructor, Extension Work
091.227-010 Teacher, Secondary School
092.227-010 Teacher, Elementary School
099.224-010 Instructor, Physical Education
099.227-014 Instructor, Correspondence School
099.227-022 Instructor, Military Science (M)
099.227-030 Teacher, Adult Education
099.327-010 Teacher Aide 1

Teaching, Vocational and Industrial

091.221-010 Teacher, Industrial Arts
097.227-014 Instructor, Vocational Training (M)
166.227-010 Training Representative (M)

Teaching, Home Economics, Agriculture, and Related

077.127-010 Community Dietitian (M)
096.121-010 County Home-Demonstration Agent
096.121-014 Home Economist
096.127-010 County-Agricultural Agent
096.127-014 Extension Service Specialist
096.127-022 Four-H Club Agent

Library Services

100.127-014 Librarian
100.167-010 Audiovisual Librarian
100.167-018 Childrens Librarian
100.167-022 Institution Librarian
100.167-026 Librarian, Special Library
100.167-030 Media Specialist, School Library
100.267-010 Acquisitions Librarian
100.367-014 Classifier
100.367-018 Library Technical Assistant
100.367-022 Music Librarian
100.387-010 Catalog Librarian
249.367-014 Career-Guidance Technician
249.367-046 Library Assistant

Social Research is to study people and the culture in which they live. Workers conduct research into all aspects of past and current human behavior. This includes abnormal behavior, politics, language, lifestyle, and work. This group includes the subgroups of:

Psychological
Sociological
Historical
Occupational
Economic

Psychological Research involves the study of human behavior and mental functions. Workers study such things as mental, physical, and social problems. They select and develop methods to conduct this research. They observe people and give psychological tests. They keep records and write reports. They also may write papers to be published.

Sociological Research is the study of the development and structure of human culture. Also included is the study of people as members of groups and of social systems. Workers conduct research on political behavior, social problems, specific languages, and the use of land. They analyze and explain the results of their research. They use their findings to develop and test theories. These workers also keep records and write reports.

Historical Research is the study of the past. Some workers trace people's ancestors. They construct charts to show lines of descent and family ties. Other workers research how the human race developed. They study fossils of human remains. They also excavate ruins and study relics. Some workers study records and old documents to appraise their value. Other workers conduct research on historic buildings. They construct exhibits to scale in dioramas (scenes with lifelike figures and surroundings).

Occupational Research involves personnel policies and the employment of workers. This includes how to recruit, select, and train people. Some researchers observe and interview workers to prepare job analyses. Their findings help place workers and make use of their skills. These workers interview people that apply for jobs. They review their skills and select the best employee for the job. They also inform new workers about such things as job duties and pay. Some workers promote and develop job training programs for the disadvantaged. They inform business, labor, and the public about these training programs. Other workers question new prison inmates to obtain data for assigning them to work and housing.

Economic Research involves economic theory. This includes how natural resources are developed and goods and services are consumed. Economists help solve problems in areas such as labor, finance, or taxes. They may conduct surveys and analyze data. Their research aids in market interpretation or solution of other economic problems.

Jobs in this group may be found with museums, schools and colleges, government agencies, and private research foundations. Some workers are self-employed. They may obtain grants from private groups or from the government to do research or to conduct special studies.

What Skills and Abilities Would Help You Succeed in This Kind of Work?

The most important skills are listed below. All of those listed do not apply to each occupation. As you explore occupations you should identify the specific ones needed.

Comprehension – to understand and use theories and methods in fields such as history, sociology, and economics.

Analytical – to examine and interpret current and historical information.

Verbalization – to express ideas through the use of words.

Organization – to keep detailed research notes and to arrange information in a way that can be understood.

Numerical – to understand advanced mathematical concepts and statistics.

Communication – to write reports related to research findings.

Do You Have or Can You Develop an Interest in This Kind of Work?

Review the following questions. Your answers can give you clues as to your interest in Social Research.

Have you been a member of a political science club? Are you interested in how government functions?

Have you taken courses in sociology, psychology, or civics? Do you like to write reports or research papers?

A social welfare research worker collects data in a field interview.

Archeologists at work at an excavation.

Have you visited museums and historical sites? Would you like to dig for artifacts? Are you interested in ancient cultures?

Have you done research projects or surveys for social science classes? Do you like this type of activity?

Have you had history courses? How were your grades? Do you like to read historical novels?

Have you read articles about the problems of society? Would you like to help solve such problems as crime and poverty? Do you keep informed of current events?

What Else Should You Know About This Group of Occupations?

Most workers keep regular business hours. They often work alone behind a desk. They may feel the pressures of deadlines, heavy workloads, and overtime work. Some workers may be required to travel to conduct research.

Workers in this group must keep up with developments and trends in their field. They may attend workshops and seminars to keep informed in their specialty.

The military services offer training and experience related to some occupations in this group. These occupations are included in the list at the end of this group description. They are identified by an (M) following the occupational title. More information about the military training and experience opportunities may be found in Appendix A.

How Can You Prepare for This Kind of Work?

Most occupations in this group require two to four years of training and experience. Others may require up to ten years. Most jobs require four or more years of college study. Advanced degrees are required for many jobs. Workers often need courses in computer science or statistics to process research data.

As you plan your high school program you should include courses related to Social Research. Next, you should include courses needed to enter college. The following list of courses and skills can help you plan your education.

Social Sciences – courses in history, geography, government, political science, anthropology, archaeology, economics, sociology, urban studies, and other cultural studies.

Psychology – courses in general and developmental psychology; experimental and clinical psychology; social, industrial, and counseling psychology; personality and psychometrics.

For occupations related to research, courses in algebra, advanced math, statistics, computer science, and research methods are very important.

Courses in language skills, composition, technical/business writing can be important for some occupations in this group. Library and archival science courses also are important for some occupations.

Courses in literature, social studies, and introductory psychology can help you determine your interest in this group of occupations.

Qualifications Profile

This section is a summary of the worker traits and work factors related to successful job performance and worker satisfaction. Try to relate your interests, abilities, aptitudes, and preferences to these traits and factors. An asterisk (*) marks those traits and factors that are related to more than 60% of the occupations listed at the end of this group. The other traits and factors listed are as important, but relate to fewer occupations. See Appendices B-G for information about all of the worker traits and work factors.

Work Activities

The most important activities related to this group involve:

5. Recognition or appreciation from others.
* 6. Communication of ideas and information.

* 7. Tasks of a scientific and technical nature.
* 8. Creative thinking.

Educational Skills

This chart shows the levels of reasoning, math, and language skills related to this group. These skills are usually developed in an educational setting. There are six levels ranging from the simple (1) to the most complex (6).

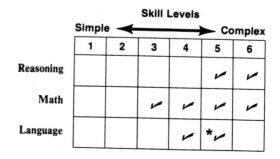

	Skill Levels					
	Simple ←			→ Complex		
	1	2	3	4	5	6
Reasoning					✔	✔
Math			✔	✔	✔	✔
Language				✔	*✔	

Aptitudes

This chart presents the most important aptitudes related to this group. The levels checked compare aptitudes needed for success in this group to aptitudes of the general working population in all occupations. For example, level 5 is low and represents the bottom 10% of the working population. Level 1 is high and represents the top 10%.

APTITUDE LEVELS COMPARED TO ALL WORKERS						
Related Aptitudes (Ability to Learn)		Lower 1/3		Middle 1/3	Upper 1/3	
		Level 5	Level 4	Level 3	Level 2	Level 1
Code	Title	10%	23%	34%	23%	10%
G	General Learning Ability				✔	✔
V	Verbal				✔	✔
N	Numerical			✔	✔	
Q	Clerical Perception		✔	✔	✔	

Working Conditions

These are the physical surroundings in which work is done. In occupations belonging to this group, work is performed:

*I – Inside — workers spend most of their time inside protected from weather conditions but not always from temperature changes.

Physical Demands

Workers in this group of occupations must be able to do:

*S – Sedentary work
L – Light work

Work Situations

Workers must be willing to:

1. Perform duties which change frequently.
3. Plan and direct an entire activity.
4. Deal with people.
* 7. Make decisions using personal judgment.
* 8. Make decisions using standards that can be measured or checked.

Personnel recruiters work in many industrial, commercial, and social fields, as well as in the military.

Data-People-Things

This chart shows the levels for these three basic elements of work as related to this group. Level means the degree of difficulty of job tasks rather than the amount of time involved. The terms low, average, and high indicate the highest level at which occupations are involved. Compare your interests and abilities with the levels checked.

Difficulty Level of Job Tasks

	Low	Avg.	High
Data			*✓
People	*✓		
Things	*✓		

Common Occupations

A full listing of all occupations belonging to this group may be found in the Guide for Occupational Exploration.

The following occupations have been selected to represent this group. They provide the major employment opportunities. However, specific job opportunities will vary according to locations of industry, geographical region, and other factors.

Information may be found in common sources of occupational information, state career information systems, and computerized guidance systems.

An (M) follows the occupational title where the military services offer training and experience.

Psychological

045.061-010 Psychologist, Developmental (M)
045.061-014 Psychologist, Engineering (M)
045.061-018 Psychologist, Experimental
045.067-010 Psychologist, Educational (M)
045.067-014 Psychologist, Social (M)
045.067-018 Psychometrist (M)
045.107-030 Psychologist, Industrial-Organizational (M)

Sociological

051.067-010 Political Scientist
054.067-010 Research Worker, Social Welfare
054.067-014 Sociologist
059.067-010 Philologist
059.067-014 Scientific Linguist
059.167-010 Intelligence Research Specialist (M)
059.267-010 Intelligence Specialist (M)
199.167-014 Urban Planner

Historical

052.067-018 Genealogist
052.067-022 Historian (M)
055.067-010 Anthropologist
055.067-018 Archeologist
055.067-022 Ethnologist
101.167-010 Archivist
109.267-010 Research Assistant

Occupational

166.067-010 Occupational Analyst (M)
166.267-010 Employment Interviewer (M)
166.267-018 Job Analyst (M)
166.267-022 Prisoner-Classification Interviewer (M)
166.267-034 Job Development Specialist
166.267-038 Personnel Recruiter (M)

Economic

050.067-010 Economist

11.04

Law

Law is to advise and represent others in legal matters. Workers use their knowledge of law to advise people of their rights and to conduct lawsuits. Some decide cases brought before a court. They define the meaning of laws used in courts, hearings, and business. This group includes the subgroups of:

Justice Administration
Legal Practice
Conciliation
Abstracting, Document Preparation

Justice Administration is to preside as an arbitrator, advisor, or administrator of the judicial system. Judges often must rule on issues that have not been heard before in court. In criminal cases, they examine the evidence and listen to the testimony given. They rule on evidence produced during a trial and settle disputes between lawyers. They also instruct the jury on the laws that apply. And, if the defendent is found guilty, the judge imposes a sentence.

Magistrates settle small civil cases. Damages in a case before them cannot exceed an amount set by state law. Also, minor cases cannot involve penitentiary sentences or large fines. Other workers involved in hearings and appeals may settle claims, give rulings, and write their views on questions appealed. They also may prepare opinions on points of law.

Legal Practice is to advise others of the law and to represent them in legal matters. Lawyers serve as the link between people and the legal justice system. They may practice one or more types of law such as criminal, patent, real estate, or tax. They prepare legal papers and advise clients on aspects of the law. Many lawyers never appear in a court.

Lawyers review past cases and research laws to prepare for a trial. When a case is tried, they examine and cross-examine witnesses. They also sum up their side of the case for the judge or jury. Other workers in this subgroup research and prepare cases for appeals. During an appeal hearing, they present arguments and evidence to support the appeal. Some research law, investigate facts, and prepare documents for Lawyers. They also may deliver subpoenas.

Conciliation is to arbitrate and settle disputes, often between labor and management. Arbitrators conduct hearings regarding disputed contracts. They study the details given, make binding decisions, and issue reports of the results. Upon request, Conciliators provide advice and counsel to settle problems and disputes.

Abstracting, Document Preparation is to analyze the law and present main points for inclusion in legal papers. Abstracters summarize sections of the law or other legal details, such as prior cases. These details are used as a reference in legal matters. Patent Agents prepare and present applications to the U.S. Patent Office. They may represent clients in patent courts, but cannot practice law or appear in other courts.

Jobs in this group may be found with law firms, government agencies, unions, and private businesses. Some workers are self-employed and have their own practices. Others may be elected or appointed to public offices.

What Skills and Abilities Would Help You Succeed in This Kind of Work?

The most important skills are listed below. All of those listed do not apply to each occupation. As you explore occupations you should identify the specific ones needed.

Comprehension – to read and understand complex laws and case histories and identify important details.

Verbalization – to speak and write clearly and communicate effectively with others.

Accuracy – to use exact legal terms and ideas to prepare contracts.

Analytical – to define problems, collect information, make inferences, establish facts, and draw valid conclusions.

Numerical – to use concepts in advanced mathematics and statistics.

Persuasiveness – to influence the opinions, attitudes, and judgments of others.

Critical Thinking – to form opinions and make decisions based upon knowledge, judgment, and experience.

Rapport – to deal with people in an effective way to inspire their trust and confidence.

Do You Have or Can You Develop an Interest in This Kind of Work?

Review the following questions. Your answers can give you clues as to your interest in Law.

Have you served as president of a club or other organization? Did you like speaking in front of a group?

Have you watched TV shows involving lawyers? Did they hold your interest? Did you understand the legal terms used?

Have you been on a debate team? Can you argue a point in an effective manner?

Have you taken speech courses? Did you enjoy talking before a group?

Have you advised friends or family members on their personal problems? Did they listen to and take your advice? Did you help them solve their problems?

Have you taken courses in journalism or composition? Can you organize and write information to present a point of view?

Have you attended a trial? Does the courtroom setting interest you?

Have you done research papers? Did you use a library card file? Did you take and use detailed notes?

Lawyers often specialize in certain types of cases as this woman counseling with her juvenile client.

What Else Should You Know About This Group of Occupations?

Most workers in this group have a great deal of responsibility. The information they obtain from clients is confidential and they must adhere to strict rules of ethics.

Lawyers often work long or irregular hours. Some jobs require them to respond to emergency calls from clients. Some are under heavy pressure when a case is being tried. They must keep up-to-date on the latest laws and judicial decisions.

Some workers in this group receive set salaries. Lawyers in private practice get their income from fees. Sometimes, the size of a fee depends upon the outcome of a case. Some lawyers have monthly or annual retainers. Clients pay these fees to have the lawyer's services available when they need them. Retainers provide a steady source of income. Lawyers in private practice determine their own workload and may practice beyond the normal retirement age.

How Can You Prepare for This Kind of Work?

Most occupations in this group require four to ten years of training and experience. Entry requirements for law schools vary. Few schools accept students directly from high school. Most require students to have two or more years of college credit. Lawyers must pass a state bar exam to get a license to practice law. Required preparation for these tests varies among states. Many states require graduation from a law school. A four-year college degree and completion of a program for law clerks is required in some states. Other states accept persons who study law with a licensed lawyer. Some states accept correspondence law courses as preparation for testing. To obtain the licenses necessary to practice law in some higher courts, lawyers must meet special requirements.

Some jobs in this group do not require a license. In these jobs, workers use a knowledge of law, but do not practice law.

Most lawyers start as junior partners in law firms, junior executives in business or industry, or workers in government agencies. A few start by establishing their own practice. However, lawyers usually need to gain experience and develop a reputation before they can become self-employed. Workers must be elected or appointed to some jobs in this group.

As you plan your high school program you should include courses related to Law. Next, you should include courses needed to enter college. The following list of courses and skills will help you plan your education.

The judge must rule on the propriety (acceptability) of evidence submitted.

Law – programs in pre-law, law, and legal assisting. This includes special areas and courses such as civil law, criminal law, contract law, constitutional law, commercial law, administrative law, legal procedures, judicial system, labor relations, business and industrial organization, legal records, bankruptcy, estates and trusts, and consumer protection.

Technical Writing – courses in professional, legal, and abstract writing.

Oral Communication – courses in speech, debate, and forensics (legal proceedings debate).

Courses in psychology, computer science, library and archival science, civics, government, sociology, and international relations can be helpful to some occupations.

Courses in social studies, composition, and speech can help you determine an interest in law.

Qualifications Profile

This section is a summary of the worker traits and work factors related to successful job performance and worker satisfaction. Try to relate your interests, abilities, aptitudes, and preferences to these traits and factors. An asterisk (*) marks those traits and factors that are related to more than 60% of the occupations listed at the end of this group. The other traits and factors listed are as important, but relate to fewer occupations. See Appendices B-G for information about all of the worker traits and work factors.

* 6. Communication of ideas and information.
8. Creative thinking.

Data-People-Things

This chart shows the levels for these three basic elements of work as related to this group. Level means the degree of difficulty of job tasks rather than the amount of time involved. The terms low, average, and high indicate the highest level at which occupations are involved. Compare your interests and abilities with the levels checked.

Work Activities

The most important activities related to this group involve:

2. Business contact.
4. Direct personal contact to help or instruct others.
* 5. Recognition or appreciation from others.

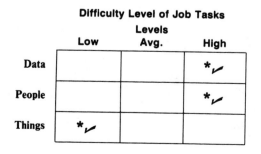

Difficulty Level of Job Tasks

	Low	Avg.	High
Data			*✓
People			*✓
Things	*✓		

Work Situations

Workers must be willing to:

1. Perform duties which change frequently.
3. Plan and direct an entire activity.
* 4. Deal with people.
* 5. Influence people's opinions, attitudes, and judgments.
7. Make decisions using personal judgment.
8. Make decisions using standards that can be measured or checked.

Working Conditions

These are the physical surroundings in which work is done. In occupations belonging to this group, work is performed:

*I – Inside — workers spend most of their time inside protected from weather conditions but not always from temperature changes.

Physical Demands

Workers in this group of occupations must be able to do:

*S – Sedentary work

Educational Skills

This chart shows the levels of reasoning, math, and language skills related to this group. These skills are usually developed in an educational setting. There are six levels ranging from the simple (1) to the most complex (6).

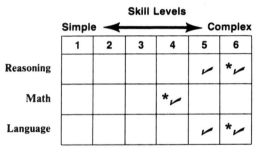

	Skill Levels					
	Simple ⟵		⟶ Complex			
	1	2	3	4	5	6
Reasoning					↙	* ↙
Math				* ↙		
Language					↙	* ↙

This man may be preparing an abstract for an attorney to include in a brief.

Aptitudes

This chart presents the most important aptitudes related to this group. The levels checked compare aptitudes needed for success in this group to aptitudes of the general working population in all occupations. For example, level 5 is low and represents the bottom 10% of the working population. Level 1 is high and represents the top 10%.

APTITUDE LEVELS COMPARED TO ALL WORKERS							
Related Aptitudes (Ability to Learn)		Lower 1/3		Middle 1/3	Upper 1/3		
		Level 5	Level 4	Level 3	Level 2	Level 1	
Code	Title	10%	23%	34%	23%	10%	
G	General Learning Ability				✔	* ✔	
V	Verbal					* ✔	
N	Numerical			✔	✔	✔	
Q	Clerical Perception		✔	* ✔	✔		

Common Occupations

A full listing of all occupations belonging to this group may be found in the Guide for Occupational Exploration.

The following occupations have been selected to represent this group. They provide the major employment opportunities. However, specific job opportunities will vary according to locations of industry, geographical region, and other factors.

Information may be found in common sources of occupational information, state career information systems, and computerized guidance systems.

An (M) follows the occupational title where the military services offer training and experience.

Justice Administration

111.107-010 Judge (M)
111.107-014 Magistrate
119.117-010 Appeals Reviewer, Veteran

Legal Practice

110.107-010 Lawyer (M)
110.107-014 Lawyer, Criminal (M)
110.117-010 District Attorney
110.117-018 Lawyer, Admiralty (M)
110.117-022 Lawyer, Corporation (M)
110.117-026 Lawyer, Patent (M)
110.117-034 Lawyer, Real Estate
110.117-038 Tax Attorney (M)
110.117-042 Title Attorney
119.267-022 Legal Investigator
119.267-026 Paralegal Assistant (M)

Conciliation

169.107-010 Arbitrator
169.207-010 Conciliator

Abstracting, Document Preparation

119.167-014 Patent Agent
119.267-010 Abstractor

11.05

Business Administration

Business Administration is to manage a public agency or private business. Workers in this group write policies and devise programs. They figure costs, prepare budgets, and control spending. They also may keep records, study data, and prepare reports. They control the work that is done. However, they often direct this work through others. They attend meetings for their company or agency. They may give speeches and meet with the press. This group includes the subgroups of:

Management Services: Nongovernment
Administrative Specialization
Management Services: Government

Management Services: Nongovernment involves directing work or services not financed with tax funds. Managers in this subgroup work in business and industry. They are the top-level people. They are in charge of the total operation of a business or facility.

Administrative Specialization involves second level managers. They manage part of a business or government facility. They are in charge of a special section or service.

Management Services: Government involves managers in federal, state, and local governments. It also includes any business or service owned and operated by a government.

Jobs in this group may be found in business, industry, and government. Labor unions and professional groups also employ these workers.

Association executives must be sure records are properly maintained.

What Skills and Abilities Would Help You Succeed in This Kind of Work?

The most important skills are listed below. All of those listed do not apply to each occupation. As you explore occupations you should identify the specific ones needed.

Comprehension – to understand all operations of a company or department.

Verbalization – to express ideas through the use of words in developing policies and programs or supervising the work of others.

Numerical – to use concepts in advanced mathematics and statistics to work with complex financial and statistical information.

Analytical – to define and analyze problems and draw valid conclusions.

Critical Thinking – to use knowledge, experience, and personal judgment to make decisions and solve problems.

Traffic management is a vital job in a shipping company.

Leadership – to plan and direct the work of others.

Rapport – to deal with people in an effective way and maintain harmony among workers.

Do You Have or Can You Develop an Interest in This Kind of Work?

Review the following questions. Your answers can give you clues as to your interest in Business Administration.

Do you read the business section of newspapers or magazines? Do you understand the terms used?

Have you taken part in Junior Achievement or a similar business program? Were you an officer? Did you plan and complete a business project?

Have you served as president of a club or other organization? Did you state your ideas in meetings? Were they understood and accepted?

Have you taken economic or business courses? Did you take part in class discussions? Did you like these subjects?

Have you helped in running a school or community fair or carnival? Can you work with others to make decisions?

Have you supervised the activities of others? Did they carry out the activities effectively?

What Else Should You Know About This Group of Occupations?

Jobs in this group usually are not entry level. Most people who become managers or administrators start their careers in other jobs. And once employed, they must compete with others seeking higher level jobs.

Workers in this group have a lot of responsibility. Since they plan, organize, and direct the major functions of a company, they work under a lot of pressure. They may have to work long hours to solve problems or meet deadlines. And, at times they may have to do a lot of traveling.

The military services offer training and experience related to some occupations in this group. These occupations are included in the list at the end of this group description. They are identified by an (M) following the occupational title. More information about military training and experience opportunities may be found in Appendix A.

How Can You Prepare
for This Kind of Work?

Occupations in this group require two to over ten years of training and experience. Some companies offer management training programs to prepare employees for jobs in this group. Employers sometimes place newly hired college graduates in these training programs.

High level administrators are usually selected on the basis of performance in lower level jobs. Management experience within the same company, agency, or industry is often re-

quired. Four or more years of college work are often required to get jobs that provide this experience. Degrees in business administration are needed for many jobs in this group. Some jobs require training and experience in such fields as engineering, chemistry, law, or sociology.

As you plan your high school program you should include courses related to Business Administration. Next, you should include courses needed to enter college. The following list of courses and skills can help you plan your education.

Business Administration and Management – courses in general business, business administration and management, human resources development, institutional management, international business, labor/industrial relations, personnel work, management science, and marketing management.

Courses in speech, technical/business writing, and economics can be helpful for some occupations in this group. Courses in journalism, communications, general mathematics, general science, social studies, and government can help you determine an interest in this group.

An executive chef must purchase, manage, and supervise - as well as prepare special sauces.

Qualifications Profile

This section is a summary of the worker traits and work factors related to successful job performance and worker satisfaction. Try to relate your interests, abilities, aptitudes, and preferences to these traits and factors. An asterisk (*) marks those traits and factors that are related to more than 60% of the occupations listed at the end of this group. The other traits and factors listed are as important, but relate to fewer occupations. See Appendices B-G for information about all of the worker traits and work factors.

Work Activities

The most important activities related to this group involve:

* * 2. Business contact.
* * 5. Recognition or appreciation from others.
* 6. Communication of ideas and information.

Working Conditions

These are the physical surroundings in which work is done. In occupations belonging to this group, work is performed:

*I – Inside — workers spend most of their time inside protected from weather conditions but not always from temperature changes.

Work Situations

Workers must be willing to:

* 1. Perform duties which change frequently.
* * 3. Plan and direct an entire activity.
* * 4. Deal with people.
* 5. Influence people's opinions, attitudes, and judgments.
* * 7. Make decisions using personal judgment.
* 8. Make decisions using standards that can be measured or checked.

Data-People-Things

This chart shows the levels for these three basic elements of work as related to this group. Level means the degree of difficulty of job tasks rather than the amount of time involved. The terms low, average, and high indicate the highest level at which occupations are involved. Compare your interests and abilities with the levels checked.

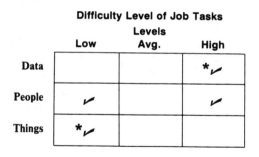

Difficulty Level of Job Tasks

	Low	Avg.	High
Data			*✓
People	✓		✓
Things	*✓		

Aptitudes

This chart presents the most important aptitudes related to this group. The levels checked compare aptitudes needed for success in this group to aptitudes of the general working population in all occupations. For example, level 5 is low and represents the bottom 10% of the working population. Level 1 is high and represents the top 10%.

		APTITUDE LEVELS COMPARED TO ALL WORKERS					
Related Aptitudes (Ability to Learn)		Lower 1/3		Middle 1/3	Upper 1/3		
		Level 5	Level 4	Level 3	Level 2	Level 1	
Code	Title	10%	23%	34%	23%	10%	
G	General Learning Ability				*✔	✔	
V	Verbal				*✔	✔	
N	Numerical			✔	✔		
Q	Clerical Perception		✔	*✔	✔		

Purchasing management is critical in service as well as resale businesses.

Physical Demands

Workers in this group of occupations must be able to do:

*S – Sedentary work

Educational Skills

This chart shows the levels of reasoning, math, and language skills related to this group. These skills are usually developed in an educational setting. There are six levels ranging from the simple (1) to the most complex (6).

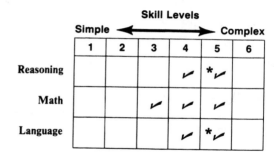

	Skill Levels					
Simple ←→ Complex						
	1	2	3	4	5	6
Reasoning				✔	*✔	
Math			✔	✔	✔	
Language				✔	*✔	

Common Occupations

A full listing of all occupations belonging to this group may be found in the Guide for Occupational Exploration.

The following occupations have been selected to represent this group. They provide the major employment opportunities. However, specific job opportunities will vary according to locations of industry, geographical region, and other factors.

Information may be found in common sources of occupational information, state career information systems, and computerized guidance systems.

An (M) follows the occupational title where the military services offer training and experience.

Management Services: Non-Government

132.017-010	Editor, Managing, Newspaper (M)
162.157-038	Purchasing Agent (M)
163.117-014	Manager, Export
163.167-018	Manager, Sales
163.167-026	Property-Disposal Officer (M)
184.117-014	Director, Transportation (M)
184.117-026	Manager, Airport
185.167-034	Manager, Merchandise
185.167-070	Wholesaler 1
186.117-034	Manager, Brokerage Office
186.117-054	President, Financial Institution
189.117-010	Association Executive
189.117-022	Manager, Industrial Organization
189.117-026	President

Management Services: Government

184.117-042	Manager, Harbor Department (M)
184.167-122	Port-Traffic Manager (M)
186.167-030	Manager, Housing Project
188.117-022	Civil Preparedness Officer (M)
188.117-070	Director, Law Enforcement
188.117-094	Director, Unemployment Insurance
188.117-102	Economic Development Coordinator
188.117-114	Manager, City
188.137-010	Supervisor
188.167-058	Manager, Office
188.167-066	Postmaster (M)
199.167-022	Environmental Analyst

Administrative Specialization

077.117-010	Dietitian, Chief
162.167-022	Manager, Procurement Services (M)
166.117-010	Director, Industrial Relations (M)
166.117-018	Manager, Personnel (M)
166.167-030	Manager, Employment (M)
166.167-034	Manager, Labor Relations
169.167-010	Administrative Assistant
183.117-010	Manager, Branch
184.117-022	Import-Export Agent
184.117-038	Manager, Flight Operations (M)
184.117-050	Manager, Operations (M)
184.117-062	Manager, Station
184.167-030	Director, Program (M)
184.167-034	Director, Sports
184.167-042	General Agent, Operations (M)
184.167-094	Manager, Traffic (M)
184.167-226	Superintendent, Transportation (M)
185.117-010	Manager, Department Store
186.117-010	Business Manager, College or University
186.117-038	Manager, Financial Institution
186.167-022	Manager, Credit Card Operations
186.167-026	Manager, Credit Union
187.117-030	Executive Vice President, Chamber of Commerce
187.161-010	Executive Chef (M)
187.167-018	Business Representative, Labor Union
189.117-030	Project Director (M)
189.167-014	Director, Service
189.167-022	Manager, Department
189.167-030	Program Manager
189.167-034	Security Officer (M)
189.167-050	Superintendent, Plant Protection (M)

Finance involves the use, control, analysis, and design of financial records. To do this, workers use logic and math skills. They also must know about the industry or government in which they work. They design and check record keeping systems for accuracy and supervise the work of others. This group includes the subgroups of:

Accounting and Auditing
Record Systems Analysis
Risk and Profit Analysis
Brokering
Budget and Financial Control

Accounting and Auditing work is to record, examine, and verify business records. Accountants prepare budgets, balance sheets, and profit and loss statements. A worker may become a specialist in one field, such as taxes. Accountants keep records and prepare reports. They often provide the financial data needed by executives to make sound business decisions. Auditors examine and verify journal and ledger entries. They make sure all records are complete and accurate.

Record Systems Analysis is to review and assess the structure of the record systems of a business or agency. Report Analysts study the goals and content of business reports. They do this to improve the format and use of the reports. Controllers direct financial affairs, prepare reports, and provide advice on matters such as taxes. They also arrange for audits of accounts.

Risk and Profit Analysis is to decide what factors lead to a profit or loss. Some workers do market research to predict sales of products or services. Others compute the degree of risk involved to extend credit or provide insurance. Still others review freight rates and tariffs. Some workers study and rate stocks or bonds for brokerage firms. Others maintain deposits in foreign banks to purchase or sell money. Bank workers review forms people fill out to apply for loans. Appraisers rate the value of real estate, personal property, and products.

Brokering is to bargain and contract for the purchase or sale of products and services. Some workers buy and sell grain on the commodities exchange. They advise clients of probable price changes and how current events will affect the market. Other workers buy and sell stocks and bonds. They represent brokerage firms. They transmit orders and compute costs involved.

Auditors make sure that all transactions are properly recorded and verify the accuracy of records.

Budget and Financial Control is to develop and manage budgets. Some workers manage trusts and other assets and prepare related legal papers. Others may assign funds and decide upon spending priorities. They may have the power to approve and sign budget requests.

Jobs in this group may be found with banks, loan companies, and investment firms. Businesses, industries, colleges, and government agencies also offer employment. Some accountants and appraisers are self-employed.

What Skills and Abilities Would Help You Succeed in This Kind of Work?

The most important skills are listed below. All of those listed do not apply to each occupation. As you explore occupations you should identify the specific ones needed.

Numerical – to understand mathematical concepts in the design of financial or economic systems and to solve math problems with speed and accuracy.

Accuracy – to see details and spot errors when working with numbers.

Verbalization – to speak and write clearly to report financial information.

Technical – to understand and use computers in problem solving and information processing.

Critical Thinking – to use personal judgment and facts to make decisions about the value of property, materials, and equipment.

Leadership – to plan, organize, and direct the work of others.

Graphic Communication – to understand technical information in mathematical or diagram form in working with real estate values, pari-mutuel betting systems, and stock market reports.

Do You Have or Can You Develop an Interest in This Kind of Work?

Review the following questions. Your answers can give you clues as to your interest in Finance.

Are you interested in the stock market? Do you listen to or read the stock reports? Do you understand the terms used?

Do you have a checking or savings account? Do you enjoy balancing your checkbook? Does your balance always agree with the bank statement?

Have you made a budget for spending your own money? Can you spend and save within that budget?

Have you had courses in accounting or bookkeeping? Are math problems easy for you? Do you like to work with details and numbers?

Have you been a treasurer of a school or community group? Did you keep accurate financial records? Did you prepare and give financial reports?

Have you filled out an income tax form? Did you understand the directions? Did you complete it correctly?

What Else Should You Know About This Group of Occupations?

Most of the work in this group of occupations is detailed. Workers can develop eyestrain if proper precautions are not taken. Computers are frequently used in accounting and auditing. However, software programs developed for this field are usually easy to learn and require few technical computer skills. Some workers must learn the total operation of a business to interpret the financial data with accuracy.

Jobs in this group are in offices. However, some require frequent travel. At certain times of the year, such as tax time, overtime work may be required. Most positions are salaried and workers are seldom paid for overtime.

The military services offer training and experience related to some occupations in this group. These occupations are included in the list at the end of this group description. They are identified by an (M) following the occupational title. More information about the military training and experience opportunities may be found in Appendix A.

How Can You Prepare for This Kind of Work?

Occupations in this group require from two to four years of education and training. Most require four to ten years. Occupations such as Investigator and Rate Reviewer only require one to two years.

Experience in keeping financial records is usually required for jobs in this group. A college degree or courses in accounting, business law, economics, and investment help prepare workers for these jobs. Some workers are promoted to these jobs within the same company. Some jobs in this group require licenses or certificates. Requirements vary from state to state.

As you plan your high school program you should include courses related to Finance. Next, you should include courses needed to enter college. The following list of courses and skills will help you plan your education.

Finance – courses in accounting, banking, finance, business economics, insurance and risk management, investments and securities, real estate, taxation, and business systems analysis.

Math – courses in algebra, advanced math, and statistics.

Courses in marketing, technical and business writing, speech, law, and business data processing are important for some occupations in this group. General math and social studies courses can help you determine an interest in this group of occupations.

A loan officer is interested in the property value as well as the buyers' finances.

Qualifications Profile

This section is a summary of the worker traits and work factors related to successful job performance and worker satisfaction. Try to relate your interests, abilities, aptitudes, and preferences to these traits and factors. An asterisk (*) marks those traits and factors that are related to more than 60% of the occupations listed at the end of this group. The other traits and factors listed are as important, but relate to fewer occupations. See Appendices B-G for information about all of the worker traits and work factors.

Work Situations

Workers must be willing to:

* * 3. Plan and direct an entire activity.
* * 4. Deal with people.
* 7. Make decisions using personal judgment.
* * 8. Make decisions using standards that can be measured or checked.

Physical Demands

Workers in this group of occupations must be able to do:

*S – Sedentary work
L – Light work

Work Activities

The most important activities related to this group involve:

1. Things and objects.
2. Business contact.
5. Recognition or appreciation from others.
6. Communication of ideas and information.
7. Tasks of a scientific and technical nature.
9. Processes, methods, or machines.

Educational Skills

This chart shows the levels of reasoning, math, and language skills related to this group. These skills are usually developed in an educational setting. There are six levels ranging from the simple (1) to the most complex (6).

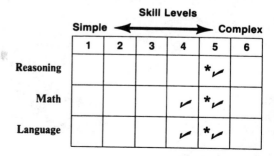

	Skill Levels Simple ← → Complex					
	1	2	3	4	5	6
Reasoning					*✓	
Math				✓	*✓	
Language				✓	*✓	

Aptitudes

This chart presents the most important aptitudes related to this group. The levels checked compare aptitudes needed for success in this group to aptitudes of the general working population in all occupations. For example, level 5 is low and represents the bottom 10% of the working population. Level 1 is high and represents the top 10%.

APTITUDE LEVELS COMPARED TO ALL WORKERS						
Related Aptitudes **(Ability to Learn)**		Lower 1/3		Middle 1/3	Upper 1/3	
		Level **5**	Level **4**	Level **3**	Level **2**	Level **1**
Code	Title	10%	23%	34%	23%	10%
G	General Learning Ability				*✔	
V	Verbal				*✔	
N	Numerical			✔	*✔	✔
Q	Clerical Perception			✔	*✔	

Working Conditions

These are the physical surroundings in which work is done. In occupations belonging to this group, work is performed:

*I – Inside — workers spend most of their time inside protected from weather conditions but not always from temperature changes.

Budget analysis is a test of the accuracy of planning compared to performance.

Data-People-Things

This chart shows the levels for these three basic elements of work as related to this group. Level means the degree of difficulty of job tasks rather than the amount of time involved. The terms low, average, and high indicate the highest level at which occupations are involved. Compare your interests and abilities with the levels checked.

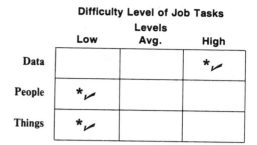

Difficulty Level of Job Tasks

	Low	Avg.	High
Data			*
People	*		
Things	*		

Common Occupations

A full listing of all occupations belonging to this group may be found in the Guide for Occupational Exploration.

The following occupations have been selected to represent this group. They provide the major employment opportunities. However, specific job opportunities will vary according to locations of industry, geographical region, and other factors.

Information may be found in common sources of occupational information, state career information systems, and computerized guidance systems.

An (M) follows the occupational title where the military services offer training and experience.

Accounting and Auditing

160.162-010 Accountant, Tax
160.162-014 Auditor (M)
160.167-010 Accountant (M)
160.167-014 Accountant, Budget (M)
160.167-018 Accountant, Cost (M)
160.167-026 Accountant, Systems (M)
160.167-030 Auditor, County or City
160.167-034 Auditor, Internal (M)
160.167-038 Auditor, Tax
160.167-050 Revenue Agent
186.167-050 Operations Officer

Records Systems Analysis

161.167-018 Manager, Records Analysis (M)
161.267-026 Reports Analyst
186.117-014 Controller (M)

Risk and Profit Analysis

050.067-014 Market-Research Analyst 1
160.267-010 Credit Analyst, Chief
161.117-018 Treasurer
162.157-042 Securities Trader 1
169.167-058 Underwriter
186.167-014 Foreign-Exchange Trader
186.267-018 Loan Officer
191.267-010 Appraiser, Real Estate
191.267-014 Credit Analyst
191.287-010 Appraiser
214.267-010 Rate Analyst, Freight
214.387-014 Rate Reviewer
241.267-030 Investigator

Brokering

162.157-010 Broker-And-Market Operator, Grain
162.157-014 Brokers Floor Representative
251.157-010 Sales Agent, Securities

Budget and Financial Control

161.117-010 Budget Officer (M)
161.267-030 Budget Analyst (M)
186.117-070 Treasurer, Financial Institution (M)
186.117-074 Trust Officer

11.07

Services Administration

Services Administration is to direct programs that provide health, welfare, education, and recreation services. Most workers are public employees. They direct programs and services provided by the local, state, and federal governments. They develop programs to carry out laws and policies. Some work in programs for private or nonprofit groups. Workers prepare and review budgets, keep records, and prepare reports. They may give speeches and meet with groups to inform the public. This group includes the subgroups of:

Social Services
Health and Safety Services
Education Services
Recreation Services

Workers in the four subgroups of Services Administration perform duties that are very much alike. They need similar skills to direct and manage programs, but the knowledge they need differs. They need to have a background related to the services provided.

Social Services provide help to people with problems. These programs may be about housing, poverty, crime, or mental health. Services may be for the aged, blind, deaf, youth groups, prison inmates, and those with drug or alcohol abuse problems.

Health and Safety Services include nursing and public health. Workers also direct emergency medical and civil disaster programs. And, directors of hospital service departments, such as medical records and outpatient, are also in this subgroup.

Education Services include programs such as vocational training, special education, and athletics. Also included are services such as guidance, financial aid, and admissions. Administrators such as deans, principals, department heads, superintendents, and presidents are also included in Educational Services.

Recreation Services are programs to help people enjoy their leisure time. These include recreation, library, and museum services.

Jobs may be found with schools, colleges, churches, libraries, museums, hospitals, prisons, and in community programs. Many government agencies also offer employment.

What Skills and Abilities Would Help You Succeed in This Kind of Work?

The most important skills are listed below. All of those listed do not apply to each occupation. As you explore occupations you should identify the specific ones needed.

Verbalization – to speak and write in a clear and effective way.

Organization – to organize the functions of various community and government service agencies.

Numerical – to work with complex financial and statistical information.

Critical Thinking – to use personal judgment to make decisions and solve problems.

Leadership – to plan and direct programs and the activities of others.

Versatile – to do a variety of tasks that may change often.

Rapport – to relate with people in an understanding way and maintain harmony among workers.

Do You Have or Can You Develop an Interest in This Kind of Work?

Review the following questions. Your answers can give you clues as to your interest in Services Administration.

Have you helped plan and arrange activities for a school or community fair or carnival? Were they successful?

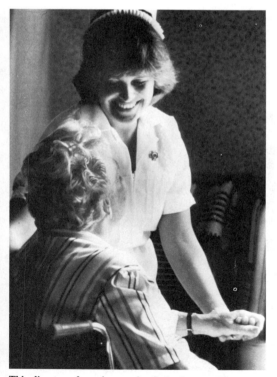

This director of nursing service finds time to visit with a patient.

Have you supervised the activities of others? Were the activities carried out effectively?

Do you take part in class discussions? Do you state your ideas in meetings? Are they understood and accepted?

Have you been active in scouting or a member of a 4-H club? Would you like to direct a program of this type?

Have you held an office in a school, church, or community group? Did you work well with others?

Have you had courses in social studies? Do you like to deal with social problems?

Have you done volunteer work for a hospital or social agency? Did you get satisfaction from helping others? Would you like a job in such as setting?

What Else Should You Know About This Group of Occupations?

Being active in social and civic affairs can be helpful for some jobs in this group. Workers often represent their agencies on radio and TV and at workshops and conventions. Their jobs often become a major part of their lives. They work under pressure and are responsible for the programs they direct. Laws and public money may affect the success of these programs. Workers may need to move to other employers or cities to get more pay and more responsible jobs.

The military services offer training and experience related to some occupations in this group. These occupations are included in the list at the end of this group description. They are identified by an (M) following the occupational title. More information about the military training and experience opportunities may be found in Appendix A.

How Can You Prepare
for This Kind of Work?

Occupations in this group require two to ten years of education and training. Some require over ten years. Work experience in a specific service field, agency, or institution is required for most jobs in this group. Degrees in social work or education are required for some jobs. Others require degrees in public administration or business management. Work experience is sometimes substituted for part of the education. Occupations in Career Area 10 (Humanitarian) provide related experience. Also, 11.02 (Education and Library Services) is related to some occupations in Services Administration. Depending on your field of interest you should review:

10.01 (Social Services).

10.02 (Nursing and Therapy Services).

10.03 (Child and Adult Care).

As you plan your high school program you should include courses related to your field of interest in Services Administration. Next, you should include courses needed to enter college. The following list of courses and skills can help you plan your education.

Communication – courses in speech, debate, and technical and business writing.

Administration – programs and courses in public administration, business administration, public affairs, community services, personnel management, institutional management, and data processing and records automation.

Psychology – courses in general psychology, organizational psychology, and social psychology. Also related areas such as human relations.

Background courses related to specialization within Services Administration are important in addition to the following.

The staff director observes an instructor working with two blind clients.

Social Services – courses in sociology, social work, consumer education, urban education, child care management, gerontology (aging), and medical social work.

Health – courses in health care, health care management, health care planning, allied health care, medical records administration, health care administration, health education, public health, and alcohol and drug abuse.

Education – courses in curriculum, instruction, education administration, educational media, evaluation and research, school psychology, social foundations, special education, student counseling and personnel services, and religious education.

Library – courses in library science, archival science, library operation, library management, and administration.

Recreation – courses in leisure and recreational activities, sports, physical education, parks and recreation, outdoor recreation, recreational therapy, recreation services marketing, and recreational enterprises management.

Qualifications Profile

This section is a summary of the worker traits and work factors related to successful job performance and worker satisfaction. Try to relate your interests, abilities, aptitudes, and preferences to these traits and factors. An asterisk (*) marks those traits and factors that are related to more than 60% of the occupations listed at the end of this group. The other traits and factors listed are as important, but relate to fewer occupations. See Appendices B-G for information about all of the worker traits and work factors.

Working Conditions

These are the physical surroundings in which work is done. In occupations belonging to this group, work is performed:

*I – Inside — workers spend most of their time inside protected from weather conditions but not always from temperature changes.

Work Activities

The most important activities related to this group involve:

* 2. Business contact.
  4. Direct personal contact to help or instruct others.
* 5. Recognition or appreciation from others.
* 6. Communication of ideas and information.

Work Situations

Workers must be willing to:

1. Perform duties which change frequently.
* 3. Plan and direct an entire activity.
* 4. Deal with people.
5. Influence people's opinions, attitudes, and judgments.
7. Make decisions using personal judgment.

Aptitudes

This chart presents the most important aptitudes related to this group. The levels checked compare aptitudes needed for success in this group to aptitudes of the general working population in all occupations. For example, level 5 is low and represents the bottom 10% of the working population. Level 1 is high and represents the top 10%.

	APTITUDE LEVELS COMPARED TO ALL WORKERS						
Related Aptitudes (Ability to Learn)		Lower 1/3		Middle 1/3	Upper 1/3		
		Level **5**	Level **4**	Level **3**	Level **2**	Level **1**	
Code	Title	10%	23%	34%	23%	10%	
G	General Learning Ability				* ✔	✔	
V	Verbal				* ✔	✔	
N	Numerical			* ✔	✔		
Q	Clerical Perception			✔	✔		

Playground locations are important to this superintendent of recreation.

Physical Demands

Workers in this group of occupations must be able to do:

*S – Sedentary work
L – Light work

Educational Skills

This chart shows the levels of reasoning, math, and language skills related to this group. These skills are usually developed in an educational setting. There are six levels ranging from the simple (1) to the most complex (6).

Skill Levels

Simple ← → Complex

	1	2	3	4	5	6
Reasoning					* ✔	✔
Math			✔	✔	✔	
Language					* ✔	

Data-People-Things

This chart shows the levels for these three basic elements of work as related to this group. Level means the degree of difficulty of job tasks rather than the amount of time involved. The terms low, average, and high indicate the highest level at which occupations are involved. Compare your interests and abilities with the levels checked.

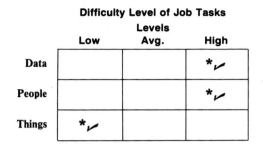

Difficulty Level of Job Tasks

| | Levels | | |
	Low	Avg.	High
Data			*⟋
People			*⟋
Things	*⟋		

Common Occupations

A full listing of all occupations belonging to this group may be found in the Guide for Occupational Exploration.

The following occupations have been selected to represent this group. They provide the major employment opportunities. However, specific job opportunities will vary according to locations of industry, geographical region, and other factors.

Information may be found in common sources of occupational information, state career information systems, and computerized guidance systems.

An (M) follows the occupational title where the military services offer training and experience.

Social Services

187.117-014 Director, Community Organization
187.117-018 Director, Institution (M)
187.117-022 District Adviser
188.117-126 Welfare Director
188.167-026 Director, Classification and Treatment
195.117-010 Administrator, Social Welfare (M)
195.167-010 Community Organization Worker
195.167-042 Alcohol-And-Drug-Abuse-Assistance Program Administrator (M)

Health and Safety Services

075.117-014 Director, Community-Health Nursing (M)
075.117-022 Director, Nursing Service (M)
075.117-030 Director, School of Nursing (M)
079.117-010 Emergency Medical Services Coordinator (M)
079.117-014 Public Health Educator
079.167-014 Medical-Record Administrator (M)
169.127-010 Civil Preparedness Training Officer (M)
187.117-010 Administrator, Hospital (M)
187.117-058 Director, Outpatient Services (M)

Education Services

045.117-010 Director of Guidance In Public Schools
090.117-010 Academic Dean (M)
090.117-022 Director, Athletic
090.117-026 Director, Extension Work (M)
090.117-030 Financial-Aids Officer
090.117-034 President, Educational Institution
090.167-010 Department Head, College or University (M)
090.167-014 Director of Admissions
090.167-030 Registrar, College or University
092.137-010 Director, Preschool
094.117-014 Director, Special Education
096.167-010 District Extension Service Agent
097.167-010 Director, Vocational Training (M)
099.117-010 Director, Educational Program (M)
099.117-018 Principal
099.117-022 Superintendent, Schools
099.117-026 Supervisor, Education (M)
099.167-018 Director, Instructional Material (M)
099.167-022 Educational Specialist (M)
129.107-022 Director, Religious Education
166.167-026 Manager, Education and Training (M)

Recreation Services

100.117-010 Library Director
102.017-010 Curator
187.117-054 Superintendent, Recreation (M)
187.137-010 Recreation Supervisor (M)

11.08

Communications

Communications involve writing, editing, reporting, and translating. Workers use language and writing skills to communicate factual information. Some workers do research or gather data. Others organize and interpret this data and write news stories, reports, and publications. Some workers consult with writers and edit their work. Some workers translate spoken or written words from one language to another. Others study secret coding systems and develop new codes. This group includes the subgroups of:

Editing
Writing
Writing and Broadcasting
Translating and Interpreting

Editing is to direct and prepare publications or scripts for radio or TV. Some workers set policy on what views may be expressed. Others follow policy to direct the work of writers. They may write lead stories, editorials, and headlines. Some may work with technical or scientific subjects. They may edit manuals, handbooks, and proposals. Some hire staff. They decide which work should be done first. Editors read copy to detect errors and may confer with authors about changes to be made in their work.

Writing is to prepare news stories for publication and for radio or TV. Workers need to verify facts from many sources. They organize these facts and write a news story.

Their story may need to be a certain length, style, and format. Some events may be assigned to them. Sometimes they get leads or tips for a story. They may also collect and analyze facts on a topic to develop a story idea. Some take pictures for their stories. Workers may do one type of reporting, such as sports, politics, or fashion.

Writing and Broadcasting is to analyze news. Some workers write a column to present a point of view. They use knowledge and experience to write the story. They may need to research the topic or interview people. They may attend an event or function to work on a story idea. Some workers present news over the radio or TV. They may assist with or prepare the scripts they use.

Translating and Interpreting involves changing spoken or written words from one language to another. Some workers translate documents and other papers. Some translate what another person is saying. This must be done without losing the meaning of what is said or written. Other workers analyze coding systems using formulas, code books, or computers. They may develop codes or new coding methods.

Jobs in this group may be found in newspapers, radio and TV stations, and publishing firms. Businesses, government agencies, and professional groups also provide job openings.

What Skills and Abilities Would Help You Succeed in This Kind of Work?

The most important skills are listed below. All of those listed do not apply to each occupation. As you explore occupations you should identify the specific ones needed.

Vocabulary – to use many different words to write or speak clearly and in an interesting way.

Organization – to arrange ideas, thoughts, and information in a way that can be understood.

Proper Form – to use the rules of grammar when speaking, writing, or translating.

Leadership (in Editing) – to plan and direct the work of others.

Interpretation – to explain ideas, information, and feelings.

Persuasiveness – to use words to influence the thinking and actions of others.

Rapport – to deal with people in an effective way and maintain harmony among workers.

Verbalization – to express ideas through the use of words.

Do You Have or Can You Develop an Interest in This Kind of Work?

Review the following questions. Your answers can give you clues as to your interest in Communications.

Have you worked for a school or community newspaper? Did you interview people and write articles?

Have you written book reports or research papers? Do you enjoy writing?

Have you spoken in front of an audience? Do you feel at ease when speaking before a group?

Have you helped others with English lessons? Can you spot errors in punctuation, spelling, or grammar?

Have you taken a foreign language course? Can you speak or write fluently in that language?

A city editor supervises reporters and rewrite staff.

This newscaster is reporting from a familiar location for the evening news.

What Else Should You Know About This Group of Occupations?

Communications is not the only Worker Trait Group that involves writing. Group 01.01 (Literary Arts) includes workers who deal with the creative expression of ideas and feelings in written form. This differs from factual writing in the communications field.

Workers in this group may have irregular hours. They may work evenings, weekends, or be on call at any time. They may work under pressure to meet deadlines. Some may have to travel locally or even great distances. They may be exposed to hazardous situations. They may be required to reflect the policies and points of view of their employers.

The military services offer training and experience related to some occupations in this group. These occupations are included in the list at the end of this group description. They are identified by an (M) following the occupational title. More information about the military training and experience opportunities may be found in Appendix A.

How Can You Prepare for This Kind of Work?

Most occupations in this group require four to ten years of education and training. Some require more than ten years. However, Research Assistants and Interpreters require only one to two years. Many jobs require college courses in English, journalism, or a foreign language. Experience and skill in writing or broadcasting is sometimes a substitute for formal education.

Some jobs require knowledge and experience in a field such as current events, sports, politics, or music.

As you plan your high school program you should include courses related to Communications. Next, you should include courses needed to enter college. The following list of courses and skills can help you plan your education.

Journalism/Communications – methods of gathering, processing, evaluating, and writing facts about current events and other topics for publication, radio, or TV. Courses in general communications, journalism (mass communications), and radio/television news broadcasting.

Technical and Business Writing – courses that describe the theory, methods, and skills need-ed for writing scientific, technical, and business papers and monographs.

Literature – study of different types of writing during periods of history. Courses in classics, comparative literature, composition, American literature, and English literature.

Speech – speaking skills including debate, persuasion, discussion, criticism, and interpretation.

Courses in economics, geography, education, government, civics, library and archival science, philosophy, religion, public affairs, and foreign languages can be helpful for some occupations in this group.

Qualifications Profile

This section is a summary of the worker traits and work factors related to successful job performance and worker satisfaction. Try to relate your interests, abilities, aptitudes, and preferences to these traits and factors. An asterisk (*) marks those traits and factors that are related to more than 60% of the occupations listed at the end of this group. The other traits and factors listed are as important, but relate to fewer occupations. See Appendices B-G for information about all of the worker traits and work factors.

Work Situations

Workers must be willing to:

1. Perform duties which change frequently.
3. Plan and direct an entire activity.
* 4. Deal with people.

5. Influence people's opinions, attitudes, and judgments.
* 7. Make decisions using personal judgment.
* 8. Make decisions using standards that can be measured or checked.
9. Interpret and express feelings, ideas, or facts.
10. Work within precise limits or standards of accuracy.

Working Conditions

These are the physical surroundings in which work is done. In occupations belonging to this group, work is performed:

*I – Inside — workers spend most of their time inside protected from weather conditions but not always from temperature changes.

A research assistant is tabulating some statistical information.

Data-People-Things

This chart shows the levels for these three basic elements of work as related to this group. Level means the degree of difficulty of job tasks rather than the amount of time involved. The terms low, average, and high indicate the highest level at which occupations are involved. Compare your interests and abilities with the levels checked.

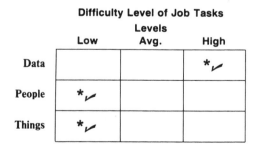

Difficulty Level of Job Tasks

	Levels		
	Low	**Avg.**	**High**
Data			*✓
People	*✓		
Things	*✓		

Physical Demands

Workers in this group of occupations must be able to do:

*S – Sedentary work

Work Activities

The most important activities related to this group involve:

* 2. Business contact.
* 5. Recognition or appreciation from others.
* 6. Communication of ideas and information.

Educational Skills

This chart shows the levels of reasoning, math, and language skills related to this group. These skills are usually developed in an educational setting. There are six levels ranging from the simple (1) to the most complex (6).

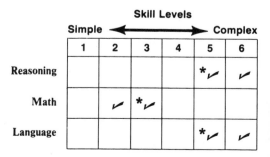

	Skill Levels					
	Simple ←				→ Complex	
	1	**2**	**3**	**4**	**5**	**6**
Reasoning					*✓	✓
Math		✓	*✓			
Language					*✓	✓

Aptitudes

This chart presents the most important aptitudes related to this group. The levels checked compare aptitudes needed for success in this group to aptitudes of the general working population in all occupations. For example, level 5 is low and represents the bottom 10% of the working population. Level 1 is high and represents the top 10%.

APTITUDE LEVELS COMPARED TO ALL WORKERS							
Related Aptitudes (Ability to Learn)		Lower 1/3		Middle 1/3	Upper 1/3		
		Level **5**	Level **4**	Level **3**	Level **2**	Level **1**	
Code	Title	10%	23%	34%	23%	10%	
G	General Learning Ability				* ✔	✔	
V	Verbal				✔	* ✔	
N	Numerical			* ✔			
Q	Clerical Perception			* ✔			

Common Occupations

A full listing of all occupations belonging to this group may be found in the Guide for Occupational Exploration.

The following occupations have been selected to represent this group. They provide the major employment opportunities. However, specific job opportunities will vary according to locations of industry, geographical region, and other factors.

Information may be found in common sources of occupational information, state career information systems, and computerized guidance systems.

An (M) follows the occupational title where the military services offer training and experience.

Editing

132.017-014   Editor, Newspaper (M)
132.017-018   Editor, Technical and Scientific Publications
132.037-014   Editor, City
132.037-018   Editor, Department (M)
132.067-026   Editor, News
132.137-010   Assignment Editor
132.267-014   Editorial Assistant (M)

Writing

131.267-014   Newswriter (M)
131.267-018   Reporter (M)
131.267-026   Writer, Technical Publications
199.267-034   Research Assistant 2

Writing and Broadcasting

131.067-010   Columnist/Commentator
131.267-010   Newscaster (M)

Translating and Interpreting

137.267-010   Interpreter (M)
137.267-018   Translator (M)
199.267-014   Cryptanalyst (M)

11.09
Promotion

Promotion involves influencing the feelings and actions of people. Workers in this group promote the sales of products and services. They solicit (seek) funds and members for organizations. Some workers have direct contact with the public and may speak to groups and visit homes or work places. Others are indirectly involved. They may plan and carry out advertising or public relations campaigns. This group includes the subgroups of:

Sales
Fund and Membership Solicitation
Public Relations

Sales involve the exchange of products or services for money. Some workers plan and direct sales programs to expand business.

Other workers promote goodwill and seek trade for local firms. They visit people new to the area or other prospects to acquaint them with local merchants. Still others promote sales with a function such as a fashion show. Some workers manage advertising programs to influence consumer preference.

Fund and Membership Solicitation involve getting people to join a group or to donate time or money. Some workers create and direct activities of a group such as the alumni of a college. These workers enlist alumni aid to recruit students and raise funds. Other workers conduct public relations programs to raise funds for social or welfare groups. They set goals for the funds needed and instruct and direct workers. They keep

A fund raising executive explains set-up desired to the operator of an office desktop publishing computer.

records of the funds raised and expenses incurred. Some disburse the funds. Other workers make appeals to employers and other groups to recruit blood donors.

Public Relations help to promote goodwill, gain support, and create a good public image. Some workers contact and "lobby" (try to influence) members of the legislature. They try to obtain legislation to meet the concerns of their clients. Other workers try to create and maintain a good public image for an employer or client. They direct such efforts as speeches, tours, and question/answer sessions. Some workers plan, schedule, and direct public service programs. Still others represent the U.S. Government and conduct relations with foreign nations and international groups.

Jobs in this group may be found with advertising agencies, business and industry, colleges, unions, professional groups, and government agencies. Some workers are self-employed.

What Skills and Abilities Would Help You Succeed in This Kind of Work?

The most important skills are listed below. All of those listed do not apply to each occupation. As you explore occupations you should identify the specific ones needed.

Creative Thinking – to create original ideas for advertising and publicity campaigns.

Leadership – to plan, direct, and supervise the work of others.

Numerical – to do math quickly and correctly.

Organization – to arrange ideas, thoughts, and information in a way that can be understood.

Persuasiveness – to use words and actions to influence the opinions of others.

Social Skills – to deal with people in an effective way to gain their trust and confidence.

Verbalization – to speak in a clear and convincing way.

Rapport – to deal with people in an effective way and maintain harmony among workers.

Do You Have or Can You Develop an Interest in This Kind of Work?

Review the following questions. Your answers can give you clues as to your interest in the Promotion field.

Have you tried selling advertising space in a school yearbook, newspaper, or magazine? Were you successful?

Have you recruited members for a club or organization? Did you enjoy that type of activity?

Have you done public speaking or been a member of a debate team? Did you like to appear before an audience?

Have you organized ticket sales for a school or community event? Did you plan the publicity? Can you lead others in this type of activity?

Have you made posters for a school or community event? Did you use your own ideas in making them? Did they attract attention?

Have you written advertising copy for a school yearbook or newspaper? Do you like this kind of writing?

Have you worked in a political campaign? Did you help think of ways to influence the opinion of the voters?

Have you sold items to raise money for a school or community group? Can you persuade people to buy things?

What Else Should You Know About This Group of Occupations?

Workers in this group may be under a great deal of pressure. They have deadlines to meet and are expected to come up with new ideas often. To prepare and deliver speeches, attend meetings, and travel out-of-town may be parts of the job. They often work long hours and on weekends. If they expect to get ahead they need to be involved in social and community affairs. Workers who build a good reputation in this field are often sought by other employers and offered better jobs.

The military services offer training and experience related to some occupations in this group. These occupations are included in the list at the end of this group description. They are identified by an (M) following the occupational title. More information about the military training and experience opportunities may be found in Appendix A.

An account executive may find airports familiar places - and perhaps lonely and tiring.

How Can You Prepare for This Kind of Work?

Most occupations in this group require four to ten years of education and training. Some jobs also require experience in a specific business or industry.

As you plan your high school education you should include courses related to Promotion, such as speech, writing, and art. Next, you should include courses needed to enter college. The following list of courses and skills can help you plan your education.

General Merchandising and Sales – courses in distributive education, marketing, advertising, fashion coordinating, and entrepreneurship.

Economics – courses based on the production, distribution, and consumption of goods and services.

Management – courses in finance, public and business management, and public relations.

Technical and Business Writing – courses that describe the theory, methods, and skills needed for writing technical and business papers, and monographs.

Courses in speech, psychology, public affairs, and sociology can be helpful for most occupations in this group. Courses in design, graphics, media, and commercial art may be helpful for some occupations in the sales subgroup.

Qualifications Profile

This section is a summary of the worker traits and work factors related to successful job performance and worker satisfaction. Try to relate your interests, abilities, aptitudes, and preferences to these traits and factors. An asterisk (*) marks those traits and factors that are related to more than 60% of the occupations listed at the end of this group. The other traits and factors listed are as important, but relate to fewer occupations. See Appendices B-G for information about all of the worker traits and work factors.

Work Activities

The most important activities related to this group involve:

* * 2. Business contact.
* * 5. Recognition or appreciation from others.
* * 6. Communication of ideas and information.

Work Situations

Workers must be willing to:

*   1. Perform duties which change frequently.
* * 3. Plan and direct an entire activity.
* * 4. Deal with people.
* * 5. Influence people's opinions, attitudes, and judgments.
* * 7. Make decisions using personal judgment.

This advertising manager is discussing an industrial control product with an agency's new copy writer.

Working Conditions

These are the physical surroundings in which work is done. In occupations belonging to this group, work is performed:

*I – Inside — workers spend most of their time inside protected from weather conditions but not always from temperature changes.

Educational Skills

This chart shows the levels of reasoning, math, and language skills related to this group. These skills are usually developed in an educational setting. There are six levels ranging from the simple (1) to the most complex (6).

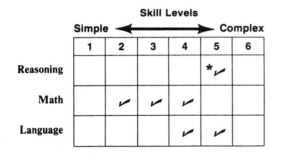

	Skill Levels					
Simple ⟷ Complex						
	1	2	3	4	5	6
Reasoning					*✓	
Math		✓	✓	✓		
Language				✓	✓	

Data-People-Things

This chart shows the levels for these three basic elements of work as related to this group. Level means the degree of difficulty of job tasks rather than the amount of time involved. The terms low, average, and high indicate the highest level at which occupations are involved. Compare your interests and abilities with the levels checked.

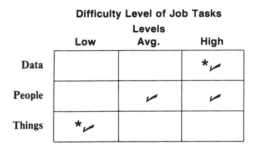

	Difficulty Level of Job Tasks		
	Levels		
	Low	Avg.	High
Data			*✓
People		✓	✓
Things	*✓		

Physical Demands

Workers in this group of occupations must be able to do:

*S – Sedentary work
L – Light work

An alumni secretary reviews a computer listing of graduates.

Aptitudes

This chart presents the most important aptitudes related to this group. The levels checked compare aptitudes needed for success in this group to aptitudes of the general working population in all occupations. For example, level 5 is low and represents the bottom 10% of the working population. Level 1 is high and represents the top 10%.

APTITUDE LEVELS COMPARED TO ALL WORKERS						
Related Aptitudes (Ability to Learn)		Lower 1/3		Middle 1/3	Upper 1/3	
		Level **5** 10%	Level **4** 23%	Level **3** 34%	Level **2** 23%	Level **1** 10%
Code	**Title**					
G	General Learning Ability			✔	*✔	
V	Verbal				*✔	✔
N	Numerical		✔	*✔	✔	
Q	Clerical Perception		✔	*✔		

Common Occupations

A full listing of all occupations belonging to this group may be found in the Guide for Occupational Exploration.

The following occupations have been selected to represent this group. They provide the major employment opportunities. However, specific job opportunities will vary according to locations of industry, geographical region, and other factors.

Information may be found in common sources of occupational information, state career information systems, and computerized guidance systems.

An (M) follows the occupational title where the military services offer training and experience.

Sales

163.117-018   Manager, Promotion
163.167-010   Manager, Advertising
164.117-010   Manager, Advertising
164.167-010   Account Executive
185.157-010   Fashion Coordinator
293.357-018   Goodwill Ambassador

Fund and Membership Solicitation

090.117-014   Alumni Secretary
165.117-010   Director, Fundraising
189.167-026   Membership Director
293.157-010   Fund Raiser 1
293.357-010   Blood-Donor Recruiter

Public Relations

165.017-010   Lobbyist
165.067-010   Public-Relations Representative (M)
166.257-010   Employer Relations Representative
184.117-010   Director, Public Service (M)
188.117-106   Foreign-Service Officer (M)
375.137-018   Police Lieutenant, Community Relations

11.10

Regulations Enforcement

Regulations Enforcement involves those laws that affect health and safety, finance, business, and people's rights. Workers in this group do not engage in police work. Some examine cases of business or tax fraud. Some inspect places of business or the quality of products or services. They may plan, organize, and carry out programs to enforce federal, state, or local laws. Some enforce the policies of a company. Some workers write reports on the cases they conduct. They may submit and discuss a case with police. They also may testify in court or serve as an expert witness. This group includes the subgroups of:

Finance
Individual Rights
Health and Safety
Immigration and Customs
Company Policy

Finance involves money or resources of a government, business, or person. Some workers in this group investigate tax, hiring, or benefit claims fraud (false or unlawful actions). Others collect late taxes or overdue accounts. Still others look into cash or product shortages in a store, office, or plant. And some workers examine cases of fraud in the use of lost or stolen charge cards.

Individual Rights involves planning and carrying out human welfare programs. Workers make sure people are treated fairly. They enforce employment, housing, and education laws. Some workers develop and conduct programs that protect the consumer.

Health and Safety concerns problems of people, animals, or business. Workers determine and set health standards. They conduct health and safety programs. They help control health hazards and diseases. Some workers investigate accidents due to working conditions. Others inspect places where food, drugs, and other consumer products are made. Some workers may inspect motor vehicles, cargoes, mines, or hazardous waste projects for safety. Others make inspections to detect fire hazards or find the cause of a fire. And, some workers deal with problems of animal cruelty and neglect.

Immigration and Customs involves enforcing the laws about people or items coming into or leaving the United States. Workers examine papers and records to see if a person can live in or visit our country. They inspect cargo, baggage, or clothes worn or carried by persons. They may inspect ships, cars, trucks, or aircraft that enter or leave. Others may patrol the border to detect illegal entry into the U.S.

Company Policy involves quality and safety standards for products and services. These standards are set and enforced by business or nongovernment groups. Some workers examine railroads, streetcars, and buses or check the conduct of employees. They may write reports and recommend ways to improve service. Some inspect and rate travel and tourist places to be listed in guides. Others may shop in a retail or service store to evaluate the store and its employees. Some workers direct programs that instruct truck drivers on traffic and safety laws.

Jobs may be found in government agencies. Businesses also hire workers in this group to enforce company policies.

What Skills and Abilities Would Help You Succeed in This Kind of Work?

The most important skills are listed below. All of those listed do not apply to each occupation. As you explore occupations you should identify the specific ones needed.

Verbalization – to express ideas through the use of words and to speak clearly and precisely.

Comprehension – to know the details of the laws or regulations that must be enforced.

Safety inspections make sure equipment is kept in top operating condition.

Empathy – to care about the welfare and needs of people and animals.

Rapport – to develop a friendly relationship with people and to deal with them in an effective way.

Composure – to be calm and self-confident in difficult situations.

Concentration – to pay attention to the details in written or numerical information.

Critical Thinking – to form opinions and make decisions based on knowledge, judgment, and experience.

Do You Have or Can You Develop an Interest in This Kind of Work?

Review the following questions. Your answers can give you clues as to your interest in Regulations Enforcement.

Have you been in charge of a group or class? Can you maintain order? Do you like to enforce rules?

Have you dealt with people who disagree with you? Can you deal with them pleasantly but firmly?

Have you been interested in consumer protection or public safety? Would you like a job to help solve problems in these areas?

Have you had summer or part-time work in a factory? Do you understand safety regulations?

Have you been a member of the school safety patrol? Can you enforce rules and regulations according to instructions?

Have you taken courses in government, political science, or environmental health? Do you think rules and regulations are important?

What Else Should You Know About This Group of Occupations?

Jobs in this group may require workers to wear uniforms. Most jobs have regular hours although some may involve evening or night shift work. Some workers are in an office all day. Others must go from place to place to inspect businesses. Still others are stationed at inspection locations, such as port-of-entry and border crossings.

The military services offer training and experience related to some occupations in this group. These occupations are included in the list at the end of this group description. They are identified by an (M) following the occupational title. More information about the military training and experience opportunities may be found in Appendix A.

How Can You Prepare For This Kind of Work?

Most occupations in this group require one to ten years of education and training. Some jobs require a college degree in accounting or other special field. Other jobs require skills and knowledge that are identified by special tests. And, some workers are promoted within a company or agency.

Most jobs in this group are in government agencies and workers must take a civil service test. Some jobs are filled by political appointments.

As you plan your high school program you should include courses related to Regulations Enforcement, such as government, math, and communications. Next, you should include courses needed to enter college, two-year technical school, or a special program. The major field of preparation should relate to your specific area of interest in Regulations Enforcement. The following list of courses and skills will help you plan your education.

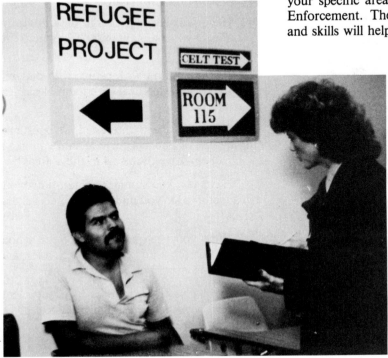

Immigration inspectors must be multi-lingual.

Finance – courses such as accounting, data processing, economics, banking, and financial systems.

Social Science – courses such as sociology, psychology, criminology, civil rights, consumer regulations, urban affairs, and introduction to contract law.

Health and Safety – courses such as public health, industrial hygiene, industrial safety, biology, chemistry, biochemistry, physiology, and toxicology.

Important courses are those related to interpersonal skills and public affairs. Courses in speech and technical/business writing can also be helpful for occupations in this group.

Qualifications Profile

This section is a summary of the worker traits and work factors related to successful job performance and worker satisfaction. Try to relate your interests, abilities, aptitudes, and preferences to these traits and factors. An asterisk (*) marks those traits and factors that are related to more than 60% of the occupations listed at the end of this group. The other traits and factors listed are as important, but relate to fewer occupations. See Appendices B-G for information about all of the worker traits and work factors.

Work Situations

Workers must be willing to:

1. Perform duties which change frequently.
3. Plan and direct an entire activity.
* 4. Deal with people.
* 7. Make decisions using personal judgment.
* 8. Make decisions using standards that can be measured or checked.
10. Work within precise limits or standards of accuracy.

Work Activities

The most important activities related to this group involve:

* 2. Business contact.
  5. Recognition or appreciation from others.
  6. Communication of ideas and information.

Physical Demands

Workers in this group of occupations must be able to do:

*L – Light work

Working Conditions

These are the physical surroundings in which work is done. In occupations belonging to this group, work is performed:

*I – Inside — workers spend most of their time inside protected from weather conditions but not always from temperature changes.

B – Both inside and outside — workers spend about equal time in each setting.

Aptitudes

This chart presents the most important aptitudes related to this group. The levels checked compare aptitudes needed for success in this group to aptitudes of the general working population in all occupations. For example, level 5 is low and represents the bottom 10% of the working population. Level 1 is high and represents the top 10%.

APTITUDE LEVELS COMPARED TO ALL WORKERS						
Related Aptitudes (Ability to Learn)		Lower 1/3		Middle 1/3	Upper 1/3	
		Level **5**	Level **4**	Level **3**	Level **2**	Level **1**
Code	Title	10%	23%	34%	23%	10%
G	General Learning Ability				✔	
N	Numerical			*✔	✔	
Q	Clerical Perception		✔	*✔		

Educational Skills

This chart shows the levels of reasoning, math, and language skills related to this group. These skills are usually developed in an educational setting. There are six levels ranging from the simple (1) to the most complex (6).

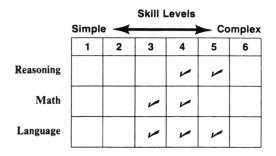

Skill Levels
Simple ⟷ Complex

	1	2	3	4	5	6
Reasoning				✔	✔	
Math			✔	✔		
Language			✔	✔	✔	

A plant safety coordinator inspects a work area.

Data-People-Things

This chart shows the levels for these three basic elements of work as related to this group. Level means the degree of difficulty of job tasks rather than the amount of time involved. The terms low, average, and high indicate the highest level at which occupations are involved. Compare your interests and abilities with the levels checked.

Difficulty Level of Job Tasks

	Low	Avg.	High
Data			*✓
People	*✓		
Things	*✓		

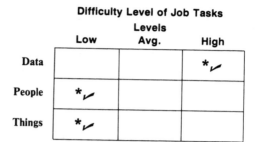

Common Occupations

A full listing of all occupations belonging to this group may be found in the Guide for Occupational Exploration.

The following occupations have been selected to represent this group. They provide the major employment opportunities. However, specific job opportunities will vary according to locations of industry, geographical region, and other factors.

Information may be found in common sources of occupational information, state career information systems, and computerized guidance systems.

An (M) follows the occupational title where the military services offer training and experience.

Finance

168.267-062	Investigator
188.167-074	Revenue Officer
376.267-010	Investigator, Cash Shortage
376.267-014	Investigator, Fraud

Individual Rights

168.167-014	Equal-Opportunity Representative (M)
188.117-046	Director, Compliance
188.117-050	Director, Consumer Affairs

Health and Safety

079.117-018	Sanitarian (M)
079.161-010	Industrial Hygienist (M)
168.161-014	Industrial-Safety-And-Health Technician
168.167-018	Health Officer, Field
168.167-042	Inspector, Health Care Facilities
168.167-062	Occupational-Safety-And-Health Inspector
168.167-078	Safety Inspector
168.264-014	Safety Inspector
168.267-042	Food and Drug Inspector (M)
168.267-058	Inspector, Motor Vehicles
168.267-074	Mine Inspector
168.267-086	Hazardous-Waste Management Specialist (M)
168.287-010	Inspector, Agricultural Commodities
373.267-010	Fire Inspector
373.267-018	Fire-Investigation Lieutenant
379.263-010	Animal Treatment Investigator
529.137-014	Sanitarian (M)

Immigration and Customs

168.167-022	Immigration Inspector
168.267-022	Customs Inspector

Company Policy

168.167-082	Transportation Inspector
168.367-014	Rater, Travel Accommodations
376.267-022	Shopping Investigator
909.127-010	Safety Coordinator

11.11
Business Management

Business Management is to manage the work of a business firm or one of its branches or units. Most of the job titles include the term "manager." Managers carry out the operating policies of the owner or other people in charge. They plan programs and schedules to make the work run smoothly and the business earn a profit. Managers resolve work problems and the complaints of workers or clients. They prepare reports, records, and budgets. Also, they must make sure that safety rules and other laws are met. Some order supplies and hire workers. This group includes the subgroups of:

Lodging
Recreation and Amusement
Transportation
Services
Wholesale-Retail

Workers in the five subgroups of Business Management perform duties that are very much alike. They differ in the knowledge and special skills needed for the type of work they manage. *Lodging* involves the managing of an apartment house, hotel, motel, trailer park, or marina. *Recreation and Amusement* includes sports arenas, golf clubs, theaters, camps, recreational centers, or health clubs. These all entertain the public. *Transportation* is concerned with the movement of people and freight by railway, highway, water, or air. The subgroups of *Services* and *Wholesale-Retail* are involved in selling products or services to the public or to retail stores.

Jobs may be found in all types of businesses as well as many government agencies.

What Skills and Abilities Would Help You Succeed in This Kind of Work?

The most important skills are listed below. All of those listed do not apply to each occupation. As you explore occupations you should identify the specific ones needed.

Leadership – to plan and direct the work of others.

Critical Thinking – to use personal judgment and information to make business decisions and solve problems.

Numerical – to complete and keep business records.

Persuasiveness – to use words to influence the thinking and actions of others.

Rapport – to deal with people in an effective way and maintain harmony among workers.

Communication – to give and exchange information orally or in records and written reports to supervisors and workers.

Organization – to arrange or set up the major elements involved in operating a business.

428

Do You Have or Can You Develop an Interest in This Kind of Work?

Review the following questions. Your answers can give you clues as to your interest in this field.

Have you been in charge of a committee or group activity? Can you lead others to work well together?

Have you planned or organized a project? Do you enjoy this type of activity?

Have you held office in a school, church, or community group? Are you able to use judgment to make decisions?

Have you taken courses in business or accounting? Do you like business?

Have you helped to operate a school or community fair or carnival? Was it successful?

What Else Should You Know About This Group of Occupations?

Some workers in this group often work long hours. They usually do this without being paid for overtime. They must cover staff shortages or meet emergencies. They may be responsible for following policies set by higher level administrators or owners. Experience in related jobs is very important for advancement to a manager's job. Some businesses have their own manager training programs. Some managers own their own businesses. Some get into a business because it is family owned. The duties of business managers are similar to those duties of managers in industry, manufacturing, and mining.

The military services offer training and experience related to some occupations in this group. These occupations are included in the list at the end of this group description. They are identified by an (M) following the occupational title. More information about the military training and experience opportunities may be found in Appendix A.

A motel manager checks a discrepancy in the daily occupancy report with a desk clerk.

How Can You Prepare
For This Kind of Work?

Occupations in this group require one to ten years of education and training, depending on the type and size of the business. Many manager jobs are filled by promotion from within a business. Although college studies are not always required, a degree in business management may be helpful. Also, vocational or technical school programs may be helpful for some jobs. Experience may be accepted as a substitute for education in some jobs.

As you plan your high school program you should include courses related to business, economics, general math, and communications. Next, you should include courses needed to enter college, technical school, or a vocational program as related to specific occupations in this group. You should take courses related to your specific interest in the subgroups within Business Management. The following list of courses and skills can help you plan your education.

Business Administration and Management – human resources development, institutional management, labor/industrial relations, management information systems, organizational behavior, personnel management, and entrepreneurship (small business ownership).

Hotel-Motel Management – marketing of hotel-motel services, institutional management, and hotel administration.

Recreation – hospitality and recreation marketing, resort management, leisure and recreational activities, sports, physical education, and arts and crafts.

Business – marketing and distribution, advertising and display, product management, salesmanship, and wholesale-retail marketing.

Courses in speech, technical/business writing, and accounting and bookkeeping are helpful for some occupations in this group.

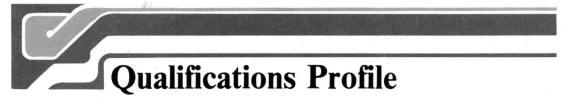

Qualifications Profile

This section is a summary of the worker traits and work factors related to successful job performance and worker satisfaction. Try to relate your interests, abilities, aptitudes, and preferences to these traits and factors. An asterisk (*) marks those traits and factors that are related to more than 60% of the occupations listed at the end of this group. The other traits and factors listed are as important, but relate to fewer occupations. See Appendices B-G for information about all of the worker traits and work factors.

Work Activities

The most important activities related to this group involve:

* * 2. Business contact.
* * 5. Recognition or appreciation from others.
* 9. Processes, methods, or machines.

Data-People-Things

This chart shows the levels for these three basic elements of work as related to this group. Level means the degree of difficulty of job tasks rather than the amount of time involved. The terms low, average, and high indicate the highest level at which occupations are involved. Compare your interests and abilities with the levels checked.

Difficulty Level of Job Tasks

	Low	Avg.	High
Data			*✔
People	*✔		
Things	*✔		

This property manager arranges maintenance services for buildings by phone.

Work Situations

Workers must be willing to:

* 1. Perform duties which change frequently.
* 3. Plan and direct an entire activity.
* 4. Deal with people.
  7. Make decisions using personal judgment.
  8. Make decisions using standards that can be measured or checked.

Physical Demands

Workers in this group of occupations must be able to do:

S – Sedentary work
*L – Light work

Educational Skills

This chart shows the levels of reasoning, math, and language skills related to this group. These skills are usually developed in an educational setting. There are six levels ranging from the simple (1) to the most complex (6).

Skill Levels

Simple ⟵⟶ Complex

	1	2	3	4	5	6
Reasoning				*✔	✔	
Math			✔	✔		
Language			✔	*✔		

Working Conditions

These are the physical surroundings in which work is done. In occupations belonging to this group, work is performed:

*I – Inside — workers spend most of their time inside protected from weather conditions but not always from temperature changes.
B – Both inside and outside — workers spend about equal time in each setting.

Aptitudes

This chart presents the most important aptitudes related to this group. The levels checked compare aptitudes needed for success in this group to aptitudes of the general working population in all occupations. For example, level 5 is low and represents the bottom 10% of the working population. Level 1 is high and represents the top 10%.

APTITUDE LEVELS COMPARED TO ALL WORKERS						
Related Aptitudes (Ability to Learn)		Lower 1/3		Middle 1/3	Upper 1/3	
		Level 5	Level 4	Level 3	Level 2	Level 1
Code	Title	10%	23%	34%	23%	10%
G	General Learning Ability			✔	* ✔	
V	Verbal			✔	* ✔	
N	Numerical			* ✔	✔	
P	Form Perception		✔	✔		
Q	Clerical Perception			* ✔		

A high-rise warehouse manager must be alert for safety violations by workers, such as this order picker.

Common Occupations

A full listing of all occupations belonging to this group may be found in the Guide for Occupational Exploration.

The following occupations have been selected to represent this group. They provide the major employment opportunities. However, specific job opportunities will vary according to locations of industry, geographical region, and other factors.

Information may be found in common sources of occupational information, state career information systems, and computerized guidance systems.

An (M) follows the occupational title where the military services offer training and experience.

Lodging

186.167-018 Manager, Apartment House
187.117-038 Manager, Hotel or Motel
187.167-046 Executive Housekeeper (M)
320.137-010 Manager, Boarding House
320.137-014 Manager, Lodging Facilities

Recreation and Amusement

187.117-042 Manager, Recreation Establishment (M)
187.167-114 Manager, Golf Club
187.167-122 Manager, Hotel Recreational Facilities
187.167-146 Manager, Skating Rink
187.167-154 Manager, Theater
195.167-018 Director, Camp
195.167-026 Director, Recreation Center
339.137-010 Manager, Health Club

Transportation

184.167-058 Manager, Cargo-And-Ramp-Services (M)
184.167-070 Manager, Flight-Reservations
184.167-082 Manager, Station (M)
184.167-110 Manager, Truck Terminal
184.167-114 Manager, Warehouse (M)
184.167-118 Operations Manager (M)
184.167-182 Superintendent, Marine (M)
184.167-214 Superintendent, Terminal (M)
185.167-018 Manager, Distribution Warehouse (M)
197.167-014 Purser
198.167-010 Conductor, Passenger Car
198.167-018 Conductor, Road Freight

Services

185.137-010 Manager, Fast Food Services
186.167-034 Manager, Insurance Office
186.167-046 Manager, Property
187.167-026 Director, Food Services
187.167-030 Director, Funeral
187.167-058 Manager, Barber or Beauty Shop
187.167-074 Manager, Cemetery
187.167-098 Manager, Employment Agency
187.167-106 Manager, Food Service (M)
187.167-126 Manager, Liquor Establishment (M)
187.167-158 Manager, Travel Agency
319.137-014 Manager, Flight Kitchen

Wholesale-Retail

185.167-010 Commissary Manager (M)
185.167-014 Manager, Automobile Service Station
185.167-026 Manager, Machinery-or-Equipment, Rental And Leasing
185.167-030 Manager, Meat Sales And Storage
185.167-038 Manager, Parts
185.167-046 Manager, Retail Store (M)
186.167-042 Manager, Market
187.167-162 Manager, Vehicle Leasing And Rental
299.137-010 Manager, Department

11.12
Contracts and Claims

Contracts and Claims involve the negotiation of contracts and the settlement of claims. Negotiation means to discuss, adjust differences, and to come to an agreement. A contract is a legal agreement. Workers who negotiate contracts help buyers and sellers come to terms and set up legal agreements. Workers who settle claims gather facts about the loss, damage, or shortage reported. They do this to see if the claim is valid and to determine the settlement to be made. This group includes the subgroups of:

Claims Settlement
Rental and Leasing
Booking
Contract Negotiations

Claims Settlement includes claims such as property damage and personal injury. Service Representatives for auto companies investigate dealer's claims for defective automobile parts. They prepare reports showing volume, types, and how claims were handled. Claim Adjusters inquire into claims filed against insurance companies and other firms. They try to settle the claim out-of-court. When they can't, they suggest litigation (legal action). Claim Examiners study an insurance claim to decide if it is covered by a policy. Then they settle the claim to comply with what the policy provides. Automobile Damage Appraisers examine damaged vehicles and estimate the cost of labor and parts to make repairs. They also decide on the salvage value of total-loss vehicles. They attempt to secure an agreement with an automobile repair shop on the cost of repairs.

Rental and Leasing are to contract for the use of property or goods for money. Real Estate Agents help owners acquire and dispose of properties. They manage other staff and direct appraisers to inspect real estate. Some act as renting agents for owners. Public Event Facilities Rental Managers negotiate contracts for leasing places where public events are held. They renew contracts and seek new business. Lease Buyers negotiate leases, options, and royalties with landowners and representatives of oil or coal producing firms. Right-of-Way Agents purchase or lease land and rights-of-way for utilities and pipelines. Property-Utilization Officers purchase and maintain property for the government. They also negotiate property transfers and sales, rental, and leasing contracts.

Booking is to schedule entertainers to perform. It is also to manage the affairs of people who are in the public eye. This includes athletes, artists, entertainers, and celebrities. Business Managers and Booking Managers negotiate contracts and fees for their clients. They advise them on various aspects of business. They often represent their clients in public contact. Literary Agents also are part of this subgroup. They read manuscripts and suggest changes. They market their clients' manuscripts to editors, publishers, studios, and other buyers. They also negotiate contracts between publishers and clients.

Contract Negotiations involve arranging contracts for the purchase of equipment, products, and supplies. Contract Administrators prepare bids, process specs (specifications), make tests, and issue any progress reports that may be required. They also review bids from other firms. Contract Specialists negotiate, direct, extend, end, and renegotiate contracts. They also evaluate how well the contract is carried out. Research Contract Supervisors direct workers who negotiate and service research contracts with agencies doing projects for the government. Contractors assess architects' plans, blueprints, codes, and specs. They also purchase materials to do the job.

Jobs may be found with insurance and transportation companies, booking agencies, industries, businesses, and government agencies. Some workers are self-employed.

What Skills and Abilities Would Help You Succeed in This Kind of Work?

The most important skills are listed below. All of those listed do not apply to each oc-cupation. As you explore occupations you should identify the specific ones needed.

Comprehension – to understand and know laws in order to prepare contracts and settle claims and to read and understand technical information.

Numerical – to do mathematics quickly and accurately to compute costs and prepare cost estimates.

Accuracy – to keep accurate records.

Persuasiveness – to get others to agree to terms.

Verbalization – to speak clearly and convincingly.

Critical Thinking – to use personal judgment to make decisions and solve problems.

Rapport – to deal with people in an effective way.

A real estate agent shows a staff member the location of a developing area.

Do You Have or Can You Develop an Interest in This Kind of Work?

Review the following questions. Your answers can give you clues as to your interest in Contracts and Claims.

Have you helped arrange for a person or group to entertain at a school or community function? Did everyone understand the arrangements? Did you enjoy this type of activity?

Have you been on a debate team? Were you persuasive? Did others accept your opinions?

Have you filed a claim with an insurance company? Did you fill out the report? Do you like this type of detailed work?

Have you read a lease or formal contract? Did you understand the terms used?

What Else Should You Know About This Group of Occupations?

Some jobs in this group require travel and odd working hours. Workers may have to call on people in the evening instead of during regular business hours. Pay may be based on salary, commission, or a combination of both. Workers usually need to take a civil service test for jobs in government agencies.

The military services offer training and experience related to some occupations in this group. These occupations are included in the list at the end of this group description. They are identified by an (M) following the occupational title. More information about the military training and experience opportunities may be found in Appendix A.

This man manages the affairs of athletes and helps them negotiate their contracts.

How Can You Prepare for This Kind of Work?

Most occupations in this group require two to four years of education and training. Some may require up to ten years. However, the type and amount of education required vary among jobs. A college degree in business or management is usually needed. Many jobs in this group also require work experience in a field such as insurance or real estate.

As you plan your high school education your should include courses in math, economics, business, and communications.

Next, you should include courses needed to enter college or a two-year technical program. The following list of courses and skills will help you plan your education.

Business Administration and Management – accounting, contract management, procurement/purchasing, product management, and small business management and ownership.

Courses related to law are important for jobs in this group. Helpful courses include speech, technical/business writing, finance, and accounting.

Qualifications Profile

This section is a summary of the worker traits and work factors related to successful job performance and worker satisfaction. Try to relate your interests, abilities, aptitudes, and preferences to these traits and factors. An asterisk (*) marks those traits and factors that are related to more than 60% of the occupations listed at the end of this group. The other traits and factors listed are as important, but relate to fewer occupations. See Appendices B-G for information about all of the worker traits and work factors.

Physical Demands

Workers in this group of occupations must be able to do:

S – Sedentary work
L – Light work

Work Activities

The most important activities related to this group involve:

* 2. Business contact.
* 5. Recognition or appreciation from others.
* 6. Communication of ideas and information.

Work Situations

Workers must be willing to:

1. Perform duties which change frequently.
* 3. Plan and direct an entire activity.
* 4. Deal with people.
* 5. Influence people's opinions, attitudes, and judgments.
7. Make decisions using personal judgment.
* 8. Make decisions using standards that can be measured or checked.

Aptitudes

This chart presents the most important aptitudes related to this group. The levels checked compare aptitudes needed for success in this group to aptitudes of the general working population in all occupations. For example, level 5 is low and represents the bottom 10% of the working population. Level 1 is high and represents the top 10%.

APTITUDE LEVELS COMPARED TO ALL WORKERS						
Related Aptitudes (Ability to Learn)		Lower 1/3		Middle 1/3	Upper 1/3	
		Level **5**	Level **4**	Level **3**	Level **2**	Level **1**
Code	Title	10%	23%	34%	23%	10%
G	General Learning Ability				*✓	
V	Verbal				*✓	
N	Numerical			*✓		
Q	Clerical Perception			*✓	✓	

Data-People-Things

This chart shows the levels for these three basic elements of work as related to this group. Level means the degree of difficulty of job tasks rather than the amount of time involved. The terms low, average, and high indicate the highest level at which occupations are involved. Compare your interests and abilities with the levels checked.

Difficulty Level of Job Tasks

	Low	Avg.	High
Data			*✓
People			*✓
Things	*✓		

A contract specialist must be aware of laws that apply and their possible tax consequences.

Working Conditions

These are the physical surroundings in which work is done. In occupations belonging to this group, work is performed:

*I – Inside — workers spend most of their time inside protected from weather conditions but not always from temperature changes.

B – Both inside and outside — workers spend about equal time in each setting.

Educational Skills

This chart shows the levels of reasoning, math, and language skills related to this group. These skills are usually developed in an educational setting. There are six levels ranging from the simple (1) to the most complex (6).

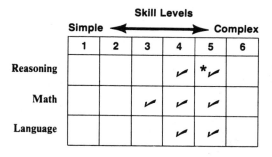

Skill Levels

| | Simple ← → Complex | | | | | |
	1	2	3	4	5	6
Reasoning				✓	*✓	
Math			✓	✓	✓	
Language				✓	✓	

Common Occupations

A full listing of all occupations belonging to this group may be found in the Guide for Occupational Exploration.

The following occupations have been selected to represent this group. They provide the major employment opportunities. However, specific job opportunities will vary according to locations of industry, geographical region, and other factors.

Information may be found in common sources of occupational information, state career information systems, and computerized guidance systems.

An (M) follows the occupational title where the military services offer training and experience.

Claims Settlement

191.167-022 Service Representative
241.217-010 Claim Adjuster
241.267-014 Appraiser, Automobile Damage
241.267-018 Claim Examiner

Rental and Leasing

186.117-058 Real-Estate Agent
186.117-062 Rental Manager, Public Events Facilities
188.117-122 Property-Utilization Officer
191.117-030 Lease Buyer
191.117-046 Right-Of-Way Agent

Booking

153.117-014 Manager, Athlete
191.117-010 Artists Manager
191.117-014 Booking Manager
191.117-018 Business Manager
191.117-034 Literary Agent

Contract Negotiations

162.117-014 Contract Administrator (M)
162.117-018 Contract Specialist (M)
162.117-030 Research-Contracts Supervisor
182.167-010 Contractor

12 PHYSICAL PERFORMING

People with an interest in Physical Performing enjoy being in front of an audience. They may participate in sports or perform physical feats. These workers must have physical skills and strength. They also need excellent eye, hand, body, and foot coordination. Their training schedules are rigid and at times they are under great mental pressure. However, workers get a reward of recognition and appreciation when they feel the excitement and enthusiasm of the crowd.

Some workers, such as athletes in sports, have a limited period of time for their careers. A career may be cut short by a physical injury. They need to plan on changing to a related occupation or have a second career field to enter.

The Physical Performing area is divided into two clusters: Sports and Physical Feats.

Sports

The Sports cluster includes professional athletes and others in organized sports. Workers play, coach, or officiate one of a wide range of sports. Coaches plan and direct the training of players, instruct players in methods of the game, and decide game strategy. Officials watch the actions of players to detect if rules are broken. They decide disputes according to set rules. Professional players take part in team or individual sports events such as football, boxing, or horse racing.

Physical Feats

The Physical Feats cluster includes workers who perform acts to entertain people. Some acts are daring and require special skills. Many workers use a gymnastics or acrobatic skill in their performance. Workers learn or polish their skills by watching others and then practicing. They work in settings such as carnivals, the circus, theme parks, rodeos, TV, and motion picture studios.

The following Worker Trait Groups and Subgroups are related to the Sports and Physical Feats clusters.

Physical Performing: an interest in physical activities performed before an audience.

Sports

12.01 Sports
    Coaching and Instructing
    Officiating
    Performing

Physical Feats

12.02 Physical Feats
    Performing

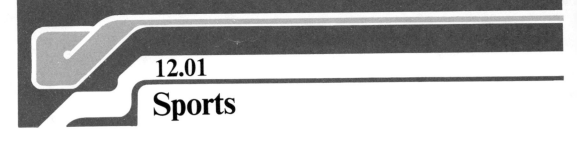

12.01
Sports

Sports include professional athletes and others in organized sports. Workers may coach players or officiate events. Some may teach skills of a sport to be played as recreation. This group includes the subgroups of:

Coaching and Instructing
Officiating
Performing

Coaching and Instructing is to plan and direct the training and performance of players. Coaches direct the conditioning of players. They assess players' skills and assign team positions. They determine game strategy and instruct players in methods of the game. Some may scout and recruit players. Some teach sports activities at private or public sports centers or schools.

Officiating is to observe actions of participants to detect the breaking of rules in sports events. Officials also decide any disputes according to the set rules of a sport. They start, stop, and time events. They may record laps, keep score or other records. They keep the sports event moving.

Performing is to take part in professional sports events. Workers entertain people in events such as football, boxing, and car or horse racing. They must use physical skills as they train and participate. They must perform under a set of rules.

Jobs may be found in all types of professional sports. Examples are football, baseball, basketball, hockey, golf, tennis, and car and horse racing. Some jobs may also be found with private or public sports centers. These may include ski resorts, skating rinks, athletic clubs, gyms, and private schools.

This defensive coach is describing how to counter an unexpected formation used by the other team.

442

What Skills and Abilities Would Help You Succeed in This Kind of Work?

The most important skills are listed below. All of those listed do not apply to each occupation. As you explore occupations you should identify the specific ones needed.

Coordination – to move the body skillfully in response to visual signals or observations.

Competitiveness – to have the desire to compete and win.

Communication – to teach or demonstrate physical skills or strategies of a sport.

Organization – to arrange ideas and information in a way that players or participants can understand.

Critical Thinking – to formulate coaching strategies and make decisions based on knowledge, judgment, and experience.

Physical Stamina – to have the strength to endure long hours of practice and performance.

Leadership – to plan and direct the work of others.

Spatial Perception – to judge distance, speed, and movement of objects or people.

Decisiveness – to make decisions quickly and firmly.

Composure – to be calm and self-confident while handling the mental pressure of competition.

Do You Have or Can You Develop an Interest in This Kind of Work?

Review the following questions. Your answers can give you clues as to your interest in Sports.

Do you enjoy watching sports events? Do you know the rules of any sport well enough to be a referee, judge, or umpire?

Have you coached children or youth in sports activities? Were your efforts effective? Do you think you would enjoy this type of work?

Have you competed against others in athletic events? Do you remain calm and alert during competition?

Do you excel in athletics? Have you won any special sports events? Have others asked you to teach them that skill?

Have you had lessons in riding? Have you competed in a horse show or race?

What Else Should You Know About This Group of Occupations?

Often sports officials must make unpopular decisions. They need to be able to stand by their decisions. Athletes must maintain or improve their physical skills to remain in competition. The risk of injury is great in sports. Physical demands may limit the number of years a worker remains a professional. Also, after reaching a certain age, many competitive players must find work in other jobs. Only a few skilled athletes reach the major leagues and top professional teams.

Many jobs in this group are seasonal. People often must find other work in the off season. Race track workers, golf and tennis pros must find other work or move to another part of the country. Frequent travel is usually involved for officials and athletes.

The military services offer training and experience related to one occupation in this group – Instructor, Sports. The occupation is included in the list at the end of this group

A major league umpire has served many years in the minors, as well as attended umpire school.

description. It is identified by an (M) following the occupational title. More information about the military training and experience opportunities may be found in Appendix A.

How Can You Prepare for This Kind of Work?

Occupations in this group require three months to four years of education and training. Others may require up to ten years. Coaches and officials in professional sports often start at the high school or college level. To be hired by professional baseball leagues, umpires must graduate from a recognized umpire training school. Then they must have experience in minor leagues. Officials in horse racing usually have some type of related work experience and receive on-the-job training.

Professional athletes often receive initial training while in high school or college. The athletes are recruited by professional clubs. Their training continues as long as they work in their jobs. Racing professionals must learn their jobs through experience over several years.

As you plan your high school program you should include courses related to Sports. Next, you should include courses needed to enter college. The following list of courses and skills can help you plan your education.

Physical Education and Recreation – courses that teach physical skills and provide instruction in athletic sports and recreational activities.

Health – courses related to health treatment and prevention practices that relate to principles and methods by which individuals can improve and maintain their physical condition.

Coaching and Officiating – courses related to coaching techniques and strategies and rules of sports events.

Courses in education may be helpful for some coaching and instructing since entry in-

to professional athletics may result from coaching and instructing in educational institutions.

Courses in the life sciences such as anatomy, physiology, and kinesiology (mechanics of human movement), may also be helpful for coaching and instructing occupations.

Qualifications Profile

This section is a summary of the worker traits and work factors related to successful job performance and worker satisfaction. Try to relate your interests, abilities, aptitudes, and preferences to these traits and factors. An asterisk (*) marks those traits and factors that are related to more than 60% of the occupations listed at the end of this group. The other traits and factors listed are as important, but relate to fewer occupations. See Appendices B-G for information about all of the worker traits and work factors.

Work Situations

Workers must be willing to:

1. Perform duties which change frequently.
3. Plan and direct an entire activity.
* 4. Deal with people.
6. Work under pressure.
* 7. Make decisions using personal judgment.
8. Make decisions using standards that can be measured or checked.

Work Activities

The most important activities related to this group involve:

2. Business contact.
* 5. Recognition or appreciation from others.
* 6. Communication of ideas and information.

Educational Skills

This chart shows the levels of reasoning, math, and language skills related to this group. These skills are usually developed in an educational setting. There are six levels ranging from the simple (1) to the most complex (6).

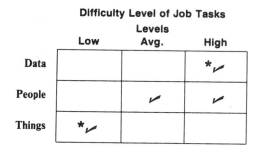

Data-People-Things

This chart shows the levels for these three basic elements of work as related to this group. Level means the degree of difficulty of job tasks rather than the amount of time involved. The terms low, average, and high indicate the highest level at which occupations are involved. Compare your interests and abilities with the levels checked.

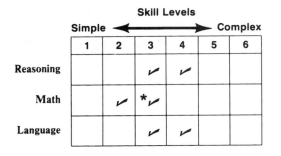

Skill Levels

| | Simple ← | | | | → Complex | |
	1	2	3	4	5	6
Reasoning			✔	✔		
Math		✔	*✔			
Language			✔	✔		

Working Conditions

These are the physical surroundings in which work is done. In occupations belonging to this group, work is performed:

O – Outside — workers spend most of their time outside with little protection from weather conditions.

B – Both inside and outside — workers spend about equal time in each setting.

Physical Demands

Workers in this group of occupations must be able to do:

L – Light work
M – Medium work

Only a small percentage achieve stardom and high pay in professional basketball.

Aptitudes

This chart presents the most important aptitudes related to this group. The levels checked compare aptitudes needed for success in this group to aptitudes of the general working population in all occupations. For example, level 5 is low and represents the bottom 10% of the working population. Level 1 is high and represents the top 10%.

APTITUDE LEVELS COMPARED TO ALL WORKERS							
Related Aptitudes **(Ability to Learn)**		Lower 1/3		Middle 1/3	Upper 1/3		
		Level **5**	Level **4**	Level **3**	Level **2**	Level **1**	
Code	Title	10%	23%	34%	23%	10%	
G	General Learning Ability			*✔	✔		
V	Verbal			✔	✔		
S	Spatial		✔	✔	✔		
P	Form Perception		✔	✔	✔		
K	Motor Coordination		✔	✔	✔		

Common Occupations

A full listing of all occupations belonging to this group may be found in the Guide for Occupational Exploration.

The following occupations have been selected to represent this group. They provide the major employment opportunities. However, specific job opportunities will vary according to locations of industry, geographical region, and other factors.

Information may be found in common sources of occupational information, state career information systems, and computerized guidance systems.

An (M) follows the occupational title where the military services offer training and experience.

Coaching and Instructing

153.117-010 Coach
153.117-018 Scout, Professional Sports
153.227-010 Coach, Professional Athletes
153.227-018 Instructor, Sports (M)

Officiating

153.267-010 Horse-Race Starter
153.267-018 Umpire
153.387-014 Scorer
379.667-010 Golf-Course Ranger

Performing

153.243-010 Automobile Racer
153.243-014 Motorcycle Racer
153.244-010 Jockey
153.341-010 Professional Athlete

Physical Feats

Physical Feats are acts that entertain people. Workers perform acts that are daring or require special skill. Some may need physical strength. Workers may perform alone or with others. This group is made up of one subgroup:

Performing

Performing includes entertaining people by doing difficult tasks. Acrobats leap, tumble, and balance. Aquatic performers do water ballets or synchronized swimming routines.

Jugglers use objects such as balls, knives, plates, and hats. They keep several objects in motion in the air at the same time. Rodeo performers use special skills in bronc (horse) riding, calf roping, and bull riding in rodeos. Stunt performers work for TV or motion pictures. They overturn cars, fall from horses, or take part in fights.

Jobs may be found with carnivals or in the circus. They also may be found with theaters, theme parks, rodeos, TV, and motion picture studios.

Powder smoke obscures this stuntman in a scene from the wild west.

What Skills and Abilities Would Help You Succeed in This Kind of Work?

The most important skills are listed below. All of those listed do not apply to each occupation. As you explore occupations you should identify the specific ones needed.

Coordination – to move the body skillfully in response to visual signals or observations.

Spatial Perception – to judge distance, speed, and movement of objects or people.

Persistence – to practice and rehearse for long periods of time.

Accuracy – to make precise body movements in a routine or act.

Composure – to be calm and self-confident in pressure situations such as performing before an audience.

Performance – to express ideas and emotions through body movements.

Boldness – to be daring and have a spirit of adventure while performing a difficult or dangerous act.

Physical Stamina – to have strength to endure long hours of practice and performance.

Do You Have or Can You Develop an Interest in This Kind of Work?

Review the following questions. Your answers can give you clues as to your interest in Physical Feats.

Have you performed stunts that require daring and skill? Did you perform them without great fear? Did you do them while others were watching?

Have you had lessons in riding? Have you competed in a horse show or rodeo?

Are you a race car fan? Have you raced go-carts, midget racers, or stock cars? Did you enjoy it?

Have you had a hobby or performed a specialty act such as juggling, gymnastics, or wire walking? Do you perform well in front of an audience?

Have you been a cheerleader? Did you do acrobatic routines?

Have you trained a dog or other animal to do tricks? Do you think you could develop a specialty act with animals?

What Else Should You Know About This Group of Occupations?

Workers in the Physical Feats group must train hard to improve and maintain their skills. Physical requirements for some jobs may limit the number of years a worker can perform. They usually are required to travel from place to place to perform.

How Can You Prepare for This Kind of Work?

Occupations in this group usually require from six months to two years of education and training. The usual method of training is by working in a related environment. Workers train by observation and practice. Another method is to work with and learn from a successful performer.

As you plan your high school program you should include courses related to Physical Feats. The following list of courses and skills can help you plan your education.

Physical Education and Recreation – courses that teach skills in group games, dance, body dynamics, aquatics, team sports, gymnastics, and outdoor recreation.

Health – courses related to health treatment and prevention practices that relate to prin-

ciples and methods by which individuals can improve and maintain their physical condition.

Courses in Dramatics can be helpful for some occupations in this group.

Qualifications Profile

This section is a summary of the worker traits and work factors related to successful job performance and worker satisfaction. Try to relate your interests, abilities, aptitudes, and preferences to these traits and factors. An asterisk (*) marks those traits and factors that are related to more than 60% of the occupations listed at the end of this group. The other traits and factors listed are as important, but relate to fewer occupations. See Appendices B-G for information about all of the worker traits and work factors.

Work Activities

The most important activities related to this group involve:

* 5. Recognition or appreciation from others.
* 6. Communication of ideas and information.
   9. Processes, methods, or machines.

Data-People-Things

This chart shows the levels for these three basic elements of work as related to this group. Level means the degree of difficulty of job tasks rather than the amount of time involved. The terms low, average, and high indicate the highest level at which occupations are involved. Compare your interests and abilities with the levels checked.

Difficulty Level of Job Tasks

	Low	Avg.	High
Data		* ✓	
People		* ✓	
Things	✓		✓

Work Situations

Workers must be willing to:

* * 1. Perform duties which change frequently.
* * 4. Deal with people.
* * 6. Work under pressure.
* * 7. Make decisions using personal judgment.
*   10. Work within precise limits or standards of accuracy.

Physical Demands

Workers in this group of occupations must be able to do:

M – Medium work

Educational Skills

This chart shows the levels of reasoning, math, and language skills related to this group. These skills are usually developed in an educational setting. There are six levels ranging from the simple (1) to the most complex (6).

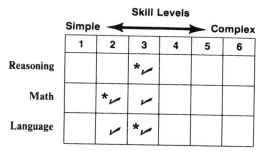

Skill Levels

Simple ← → Complex

	1	2	3	4	5	6
Reasoning			*✔			
Math		*✔	✔			
Language		✔	*✔			

Rodeo performers compete for prize money, pay their own expenses, and put up an entry fee.

Aptitudes

This chart presents the most important aptitudes related to this group. The levels checked compare aptitudes needed for success in this group to aptitudes of the general working population in all occupations. For example, level 5 is low and represents the bottom 10% of the working population. Level 1 is high and represents the top 10%.

APTITUDE LEVELS COMPARED TO ALL WORKERS						
Related Aptitudes (Ability to Learn)		Lower 1/3		Middle 1/3	Upper 1/3	
		Level 5	Level 4	Level 3	Level 2	Level 1
Code	Title	10%	23%	34%	23%	10%
G	General Learning Ability			*✔		
V	Verbal			*✔		
S	Spatial				*✔	
P	Form Perception		✔	*✔	✔	
K	Motor Coordination			✔	*✔	
F	Finger Dexterity			*✔	✔	
M	Manual Dexterity			✔	*✔	✔

Acrobats practice long hours to perfect a stunt before performing in public.

Working Conditions

These are the physical surroundings in which work is done. In occupations belonging to this group, work is performed:

*I – Inside — workers spend most of their time inside protected from weather conditions but not always from temperature changes.

B – Both inside and outside — workers spend about equal time in each setting.

Common Occupations

A full listing of all occupations belonging to this group may be found in the Guide for Occupational Exploration.

The following occupations have been selected to represent this group. They provide the major employment opportunities. However, specific job opportunities will vary according to locations of industry, geographical region, and other factors.

Information may be found in common sources of occupational information, state career information systems, and computerized guidance systems.

An (M) follows the occupational title where the military services offer training and experience.

Performing

159.247-010 Acrobat
159.341-010 Juggler
159.341-014 Stunt Performer
159.344-014 Rodeo Performer
159.347-014 Aquatic Performer

Appendices....

Occupations With Military Counterparts

The military services offer training, experience, and career opportunities related to many occupations. In the list of occupations at the end of each Worker Trait Group (WTG) description, the civilian occupations with military counterparts are identified by an (M) following the title. This appendix lists these occupations by Worker Trait Group.

The "O" and "E" in front of the nine-digit occupational code indicate that the opportunity is as an officer, enlisted person, or both. The letters following the occupational title identify the branches of services: AR - Army;

NA - Navy; AF - Air Force; MC - Marine Corps; and CG - Coast Guard.

The Military Career Guide gives more information about opportunities in the military services. Occupations related to enlisted classifications are found in the DOT Code Index of the Military Career Guide. Use the Index to look up the code for the occupation of interest. Following the code and title is the page number where information may be found. Information about officer related classifications may be found in the officer section of the Military Career Guide.

01 - ARTISTIC

01.01 – LITERARY ARTS

	E	131.067-022	Editorial Writer	AR	NA	AF	MC	CG
	E	131.087-018	Screen Writer	AR	NA	AF	MC	CG
O	E	132.037-022	Editor, Publications	AR	NA	AF	MC	CG
O		187.167-174	Producer	AR	NA	AF	MC	..
	E	962.264-010	Editor, Film	AR	NA	AF	MC	CG

01.02 - VISUAL ARTS

	E	141.061-018	Graphic Designer	AR	NA	AF	MC	..
	E	141.061-022	Illustrator	AR	NA	AF	MC	..
	E	141.061-026	Illustrator, Medical and Scientific	AR	NA	AF	MC	..
O		143.062-010	Director of Photography	AR	NA	AF	MC	..
	E	143.062-022	Photographer, Motion Picture	AR	NA	AF	MC	CG
	E	143.062-030	Photographer, Still	AR	NA	AF	MC	CG
	E	143.062-034	Photojournalist	AR	NA	AF	MC	CG
	E	149.061-010	Audiovisual Production Specialist	AR	NA	AF	MC	CG

01.03 - PERFORMING ARTS: DRAMA

O		159.067-010	Director, Motion Picture	AR	NA	AF	MC	..
O		159.067-014	Director, Television	AR	NA	AF	MC	..
O		159.117-010	Producer	AR	NA	AF	MC	..
	E	159.147-010	Announcer	AR	NA	AF	MC	CG
	E	159.147-014	Disk Jockey	AR	NA	AF	MC	CG
O		159.167-014	Director, Radio	AR	NA	AF	MC	..

455

01.04 - PERFORMING ARTS: MUSIC

	E	152.041-010	Musician, Instrumental	AR	NA	AF	MC	CG
O	E	152.047-010	Choral Director	AR	NA	AF	NC	CG
O	E	152.047-014	Conductor, Orchestra	AR	NA	AF	MC	CG
	E	152.047-022	Singer	AR	NA	AF	MC	CG
O	E	152.067-010	Arranger	AR	NA	AF	MC	CG
O	E	152.067-014	Composer	AR	NA	AF	MC	CG

01.06 - TECHNICAL ARTS

	E	143.062-014	Photographer, Aerial	AR	NA	AF	MC	CG
	E	962.382-014	Sound Cutter	AR	NA	AF	MC	..
	E	972.381-010	Lithographic Plate Maker	AR	NA	AF	MC	..
	E	972.381-022	Stripper, Photolithographic	AR	NA	AF	MC	..
	E	972.382-014	Photographer, Lithographic	AR	NA	AF	MC	..
	E	979.382-018	Graphic Arts Technician	AR	NA	AF	MC	..

02 - SCIENTIFIC

02.01 - PHYSICAL SCIENCES

O		020.067-014	Mathematician	AR	NA	AF	MC	CG
O		022.061-010	Chemist	AR	NA	AF	MC	CG
O		023.061-014	Physicist	AR	NA	AF	..	CG
O		024.061-018	Geologist	..	NA	..	..	CG
O		024.061-030	Geophysicist	..	NA	..	..	CG
O		024.061-034	Hydrologist	..	NA	..	..	CG
O		025.062-01	Meteorologist	AR	NA	AF	MC	..
O		029.081-010	Environmental Analyst	AR	NA	AF	..	CG
O	E	029.167-010	Aerial-Photograph Interpreter	AR	NA	AF	MC	CG

02.02 - LIFE SCIENCES

O		019.061-010	Biomedical Engineer	AR	NA	AF	..	CG
O		040.061-010	Agronomist	AR	NA	AF	..	..
O		041.061-026	Biochemist	AR	NA	AF	..	..
O		041.061-046	Entomologist	AR	NA	AF	..	..
O		041.061-058	Microbiologist	AR	NA	AF	..	..
O		041.061-070	Parasitologist	AR	NA	AF	..	..
O		041.061-074	Pharmacologist	AR	NA	AF	..	..
O		041.061-078	Physiologist	AR	NA	AF	..	..
O		041.061-094	Staff Toxicologist	AR	NA	AF	..	..
O		041.167-010	Environmental Epidemiologist	AR	NA	AF	..	..
O		070.061-010	Pathologist	AR	NA	AF	..	..
O		073.061-010	Veterinarian, Lab Animal Care	AR	..	..	..	..
O		073.061-014	Veterinary Anatomist	AR	..	..	..	..
O		073.061-018	Veterinary Bacteriologist	AR	..	..	..	..
O		073.061-022	Veterinary Epidemiologist	AR	..	..	..	..
O		073.061-026	Veterinary Parasitologist	AR	..	..	..	..
O		073.061-030	Veterinary Pathologist	AR	..	..	..	..
O		073.061-034	Veterinary Pharmacologist	AR	..	..	..	..
0		073.061-038	Veterinary Physiologist	AR	..	..	..	..
O		073.061-042	Veterinary Virologist	AR	..	..	..	..
O		079.021-014	Medical Physicist	AR	NA	AF	..	CG

02.03 - MEDICAL SCIENCES

O	070.101-010	Anesthesiologist	AR	NA	AF	..	..
O	070.101-014	Cardiologist	AR	NA	AF	..	..
O	070.101-018	Dermatologist	AR	NA	AF	..	..
O	070.101-022	General Practitioner	AR	NA	AF	..	..
O	070.101-026	Family Practitioner	AR	NA	AF	..	..
O	070.101-030	Flight Surgeon	AR	NA	AF	..	..
O	070.101-034	Gynecologist	AR	NA	AF	..	..
O	070.101-038	Intern	AR	NA	AF	..	..
O	070.101-042	Internist	AR	NA	AF	..	..
O	070.101-046	Medical Officer	AR	NA	AF	..	..
O	070.101-050	Neurologist	AR	NA	AF	..	..
O	070.101-054	Obstetrician	AR	NA	AF	..	..
O	070.101-058	Ophthalmologist	AR	NA	AF	..	..
O	070.101-062	Otolaryngologist	AR	NA	AF	..	..
O	070.101-066	Pediatrician	AR	NA	AF	..	..
O	070.101-070	Physiatrist	AR	NA	AF	..	..
O	070.101-074	Physician, Head	AR	NA	AF	..	..
O	070.101-078	Physician, Occupational	AR	NA	AF	..	..
O	070.101-090	Radiologist	AR	NA	AF	..	..
O	070.101-094	Surgeon 1	AR	NA	AF	..	..
O	070.101-098	Urologist	AR	NA	AF	..	..
O	070.107-010	Allergist-Immunologist	AR	NA	AF	..	..
O	070.107-014	Psychiatrist	AR	NA	AF	..	..
O	072.061-010	Oral Pathologist	AR	NA	AF	..	..
O	072.101-010	Dentist	AR	NA	AF	..	..
O	072.101-014	Endodontist	AR	NA	AF	..	..
O	072.101-018	Oral Surgeon	AR	NA	AF	..	..
O	072.101-022	Orthodontist	AR	NA	AF	..	..
O	072.101-026	Pedodontist	AR	NA	AF	..	..
O	072.101-030	Periodontist	AR	NA	AF	..	..
O	072.101-034	Prosthodontist	AR	NA	AF	..	..
O	072.101-038	Public-Health Dentist	AR	NA	AF	..	..
O	072.117-010	Director, Dental Services	AR	NA	AF	..	..
O	073.101-010	Veterinarian	AR	..	..	..	..
O	073.101-018	Zoo Veterinarian	AR	..	..	..	..
O	076.101-010	Audiologist	AR	NA	AF	..	..
O	076.107-010	Speech Pathologist	AR	NA	AF	..	..
E	078.361-034	Radiation-Therapy Technologist	AR	NA	AF	..	CG
O	079.101-018	Optometrist	AR	NA	AF	..	..
O	079.101-022	Podiatrist	AR	NA	AF	..	..

02.04 - LABORATORY TECHNOLOGY

E	011.281-014	Spectroscopist	AR	NA	AF	MC	CG
E	019.261-010	Biomedical Equipment Technician	AR	NA	AF	MC	CG
E	022.261-010	Chemical-Laboratory Technician	AR	NA	AF	MC	CG
E	025.267-010	Oceanographer, Assistant	AR	NA	AF	MC	CG
E	025.267-014	Weather Observer	AR	NA	AF	MC	CG
E	029.261-010	Laboratory Tester	AR	NA	AF	MC	CG

O		074.131-010	Director, Pharmacy Services	AR	NA	AF	..	..
O		074.161-010	Pharmacist	AR	NA	AF	..	..
	E	074.381-010	Pharmacist Assistant	AR	NA	AF	..	CG
	E	078.221-010	Immunohematologist	AR	NA	AF	..	CG
	E	078.281-010	Cytotechnologist	AR	NA	AF	..	CG
	E	078.361-014	Medical Technologist	AR	NA	AF	..	CG
	E	078.361-030	Tissue Technologist	AR	NA	AF	..	CG
	E	078.381-010	Medical-Laboratory Assistant	AR	NA	AF	..	CG
	E	078.381-014	Medical-Laboratory Technician	AR	NA	AF	..	CG
	E	143.362-010	Biological Photographer	AR	NA	AF	MC	CG
O		199.267-010	Ballistics Expert, Forensic	AR	NA	AF	MC	CG
O		199.267-026	Polygraph Examiner	AR	NA	AF	MC	CG
	E	199.384-010	Decontaminator	AR	NA	AF	MC	CG
O		375.387-010	Fingerprint Classifier	AR	NA	AF	MC	CG

03 - NATURE

03.04 - ELEMENTAL WORK: NATURE

	E	454.684-018	Logger, All-Round	AR	..	..	MC	..

04 - AUTHORITY

04.01 - SAFETY AND LAW ENFORCEMENT

	E	059.267-014	Intelligence Specialist	AR	NA	AF	MC	CG
O		168.167-010	Customs Patrol Officer	AR	NA	AF	MC	CG
O		375.117-010	Police Chief	AR	NA	AF	MC	CG
O		375.167-026	Harbor Master	AR	NA	AF	MC	CG
O		375.167-034	Police Captain, Precinct	AR	NA	AF	MC	CG
O		375.167-042	Special Agent	AR	NA	AF	MC	CG
	E	375.263-014	Police Officer 1	AR	NA	AF	MC	CG
	E	375.263-018	State-Highway Police Officer	AR	NA	AF	MC	CG
	E	375.267-010	Detective	AR	NA	AF	MC	CG
	E	376.267-018	Investigator, Private	AR	NA	AF	MC	CG
O		377.117-010	Sheriff, Deputy, Chief	AR	NA	AF	MC	CG
O		377.137-014	Deputy Sheriff, Commander, Criminal, and Patrol Division	AR	NA	AF	MC	CG
O		377.167-010	Deputy Sheriff, Chief	AR	NA	AF	MC	CG
	E	377.263-010	Sheriff, Deputy	AR	NA	AF	MC	CG
	E	378.267-010	Counterintelligence Agent	AR	NA	AF	MC	CG

04.02 - SECURITY SERVICES

	E	372.667-018	Correction Officer	AR	NA	AF	MC	..
	E	372.667-034	Guard, Security	AR	NA	AF	MC	CG
	E	372.667-038	Merchant Patroller	AR	NA	AF	MC	CG
	E	373.364-010	Fire Fighter	AR	NA	AF	MC	CG
	E	373.367-010	Fire Inspector	AR	NA	AF	MC	CG
	E	373.663-010	Fire Fighter, Crash, Fire, and Rescue	AR	NA	AF	MC	CG

05 - MECHANICAL

05.01 - ENGINEERING

O	001.061-010	Architect	AR	NA	AF	..	CG
O	001.061-014	Architect, Marine	..	NA	..	..	CG
O	002.061-010	Aerodynamist	..	NA	AF	MC	CG
O	002.061-014	Aeronautical Engineer	..	NA	AF	MC	CG
O	002.061-018	Aeronautical Test Engineer	..	NA	AF	MC	CG
O	002.061-022	Aeronautical-Design Engineer	..	NA	AF	MC	CG
O	002.061-026	Aeronautical-Research Engineer	..	NA	AF	MC	CG
O	002.061-030	Stress Analyst	..	NA	AF	MC	CG
O	002.167-018	Aeronautical Project Engineer	..	NA	AF	MC	CG
O	003.061-010	Electrical Engineer	AR	NA	AF	MC	CG
O	003.061-030	Electronics Engineer	AR	NA	AF	MC	CG
O	003.061-034	Electronics-Design Engineer	AR	NA	AF	MC	CG
O	003.061-042	Electronics-Test Engineer	AR	NA	AF	MC	CG
O	003.167-062	Systems Engineer, Electronic Data Processing	AR	NA	AF	MC	CG
O	005.061-014	Civil Engineer	AR	NA	AF	..	CG
O	005.061-030	Sanitary Engineer	AR	NA	AF	..	CG
O	012.061-014	Safety Engineer	AR	NA	AF	MC	CG
O	012.067-010	Meteorologist	AR	NA	AF	MC	CG
O	012.167-022	Fire-Prevention Research Engineer	AR	NA	AF	MC	CG
O	012.167-026	Fire-Protection Engineer	AR	NA	AF	MC	CG
O	012.167-030	Industrial Engineer	AR	NA	AF	MC	CG
O	012.167-034	Industrial-Health Engineer	AR	NA	AF	MC	CG
O	012.167-042	Manufacturing Engineer	AR	NA	AF	MC	CG
O	012.167-046	Production Engineer	AR	NA	AF	MC	CG
O	012.167-050	Production Planner	AR	NA	AF	MC	CG
O	012.167-054	Quality-Control Engineer	AR	NA	AF	MC	CG
O	012.167-058	Safety Manager	AR	NA	AF	MC	CG
O	014.061-010	Design Engineer, Marine Equipment	..	NA	..	..	CG
O	014.061-014	Marine Engineer	..	NA	..	..	CG
O	014.061-018	Research Engineer, Marine Equip.	..	NA	..	..	CG
O	014.061-022	Test Engineer, Marine Equipment	..	NA	..	..	CG
O	014.167-014	Port Engineer	..	NA	..	..	CG
O	015.061-014	Nuclear Engineer	AR	NA	AF	MC	..
O	015.061-018	Research Engineer, Nuclear Equip.	AR	NA	AF	MC	..
O	018.167-018	Land Surveyor	AR	NA	AF	MC	CG
O	019.061-022	Ordnance Engineer	AR	NA	..	..	CG
O	019.167-010	Logistics Engineer	AR	NA	AF	MC	CG
O	079.021-010	Health Physicist	AR	NA	AF	..	CG
O	161.167-010	Management Analyst	AR	NA	AF	MC	CG

05.02 - MANAGERIAL WORK: MECHANICAL

O	018.167-022	Manager, Land Surveying	AR	NA	AF	MC	CG
O	181.117-010	Manager, Bulk Plant	AR	NA	AF	MC	CG
O	184.117-082	Superintendent, Communications	AR	NA	AF	MC	CG
O	184.167-062	Manager, Communications Station	AR	NA	AF	MC	CG

O		184.167-066	Manager, Flight Control	AR	NA	AF	MC	CG
O		184.167-174	Superintendent, Maintenance	AR	NA	AF	MC	CG
O		184.167-186	Superintendent, Marine Oil Terminal	AR	NA	AF	MC	CG
O		184.167-230	Supervisor of Communications	AR	NA	AF	MC	CG
O		184.167-266	Transportation-Maintenance Supv.	AR	NA	AF	MC	CG
O		189.167-038	Superintendent, Ammunition Storage	AR	NA	AF	MC	CG
O		193.167-018	Superintendent, Radio Comm.	AR	NA	AF	MC	CG
	E	914.167-014	Dispatcher, Oil	AR	NA	AF	MC	CG

05.03 - ENGINEERING TECHNOLOGY

	E	005.281-010	Drafter, Civil	AR	NA	AF	MC	CG
	E	005.281-014	Drafter, Structural	AR	NA	AF	MC	CG
O		012.167-062	Supervisor, Vendor Quality	AR	NA	AF	MC	CG
O		018.131-010	Supervisor, Cartography	AR	NA	AF	MC	CG
	E	018.167-010	Chief of Party	AR	NA	AF	MC	CG
	E	018.167-014	Geodetic Computer	AR	NA	AF	MC	CG
O		018.167-026	Photogrammetric Engineer	AR	NA	AF	MC	CG
	E	018.167-034	Surveyor Assistant, Instruments	AR	NA	AF	MC	CG
O	E	018.167-038	Surveyor, Geodetic	AR	NA	AF	MC	CG
	E	018.167-046	Surveyor, Marine	AR	NA	AF	MC	..
	E	018.261-010	Drafter, Cartographic	AR	NA	AF	MC	..
	E	018.261-014	Drafter, Topographical	AR	NA	AF	MC	..
	E	018.261-018	Editor, Map	AR	NA	AF	MC	..
	E	018.261-022	Mosaicist	AR	NA	AF	MC	..
	E	018.261-026	Photogrammetrist	AR	NA	AF	MC	..
	E	018.281-010	Stereo-Plotter Operator	AR	NA	AF	MC	..
O	E	168.267-054	Inspector, Industrial Waste	AR	NA	AF	MC	CG
O		184.167-026	Director, Photogrammetry Flight Operations	AR	NA	AF	MC	CG
	E	193.162-018	Air-Traffic-Control Spec., Tower	AR	NA	AF	MC	..
O		193.167-010	Chief Controller	AR	NA	AF	MC	..
	E	193.262-034	Radiotelephone Operator	AR	NA	AF	MC	CG
	E	193.362-014	Radio-Intelligence Operator	AR	NA	AF	MC	CG
	E	193.382-010	Electronic Intelligence Op. Spec.	AR	NA	AF	MC	CG
	E	194.282-010	Video Operator	AR	NA	AF	MC	..
O		196.167-014	Navigator	..	NA	AF	MC	CG
	E	199.361-010	Radiographer	..	NA	AF	MC	..
	E	621.261-018	Flight Engineer	..	NA	AF	MC	CG
	E	912.167-010	Dispatcher	AR	NA	AF	MC	..

05.04 - AIR AND WATER TRANSPORTATION

O		196.223-010	Instructor, Flying 1	AR	NA	AF	MC	CG
O		196.223-014	Instructor, Pilot	AR	NA	AF	MC	CG
O		196.263-014	Airplane Pilot, Commercial	AR	NA	AF	MC	CG
O		196.263-038	Helicopter Pilot	AR	NA	AF	MC	CG
O		196.263-042	Test Pilot	AR	NA	AF	MC	CG
	E	197.133-026	Pilot, Ship	AR	NA	AF	..	CG
	E	197.133-030	Tugboat Captain	AR	NA	AF	..	CG
O		197.167-010	Master, Ship	AR	NA	..	..	CG
	E	911.363-014	Quartermaster	AR	NA	AF	..	CG

05.05 - CRAFT TECHNOLOGY

O		077.127-014	Dietitian, Clinical	AR	NA	AF	..	..
O		077.127-018	Dietitian, Consultant	AR	NA	AF	..	..
	E	078.261-018	Orthotist	AR	..	AF	..	..
	E	078.361-022	Orthotics Assistant	AR	..	AF	..	..
	E	313.131-014	Chef	AR	NA	AF	MC	CG
	E	313.361-014	Cook	AR	NA	AF	MC	CG
	E	600.280-022	Machinist	AR	NA	AF	MC	CG
	E	600.280-042	Maintenance Machinist	AR	NA	AF	MC	CG
	E	620.261-010	Automobile Mechanic	AR	NA	AF	MC	CG
	E	620.261-022	Construction-Equipment Mechanic	AR	NA	AF	MC	CG
	E	620.281-010	Air-Conditioning Mechanic	AR	NA	AF	MC	CG
	E	620.281-058	Tractor Mechanic	AR	NA	AF	MC	CG
	E	620.381-014	Mechanic, Endless Track Vehicle	AR	NA	AF	MC	CG
	E	621.281-014	Airframe-And-Power-Plant Mechanic	AR	NA	AF	MC	CG
	E	623.281-026	Machinist, Marine Engine	AR	NA	AF	MC	CG
	E	623.281-034	Maintenance Mechanic, Engine	AR	NA	AF	..	CG
	E	623.281-038	Motorboat Mechanic	AR	NA	AF	MC	CG
	E	625.281-010	Diesel Mechanic	AR	NA	AF	MC	CG
	E	625.281-026	Gas-Engine Repairer	AR	NA	AF	MC	CG
	E	630.281-034	Service Mech., Compressed-Gas Eqp.	AR	NA	AF	MC	..
	E	631.261-014	Powerhouse Mechanic	AR	NA	AF	..	CG
	E	632.261-010	Aircraft-Armament Mechanic	AR	NA	AF	MC	CG
	E	632.261-014	Fire-Control Mechanic	AR	NA	AF	MC	CG
	E	632.281-010	Gunsmith	AR	NA	AF	MC	CG
	E	633.281-018	Office-Machine Servicer	AR	NA	..	MC	..
	E	633.281-030	Statistical-Machine Servicer	AR	NA	..	MC	..
	E	637.261-014	Environmental-Control-System Installer-Servicer	AR	NA	AF	MC	CG
	E	637.261-026	Refrigeration Mechanic	AR	NA	AF	MC	CG
	E	638-381-010	Fuel-System-Maintenance Worker	AR	NA	AF	MC	CG
	E	651.482-010	Offset-Press Operator 1	AR	NA	AF	MC	..
	E	710.281-026	Instrument Mechanic	AR	NA	AF	MC	..
	E	710.281-030	Instrument Technician	AR	NA	AF	MC	..
	E	711.281-014	Instrument Mechanic, Weapons Syst.	AR	NA	AF	MC	..
	E	712.381-018	Dental-Laboratory Technician	AR	NA	AF	..	CG
	E	712.381-034	Orthotics Technician	AR	..	AF	..	..
	E	713.361-014	Optician, Dispensing 1	AR	NA	..	..	..
	E	714.281-014	Camera Repairer	AR	NA	AF	MC	..
	E	714.281-018	Machinist, Motion-Picture Equip.	AR	NA	AF	MC	..
	E	714.281-022	Photographic Equipment Technician	AR	NA	AF	MC	..
	E	714.281-026	Photographic-Equipment-Maintenance Technician	AR	NA	AF	MC	..
	E	715.281-010	Watch Repairer	AR	NA	AF	MC	..
	E	716.280-014	Optician	AR	NA	..	..	..
	E	719.261-010	Biomedical Equipment Technician	AR	NA	AF	MC	CG
	E	719.261-014	Radiological-Equipment Specialist	AR	NA	AF	MC	CG
	E	721.281-018	Electric-Motor Repairer	AR	NA	AF	MC	CG
	E	729.281-010	Audio-Video Repairer	AR	NA	AF	MC	CG
	E	729.281-026	Electrical-Instrument Repairer	AR	NA	AF	MC	CG
	E	729.281-030	Electromedical-Equipment Repairer	AR	NA	AF	MC	CG

E	785.261-010	Alteration Tailor	AR	NA	AF	MC	..
E	785.361-014	Garment Fitter	AR	NA	AF	MC	..
E	785.361-022	Shop Tailor	AR	NA	AF	MC	..
E	801.361-014	Structural-Steel Worker	AR	NA	..	..	..
E	801.684-026	Reinforcing-Metal Worker	AR	NA	..	..	..
E	804.281-010	Sheet-Metal Worker	AR	NA	AF	MC	CG
E	805.261-014	Boilermaker 1	..	NA	..	..	CG
E	805.361-010	Boilerhouse Mechanic	..	NA	..	..	CG
E	806.261-026	Marine-Services Technician	AR	NA	..	..	CG
E	806.381-046	Shipfitter	AR	NA	..	..	CG
E	807.261-010	Aircraft Body Repairer	AR	NA	AF	MC	CG
E	807.381-010	Automobile-Body Repairer	AR	NA	AF	MC	..
E	810.384-014	Welder, Arc	AR	NA	AF	MC	CG
E	819.361-010	Welder-Fitter	AR	NA	AF	MC	CG
E	819.384-010	Welder, Combination	AR	NA	AF	MC	CG
E	820.261-014	Electrician, Powerhouse	AR	NA	AF	MC	CG
E	821.261-014	Line Maintainer	AR	NA	AF	MC	CG
E	821.361-010	Cable Installer-Repairer	AR	NA	AF	MC	CG
E	821.361-018	Line Erector	AR	NA	AF	MC	CG
E	821.361-026	Line Repairer	AR	NA	AF	MC	CG
E	822.261-010	Electrician, Office	AR	NA	AF	MC	CG
E	822.261-022	Station Installer-And-Repairer	AR	NA	AF	MC	CG
E	822.281-010	Automatic-Equipment Technician	AR	NA	AF	MC	CG
E	822.281-014	Central-Office Repairer	AR	NA	AF	MC	CG
E	822.281-018	Maintenance Mechanic, Telephone	AR	NA	AF	MC	CG
E	822.281-022	Private-Branch-Exchange Repairer	AR	NA	AF	MC	CG
E	822.361-010	Cable Tester	AR	NA	AF	MC	CG
E	822.361-014	Central-Office Installer	AR	NA	AF	MC	CG
E	822.381-014	Line Installer-Repairer	AR	NA	AF	MC	CG
E	822.381-018	Private-Branch-Exchange Installer	AR	NA	AF	MC	CG
E	823.261-018	Radio Mechanic	AR	NA	AF	MC	CG
E	823.281-010	Avionics Technician	AR	NA	AF	MC	CG
E	823.281-014	Electrician, Radio	AR	NA	AF	MC	CG
E	823.281-018	Meteorological-Equipment Repairer	AR	NA	AF	MC	CG
E	823.281-022	Rigger	AR	NA	AF	MC	CG
E	824.261-010	Electrician	AR	NA	AF	MC	CG
E	825.281-014	Electrician	..	NA	..	..	CG
E	825.281-018	Electrician, Airplane	AR	NA	AF	MC	CG
O	828.161-010	Supervisor, Electronics Systems Maintenance	AR	NA	..	..	CG
E	828.281-010	Electronics Mechanic	AR	NA	AF	MC	CG
E	829.281-014	Electrical Repairer	AR	NA	AF	MC	CG
E	829.281-022	Sound Technician	AR	NA	AF	MC	CG
E	829.361-010	Cable Splicer	AR	NA	AF	MC	CG
E	844.364-010	Cement Mason	AR	NA	AF	MC	..
E	860.381-022	Carpenter	AR	NA	AF	MC	CG
E	861.381-018	Bricklayer	AR	NA	AF	MC	..
E	862.261-010	Pipe Fitter	AR	NA	AF	MC	CG
E	862.381-018	Pipe Fitter	AR	NA	AF	MC	CG
E	862.381-030	Plumber	AR	NA	AF	MC	CG
E	869.281-010	Furance Installer-And-Repairer, Hot Air	AR	NA	AF	MC	CG

05.06 - SYSTEMS OPERATION

O	197.130-010	Engineer	AR	NA	..	..	CG
E	914.382-014	Pumper-Gager	AR	NA	AF	MC	CG
E	914.384-010	Gager	AR	NA	AF	MC	CG
E	950.382-010	Boiler Operator	AR	NA	AF	MC	CG
E	950.382-018	Gas-Engine Operator	AR	NA	AF	MC	CG
E	950.382-026	Stationary Engineer	AR	NA	AF	MC	CG
E	952.362-010	Auxiliary-Equipment Operator	AR	NA	AF	MC	CG
E	952.362-022	Power-Reactor Operator	AR	NA	AF	MC	CG
E	952.382-010	Diesel-Plant Operator	AR	NA	AF	MC	CG
E	954.382-010	Pump-Station Operator, Waterworks	AR	NA	AF	MC	CG
E	954.382-014	Water-Treatment-Plant Operator	AR	NA	AF	MC	CG
E	955.362-010	Wastewater-Treatment-Plant Op.	AR	NA	AF	MC	CG

05.07 - QUALITY CONTROL

E	011.261-018	Nondestructive Tester	..	NA	AF	MC	..
E	549.387-010	Cargo Inspector	AR	NA	AF	MC	CG
E	621.261-010	Airplane Inspector	AR	NA	AF	MC	CG

05.08 - LAND AND WATER VEHICLE OPERATION

E	903.683-018	Tank-Truck Driver	AR	NA	AF	MC	CG
E	904.383-010	Tractor-Trailer-Truck Driver	AR	NA	AF	MC	CG
E	905.663-014	Truck Driver, Heavy	AR	NA	AF	MC	CG
E	906.683-022	Truck Driver, Light	AR	NA	AF	MC	CG
E	911.663-010	Motorboat Operator	AR	NA	AF	..	CG
E	911.687-022	Deckhand	AR	NA	AF	..	CG

05.09 - MATERIAL   CONTROL

E	074.387-010	Pharmacy Helper	AR	NA	AF	..	CG
O	222.137-030	Shipping-And-Receiving Supervisor	AR	NA	AF	MC	CG
E	222.367-038	Magazine Keeper	AR	NA	AF	MC	CG
E	222.367-042	Parts Clerk	AR	NA	AF	MC	CG
E	222.387-026	Inventory Clerk	AR	NA	AF	MC	CG
E	222.387-034	Material Clerk	AR	NA	AF	MC	CG
E	222.387-050	Shipping And Receiving Clerk	AR	NA	AF	MC	CG
E	222.387-058	Stock Clerk	AR	NA	AF	MC	CG
E	222.387-062	Storekeeper	AR	NA	AF	MC	CG
E	248.367-018	Cargo Agent	AR	NA	AF	MC	CG
E	299.367-014	Stock Clerk, Self-Service Store	AR	NA	AF	MC	CG
E	782.684-042	Mender	AR	NA	AF	MC	..

05.10 - SKILLED HAND AND MACHINE WORK

E	194.262-010	Audio Operator	AR	NA	AF	MC	..
E	194.262-018	Sound Mixer	AR	NA	AF	MC	..
E	194.362-010	Recording Engineer	AR	NA	AF	MC	..
E	313.381-010	Baker	AR	NA	AF	MC	CG
E	313.381-030	Cook, School Cafeteria	AR	NA	AF	MC	CG
E	315.361-010	Cook	AR	NA	AF	MC	CG
E	316.681-010	Butcher, Meat	AR	NA	AF	MC	CG
E	316.684-018	Meat Cutter	AR	NA	AF	MC	CG

E	379.384-010	Scuba Diver	AR	NA	AF	MC	..
E	620.281-034	Carburetor Mechanic	AR	NA	AF	MC	CG
E	620.381-010	Automobile-Radiator Mechanic	AR	NA	AF	MC	CG
E	632.261-018	Ordnance Artificer	AR	NA	AF	MC	CG
E	720.281-018	Television-And-Radio Repairer	AR	NA	AF	MC	CG
E	729.281-022	Electric-Tool Repairer	AR	NA	AF	MC	CG
E	739.381-054	Survival-Equipment Repairer	AR	NA	AF	MC	CG
E	789.684-038	Parachute Mender	AR	NA	AF	MC	CG
E	829.261-014	Dental-Equip. Installer And Serv.	AR	NA	AF	MC	CG
E	845.381-014	Painter, Transportation Equipment	AR	NA	AF	MC	..
E	859.261-010	Blaster	AR	NA	AF	MC	..
E	862.381-010	Aircraft Mechanic, Plumbing and Hydraulics	AR	NA	AF	MC	CG
E	899.261-010	Diver	AR	NA	..	MC	CG
E	910.384-010	Tank-Car Inspector	AR	NA	AF	MC	CG
E	931.261-010	Blaster	AR	NA	AF	MC	..
E	962.382-010	Recordist	AR	NA	AF	MC	..
E	976.267-010	Quality-Control Technician	AR	NA	AF	MC	..
E	976.382-014	Color-Printer Operator	AR	NA	AF	MC	..
E	976.382-018	Film Developer	AR	NA	AF	MC	..
E	976.681-010	Developer	AR	NA	AF	MC	..

05.11 - EQUIPMENT OPERATION

E	850.683-010	Bulldozer Operator 1	AR	NA	AF	MC	..
E	850.683-030	Power-Shovel Operator	AR	NA	AF	MC	..
E	850.683-038	Scraper Operator	AR	NA	AF	MC	..
E	850.683-046	Utility-Tractor Operator	AR	NA	AF	MC	..
E	853.663-010	Asphalt-Paving-Machine Operator	AR	NA	AF	MC	..
E	853.663-014	Concrete-Paving-Machine Operator	AR	NA	AF	MC	..
E	859.362-010	Well-Drill Operator	AR	NA	..	MC	..
E	859.682-010	Earth-Boring-Machine Operator	AR	NA	AF	MC	..
E	859.683-010	Operating Engineer	AR	NA	AF	MC	..
E	859.683-030	Road-Roller Operator	AR	NA	AF	MC	..
E	869.683-014	Rigger	AR	NA	AF	MC	CG
E	911.663-014	Stevedore 1	AR	NA	AF	MC	CG
E	921.260-010	Rigger	AR	NA	AF	MC	CG
E	921.663-058	Tractor-Crane Operator	AR	NA	AF	MC	..
E	921.663-062	Truck-Crane Operator	AR	NA	AF	MC	CG
E	921.683-082	Winch Driver	AR	NA	AF	MC	CG

05.12 - ELEMENTAL WORK: MECHANICAL

O	079.164-010	Supervisor, Central Supply	AR	NA	AF	MC	CG
E	381.687-010	Central-Supply Worker	AR	NA	AF	MC	CG
E	869.687-026	Construction Worker 2	AR	..	..	MC	..
E	891.687-022	Tank Cleaner	AR	NA	AF	MC	CG
E	911.131-010	Boatswain	AR	NA	AF	..	CG
E	911.364-010	Able Seaman	AR	NA	AF	..	CG
E	911.364-014	Boat Loader 1	AR	NA	AF	..	CG
E	911.687-030	Ordinary Seaman	AR	NA	AF	..	CG
E	922.687-090	Stevedore 2	AR	NA	AF	MC	CG
E	929.687-030	Material Handler	AR	NA	AF	MC	CG

06 - INDUSTRIAL

06.01 - PRODUCTION TECHNOLOGY

E	600.380-018	Machine Set-Up Operator	AR	NA	AF	MC	CG
E	621.261-014	Engine Tester	AR	NA	AF	MC	CG
E	621.281-010	Air-Conditioning Check-Out Mechanic	AR	NA	AF	MC	CG
E	651.380-010	Printer 2	AR	NA	AF	MC	..
E	710.381-042	Instrument Mechanic	AR	NA	AF	MC	..
E	710.681-014	Calibrator 1	AR	NA	AF	MC	..
E	711.281-010	Inspector, Optical Instrument	AR	NA	AF	MC	..
O	726.130-010	Supervisor, Electronics	AR	NA	AF	MC	CG
E	726.281-014	Electronics Tester 1	AR	NA	AF	MC	..
E	806.261-010	Internal-Combustion-Engine Inspct.	AR	NA	AF	MC	CG
E	806.281-030	Inspector, Missile	AR	NA	AF	MC	CG
E	806.281-054	Tester, Plumbing Systems	AR	NA	AF	MC	CG
E	806.381-014	Aircraft Mechanic, Heat And Vent	AR	NA	AF	MC	CG
E	806.381-054	Skin Fitter	AR	NA	AF	MC	CG
E	819.281-018	Weld Inspector 1	AR	NA	AF	MC	CG
E	976.360-010	Print Controller	AR	NA	AF	MC	..

06.02 - PRODUCTION WORK

O	222.137-018	Magazine Supervisor	AR	NA	AF	MC	CG
E	552.362-014	Oxygen-Plant Operator	AR	NA	AF	MC	..
E	721.484-010	Electric-Motor Winder	AR	NA	AF	MC	CG
E	724.684-018	Armature Winder, Repair	AR	NA	AF	MC	CG
E	787.682-030	Mender	AR	NA	AF	MC	..

06.03 - PRODUCTION CONTROL

E	549.364-010	Tester, Compressed Gases	AR	NA	AF	MC	..
E	789.687-114	Parachute Inspector	AR	NA	AF	MC	CG

06.04 - ELEMENTAL WORK: INDUSTRIAL

E	549.587-010	Compressed-Gas-Plant Worker	AR	NA	AF	MC	..
E	559.665-030	Press Operator	AR	NA	AF	MC	..
E	653.685-010	Bindery Worker	AR	NA	AF	MC	..
E	782.684-010	Canvas Repairer	AR	NA	AF	MC	..
E	789.684-034	Parachute Folder	AR	NA	AF	MC	CG
E	912.684-010	Parachute Rigger	AR	NA	AF	MC	CG
E	914.667-010	Loader 1	AR	NA	AF	MC	CG
E	920.484-010	Crater	AR	NA	AF	MC	CG
E	920.587-018	Packager, Hand	AR	NA	AF	MC	CG
E	920.685-078	Packager, Machine	AR	NA	AF	MC	CG
E	921.683-050	Industrial-Truck Operator	AR	NA	AF	MC	CG
E	976.685-026	Print Developer, Automatic	AR	NA	AF	MC	..

07 - BUSINESS DETAIL

07.01 - ADMINISTRATIVE DETAIL

O		169.167-034	Manager, Office	AR	NA	..	..	CG
	E	201.362-010	Legal Secretary	AR	NA	..	MC	CG
	E	201.362-030	Secretary	AR	NA	..	MC	CG
	E	216.382-022	Budget Clerk	AR	NA	AF	MC	CG
	E	219.362-010	Administrative Clerk	AR	NA	AF	MC	CG
	E	243.362-010	Court Clerk	AR	NA	AF	MC	CG
	E	249.367-066	Procurement Clerk	AR	NA	AF	MC	CG

07.02 - MATHEMATICAL DETAIL

	E	210.382-010	Audit Clerk	AR	NA	AF	MC	CG
	E	210.382-014	Bookkeeper 1	AR	NA	AF	MC	CG
	E	215.482-010	Payroll Clerk	AR	NA	AF	MC	CG
	E	216.382-010	Accounting Clerk, Data Processing	AR	NA	AF	MC	CG
	E	216.382-034	Cost Clerk	AR	NA	AF	MC	CG
	E	216.382-062	Statistical Clerk	AR	NA	AF	MC	CG
	E	216.482-010	Accounting Clerk	AR	NA	AF	MC	CG

07.03 - FINANCIAL DETAIL

	E	243.367-014	Post-Office Clerk	AR	NA	AF	MC	CG

07.04 - ORAL COMMUNICATIONS

	E	193.262-022	Radio Officer	AR	NA	AF	MC	CG
	E	193.262-030	Radiotelegraph Operator	AR	NA	AF	MC	CG
	E	205.362-010	Civil-Service Clerk	AR	NA	AF	MC	CG
	E	205.362-014	Employment Clerk	AR	NA	AF	MC	CG
	E	205.362-018	Hospital-Admitting Clerk	AR	NA	AF	..	CG
	E	205.362-030	Outpatient-Admitting Clerk	AR	NA	AF	..	CG
	E	235.462-010	Central-Office Operator	AR	NA	AF	MC	..
	E	235.662-022	Telephone Operator	AR	NA	AF	MC	..
	E	238.362-010	Hotel Clerk	AR	NA	AF	MC	CG
	E	912.367-010	Flight-Information Expediter	AR	NA	AF	MC	CG

07.05 - RECORDS PROCESSING

	E	079.367-014	Medical Record Technician	AR	NA	AF	..	CG
	E	202.362-010	Shorthand Reporter	AR	NA	AF	MC	CG
	E	202.362-014	Stenographer	AR	NA	..	MC	CG
	E	202.362-022	Stenotype Operator	AR	NA	AF	MC	CG
	E	209.362-026	Personnel Clerk	AR	NA	AF	MC	CG
	E	219.367-034	Stock-Control Clerk	AR	NA	AF	MC	CG
	E	221.362-010	Aircraft-Log Clerk	AR	NA	AF	MC	CG
	E	221.367-066	Scheduler, Maintenance	AR	NA	AF	MC	..
O		222.137-038	Stock-Control Supervisor	AR	NA	AF	MC	CG
	E	238.167-010	Travel Clerk	AR	NA	AF	MC	CG
	E	238.362-014	Reservation Clerk	AR	NA	AF	MC	CG
	E	245.362-010	Medical-Record Clerk	AR	NA	AF	..	CG
	E	245.362-014	Ward Clerk	AR	NA	AF	..	CG
	E	248.367-010	Airplane-Dispatch Clerk	AR	NA	AF	MC	CG
	E	249.167-014	Dispatcher, Motor Vehicle	AR	NA	AF	MC	..
	E	912.367-014	Transportation Agent	AR	NA	AF	MC	CG

07.06 - CLERICAL MACHINE OPERATION

E	206.362-010	Clerk-Typist	AR	NA	AF	MC	CG
E	203.362-022	Word-Processing-Machine Operator	AR	NA	AF	MC	CG
E	203.582-018	Cryptographic-Machine Operator	AR	NA	AF	MC	CG
E	203.582-026	Data-Coder Operator	AR	NA	AF	MC	CG
E	203.582-030	Keypunch Operator	AR	NA	AF	MC	CG
E	203.582-050	Telegraphic-Typewriter Operator	AR	NA	AF	MC	CG
E	203.582-070	Verifier Operator	AR	NA	AF	MC	CG
E	203.582-078	Notereader	AR	NA	AF	MC	CG
O	213.132-010	Supervisor, Computer Operations	AR	NA	AF	MC	CG
E	213.362-010	Computer Operator	AR	NA	AF	MC	CG
E	213.382-010	Computer-Peripheral-Equip. Op.	AR	NA	AF	MC	CG

07.07 - CLERICAL HANDLING

E	209.562-010	Clerk, General	AR	NA	AF	MC	CG
E	248.362-014	Weather Clerk	AR	NA	AF	MC	CG

09 - ACCOMMODATING

09.01 - HOSPITALITY SERVICES

E	195.227-014	Recreation Leader	AR	..	AF	MC	..
E	352.367-010	Airplane-Flight Attendant	AR	NA	AF	MC	CG
E	352.377-010	Host/Hostess, Ground	AR	NA	AF	MC	CG

09.02 - BARBERING AND BEAUTY SERVICES

E	330.371-010	Barber	..	NA	..	..	CG

09.03 - PASSENGER SERVICES

E	913.463-010	Bus Driver	AR	NA	AF	MC	CG

09.04 - CUSTOMER SERVICES

E	290.477-014	Sales Clerk	AR	NA	AF	MC	CG

09.05 - ATTENDANT SERVICES

E	238.367-010	Gate Agent	AR	NA	AF	MC	CG

10 - HUMANITARIAN

10.01 - SOCIAL SERVICES

O		045.107-018	Director of Counseling	AR	NA	AF	MC	CG
O		045.107-022	Psychologist, Clinical	AR	NA	AF	..	..
O		045.107-026	Psychologist, Counseling	AR	NA	AF	..	..
O		045.107-046	Psychologist, Chief	AR	NA	AF	..	..
O		090.117-018	Dean of Students 1	AR	NA	AF	MC	CG
O		120.007-010	Clergy Member	AR	NA	AF	..	..
	E	129.107-018	Director of Religious Activities	AR	NA	AF	MC	CG
	E	187.167-198	Veterans Contact Representative	AR	NA	AF	MC	CG
	E	195.107-010	Caseworker	AR	NA	AF	MC	CG
O		195.107-022	Social Group Worker	AR	NA	AF	..	..
O		195.107-030	Social Worker, Medical	AR	NA	AF	..	..
O		195.107-034	Social Worker, Psychiatric	AR	NA	AF	..	..
O	E	195.267-014	Human Relations or Drug and Alcohol Counselor	AR	NA	AF	MC	CG
	E	195.367-034	Social-Services Aide	AR	NA	AF	MC	CG

10.02 - NURSING AND THERAPY SERVICES

O	075.117-018	Director, Educational, Community-Health Nursing	AR	NA	AF	MC	CG
O	075.121-010	Nurse, Instructor	AR	NA	AF	MC	CG
O	075.124-014	Nurse, Staff, Community Health	AR	NA	AF	..	..
O	075.127-018	Nurse, Head	AR	NA	AF	..	..
O	075.127-022	Nurse, Supervisor	AR	NA	AF	..	..
O	075.127-026	Nurse, Supervisor, Community-Health Nursing	AR	NA	AF	..	..
O	075.137-010	Nurse, Supervisor, Occupational Health Nursing	AR	NA	AF	..	..

10 - HUMANITARIAN

10.02 - NURSING AND THERAPY SERVICES

O		075.264-010	Nurse Practitioner	AR	NA	AF	..	..
O		075.264-014	Nurse-Midwife	AR	NA	AF	..	..
O		075.371-010	Nurse Anesthetist	AR	NA	AF	..	..
O		075.374-010	Nurse, General Duty	AR	NA	AF	..	..
O		075.374-014	Nurse, Office	AR	NA	AF	..	..
O		075.374-022	Nurse, Staff, Occupational Health Nursing	AR	NA	AF	..	..
O		076.121-010	Occupational Therapist	AR	NA	AF	..	..
O		076.121-014	Physical Therapist	AR	NA	AF	..	..
	E	076.224-010	Physical Therapist Assistant	AR	NA	AF	..	CG
	E	076.264-010	Physical-Integration Practitioner	AR	NA	AF	..	CG
	E	076.364-010	Occupational Therapy Assistant	AR	NA	AF	..	CG
	E	078.361-010	Dental Hygienist	AR	NA	AF	..	CG
	E	078.361-018	Nuclear Medical Technologist	AR	NA	AF	..	CG
	E	078.362-026	Radiologic Technologist	AR	NA	AF	..	CG
	E	079.361-010	Respiratory Therapist	AR	NA	AF	..	..
O	E	079.364-018	Physician Assistant	AR	NA	AF	..	CG
	E	079.374-014	Nurse, Licensed Practical	AR	NA	AF	..	..
	E	079.374-026	Psychiatric Technician	AR	NA	AF	..	..
O	E	153.227-014	Instructor, Physical	AR	NA	AF	MC	CG

10.03 - CHILD AND ADULT CARE

E	078.262-010	Pulmonary-Function Technician	AR	NA	AF	..	..
E	078.362-010	Audiometrist	AR	NA	AF	..	CG
E	078.362-018	Electrocardiograph Technican	AR	NA	AF	..	..
E	078.362-022	Electroencephalographic Tech.	AR	NA	AF	..	..
E	078.362-030	Cardiopulmonary Technologist	AR	NA	AF	..	..
E	079.364-014	Optometric Assistant	AR	NA	AF	..	..
E	079.367-010	Medical Assistant	AR	NA	AF	..	CG
E	079.371-010	Dental Assistant	AR	NA	AF	..	CG
E	079.374-010	Emergency Medical Technician	AR	NA	AF	..	CG
E	079.374-022	Surgical Technician	AR	NA	AF	..	CG
E	355.354-010	Physical Therapy Aide	AR	NA	AF	..	CG
E	355.374-014	Medication Aide	AR	NA	AF	..	CG
E	355.377-010	Occupational Therapy Aide	AR	NA	AF	..	CG
E	355.377-014	Psychiatric Aide	AR	NA	AF	..	..
E	355.674-014	Nurse Aide	AR	NA	AF	..	..
E	355.674-018	Orderly	AR	NA	AF	..	..
E	712.661-010	Orthopedic Assistant	AR	NA	AF	..	..

11 - SOCIAL/BUSINESS

11.01 - MATHEMATICS AND STATISTICS

O	E	012.167-066	Systems Analyst, Electronic Data Processing	AR	NA	AF	MC	CG
O		020.067-018	Operations-Research Analyst	AR	NA	AF	MC	CG
O	E	020.162-014	Programer, Business	AR	NA	AF	MC	CG
O		020.167-018	Programer, Chief, Business	AR	NA	AF	MC	CG
O		020.167-026	Statistician, Applied	AR	NA	AF	MC	CG
O		020.187-010	Programer, Information System	AR	NA	AF	MC	CG
O		109.067-010	Information Scientist	AR	NA	AF	MC	CG
O		161.117-014	Director, Records Management	AR	NA	AF	MC	CG
O		169.167-030	Manager, Electronic Data Processing	AR	NA	AF	MC	CG
	E	219.367-026	Programer, Detail	AR	NA	AF	MC	CG

11.02 - EDUCATION AND LIBRARY SERVICES

O		077.127-010	Community Dietitian	AR	NA	AF	..	..
O		090.227-010	Faculty Member, College or Univ.	AR	NA	AF	MC	CG
	E	097.227-014	Instructor, Vocational Training	AR	NA	AF	MC	CG
O		099.227-022	Instructor, Military Science	AR	NA	AF	MC	CG
O	E	166.227-010	Training Representative	AR	NA	AF	MC	CG

11.03 - SOCIAL RESEARCH

O		045.061-010	Psychologist, Developmental	AR	NA	AF	..	..
O		045.061-014	Psychologist, Engineering	AR	NA	AF	..	..
O		045.067-010	Psychologist, Educational	AR	NA	AF	..	..
O		045.067-014	Psychologist, Social	AR	NA	AF	..	..
O		045.067-018	Psychometrist	AR	NA	AF	..	..
O		045.107-030	Psychologist, Industrial-Org.	AR	NA	AF	..	..
O		052.067-022	Historian	AR	NA	AF	MC	CG
O		059.167-010	Intelligence Research Specialist	AR	NA	AF	MC	CG
O	E	059.267-010	Intelligence Specialist	AR	NA	AF	MC	CG
O		166.067-010	Occupational Analyst	AR	NA	AF	MC	CG
O	E	166.267-010	Employment Interviewer	AR	NA	AF	MC	CG
O		166.267-018	Job Analyst	AR	NA	AF	MC	CG
O	E	166.267-022	Prisoner-Classification Interviewer	AR	NA	AF	MC	CG
O	E	166.267-038	Personnel Recruiter	AR	NA	AF	MC	CG

11.04 - LAW

O		110.107-010	Lawyer	AR	NA	AF	MC	CG
O		110.107-014	Lawyer, Criminal	AR	NA	AF	MC	CG
O		110.117-018	Lawyer, Admiralty	AR	NA	AF	MC	CG
O		110.117-022	Lawyer, Corporation	AR	NA	AF	MC	CG
O		110.117-026	Lawyer, Patent	AR	NA	AF	MC	CG
O		110.117-038	Tax Attorney	AR	NA	AF	MC	CG
O		111.107-010	Judge	AR	NA	AF	MC	CG
	E	119.267-026	Paralegal Assistant	AR	NA	AF	MC	..

11.05 - BUSINESS ADMINISTRATION

	E	132.017-010	Editor, Managing, Newspaper	AR	NA	AF	MC	CG
O		162.157-038	Purchasing Agent	AR	NA	AF	MC	CG
O		162.167-022	Manager, Procurement Services	AR	NA	AF	MC	CG

O		163.167-026	Property-Disposal Officer	AR	NA	AF	MC	CG
O		166.117-010	Director, Industrial Relations	AR	NA	AF	MC	CG
O		166.117-018	Manager, Personnel	AR	NA	AF	MC	CG
O		166.167-030	Manager, Employment	AR	NA	AF	MC	CG
O		184.117-014	Director, Transportation	AR	NA	AF	MC	CG
O		184.117-038	Manager, Flight Operations	AR	NA	AF	MC	CG
O		184.117-042	Manager, Harbor Department	AR	NA	AF	MC	CG
O		184.117-050	Manager, Operations	AR	NA	AF	MC	CG
O		184.167-030	Director, Program	AR	NA	AF	MC	..
O		184.167-042	General Agent, Operations	AR	NA	AF	MC	CG
O		184.167-094	Manager, Traffic	AR	NA	AF	MC	CG
O		184.167-122	Port-Traffic Manager	AR	NA	AF	MC	CG
O		184.167-226	Superintendent, Transportation	AR	NA	AF	MC	CG
O		187.161-010	Executive Chef	AR	NA	AF	MC	CG
O		188.117-022	Civil Preparedness Officer	AR	NA	AF	MC	CG
O		188.167-066	Postmaster	AR	NA	AF	MC	..
O		189.117-030	Project Director	AR	NA	AF	..	CG
O		189.167-034	Security Officer	AR	NA	AF	MC	CG
O		189.167-050	Superintendent, Plant Protection	AR	NA	AF	MC	CG

11.06 - FINANCE

O		160.162-014	Auditor	AR	NA	AF	MC	CG
O		160.167-010	Accountant	AR	NA	AF	MC	CG
O		160.167-014	Accountant, Budget	AR	NA	AF	MC	CG
O		160.167-018	Accountant, Cost	AR	NA	AF	MC	CG
O		160.167-026	Accountant, Systems	AR	NA	AF	MC	CG
O		160.167-034	Auditor, Internal	AR	NA	AF	MC	CG
O		161.117-010	Budget Officer	AR	NA	AF	MC	CG
O		161.167-018	Manager, Records Analysis	AR	NA	AF	MC	CG
O		161.267-030	Budget Analyst	AR	NA	AF	MC	CG
O		186.117-014	Controller	AR	NA	AF	MC	CG
O		186.117-070	Treasurer, Financial Institution	AR	NA	AF	MC	CG

11.07 - SERVICES ADMINISTRATION

O		075.117-014	Director, Community-Health Nursing	AR	NA	AF	..	CG
O		075.117-022	Director, Nursing Service	AR	NA	AF	..	CG
O		075.117-030	Director, School of Nursing	AR	NA	AF	..	..
O		079.117-010	Emergency Medical Services Coord.	AR	NA	AF	..	CG
O		079.167-014	Medical-Record Administrator	AR	NA	AF	..	CG
O		090.117-010	Academic Dean	AR	NA	AF	MC	CG
O		090.117-026	Director, Extension Work	AR	NA	AF	MC	CG
O		090.167-010	Department Head, College or Univ.	AR	NA	AF	MC	CG
O		090.167-010	Director, Vocational Training	AR	NA	AF	MC	CG
O		099.117-010	Director, Educational Program	AR	NA	AF	MC	CG
O		099.117-026	Supervisor, Education	AR	NA	AF	MC	CG
O		099.167-018	Director, Instructional Material	AR	NA	AF	MC	CG
	E	099.167-022	Educational Specialist	AR	NA	AF	MC	CG
O		166.167-026	Manager, Education and Training	AR	NA	AF	MC	CG
O		169.127-010	Civil Preparedness Training Officer	AR	NA	AF	MC	CG
O		187.117-010	Administrator, Hospital	AR	NA	AF	..	CG
O		187.117-018	Director, Institution	AR	NA	AF	MC	CG
O		187.117-054	Superintendent, Recreation	AR	NA	AF	MC	..
O		187.117-058	Director, Outpatient Services	AR	NA	AF	..	CG

O		187.137-010	Recreation Supervisor	AR	NA	AF	MC	..
O		195.117-010	Administrator, Social Welfare	AR	NA	AF	MC	CG
O		195.167-042	Alcohol-And-Drug-Abuse-Assistance Program Administration	AR	NA	AF	..	..

11.08 - COMMUNICATIONS

	E	131.267-010	Newscaster	AR	NA	AF	MC	CG
	E	131.267-014	Newswriter	AR	NA	AF	MC	CG
	E	131.267-018	Reporter	AR	NA	AF	MC	CG
	E	132.017-014	Editor, Newspaper	AR	NA	AF	MC	CG
O	E	132.037-018	Editor, Department	AR	NA	AF	MC	CG
	E	132.267-014	Editorial Assistant	AR	NA	AF	MC	CG
O	E	137.267-010	Interpreter	AR	NA	AF	MC	CG
	E	137.267-018	Translator	AR	NA	AF	MC	..
O	E	199.267-014	Cryptanalyst	AR	NA	AF	MC	CG

11.09 - PROMOTION

O		165.067-010	Public-Relations Representative	AR	NA	AF	MC	CG
O		184.117-010	Director, Public Service	AR	NA	AF	MC	CG
O		188.117-106	Foreign-Service Officer	AR	NA	AF	MC	..

11.10 - REGULATIONS ENFORCEMENT

O		079.117-018	Sanitarian	AR	NA	AF	..	CG
O		079.161-010	Industrial Hygientist	AR	NA	AF	..	CG
O		168.167-014	Equal-Opportunity Representative	AR	NA	AF	MC	CG
	E	168.267-042	Food And Drug Inspector	AR	NA	AF	MC	CG
O	E	168.267-086	Hazardous-Waste Management Spec.	AR	NA	AF	MC	CG
O	E	529.137-014	Sanitarian	AR	NA	AF	MC	CG

11.11 - BUSINESS MANAGEMENT

O		184.167-058	Manager, Cargo-And-Ramp Services	AR	NA	AF	MC	CG
O		184.167-082	Manager, Station	AR	NA	AF	MC	CG
O		184.167-114	Manager, Warehouse	AR	NA	AF	MC	CG
O		184.167-118	Operations Manager	AR	NA	AF	MC	CG
O		184.167-182	Superintendent, Marine	AR	NA	AF	MC	CG
O		184.167-214	Superintendent, Terminal	AR	NA	AF	MC	CG
O	E	185.167-010	Commissary Manager	AR	NA	AF	MC	CG
O		185.167-018	Manager, Distribution Warehouse	AR	NA	AF	MC	CG
O	E	185.167-046	Manager, Retail Store	AR	NA	AF	MC	CG
O		187.117-042	Manager, Recreation Establishment	AR	NA	AF	MC	..
O		187.167-046	Executive Housekeeper	AR	NA	AF	..	CG
O		187.167-106	Manager, Food Service	AR	NA	AF	MC	CG
O		187.167-126	Manager, Liquor Establishment	AR	NA	AF	MC	CG

11.12 - CONTRACTS AND CLAIMS

O		162.117-014	Contract Administrator	AR	NA	AF	MC	CG
O		162.117-018	Contract Specialist	AR	NA	AF	MC	CG

12 - PHYSICAL PERFORMING

12.01 - SPORTS

	E	153.227-018	Instructor, Sports	AR	NA	AF	MC	CG

APPENDIX B
Work Activities

Everyone has preferences for certain types of activities. These preferences may be shown in leisure-time activities or tasks one does as part of a job. Activity preferences are part of the interests that people have - the things they like and enjoy doing. Interests play an important role in a person's career satisfaction and success. They are related to motivation. People are more likely to do a task better if they like what they are doing than if they do not enjoy the activity.

The tasks performed by workers can be grouped into ten broad types of activities. These ten types of work activities also are related to nonwork activities. Therefore, you have experienced many of them. By assessing how you feel about your experiences, you can project how you might feel about doing similar types of activities in a work situation. These activities have been related to the 66 Worker Trait Groups to help you in career exploration.

The following is a listing and brief description of the ten types of work activities.

1. Things and Objects:

Workers do physical work with things and objects such as materials, products, tools, instruments, machines, and vehicles. The tasks they do may be complex and involve adjusting, testing, and researching. Such precision work uses knowledge and judgment in making decisions. Working with things and objects also involves less complex tasks such as handling, driving, and operating.

2. Business Contact:

Workers make contact with people to buy, sell, talk, listen, promote, and negotiate. They gather, exchange, or present ideas and facts. A wide variety of businesses that provide services or products use business contact workers. Business contact also involves giving instructions, leading a work activity, managing, and supervising.

3. Tasks of A Routine, Definite Nature:

Workers repeat the same tasks over and over, usually each cycle takes a short period of time. The work is most often organized to get the most done in a short period of time. Work assignments and methods are set up in advance with little opportunity for making decisions.

4. Direct Personal Contact to Help or Instruct Others:

Workers help people improve or maintain their physical, mental, emotional, or spiritual well-being. They also teach, train, or help people in other ways. Workers use communication skills and knowledge of human growth and development. Also included is working with animals to help them or change their behavior.

5. Recognition or Appreciation From Others:

Workers gain recognition and prestige through leading or managing the work of others. Involvement in acting, sports, art, or music also provides status. Workers gain recognition and appreciation in a leadership position, or performing where their work and skills are viewed by the public.

6. Communication of Ideas and Information:

Workers communicate ideas and information to people through writing, acting, music, or other artistic forms. They need to be perceptive (sensitive) and understand the interests, needs, and desires of others. Their involvement with people may be indirect such as through radio, TV, or the newspaper. Or, their involvement with people may be direct such as in educational, financial, sales, law, or social services.

7. Tasks of A Scientific and Technical Nature:

Workers conduct research and analyze, evaluate, explain, and record scientific information. Also involved is the technical application of scientific knowledge in practical ways. Workers use scientific instruments and equipment in their work.

8. Creative Thinking:

Workers use complex mental skills and thinking processes to create new knowledge or new ways to apply what is known. They express ideas, feelings, and moods. They also use imagination to create ideas, solve difficult problems, or design projects and methods.

9. Processes, Methods, or Machines:

Workers are involved with processes and methods and use machines and instruments in their work. Their major work tasks involve planning, scheduling, processing, controlling, and evaluating data and things.

10. Working On or Producing Things:

Workers are involved in making or creating things. They also may use their skills to repair, alter, or restore something that is old, damaged, or that needs to be changed. Products may be handcrafted or produced using equipment, tools, and machines. Workers may create products from ideas and they may be involved in writing, designing, or other artistic expression. They feel a degree of identification with their work and pride in their craftsmanship. Working on products that are mass produced is not included.

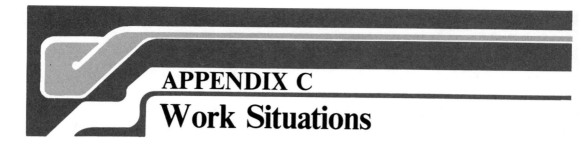

APPENDIX C
Work Situations

Career satisfaction and/or successful job performance involves more than knowledge and skills and liking what you do. Workers must be willing to adapt to or cope with the many kinds of situations they encounter on their jobs. The personal traits related to a worker's ability to adapt to *work situations* are called *temperaments*.

Occupations differ in the situations involved. These situations can be grouped into ten broad types, which can also be related to non-work experiences. Therefore, you can review the many kinds of experiences you have had. Look at those you liked or disliked in terms of the situations involved and what caused you to feel the way you did. You can then look for or avoid similar work and nonwork experiences.

The ten types of work situations are related to the 66 Worker Trait Groups. You can use your feelings about the types of situations to identify Worker Trait Groups that involve situations you wish to avoid or those that you like.

The following is a listing and brief description of the ten types of work situations.

1. Perform Duties Which Change Frequently:

Workers perform a variety of duties, often changing from one task to another. This change in job tasks requires workers to use different skills, knowledge, and abilities. They may need to use different materials or methods, change work locations, or be involved with people in a different way.

2. Perform Routine Tasks:

Workers do the same tasks every day with little or no opportunity for change. Work assignments can be completed in a short period of time and follow a specified method or sequence. Very little judgment is involved. Sometimes a machine sets the pace of the work.

3. Plan and Direct an Entire Activity:

Workers are responsible for planning, directing, or controlling an entire activity, project, or program. As leaders, they are responsible for making decisions and supervising the work of others. They must keep up-to-date on information about their work.

4. Deal With People:

Workers interact with people at a higher level than giving or receiving instructions. This interaction is a major job responsibility. The ability to meet people and cooperate with other workers is important. This must be done in a pleasant and friendly manner.

5. Influence People's Opinions, Attitudes, and Judgments:

Workers influence others by changing their thinking and behavior. They must be able to understand and communicate with people. They influence how others feel about a product, service, an issue, or other people. Influencing people may be through direct contact or indirect through a form of media.

6. Work Under Pressure:

Workers deal with situations that involve potential danger or risk. They must have the ability to work under stress and tension. They must be able to maintain self-control and take decisive action in unexpected or critical situations. Workers must be able to do job tasks well in emergencies. Working speed and sustained attention also are important.

7. Make Decisions Using Personal Judgment:

Workers make evaluations and decisions. They use personal judgment or sensory data received from one or more of the physical senses. The worker relies on knowledge gained from experience and aesthetic values. Decisions may need to be made without specific information or proof and with the outcome uncertain.

8. Make Decisions Using Standards That Can Be Measured or Checked:

Workers make decisions based upon information or standards that can be measured or checked. Decisions are made on concrete evidence and are not open to personal interpretation. Where judgment is needed, facts and set standards are used to make decisions.

9. Interpret and Express Feelings, Ideas, or Facts:

Workers express their concept of a feeling, idea, or fact from a personal point of view. They use creativity, self-expression, and imagination to develop and communicate their views through writing, music, or some form of art. Some workers focus on the process they use to communicate, such as speaking, singing, or acting. Others communicate through such products as photographs, designs, poems, prose writings, songs, or paintings.

10. Work Within Precise Limits or Standards of Accuracy:

Workers must pay strict attention to details and be very precise and thorough in their work. Tasks must be completed within exact standards. Standards may include precise body movements, use of words, time limits, size, weight, or accuracy of math computations. The quality of the product, service, or work task is directly related to the performance of the worker.

APPENDIX D
Data-People-Things

All work may be described in relation to three basic elements – data, people, and things. Every work task involves each element to some extent. There are two kinds of involvement: (1) *orientation* – the amount of time the worker is involved, and (2) *complexity* – the level or degree of difficulty of the involvement. The degree of difficulty is related to the level of knowledge and skill needed to perform the work task.

The orientation (time) involvement with data, people, and things differs by occupation. For example, teachers spend a large part of their time working with people, but plumbers do not. Also, the complexity (level) of involvement may differ from the amount of time spent. For example, toll collectors spend a large amount of contact time with people, but at a very low level.

All occupations have been rated on the highest level of involvement workers have with data, people, and things. It is assumed that workers who can perform work tasks at a highly complex level can also perform tasks at lower levels. For example, if workers can solve math problems they can copy them. Thus, only the most difficult levels of data, people, and things need to be identified. Successful performance at lower levels can be assumed.

The following provides a definition of each element and a description of each level of complexity from high to low. Note that *the lower the number assigned, the higher the level of complexity.*

DATA

Definition:

Data include information, knowledge, and ideas about known facts, people, animals, or objects such as materials, machines, and products. Data may be gathered, observed, investigated, interpreted, and thought about. Data cannot be touched or handled. However, data can be expressed in numbers, spoken and written words, symbols, or in the form of thoughts and ideas.

Levels of Data Involvement:

Rated on a scale of 0 (most difficult) to 6 (simplest).

0 – Synthesizing:

Examine and evaluate information to develop logical conclusions or interpretations of ideas or fact.

1 – Coordinating:

Determining the time, place, and order of operations or actions to be performed. Also includes carrying out and/or reporting on actions decided upon.

2 – Analyzing:

Examining and determining the value of data, which sometimes results in a need to choose the best course of action to be taken.

3 – Compiling:

Gathering information and putting it together in proper order. Frequently involves reporting and/or carrying out activities indicated by the information.

4 – Computing:

Performing arithmetic operations. Also may include reporting results or carrying out activities as indicated by the results.

5 – Copying:

Transcribing data (rewriting from other copy or from shorthand notes), or posting data (entering it in ledgers or account books).

6 – Comparing:

Judging events or situations according to what can be readily observed such as actions, appearances, and differences from the usual.

PEOPLE

Definition:

People, as used in defining work functions, also include animals when they are given care and consideration similar to that given human beings.

Levels of People Involvement:

Rated on a scale of 0 (most difficult) to 8 (simplest).

0 – Mentoring:

Dealing with people in terms of their total personality to advise or counsel them on problems. This is accomplished by using principles of law, science, medicine, religion, or education.

1 – Negotiating:

Exchanging ideas, information, and opinions with others to make policies, plan programs, and/or arrive jointly at decisions, conclusions, or solutions.

2 – Instructing:

Teaching subject matter to others or training others (including animals) through explaining, demonstrating, or supervised practice.

3 – Supervising:

Determining or explaining work procedures for a group of workers and assigning tasks to them. Encouraging workers to get along well with each other and to do their best work.

4 – Diverting:

Amusing others.

5 – Persuading:

Influencing the feelings of others about a product, service, or opinion.

6 – Speaking/Signaling:

Talking with and/or signaling people to give or exchange information. Assigning tasks or giving directions to helpers or assistants.

7 – Serving:

Attending to the requests or needs of people or animals. Carrying out the wishes of people, either expressed or understood without being expressed. Immediate response is involved.

8 – Taking Instructions:

Carrying out work instructions or orders of supervisor. Immediate response is not necessarily involved.

THINGS

Definition:

Things are lifeless objects as distinguished from people or animals. This includes such substances as materials, machines, tools, equipment, and products. They have shape, form, weight, and texture and can be touched or handled.

Levels of Things Involvement:

Rated on a scale of 0 (most difficult) to 7 (simplest).

0 – Setting Up:

Adjusting machines or equipment by replacing or altering jigs, fixtures, and attachments. Adjusting is done to prepare machines or equipment to perform their functions, change their performance, or restore their proper functioning if there is a breakdown.

1 – Precision Working:

Using parts of the body and tools to work, guide, or place objects or materials in such a way that rigid standards for the product or process will be met. Precision workers use considerable judgment to select the right tools, objects, or materials and to apply them correctly.

2 – Operating/Controlling:

Starting, stopping, controlling, and adjusting machines or equipment designed to manufacture and/or process products or materials.

3 – Driving/Operating:

Starting, stopping, and controlling machines or equipment to manufacture, process, and/or move things or people. (This does not include machines powered by hand such as handtrucks and dollies, or such machines as electric wheelbarrows or handtrucks.)

4 – Manipulating:

Using tools, special devices, or parts of the body to work, move, guide, or place objects or materials. Workers use some judgment to maintain the needed degree of accuracy and to select the proper tools, objects, or materials. However, such judgments are usually not difficult to make.

5 – Tending:

Starting, stopping, and watching the operation of machines and equipment. It may involve adjusting materials or controls of machines. Little judgment is involved in making these adjustments.

6. Feeding/Offbearing:

Throwing, dumping, inserting, or feeding materials into or removing them from machines or equipment. These machines or equipment may be automatic or may be tended or operated by other workers.

7 – Handling:

Using parts of the body, handtools, and/or special devices to work, move, or carry objects or materials. Little or no judgment is involved in meeting standards or in selecting the proper tools, objects, or materials.

DATA — PEOPLE — THINGS STRUCTURE

Level		Data	People	Things
Difficult **High**		0 Synthesizing 1 Coordinating 2 Analyzing	0 Mentoring 1 Negotiating 2 Instructing	0 Setting-Up 1 Precision Working
Average		3 Compiling 4 Computing	3 Supervising 4 Diverting 5 Persuading	2 Operating - Controlling 3 Driving - Operating 4 Manipulating
Low **Simple**		5 Copying 6 Comparing	6 Speaking - Signaling 7 Serving 8 Taking Instructions - Helping	5 Tending 6 Feeding - Offbearing 7 Handling

A nine digit code is included with each occupational title in the list of occupations at the end of each Worker Trait Group description. The middle three digits of the code represent the data, people, and things level of the occupation as illustrated below.

Telephone Solicitor

299.357-014
/ ↑ \
Data – People – Things

In the example above for Telephone Solicitor, the highest level of *data* is 3 (compiling), *people* 5 (persuading), and *things* 7 (handling). The code numbers for data, people, things always indicate the highest level of involvement a worker has with each element. However, a worker also may be involved at lower levels. The following table shows the data, people, and things levels of involvement for each code number.

The table also groups the data, people, and things levels into high, average, and low. These are the level designations used in this book to represent the levels of data, people, and things for each Worker Trait Group as reported in the Qualifications Profile. For example, the data-people-things chart for WTG 01.01 is shown below.

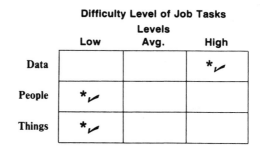

Difficulty Level of Job Tasks

	Levels		
	Low	**Avg.**	**High**
Data			*✓
People	*✓		
Things	*✓		

APPENDIX E
Physical Demands and Working Conditions

Physical demands are the moving and sensing needs of an occupation. Working conditions are the surroundings of a worker in a job setting. The physical demands and working conditions make specific demands on a worker. In addition to job knowledge and skills, workers must have the physical abilities to perform major work tasks and be able to cope with the environmental conditions.

PHYSICAL DEMANDS

In addition to physical strength and coordination, the five physical senses of sight, hearing, touch, taste, and smell are used in varying degrees in performing work tasks. Many workers' disabilities or limitations may be corrected or compensated for by modifying work tasks or through the use of special equipment or apparatus.

The most important physical strength activities associated with occupations are lifting, carrying, pushing, and pulling. If a worker is able to perform one, they are generally able to do them all. The strength capacities of workers are divided into the following levels of work requirements.

S – Sedentary Work:

Usually involves sitting, but also may involve walking and standing. Objects involved in work tasks generally weigh less than ten pounds.

L – Light Work:

Objects involved in work tasks usually weigh less than twenty pounds. Work tasks may involve frequent lifting and carrying of objects up to ten pounds. Work is considered light even if a lot of walking or standing is required. Some jobs may involve sitting most of the time while using arms and legs for pushing and pulling.

M – Medium Work:

Lifting objects weighing up to fifty pounds is involved. Also, frequent lifting and carrying of objects weighing up to twenty-five pounds is usually involved.

H – Heavy Work:

Lifting objects weighing up to one hundred pounds is involved. Frequent lifting and carrying of objects up to fifty pounds is usually involved.

V – Very Heavy Work:

Lifting objects weighing more than one hundred pounds and frequent lifting and carrying of objects weighing fifty pounds or more.

WORKING CONDITIONS

Workers must be able to cope with the environmental conditions involved in a work setting. These may include heat, cold, wet, humid, noise, vibrations, odors, dust, or other conditions which may make the worker uncomfortable. Also included are conditions that expose workers to the risk of bodily injury. The setting of work performed - inside or outside - controls some of the major working conditions. The following are used to define inside and outside settings associated with occupations and Worker Trait Groups.

I – Inside:

Where workers spend seventy-five percent or more of their time on work tasks inside. This may provide protection from the sun, rain, snow, and wind, but not always from temperature changes.

O – Outside:

Where workers spend seventy-five percent or more of their time on work tasks outside, with little effective protection from weather conditions.

B – Both:

Where workers spend about half of their time inside and half outside.

Educational Skills

Educational skills are important considerations in career planning. Three types of information are provided with each Worker Trait Group description. This will help you identify the related skills and educational programs needed to prepare for work in each group. These are briefly described below.

SKILLS AND ABILITIES

The most important skills and abilities needed by occupations in each Worker Trait Group are listed and defined in response to the question "What Skills and Abilities Would Help You Succeed in This Kind of Work?" All of the skills and abilities listed do not apply for each occupation. As you explore an occupation you need to identify those needed.

PREPARATION

Basic information on preparation for occupations in each Worker Trait Group is provided in response to the question "How Can You Prepare for This Type of Work?" The general amount of training and experience related to most of the occupations in each group is identified. The most common way to prepare for the field is described. Also included is a listing of related educational programs and courses.

GENERAL EDUCATIONAL DEVELOPMENT

In the Qualifications Profile section of each Worker Trait Group description is a chart that shows the general level of educational skills needed by most occupations in the group. As an example, the chart from 01.01 is shown below.

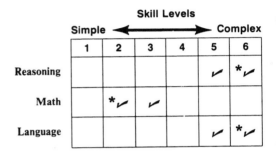

These educational skills are called *General Educational Development (GED)*. GED is education of a general academic nature that does not have a specific occupational objective. It is usually obtained in elementary and high school and in college. However, it may be acquired from experience and self-directed study. GED as used in the Worker Trait Group Guide is not related to the GED high school equivalency testing program.

General Educational Development refers to the educational background that helps increase a worker's reasoning, math, and language skills. These are briefly described below.

Reasoning Development:

The ability to understand concepts and systems, solve problems, and exercise judgment. Also includes the ability to understand and carry out instructions as well as to adapt to social and work environments.

Mathematical Development:

Attaining basic math skills such as solving arithmetic, algebraic, and geometric problems. Also included at the higher levels is the application of statistical and mathematical concepts to the analysis and evaluation of data and to research.

Language Development:

Acquiring language skills such as mastery of an extensive vocabulary and use of correct sentence structure, punctuation, and spelling. Also included at the higher levels is the appreciation of literature and the application of language skills to persuasive or effective speaking, composition and logic, and creative and narrative writing.

The level of reasoning, math, and language skills for each Worker Trait Group has been reported on a six level scale from 1 (simple skills) to 6 (complex skills). These skill levels, as represented by typical curriculums in schools throughout the United States, are related to the following educational levels.

Level 1: grades one to three.

Level 2: grades four to six.

Level 3: grades seven and eight.

Level 4: grades nine to twelve.

Level 5: college years one and two.

Level 6: college years three and four.

APPENDIX G
Aptitudes

Aptitude is the quickness or ease with which you can learn to do something. There are different types of aptitudes. Some aptitudes make it easy for you to understand a novel or solve math problems. Others are concerned with doing very fine work with your hands or fingers. Some other aptitudes are used in tasks requiring fast and accurate body movements. Still other aptitudes make seeing differences in size or shape quick and easy. Knowing as much as possible about your aptitudes can help you in career exploration and planning.

People differ from one another in aptitude just as they differ in looks, height, weight, or interests. You may be able to learn some things quite easily. Other things may be more difficult for you to learn. For example, only a few people become basketball stars, get the lead in a class play, or an "A" in physics.

There are nine aptitudes related to occupations and to Worker Trait Groups. The aptitudes significant to the Worker Trait Groups are included as part of the Qualifications Profile section of each Worker Trait Group description. The aptitude level or levels needed for average successful performance are also reported. The following statements describe the nine aptitudes.

G – General:

Understanding instructions, facts, and underlying reasonings. Being able to reason and make judgments. Closely related to school achievement.

V – Verbal:

Understanding meanings of words and ideas. Using them to present information or ideas clearly.

N – Numerical:

Doing arithmetic operations quickly and correctly.

S – Spatial:

Looking at flat drawings or pictures of objects and forming mental images of them in three dimensions - height, width, and depth.

P – Form Perception:

Observing detail in objects or drawings. Noticing differences in shapes or shadings.

Q – Clerical Perception:

Observing details and recognizing errors in numbers, spelling, and punctuation in written materials, charts, and tables. Avoiding errors when copying materials.

K – Motor Coordination:

Using eyesight and coordinating the movement of hands and fingers to perform a task rapidly and correctly.

F – Finger Dexterity:

Moving the fingers to work with small objects rapidly and correctly.

M – Manual Dexterity:

Moving the hands with ease and skill. Working with the hands in placing and turning motions.

LEVELS OF APTITUDES

There are five levels of aptitudes. These levels represent the aptitudes of the adult working population. The following statements describe the five aptitude levels.

Level 1:

The top ten percent of the population - a very high degree of aptitude.

Level 2:

The rest of the highest third of the population, not including the highest ten percent - an above average or high degree of the aptitude.

Level 3:

The middle third of the population - an average or medium degree of the aptitude.

Level 4:

The lowest third of the population, but not including the lowest ten percent - a below average or low degree of the aptitude.

Level 5:

The lowest ten percent of the population - a very low degree of the aptitude.

APPENDIX H
Acknowledgments

The *Worker Trait Group Guide,* Revised Edition, was developed by the Appalachia Educational Laboratory (AEL) under the direction of David W. Winefordner, Director, Division of Career Guidance.

AEL staff member Phyllis Stowers served as writer/editor for the development of this publication. Her contributions to the Revised Edition reflect twenty years of work at AEL in assisting with the research and development of career guidance materials. She was involved in the development of the original *Worker Trait Group Guide* and has been a major contributor to this revision.

Many others contributed to the development of the Revised Edition. Rex Clay, Executive Director, West Virginia Occupational Information Coordinating Committee, provided technical and data processing assistance for the development of the core occupations and base data included in the Qualifications Profiles. Todd Strohmenger, an AEL staff member, also provided data processing technical assistance. Walter Adams, Charleston, West Virginia, served as a consultant and assisted in the development of educational information. Don Winefordner, teacher at Andrew Jackson Junior High School, Kanawha County, West Virginia, served as a summer intern with the project and assisted in the writing of Career Area and Worker Trait Group descriptions.

It is impossible to personally acknowledge all AEL staff and consultants who contributed to the development of the original Worker Trait Group Guide. In addition, there have been hundreds of significant contributors over the past half century to the research, development, and publication of the *Dictionary of Occupational Titles (DOT).* The *Worker Trait Group Guide* is based upon this original research and development work.

Beginning with the first edition, published in 1939, the DOT has been the most widely used reference resource on occupations. The continuous program of research and occupational analysis of the U.S. Department of Labor has resulted in major improvements with each new edition. In addition to the expansion and refinement of information, coding and occupational grouping structures have been developed that make the information more usable for career exploration and decision-making as well as for employment placement.

The most notable of the DOT changes resulted from the functional job analysis research that led to the development of the Worker Trait Group structure. This structure changed the focus of work from products and services to the workers and what they do. This research identified the significant work factors and worker characteristics related to worker satisfaction and successful performance of job tasks. The Worker Trait Group structure was incorporated into the third edition of the DOT in 1965.

In the early 1970's, as part of the cooperative efforts between the Department of Labor, the National Institute of Education, and the Department of Education, the Appalachia Educational Laboratory (AEL) was

486

funded to develop techniques, procedures, and materials for improving the use of the DOT Worker Trait Group structure in educational settings.

Some of the AEL work was incorporated into the fourth edition revision of the DOT. The major AEL contributions were: the separation of the Worker Trait Group structure from the DOT into a separate publication, the *Guide for Occupational Exploration (GOE);* and changes in the format, reading level, and content to make the publication "client centered" and more usable for career exploration and planning.

In addition to assisting the Department of Labor with the development of the GOE, AEL developed a separate publication, the *Worker Trait Group Guide.* This Guide focused on the career exploration and educational planning needs of students in educational settings.

After ten years of successful use of the *Worker Trait Group Guide* by youth and adults in a variety of settings, this Revised Edition (1988) of the Guide contains many improvements and additions. These changes focus on a more friendly user format; expanded Career Area and Worker Trait Group descriptions; identification of programs and courses related to exploring or preparing for occupations in each WTG; and a refinement of the "core" occupations to include all occupations with military counterparts and the most common occupations in state career information delivery systems.

Illustrations have been selected to show work activities and work situations. Most of these came from the author's and the publisher's extensive files, but a number were obtained from firms and associations in various occupational fields. Following is a list of Worker Trait Groups and those who supplied photographs. Their cooperation and helpfulness contribute significantly to the usefulness of this book.

01.01	Hershey Foods Corporation
	Illinois Wesleyan University (Drama)
01.02	American Greetings (Cartoonist)
	Kemper Group (Merchandise Display)
	Tribute Company (Designer)
01.03	Tribune Company (Clown)
	Illinois Wesleyan University (Drama)
	Tribune Company (TV Production)
01.04	Impact Communications (Composer)
01.05	Buddy Myers (Dance)
01.06	Arvin/Calspan, AEDC Division (Model maker)
	Amir Pishdahl, Media General, Inc. (Lasar Scanner)
	Tribune Company (Stripper)
01.07	Illinois State University (Ring Conductor)
01.08	Impact Communications (Modeling Instructor) (Models)
	Michael Jenkins (Model)
02.01	British Petroleum Company, p.l.c. (Geologist)
02.02	Campbell Soup Co.,/Mark Seliger (Botanist)
	The Catfish Institute (Food Technologists)
	Illinois Department of Conservation (Pathologist)
02.04	The Kroger Company (Pharmacist)
03.01	The Catfish Institute (Fish farmer)
	Illinois Department of Conservation (Game farm manager)

03.02	Illinois Department of Conservation (Fish Hatchery)
	Illinois Department of Conservation (Tree Seedlings)
	Illinois Department of Conservation (Log markings)
03.04	Illinois Department of Conservation (Log Stacker)
	The Catfish Institute (Harvesting Fish)
	Illinois Department of Conservation (Free-flight pen)
04.01	Illinois Department of Conservation (Officer Training)
	The British Petroleum Company, p.l.c. (Fire Team)
	Illinois Department of Conservation (Game Warden)
05.01	Motorola, Inc. (Aeronautical Engineer)
	The Upjohn Company (Chemical Engineer)
	Tracor, Inc. (Submarine Engineers)
	Sealed Power Corporation, Tim Bieber (Electronics Test Engineer)
05.03	Sun Company, Inc. (Geodetic Surveyor) (Mine Surveyor)
05.04	Tracor, Inc. (Ship's Pilot)
05.05	Houston Industries, Inc., Bryant Smothers, Photographer (Linemen)
	Tribune Company (Multi-Color Press Control Panel)
05.06	Alexander Baldwin, Inc. (Switchboard)
	Great American Savings Bank (Stationary Engineer)
	Sun Company, Inc. (Oil Pumper)
05.07	Impact Communications (Service Manager, Elevator Examiner)
05.09	Reynolds Aluminum (Inventory Clerk)
	Illinois Power Company (Meter Reader)
05.10	Rohr Industries, Inc. (Aircraft Mechanic)
05.11	Mapco, Inc. (Long-Wall Mining Machine)
05.12	Sonoco Products Company, David Dobbs (Truck Driver's Helper)
06.01	Phillips Petroleum Company (Refinery Operator)
	Rohr Industries, Inc. (Aircraft Assembler)
06.02	Schering-Plough Corp., Bob Kaist Photo (Pill Making Machine)
06.03	Raytheon Company (Refrigerator Compressors)
	Chrysler Corporation (Final Inspection)
	Echlin, Inc. (Printed Circuit Boards)
07.01	Impact Communications (Title Examiner)
07.03	Impact Communications (Cashier)
07.04	General Motors Corp., (Price Quotations)
07.06	Ace Hardware Corporation (Word Processor)
09.01	Impact Communications (Hostess)
09.03	Impact Communications (Driver Education)
09.05	Impact Communications (Manicurist)
10.02	Worthington Industries, Inc. (Nurse Taking Pressure)
11.01	General Motors Corp. (Financial Analyst at Keyboard)
11.05	Carolina Freight Carriers Corporation (Traffic Manager)
	Owens-Illinois (Executive Chef)
11.09	Impact Communications (Advertising Manager)
11.10	Impact Communications (Safety Coordinator)

APPENDIX I

Use of the WTG Guide With Other Career Exploration Resources

As you explore Worker Trait Groups, you may want to locate information about a specific occupation or groups of occupations. The *Worker Trait Group (WTG) Guide* may be easily used with common sources of occupational and career information. The following provides an overview of commonly used sources of career information and how you may use these materials.

The three most widely used and most comprehensive sources of career information are the *Dictionary of Occupational Titles (DOT)*, the *Guide for Occupational Exploration (GOE)*, and the *Occupational Outlook Handbook (OOH)*. These publications were developed as part of an extensive and continuous program of research and occupational analysis by the U.S. Employment Service and the Bureau of Labor Statistics of the Department of Labor.

Dictionary of Occupational Titles

The major use of the DOT with the WTG Guide is to look up the description of a single occupation. The DOT is the only reference that contains descriptions of each of the thousands of occupations in the world of work. These descriptions are brief, but include a lot of information.

Each occupation in the DOT has a nine-digit code. The occupational descriptions are organized in the numerical sequence of these codes. To locate a description you use the nine-digit code as you use the page numbers in a book.

A nine-digit occupational code appears on the top outside corner of each DOT page. On the left-hand page, the code represents the first occupation described. On the right-hand page, the code is that of the last occupation. So, if the code number of the occupation you are seeking is between these two reference numbers you will find it on one of the two pages. The WTG Guide lists the nine-digit code with each occupational title for easy use with the DOT.

There is a second purpose for using the DOT with the WTG Guide. The occupations are grouped in a structure that is different from the Career Area/Worker Trait Groups. This structure is called the *Occupational Group Arrangement (OGA)*. The first three digits of the nine-digit occupational code represent the OGA structure. This structure organizes occupations into groups based on similar: (1) knowledge and skills; (2) work tasks and their purpose; (3) machines, tools, equipment, and other work aids used; (4) materials or subject matter involved; and (5) products made or services offered. Thus, occupations with the same first three digits have similar characteristics. Occupations with the same first one or two digits have fewer similarities than occupations with all three digits the same.

The OGA structure helps to identify other occupations related to the transferable skills of a specific occupation. This means that if workers become unemployed, they may be able to use the knowledge and skills they already have in another occupation in the OGA group. However, they may need additional training. The lower the skills involved in an occupation, the easier the transfer of skills. All that may be needed is a period of on-the-job training. The professional and technical level occupations may require more formalized training to transfer, unless it is to occupations at lower skill levels.

The DOT is updated periodically with a supplement. This supplement includes new occupations and makes the necessary changes in existing ones. If you cannot find the occupation you are looking for in the DOT, check the supplement. It is organized in the same nine-digit code sequence.

Guide for Occupational Exploration

The *WTG Guide* is an educational version of the GOE. It contains the same base data, expanded area and group descriptions, and identifies the work factors and worker characteristics for each WTG. These work factors and worker characteristics are associated with job success and worker satisfaction. These factors and characteristics are not included in the GOE descriptions.

The *WTG Guide* lists only occupations that represent major employment opportunities. The GOE lists all occupations belonging to a Worker Trait Group.

Occupational Outlook Handbook

The OOH, published every two years, provides one of the most current sources of information about employment trends in occupations. Although the OOH does not provide information about all of the occupations in the

world of work, it does include the ones that provide the major employment opportunities. Detailed information is usually provided for about 200 occupational clusters made up of similar occupations, such as all architects or all surveyors.

In addition to the listing of occupational clusters in the OOH Table of Contents, there is a DOT Index. This Index lists occupational titles in the numerical sequence of their nine-digit DOT code. The titles listed are specific occupational titles included in the occupational cluster information. The nine-digit code, provided with occupational titles in the *WTG Guide*, also can be used to access information in the OOH. If the code you are looking for is not listed in the OOH, use its table of contents and alphabetical index to identify the related clusters. This is necessary especially for some clusters related to construction and manufacturing where occupational titles are too numerous to list.

Commercial and Other Materials

In addition to government publications, there is a wide variety of other occupational and career information. These include resources such as books, audiovisuals, and occupational briefs. They are developed and published by many different organizations. However, most of the materials are produced by commercial publishers.

Other than for specific occupational briefs, these materials usually contain information about many occupations. Therefore, it may be necessary for you to use alphabetical indexes, tables of contents, and other cross-references to find information about a specific occupation. Many publishers of career information resources are including cross-reference codes and indexes as part of their materials.

Many career resource centers organize, file, and code materials for easy access. Most of these filing and indexing systems include the DOT nine-digit occupational code. Most of the systems also use the Career Area/Worker Trait Group and/or Occupational Group Arrangement codes. You should check to see how the materials available for your use are organized.

State and Other Career Information Systems

Each state has an Occupational Information Coordinating Committee (SOICC). This committee is responsible for organizing and merging the data from various state sources of occupational and career information for efficient use by state agencies, school systems, and other organizations providing career exploration and employment services to youth and adults.

Many states have developed a Career Information Delivery System (CIDS). These systems deliver career information by computer, microfilm, print materials, and audiovisuals to provide specific information for their state and region. They also may include information on a national level.

The SOICCs and CIDS include many cross-reference codes for occupations, training programs, and other types of career information. The nine-digit DOT code for occupations is included in most systems. You need to become familiar with the access and cross-reference structure built into the system available to you.

In addition to state systems of career information, there are commercial computerized systems that provide information on a national basis. These systems are similar to state systems and use the same access and cross-reference codes.

Exploration Worksheets

As you use resources to explore Worker Trait Groups and occupations, you should summarize and record key points. This will help you identify the most important information. It will also make it easier for you to compare Worker Trait Groups or occupations. These worksheets provide a personal copy of information you may wish to keep for later use.

On the following pages are illustrations of two worksheets that can be used. DO NOT WRITE ON THESE PAGES. Check with your counselor or teacher to see if printed forms are available. If not, a copying machine may be available or you can use the headings to develop your own worksheets.

NOTE: For reproducing the worksheet illustrations on 8 1/2 x 11 inch paper, enlarge to 130 percent. The forms can be reproduced front-and-back to keep information about a WTG or occupation on one sheet. Permission is granted for reproducing the worksheets for individual use. However, the worksheets may not be reproduced for sale, used in any other form, or included in other materials without written permission of the publisher.

WTG Exploration Worksheet

WTG Title _____   WTG# _____

Directions: As you read information about a Worker Trait Group, use the space provided to summarize information about each topic.

Work Performed (What types of work interest you the most? Which sub-groups do you like best?)

Skills and Abilities (Do you have the skills and abilities listed? Which ones are your strengths? Which ones are your weaknesses?)

Interests (What clues are related to your interests? Are there other clues in addition to those listed?)

Other Information (What else should you know and is important to you?)

Preparation (How can you prepare? What courses and skills are important? What else is needed?)

Qualifications Profile

Directions: Using the WTG Guide, circle the number or letter of each qualification below that applies. Where an asterisk (*) is included in the Guide, mark an asterisk above the number or letter you circled.

Work Activities: 1 2 3 4 5 6 7 8 9 10

Work Situations: 1 2 3 4 5 6 7 8 9 10

Data-People-Things: Data L A H - People L A H - Things L A H

Physical Demands: S L M H VH

Working Conditions: I O B

Educational Skills: Reasoning 1 2 3 4 5 6

Math 1 2 3 4 5 6

Language 1 2 3 4 5 6

Aptitudes: First, circle the letters below for the aptitudes listed in the WTG Guide. Then circle the levels reported for each. Remember to mark an asterisk (*) above the level circled if one is reported in the Guide.

G - General 5 4 3 2 1

V - Verbal 5 4 3 2 1

N - Numerical 5 4 3 2 1

S - Spatial 5 4 3 2 1

P - Form Perception 5 4 3 2 1

Q - Clerical Perception 5 4 3 2 1

K - Motor Coordination 5 4 3 2 1

F - Finger Dexterity 5 4 3 2 1

M - Manual Dexterity 5 4 3 2 1

Occupation Codes and Titles

(What occupations in the WTG Guide do you want to explore? Is it an occupation with a military counterpart?)

Occupation Exploration Worksheet

**Title of
Occupation** _____

Code _____   **WTG#** _____

Directions: As you read the information about an occupation, write down a summary of the important points related to the following categories. You may need more than one source to find all the information.

Source/Reference

**Specific Work
Performed**   (What kind of work would you do?)

**Required
Knowledge,
Skills, and
Abilities**   (What are they? How do you develop them?)

**Education,
Training, and
Entry**   (What kind of courses or programs should you take? Are
there different ways to enter the occupation?)

Work Setting (Where would you work? Under what conditions?)

Employment Outlook (Are there job openings now? In the future? Where are they?)

Advancement Opportunities (What jobs can you advance with? What is the typical way to advance?)

Special Qualifications (Do you need credentials or licenses? What are they? How do you get them?)

Earnings and Rewards (How much does the work usually pay? What are the chances for overtime, bonuses, or special rewards?)

More Information (Where can you write or go for further information?)